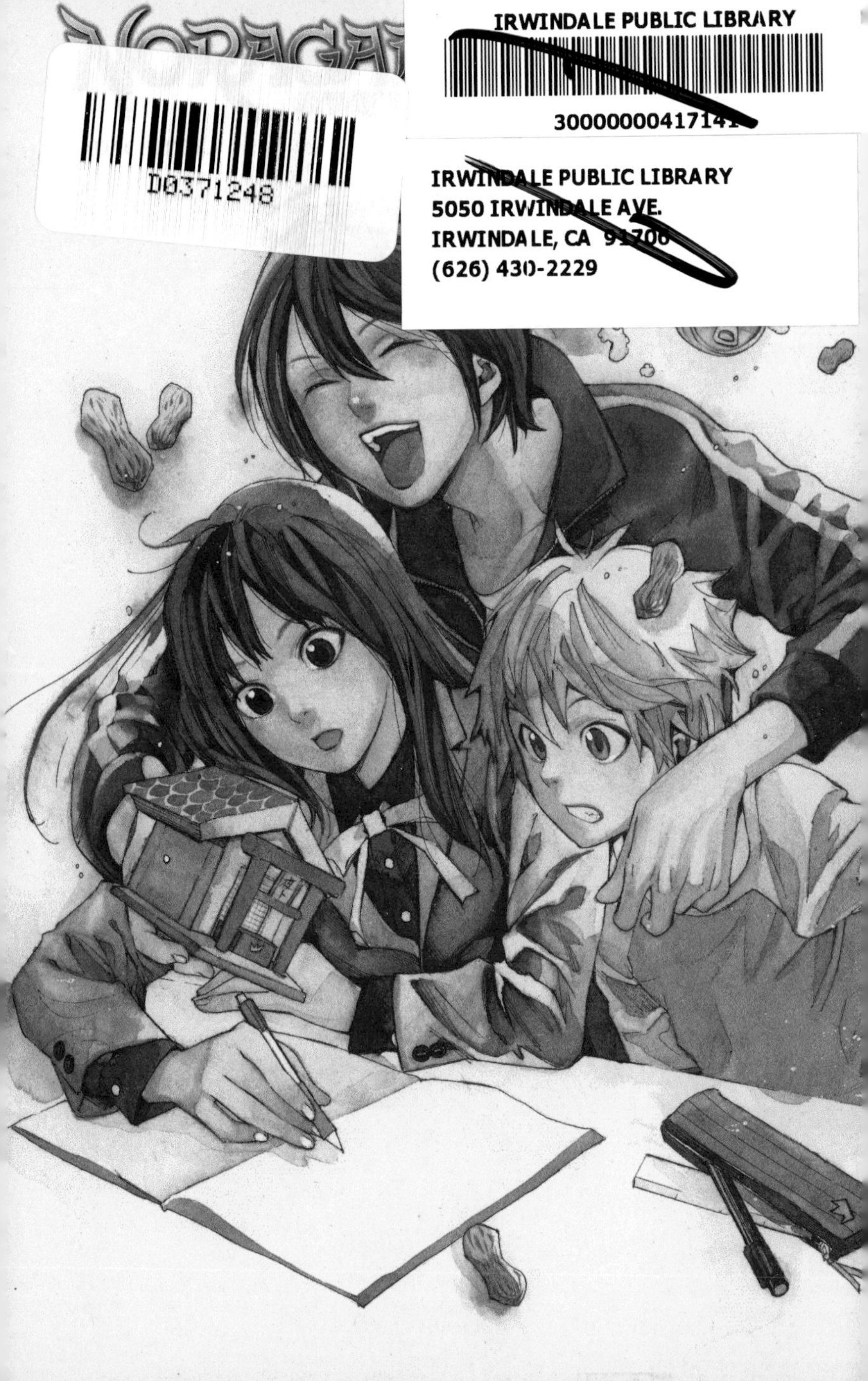

Characters

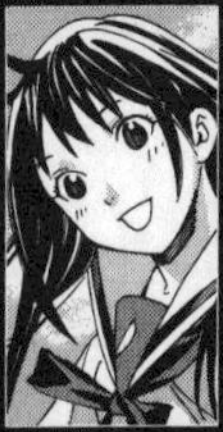

HIYORI IKI

A middle school student who has become half ayakashi.

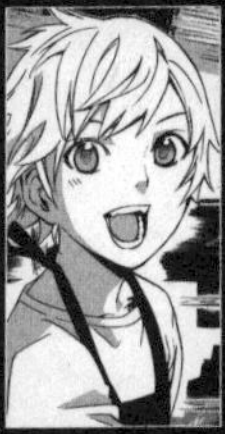

YUKINÉ

Yato's shinki who turns into a sword.

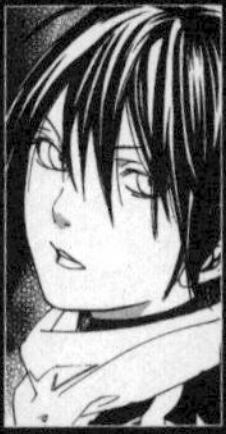

YATO

A minor deity who always wears a sweatsuit.

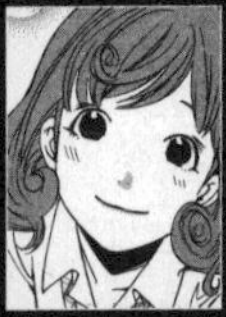

KOFUKU

A goddess of poverty who calls herself Ebisu after the god of fortune.

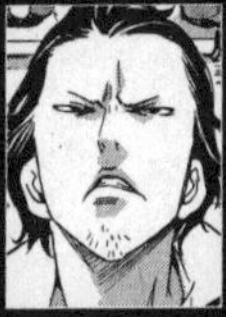

DAIKOKU

Kofuku's shinki who summons storms.

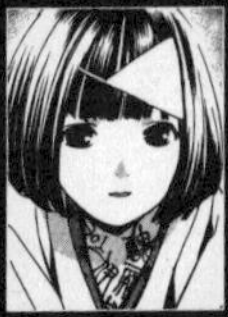

STRAY

A shinki who serves an unspecified number of deities

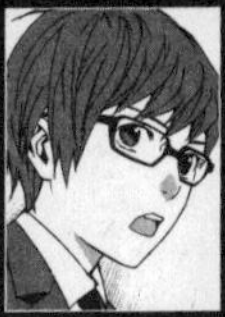

KAZUMA

A navigational shinki who serves as guide to Bishamon.

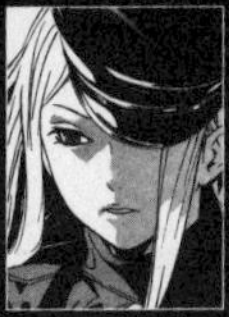

BISHAMONTEN

A powerful warrior god, one of the Seven Gods of Fortune.

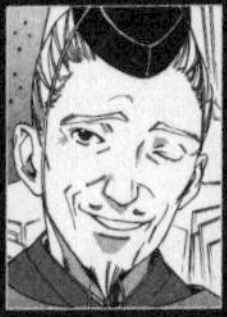

TENJIN

The God of Learning, Sugawara no Michizane.

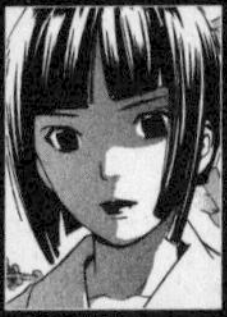

MAYU

Formerly Yato's shinki, now Tenjin's shinki.

經

[illegible]

神

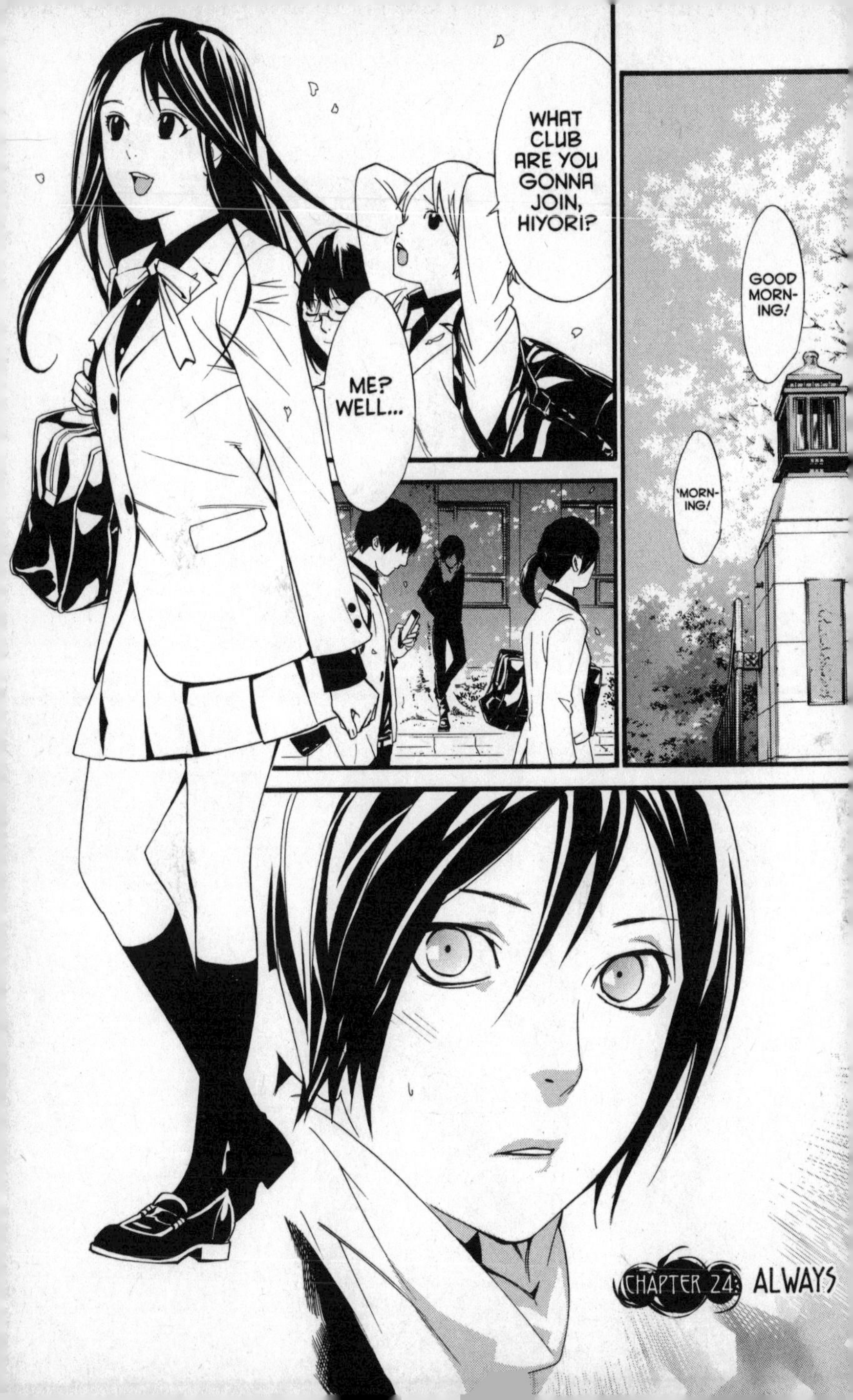
GOOD MORNING!
'MORNING!
WHAT CLUB ARE YOU GONNA JOIN, HIYORI?
ME? WELL...
CHAPTER 24: ALWAYS

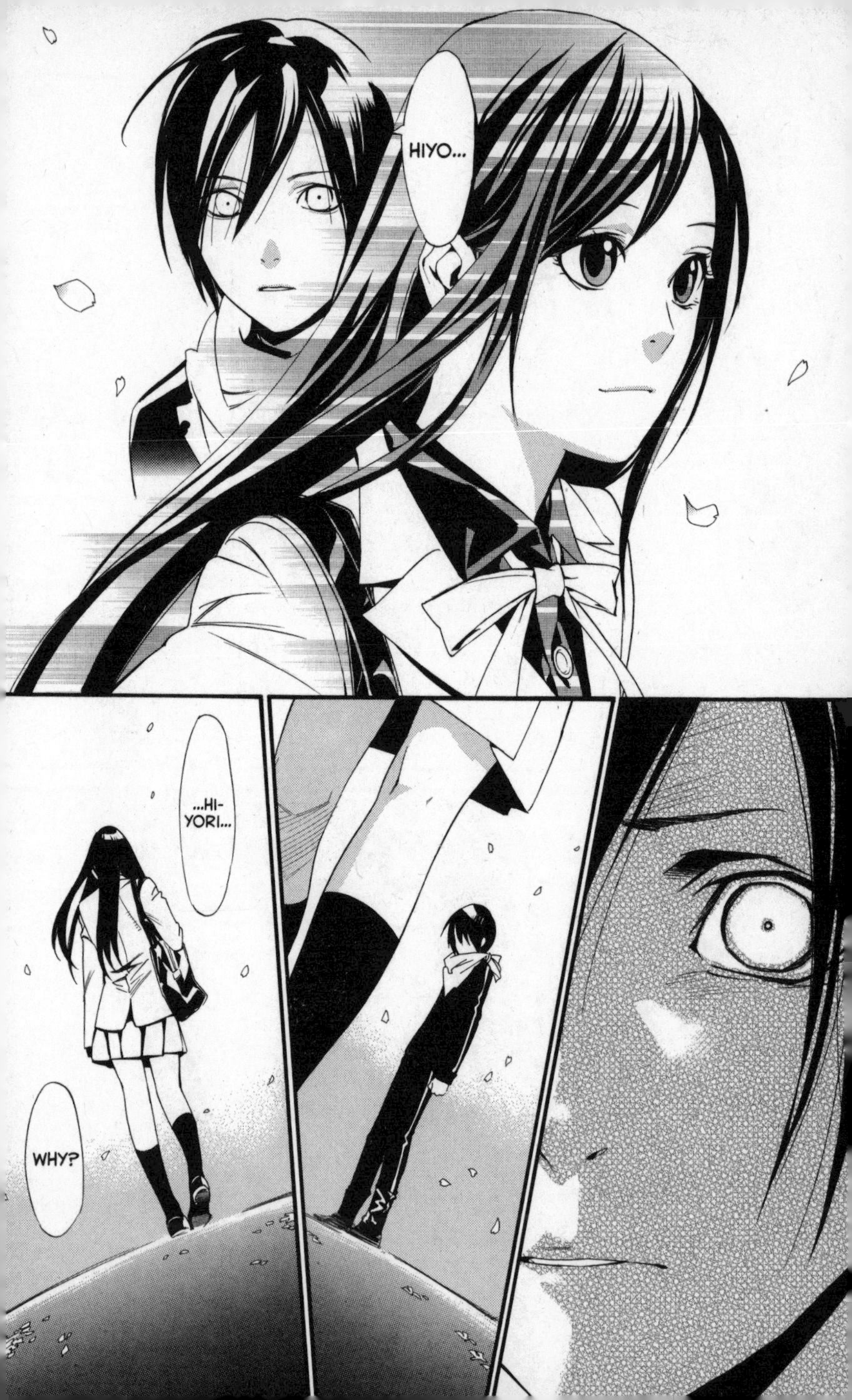
HIYO...
...HI-YORI...
WHY?

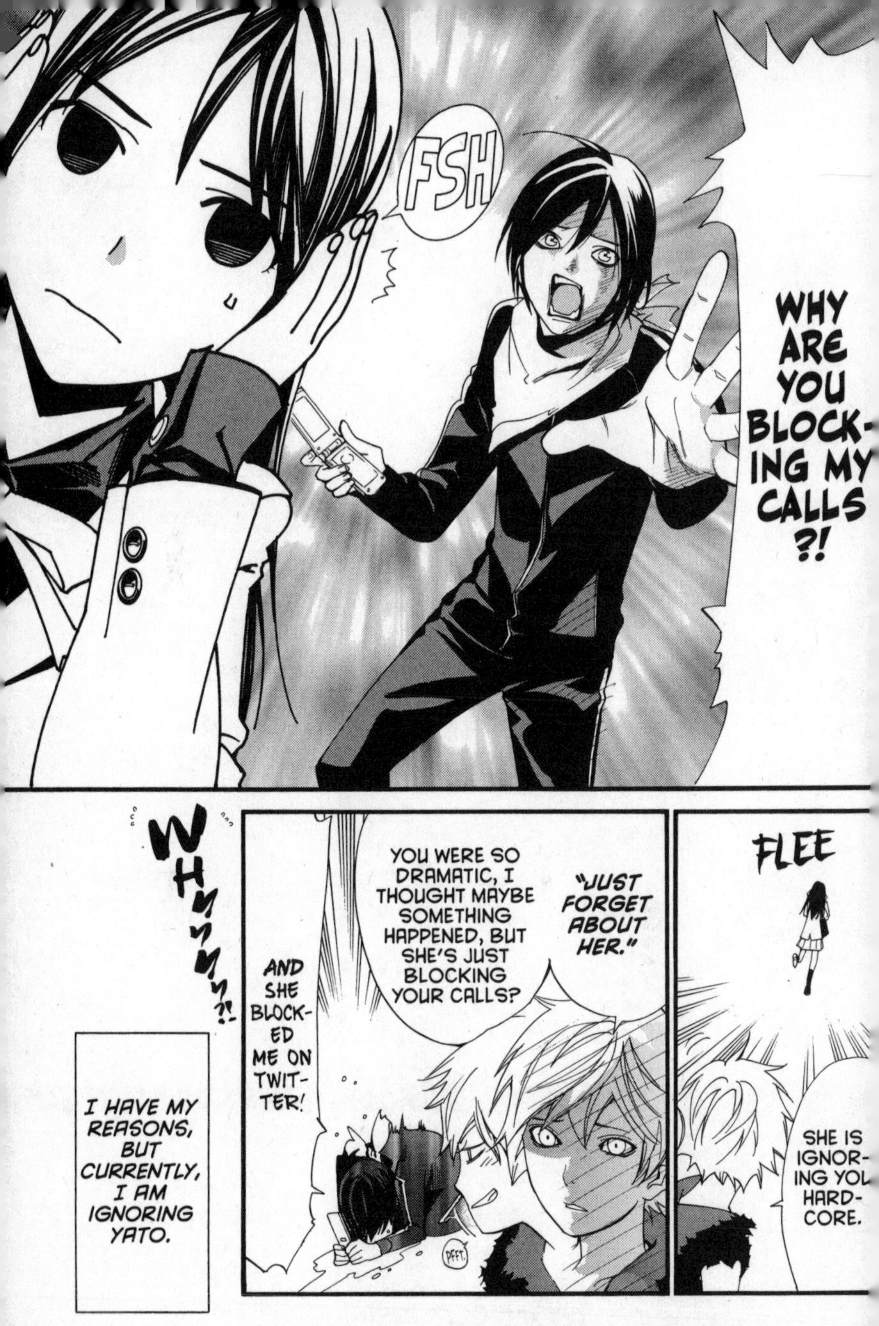
WHY ARE YOU BLOCKING MY CALLS?!
FSH
FLEE
SHE IS IGNORING YOU HARDCORE.
"JUST FORGET ABOUT HER."
YOU WERE SO DRAMATIC, I THOUGHT MAYBE SOMETHING HAPPENED, BUT SHE'S JUST BLOCKING YOUR CALLS?
AND SHE BLOCKED ME ON TWITTER!
PFFT.
WHMMM?!
I HAVE MY REASONS, BUT CURRENTLY, I AM IGNORING YATO.

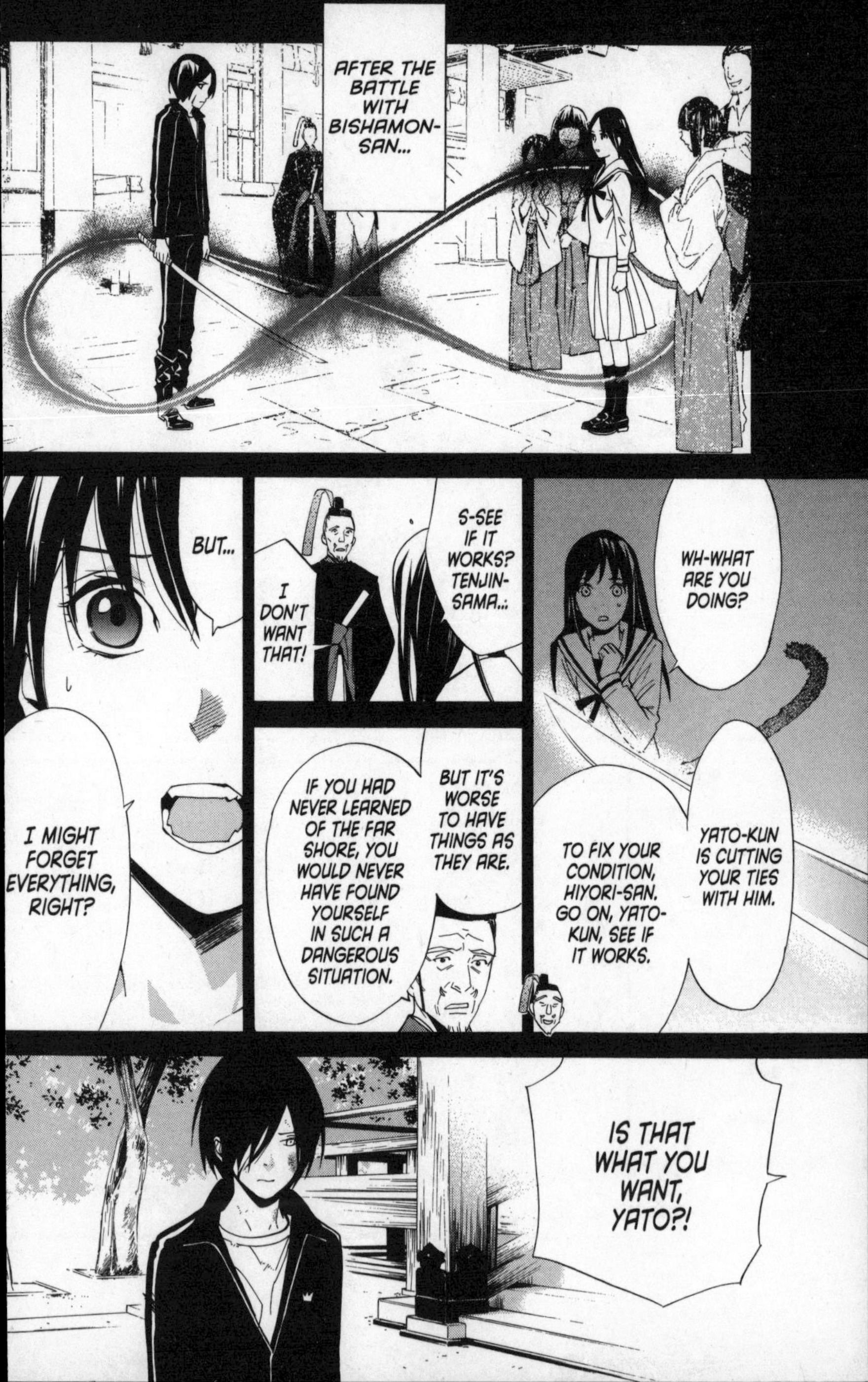
AFTER THE BATTLE WITH BISHAMON-SAN...
WH-WHAT ARE YOU DOING?
YATO-KUN IS CUTTING YOUR TIES WITH HIM.
TO FIX YOUR CONDITION, HIYORI-SAN. GO ON, YATO-KUN, SEE IF IT WORKS.
S-SEE IF IT WORKS? TENJIN-SAMA...
I DON'T WANT THAT!
BUT IT'S WORSE TO HAVE THINGS AS THEY ARE.
IF YOU HAD NEVER LEARNED OF THE FAR SHORE, YOU WOULD NEVER HAVE FOUND YOURSELF IN SUCH A DANGEROUS SITUATION.
BUT...
I MIGHT FORGET EVERYTHING, RIGHT?
IS THAT WHAT YOU WANT, YATO?!

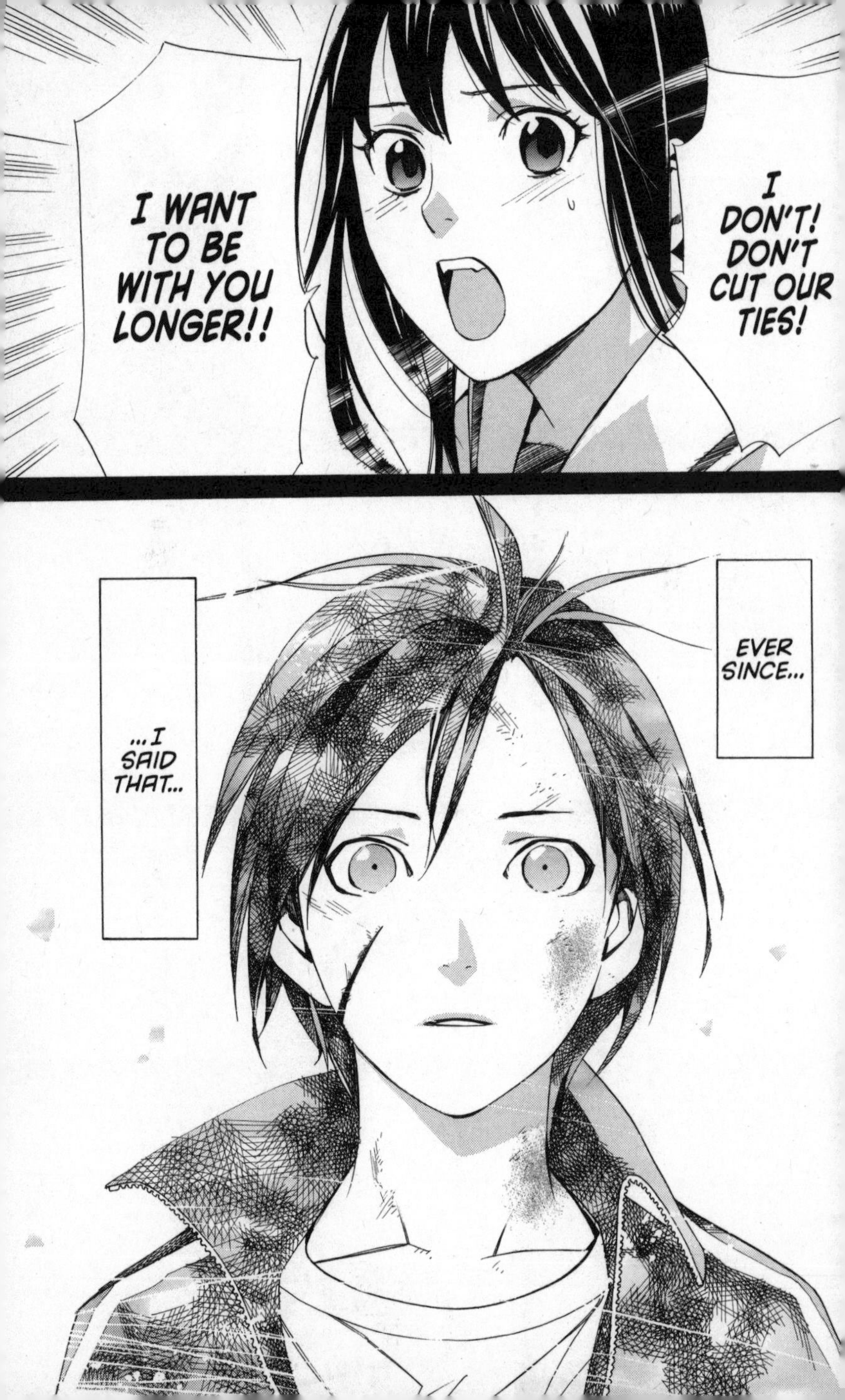
I DON'T! DON'T CUT OUR TIES!
I WANT TO BE WITH YOU LONGER!!
EVER SINCE...
...I SAID THAT...

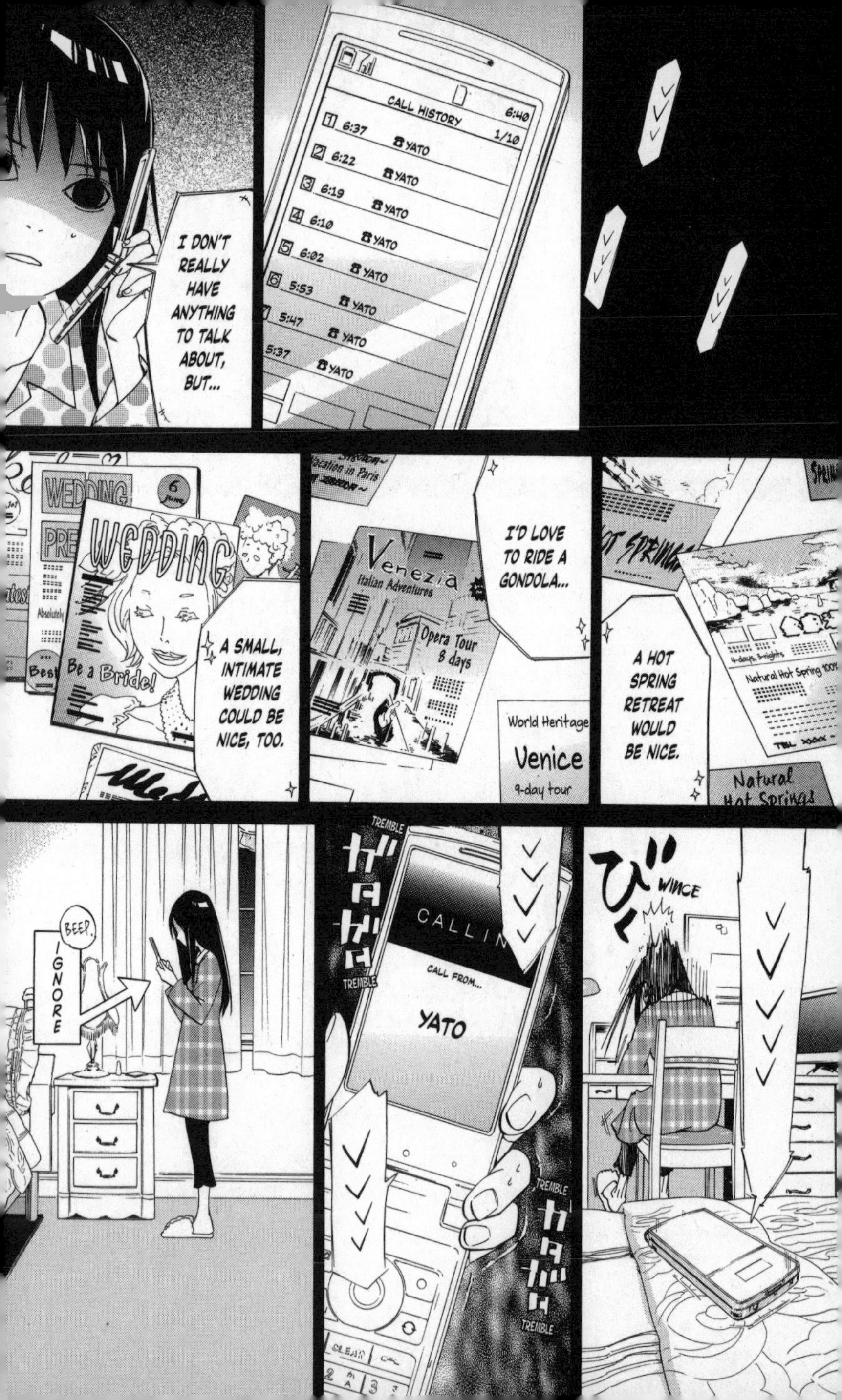
CALL HISTORY 6:40
1/10
1 6:37 YATO
2 6:22 YATO
3 6:19 YATO
4 6:10 YATO
5 6:02 YATO
6 5:53 YATO
5:47 YATO
5:37 YATO
I DON'T REALLY HAVE ANYTHING TO TALK ABOUT, BUT...
HOT SPRINGS
4-days, 3-nights
Natural Hot Spring 100%
TEL xxxx
Natural Hot Springs
A HOT SPRING RETREAT WOULD BE NICE.
Vacation in Paris
Venezia
Italian Adventures
Opera Tour 8 days
World Heritage
Venice
9-day tour
I'D LOVE TO RIDE A GONDOLA...
WEDDING
WEDDING
Be a Bride!
A SMALL, INTIMATE WEDDING COULD BE NICE, TOO.
WINCE
TREMBLE
TREMBLE
CALLIN
CALL FROM...
YATO
CLEAR
TREMBLE
TREMBLE
BEEP.
IGNORE

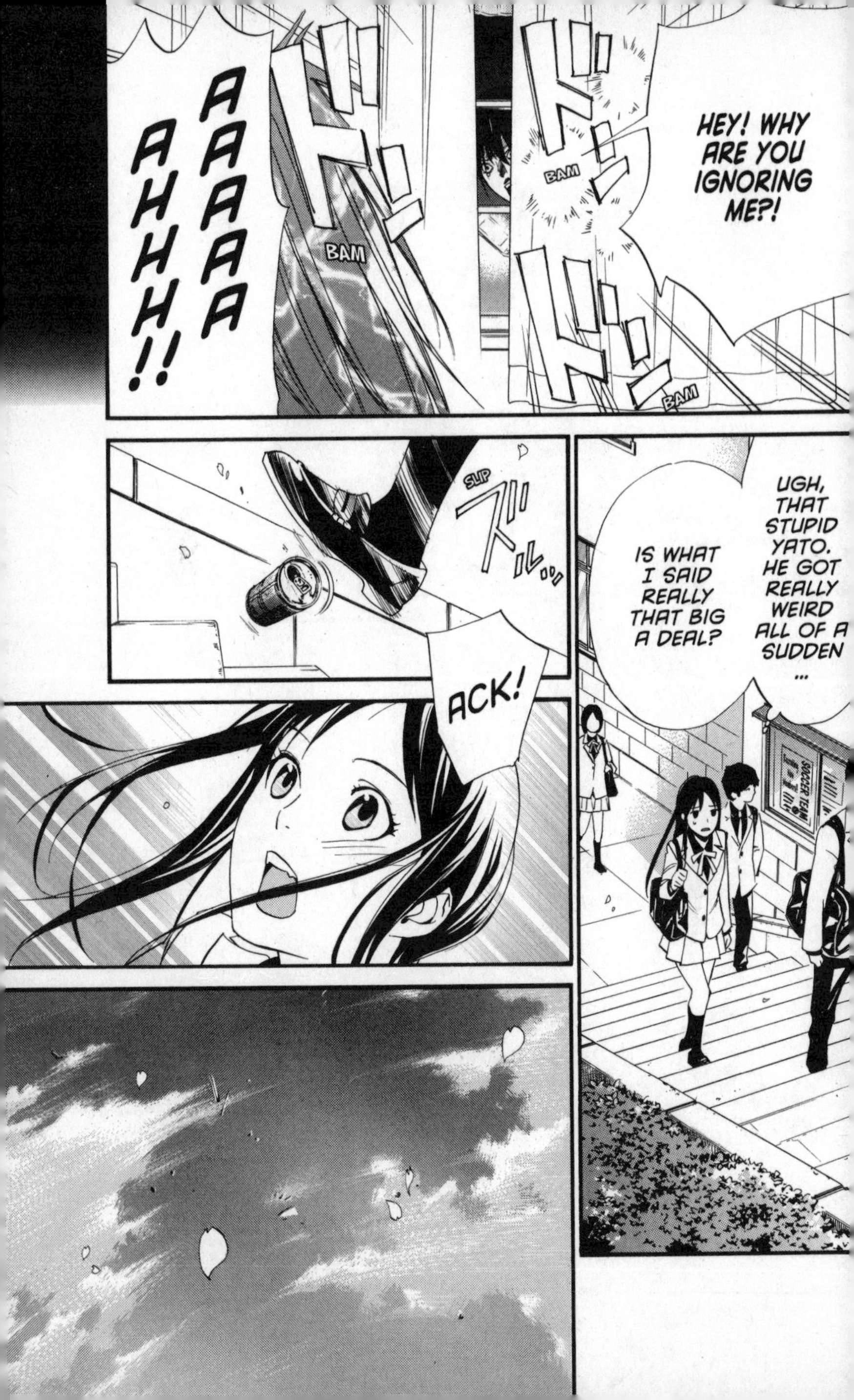

HEY! WHY ARE YOU IGNORING ME?!
BAM
BAM
BAM
AAAAAA
AHHHH!!
UGH, THAT STUPID YATO. HE GOT REALLY WEIRD ALL OF A SUDDEN ...
IS WHAT I SAID REALLY THAT BIG A DEAL?
SOCCER TEAM
SLIP
ACK!

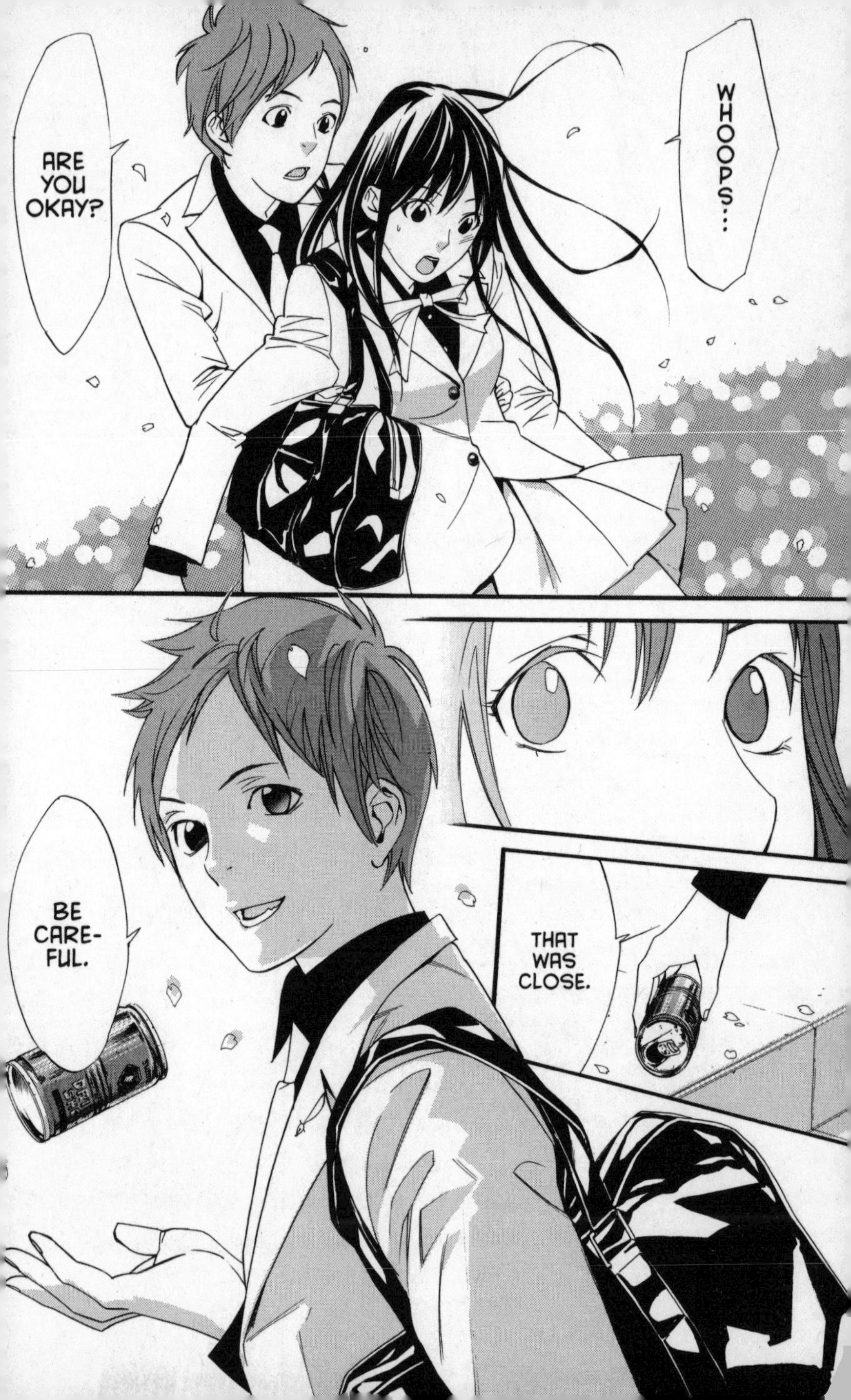
WHOOPS...
ARE YOU OKAY?
THAT WAS CLOSE.
BE CARE-FUL.

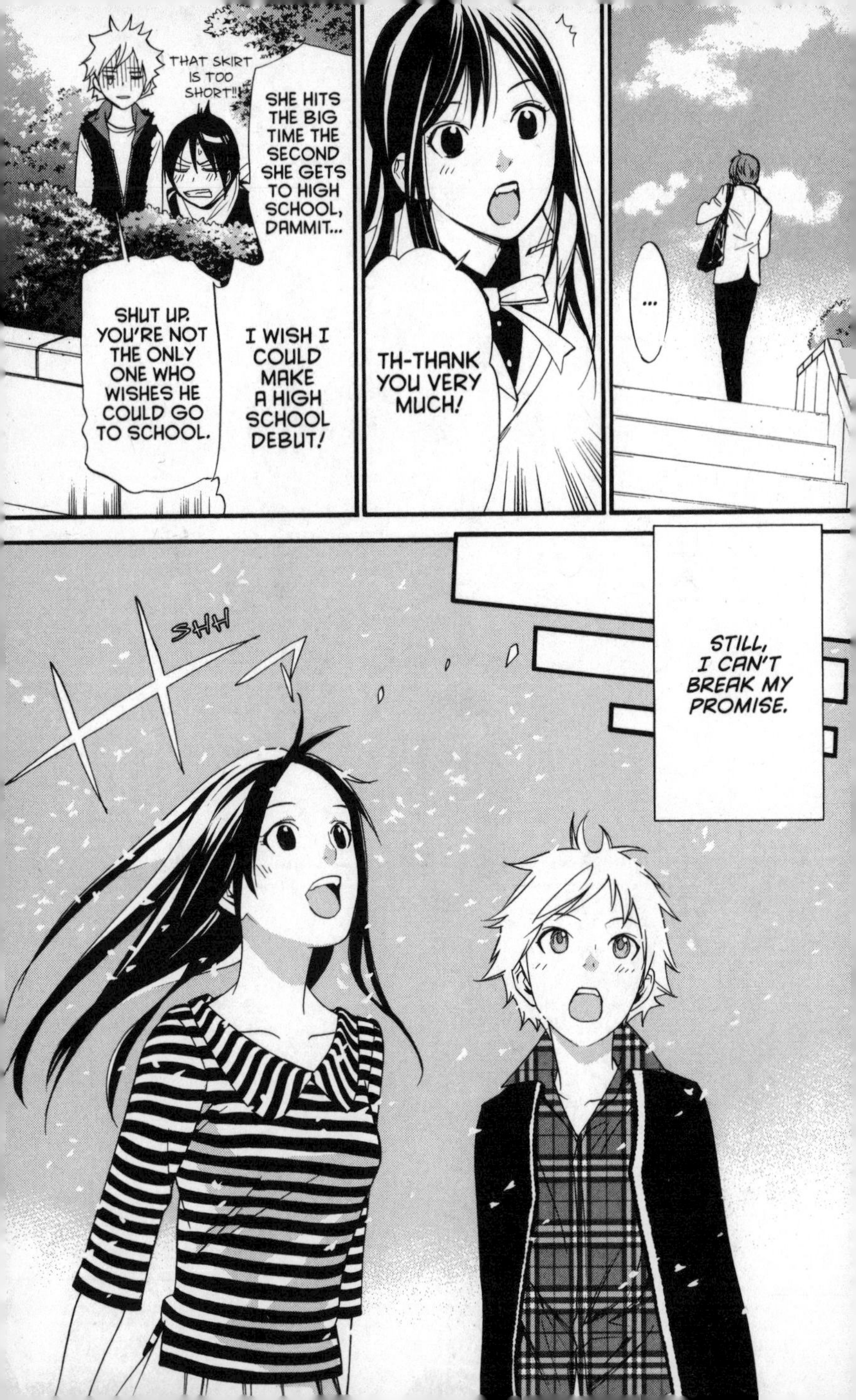
...
TH-THANK YOU VERY MUCH!
SHE HITS THE BIG TIME THE SECOND SHE GETS TO HIGH SCHOOL, DAMMIT...
THAT SKIRT IS TOO SHORT!!
I WISH I COULD MAKE A HIGH SCHOOL DEBUT!
SHUT UP. YOU'RE NOT THE ONLY ONE WHO WISHES HE COULD GO TO SCHOOL.
STILL, I CAN'T BREAK MY PROMISE.
SHH

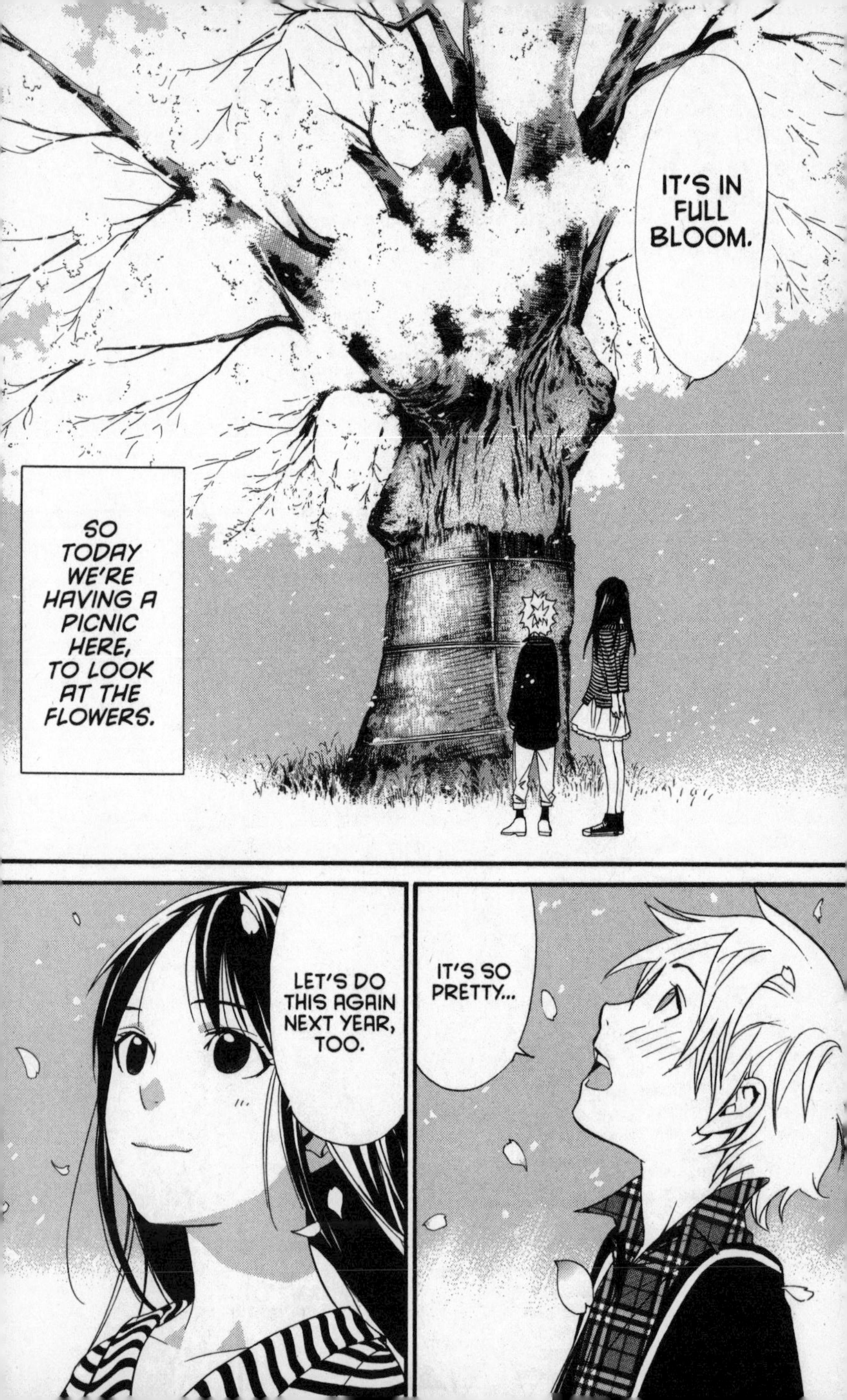
IT'S IN FULL BLOOM.
SO TODAY WE'RE HAVING A PICNIC HERE, TO LOOK AT THE FLOWERS.
IT'S SO PRETTY...
LET'S DO THIS AGAIN NEXT YEAR, TOO.

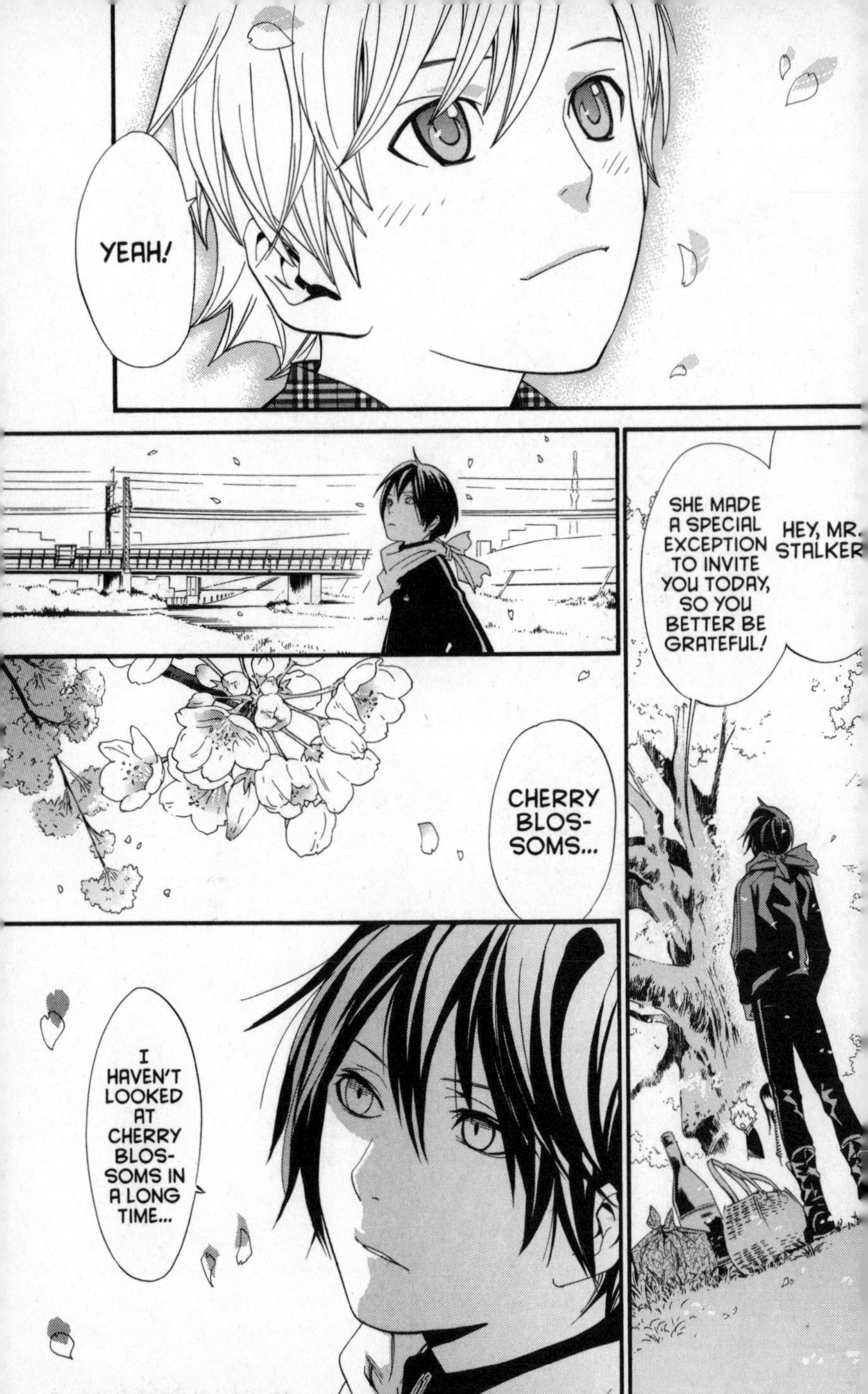
YEAH!
HEY, MR. STALKER
SHE MADE A SPECIAL EXCEPTION TO INVITE YOU TODAY, SO YOU BETTER BE GRATEFUL!
CHERRY BLOSSOMS...
I HAVEN'T LOOKED AT CHERRY BLOSSOMS IN A LONG TIME...

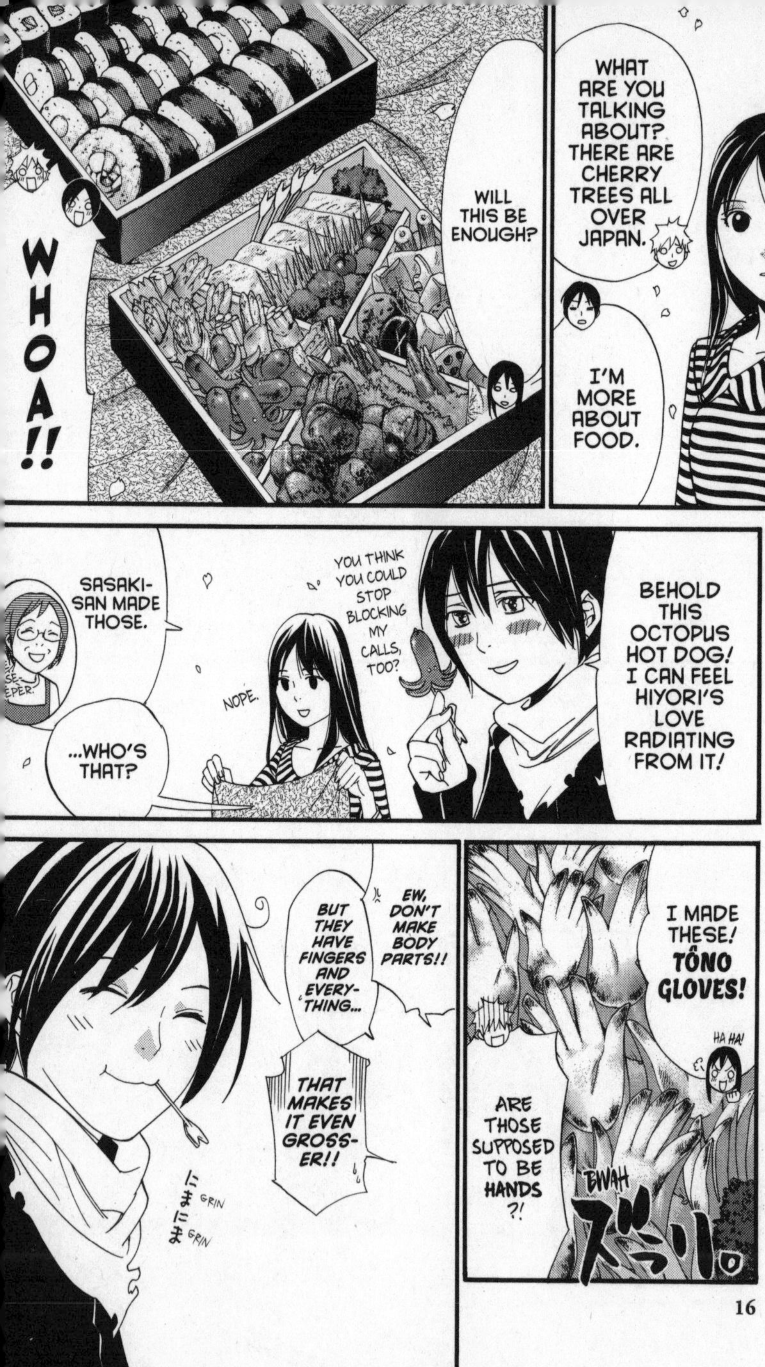
WHAT ARE YOU TALKING ABOUT? THERE ARE CHERRY TREES ALL OVER JAPAN.
I'M MORE ABOUT FOOD.
WILL THIS BE ENOUGH?
WHOA!!
BEHOLD THIS OCTOPUS HOT DOG! I CAN FEEL HIYORI'S LOVE RADIATING FROM IT!
YOU THINK YOU COULD STOP BLOCKING MY CALLS, TOO?
NOPE.
SASAKI-SAN MADE THOSE.
...WHO'S THAT?
I MADE THESE! **TÔNO GLOVES!**
HA HA!
ARE THOSE SUPPOSED TO BE **HANDS**?!
BWAH
EW, DON'T MAKE BODY PARTS!!
BUT THEY HAVE FINGERS AND EVERY-THING...
THAT MAKES IT EVEN GROSSER!!
にまにま GRIN GRIN

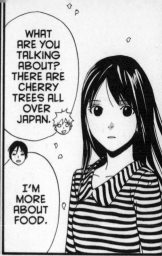

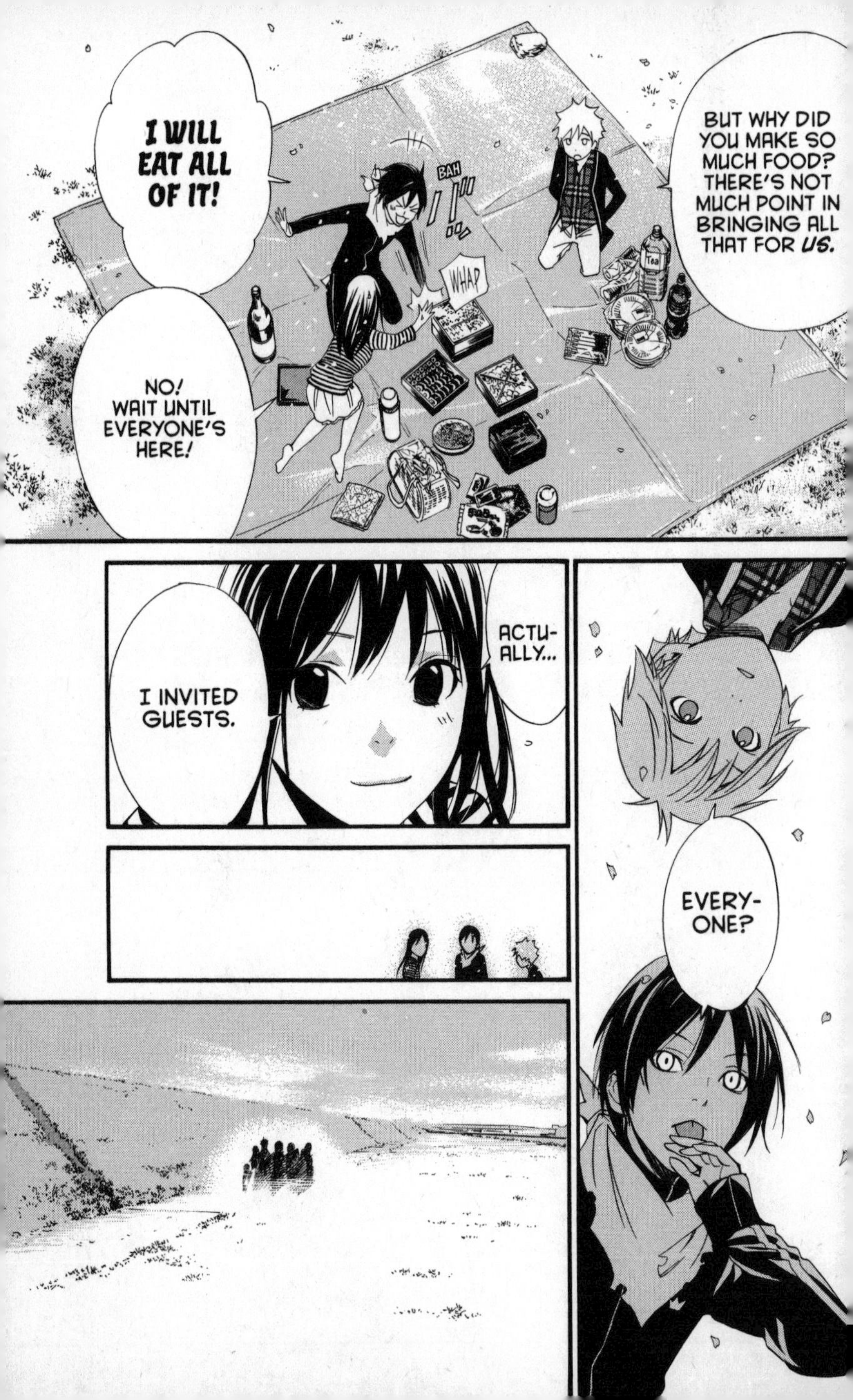
BUT WHY DID YOU MAKE SO MUCH FOOD? THERE'S NOT MUCH POINT IN BRINGING ALL THAT FOR *US.*
I WILL EAT ALL OF IT!
BAH
WHAP
NO! WAIT UNTIL EVERYONE'S HERE!
EVERY-ONE?
ACTU-ALLY...
I INVITED GUESTS.

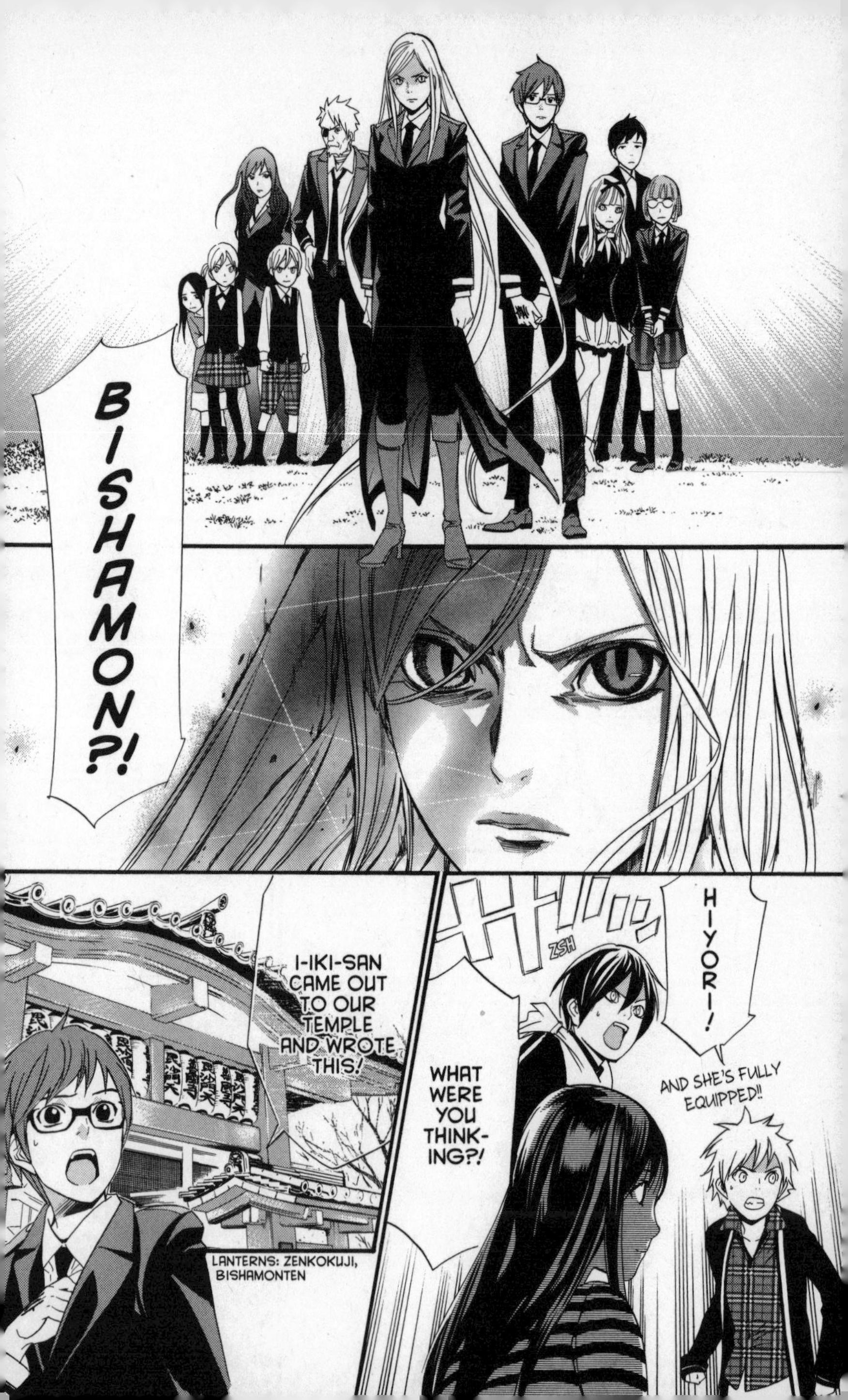
BISHAMON?!
HIYORI!
ZSH
AND SHE'S FULLY EQUIPPED!!
WHAT WERE YOU THINKING?!
I-IKI-SAN CAME OUT TO OUR TEMPLE AND WROTE THIS!
LANTERNS: ZENKOKUJI, BISHAMONTEN

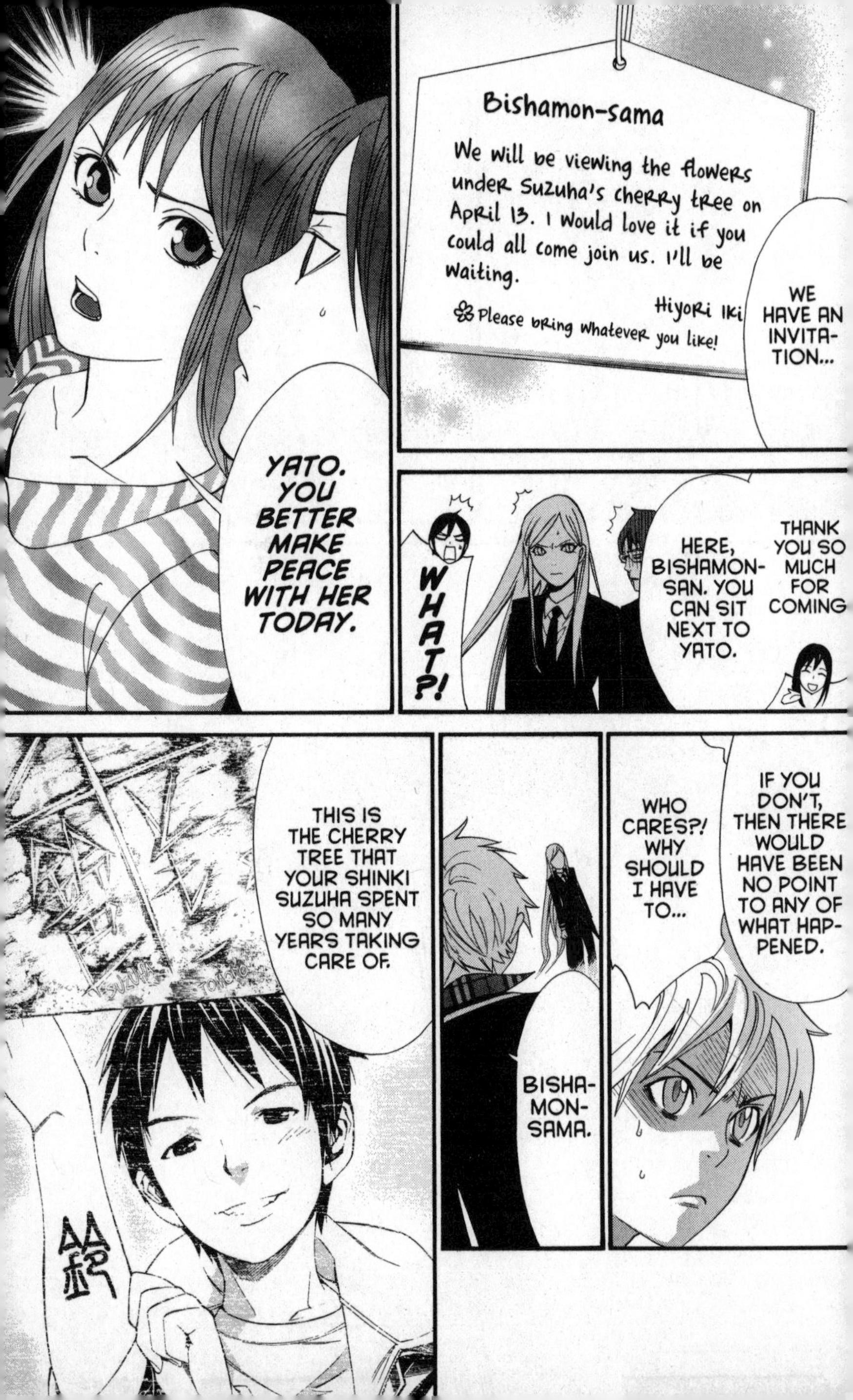

Bishamon-sama
We will be viewing the flowers under Suzuha's cherry tree on April 13. I would love it if you could all come join us. I'll be waiting.
Hiyori Iki
Please bring whatever you like!
WE HAVE AN INVITATION...
THANK YOU SO MUCH FOR COMING
HERE, BISHAMON-SAN. YOU CAN SIT NEXT TO YATO.
WHAT?!
YATO. YOU BETTER MAKE PEACE WITH HER TODAY.
IF YOU DON'T, THEN THERE WOULD HAVE BEEN NO POINT TO ANY OF WHAT HAPPENED.
WHO CARES?! WHY SHOULD I HAVE TO...
BISHAMON-SAMA.
THIS IS THE CHERRY TREE THAT YOUR SHINKI SUZUHA SPENT SO MANY YEARS TAKING CARE OF.

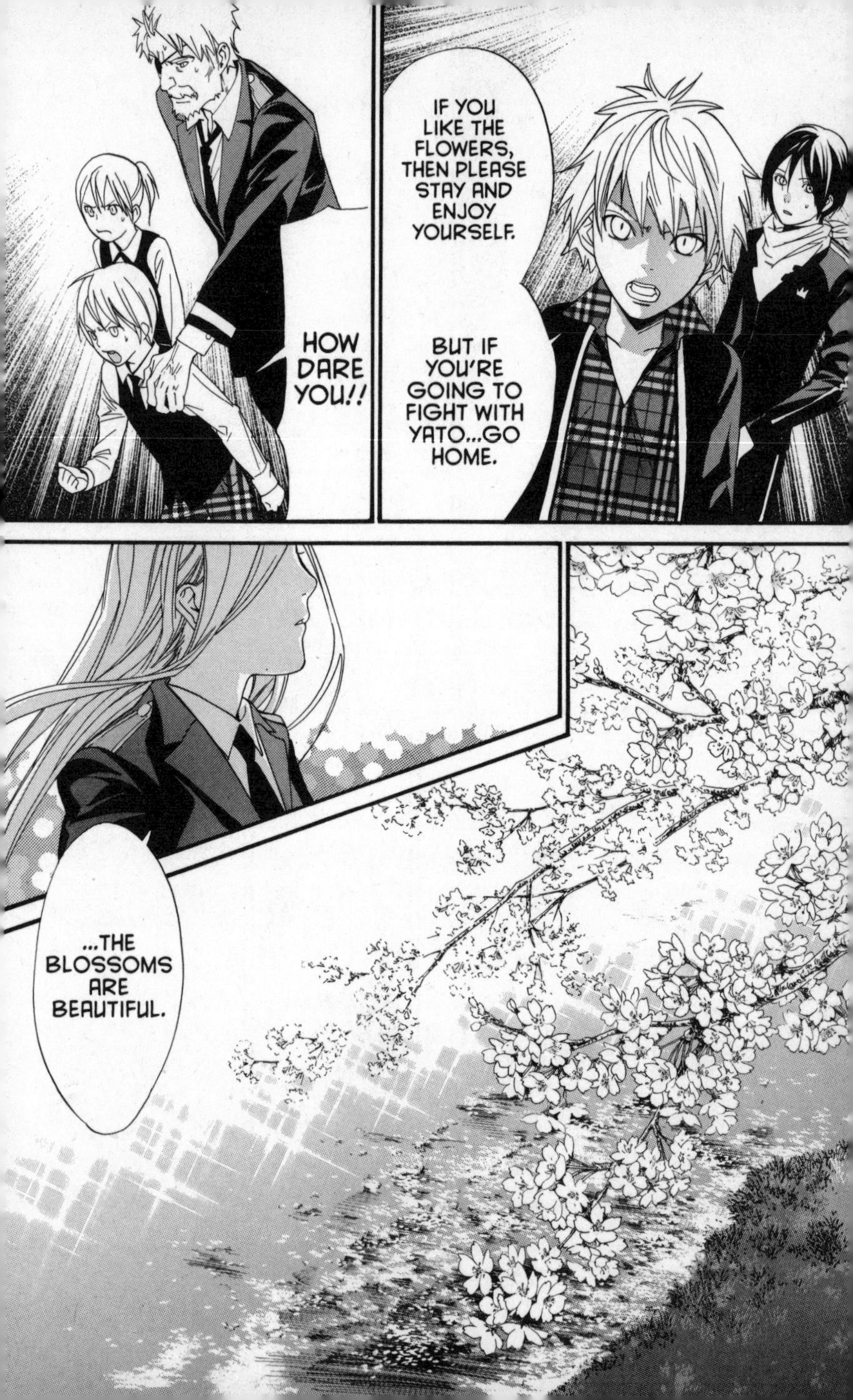
IF YOU LIKE THE FLOWERS, THEN PLEASE STAY AND ENJOY YOURSELF.
BUT IF YOU'RE GOING TO FIGHT WITH YATO...GO HOME.
HOW DARE YOU!!
...THE BLOSSOMS ARE BEAUTIFUL.

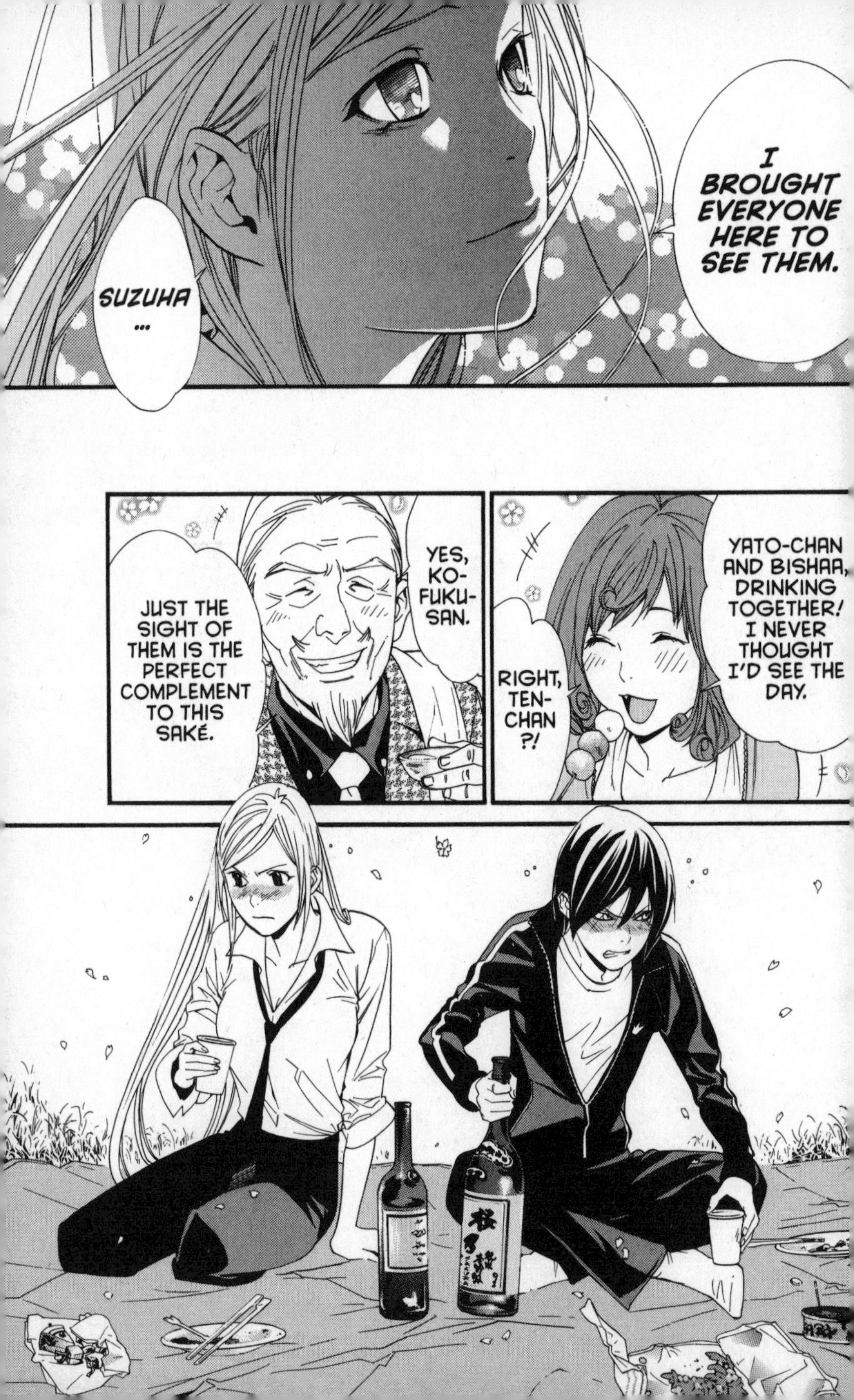
I BROUGHT EVERYONE HERE TO SEE THEM.
SUZUHA...
YATO-CHAN AND BISHAA, DRINKING TOGETHER! I NEVER THOUGHT I'D SEE THE DAY.
RIGHT, TEN-CHAN?!
YES, KO-FUKU-SAN.
JUST THE SIGHT OF THEM IS THE PERFECT COMPLEMENT TO THIS SAKÉ.

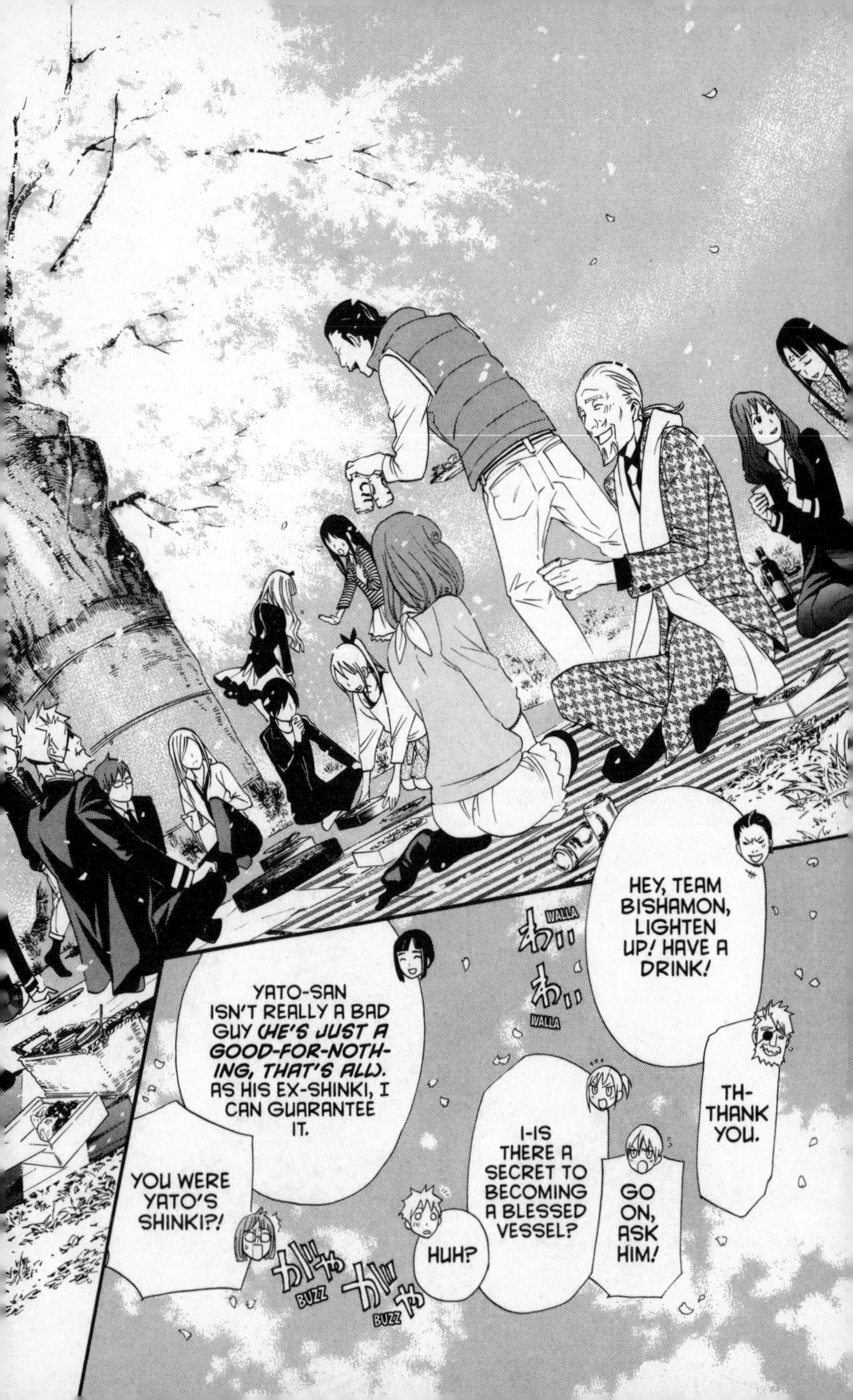
HEY, TEAM BISHAMON, LIGHTEN UP! HAVE A DRINK!
WALLA
WALLA
YATO-SAN ISN'T REALLY A BAD GUY (*HE'S JUST A GOOD-FOR-NOTHING, THAT'S ALL*). AS HIS EX-SHINKI, I CAN GUARANTEE IT.
TH-THANK YOU.
GO ON, ASK HIM!
I-IS THERE A SECRET TO BECOMING A BLESSED VESSEL?
HUH?
YOU WERE YATO'S SHINKI?!
BUZZ
BUZZ

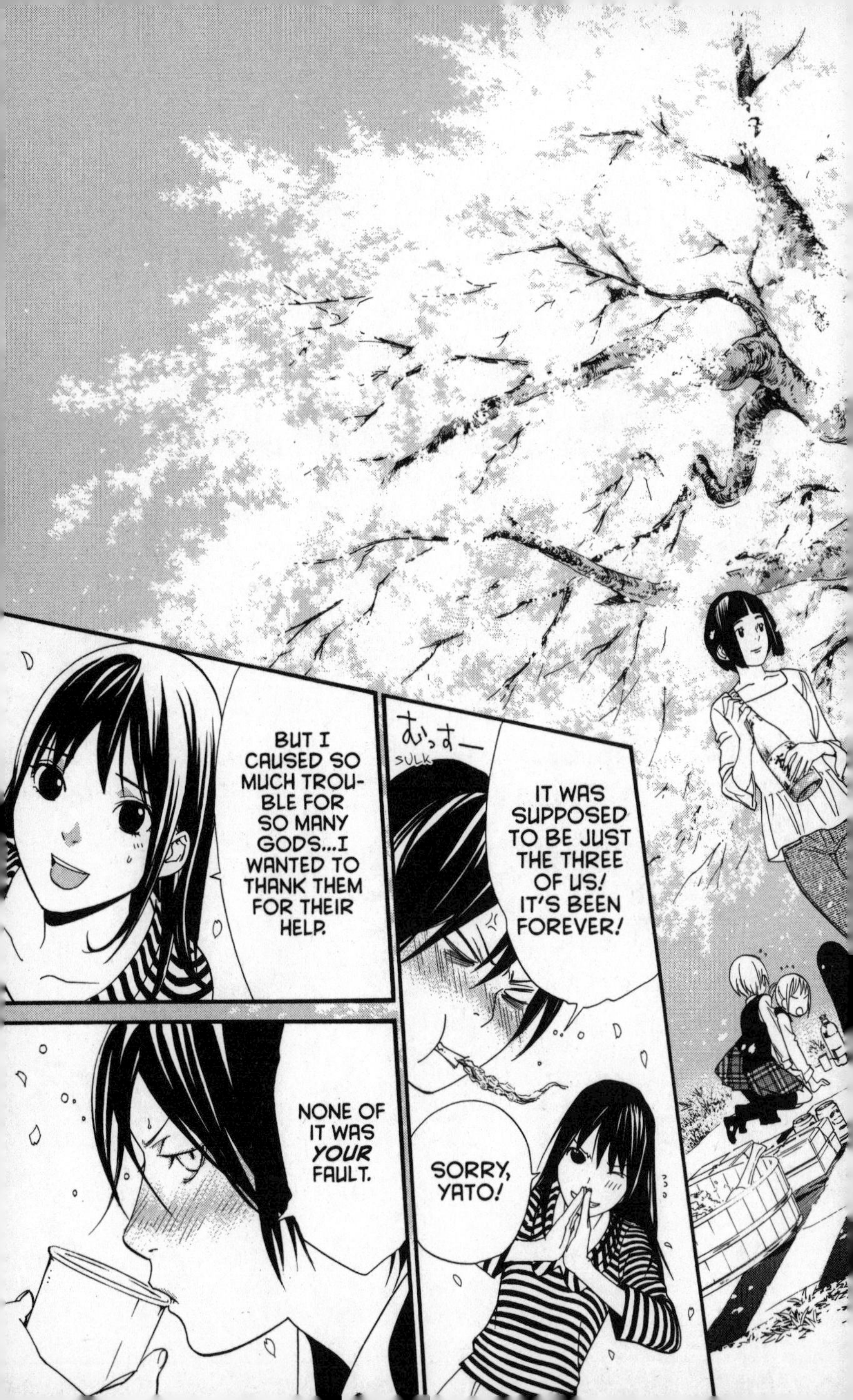
むっすー
SULK
IT WAS SUPPOSED TO BE JUST THE THREE OF US! IT'S BEEN FOREVER!
SORRY, YATO!
BUT I CAUSED SO MUCH TROU-BLE FOR SO MANY GODS...I WANTED TO THANK THEM FOR THEIR HELP.
NONE OF IT WAS *YOUR* FAULT.

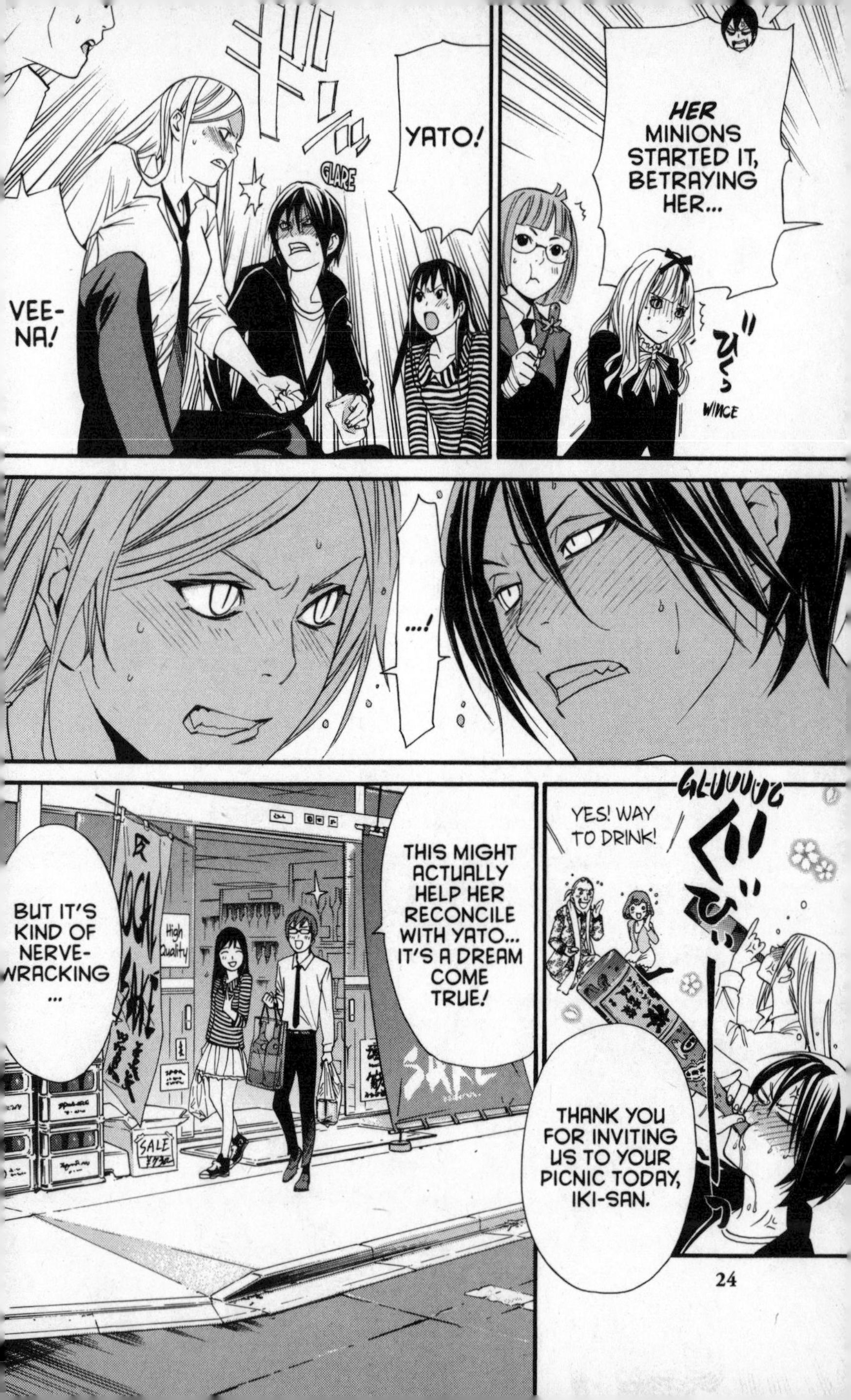

HER MINIONS STARTED IT, BETRAYING HER...
WINCE
YATO!
GLARE
VEE-NA!
...!
GL-UUUUG
YES! WAY TO DRINK!
THANK YOU FOR INVITING US TO YOUR PICNIC TODAY, IKI-SAN.
THIS MIGHT ACTUALLY HELP HER RECONCILE WITH YATO... IT'S A DREAM COME TRUE!
BUT IT'S KIND OF NERVE-WRACKING ...

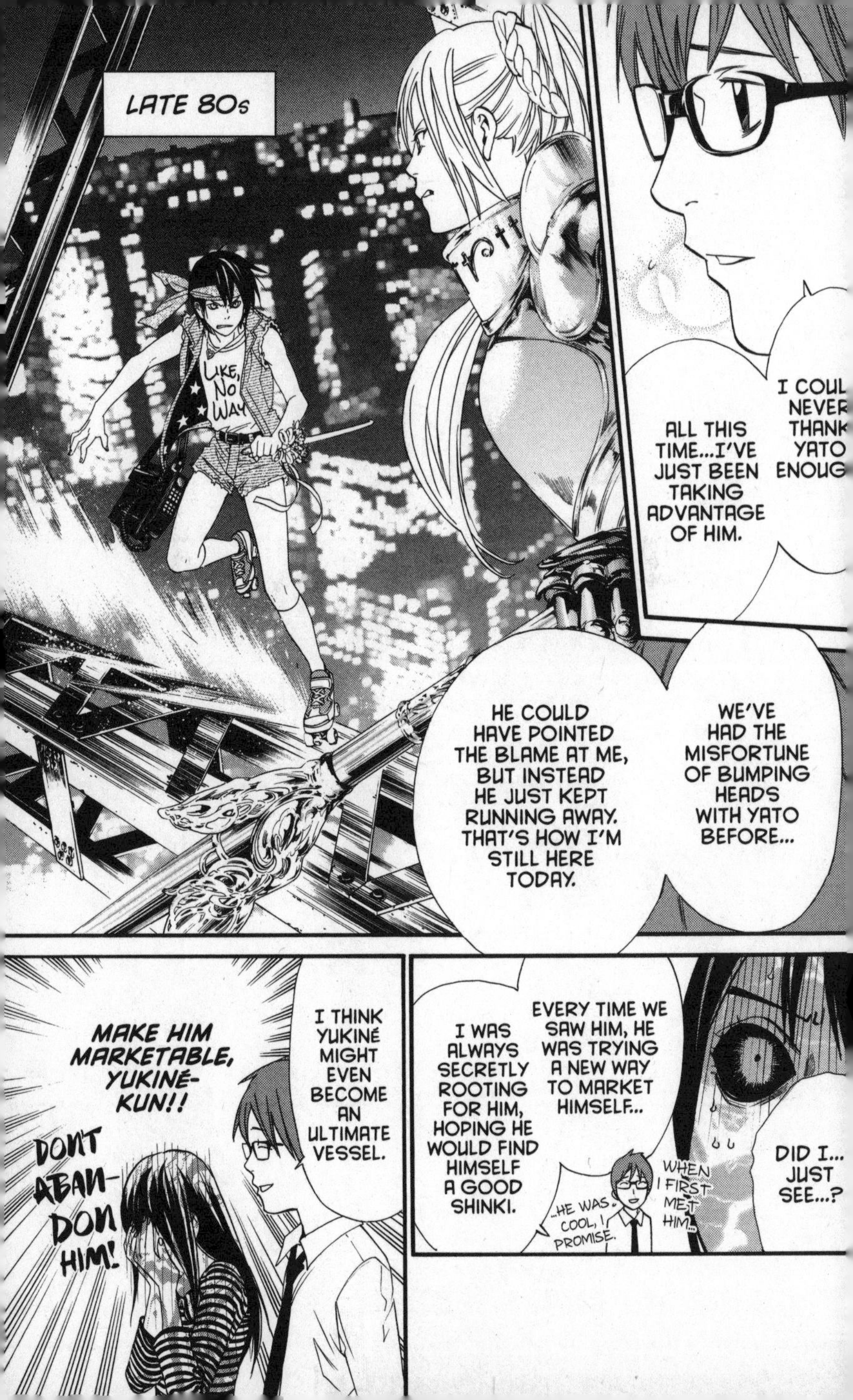

I COUL NEVER THANK YATO ENOUG
ALL THIS TIME...I'VE JUST BEEN TAKING ADVANTAGE OF HIM.
LATE 80s
WE'VE HAD THE MISFORTUNE OF BUMPING HEADS WITH YATO BEFORE...
HE COULD HAVE POINTED THE BLAME AT ME, BUT INSTEAD HE JUST KEPT RUNNING AWAY. THAT'S HOW I'M STILL HERE TODAY.
LIKE, NO WAY
DID I... JUST SEE...?
EVERY TIME WE SAW HIM, HE WAS TRYING A NEW WAY TO MARKET HIMSELF...
I WAS ALWAYS SECRETLY ROOTING FOR HIM, HOPING HE WOULD FIND HIMSELF A GOOD SHINKI.
WHEN I FIRST MET HIM...
...HE WAS COOL, I PROMISE.
I THINK YUKINÉ MIGHT EVEN BECOME AN ULTIMATE VESSEL.
MAKE HIM MARKETABLE, YUKINÉ-KUN!!
DON'T ABAN-DON HIM!

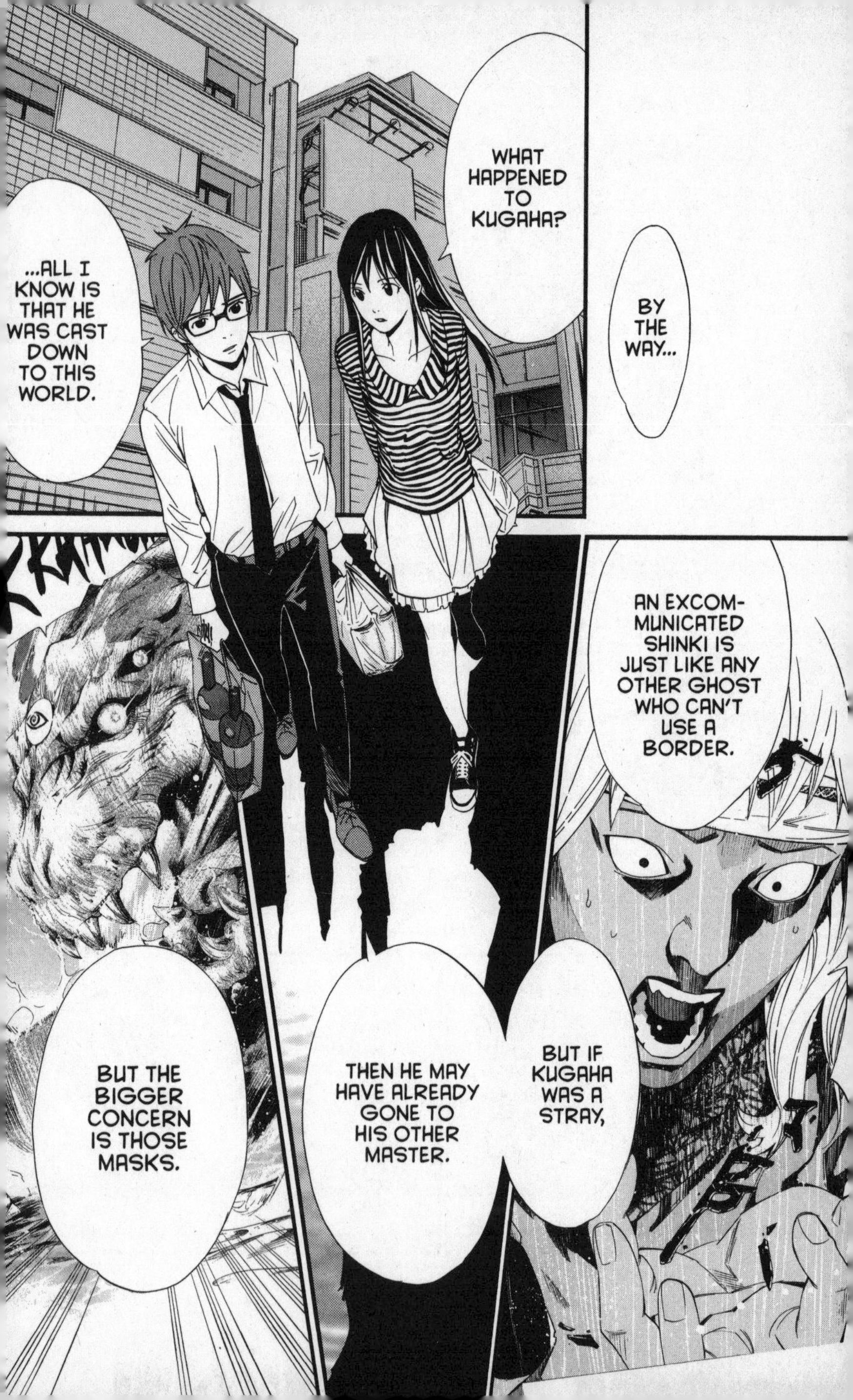
BY THE WAY...
WHAT HAPPENED TO KUGAHA?
...ALL I KNOW IS THAT HE WAS CAST DOWN TO THIS WORLD.
AN EXCOM-MUNICATED SHINKI IS JUST LIKE ANY OTHER GHOST WHO CAN'T USE A BORDER.
BUT IF KUGAHA WAS A STRAY,
THEN HE MAY HAVE ALREADY GONE TO HIS OTHER MASTER.
BUT THE BIGGER CONCERN IS THOSE MASKS.

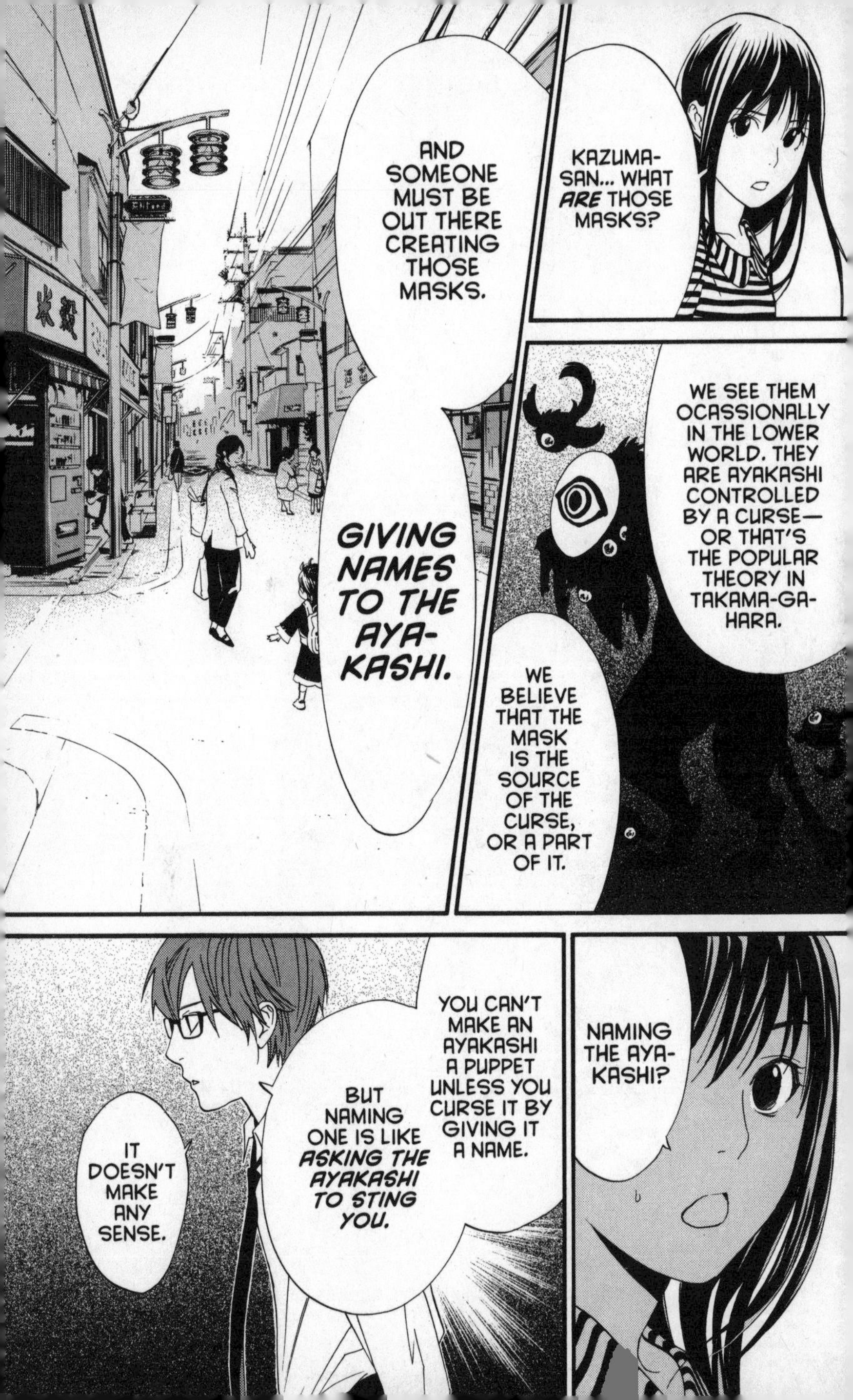
KAZUMA-SAN... WHAT *ARE* THOSE MASKS?
WE SEE THEM OCASSIONALLY IN THE LOWER WORLD. THEY ARE AYAKASHI CONTROLLED BY A CURSE— OR THAT'S THE POPULAR THEORY IN TAKAMA-GA-HARA.
WE BELIEVE THAT THE MASK IS THE SOURCE OF THE CURSE, OR A PART OF IT.
AND SOMEONE MUST BE OUT THERE CREATING THOSE MASKS.
GIVING NAMES TO THE AYA-KASHI.
NAMING THE AYA-KASHI?
YOU CAN'T MAKE AN AYAKASHI A PUPPET UNLESS YOU CURSE IT BY GIVING IT A NAME.
BUT NAMING ONE IS LIKE *ASKING THE AYAKASHI TO STING YOU.*
IT DOESN'T MAKE ANY SENSE.

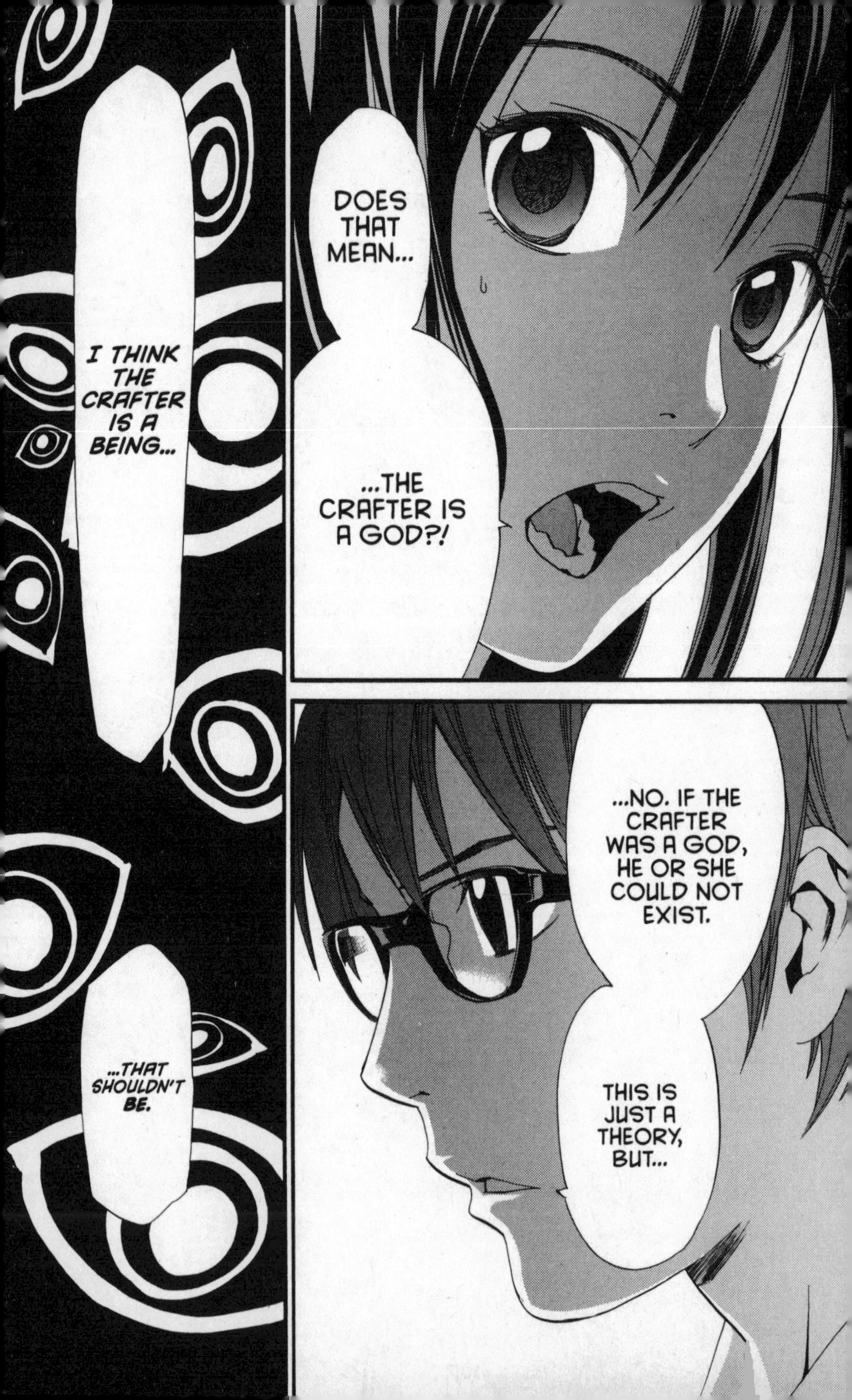
DOES THAT MEAN...
...THE CRAFTER IS A GOD?!
...NO. IF THE CRAFTER WAS A GOD, HE OR SHE COULD NOT EXIST.
THIS IS JUST A THEORY, BUT...
I THINK THE CRAFTER IS A BEING...
...THAT SHOULDN'T BE.

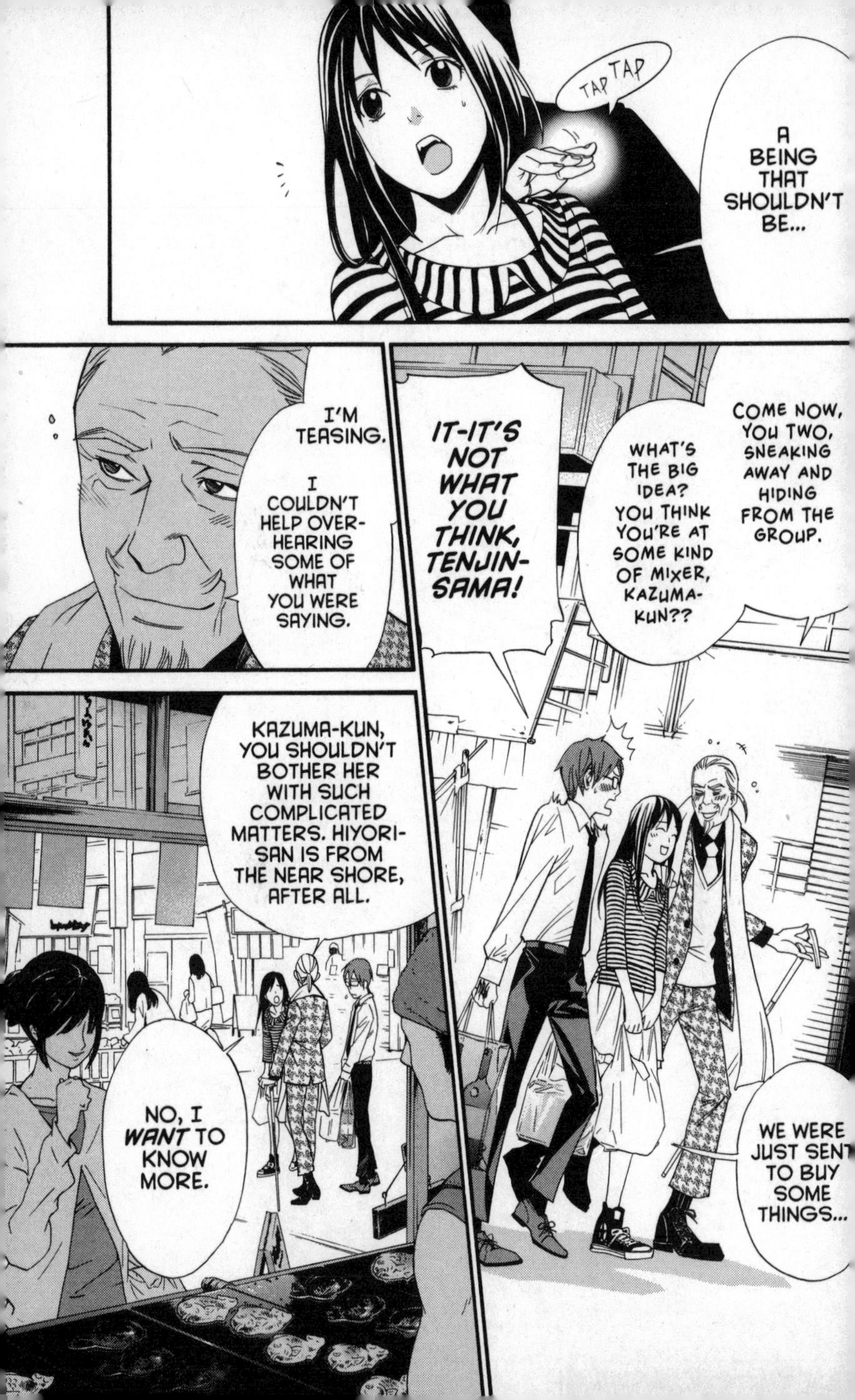
TAP TAP
A BEING THAT SHOULDN'T BE...
COME NOW, YOU TWO, SNEAKING AWAY AND HIDING FROM THE GROUP.
WHAT'S THE BIG IDEA? YOU THINK YOU'RE AT SOME KIND OF MIXER, KAZUMA-KUN??
IT-IT'S NOT WHAT YOU THINK, TENJIN-SAMA!
WE WERE JUST SENT TO BUY SOME THINGS...
I'M TEASING.
I COULDN'T HELP OVER-HEARING SOME OF WHAT YOU WERE SAYING.
KAZUMA-KUN, YOU SHOULDN'T BOTHER HER WITH SUCH COMPLICATED MATTERS. HIYORI-SAN IS FROM THE NEAR SHORE, AFTER ALL.
NO, I *WANT* TO KNOW MORE.

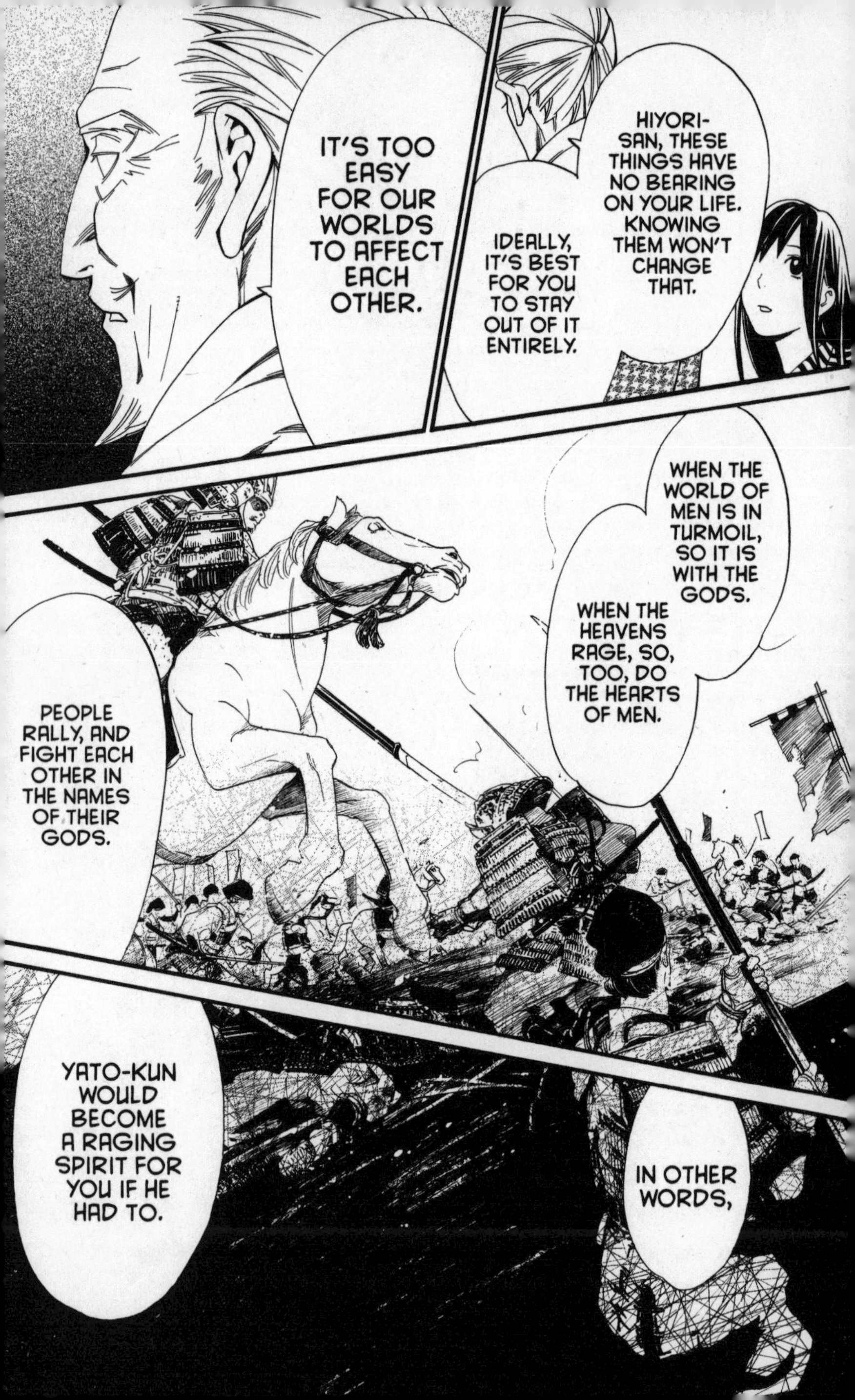
HIYORI-SAN, THESE THINGS HAVE NO BEARING ON YOUR LIFE. KNOWING THEM WON'T CHANGE THAT.
IDEALLY, IT'S BEST FOR YOU TO STAY OUT OF IT ENTIRELY.
IT'S TOO EASY FOR OUR WORLDS TO AFFECT EACH OTHER.
WHEN THE WORLD OF MEN IS IN TURMOIL, SO IT IS WITH THE GODS.
WHEN THE HEAVENS RAGE, SO, TOO, DO THE HEARTS OF MEN.
PEOPLE RALLY, AND FIGHT EACH OTHER IN THE NAMES OF THEIR GODS.
IN OTHER WORDS,
YATO-KUN WOULD BECOME A RAGING SPIRIT FOR YOU IF HE HAD TO.

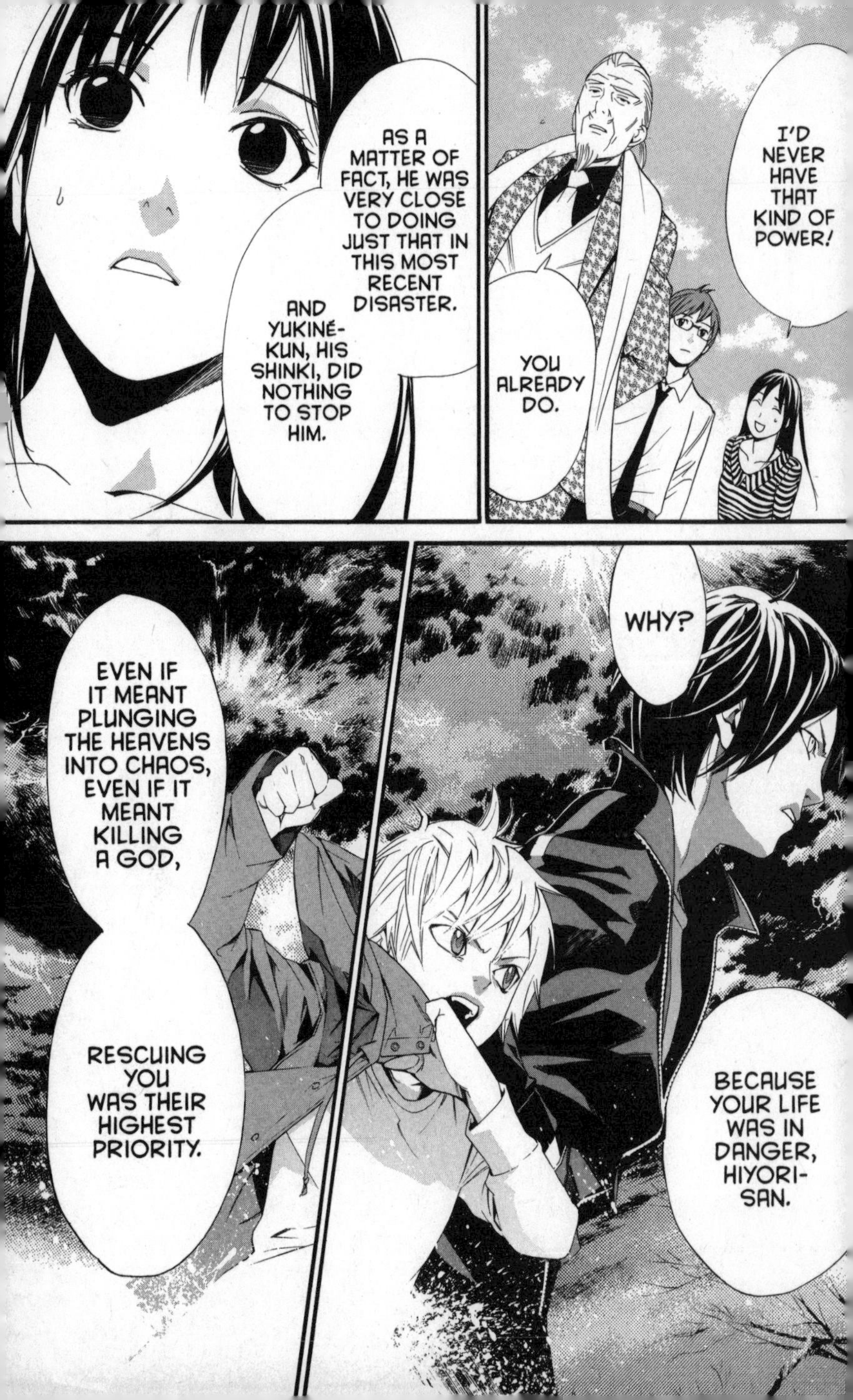
I'D NEVER HAVE THAT KIND OF POWER!
YOU ALREADY DO.
AS A MATTER OF FACT, HE WAS VERY CLOSE TO DOING JUST THAT IN THIS MOST RECENT DISASTER.
AND YUKINÉ-KUN, HIS SHINKI, DID NOTHING TO STOP HIM.
WHY?
BECAUSE YOUR LIFE WAS IN DANGER, HIYORI-SAN.
EVEN IF IT MEANT PLUNGING THE HEAVENS INTO CHAOS, EVEN IF IT MEANT KILLING A GOD,
RESCUING YOU WAS THEIR HIGHEST PRIORITY.

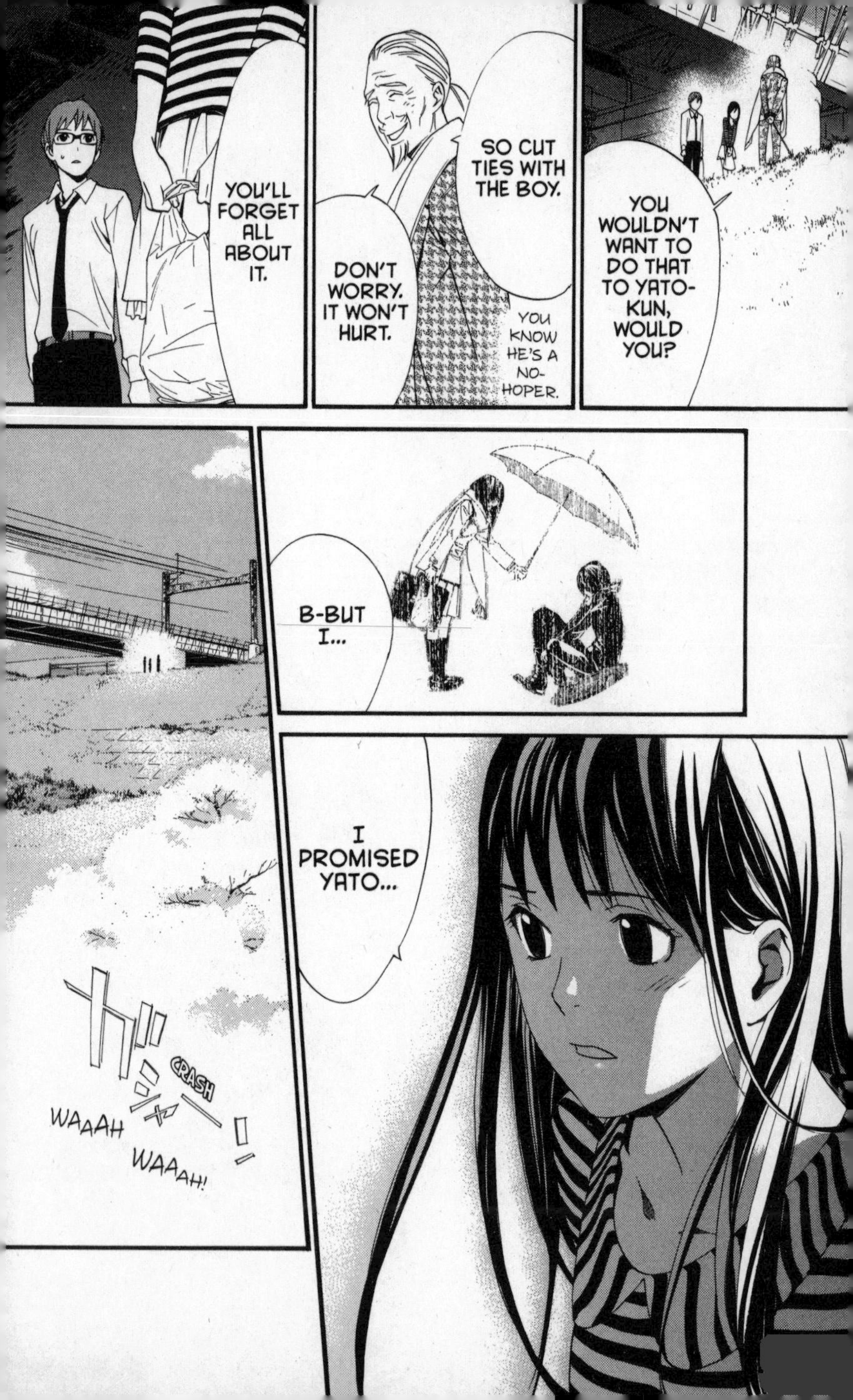
YOU WOULDN'T WANT TO DO THAT TO YATO-KUN, WOULD YOU?
SO CUT TIES WITH THE BOY.
YOU KNOW HE'S A NO-HOPER.
DON'T WORRY. IT WON'T HURT.
YOU'LL FORGET ALL ABOUT IT.
B-BUT I...
I PROMISED YATO...
CRASH
WAAAH
WAAAH!

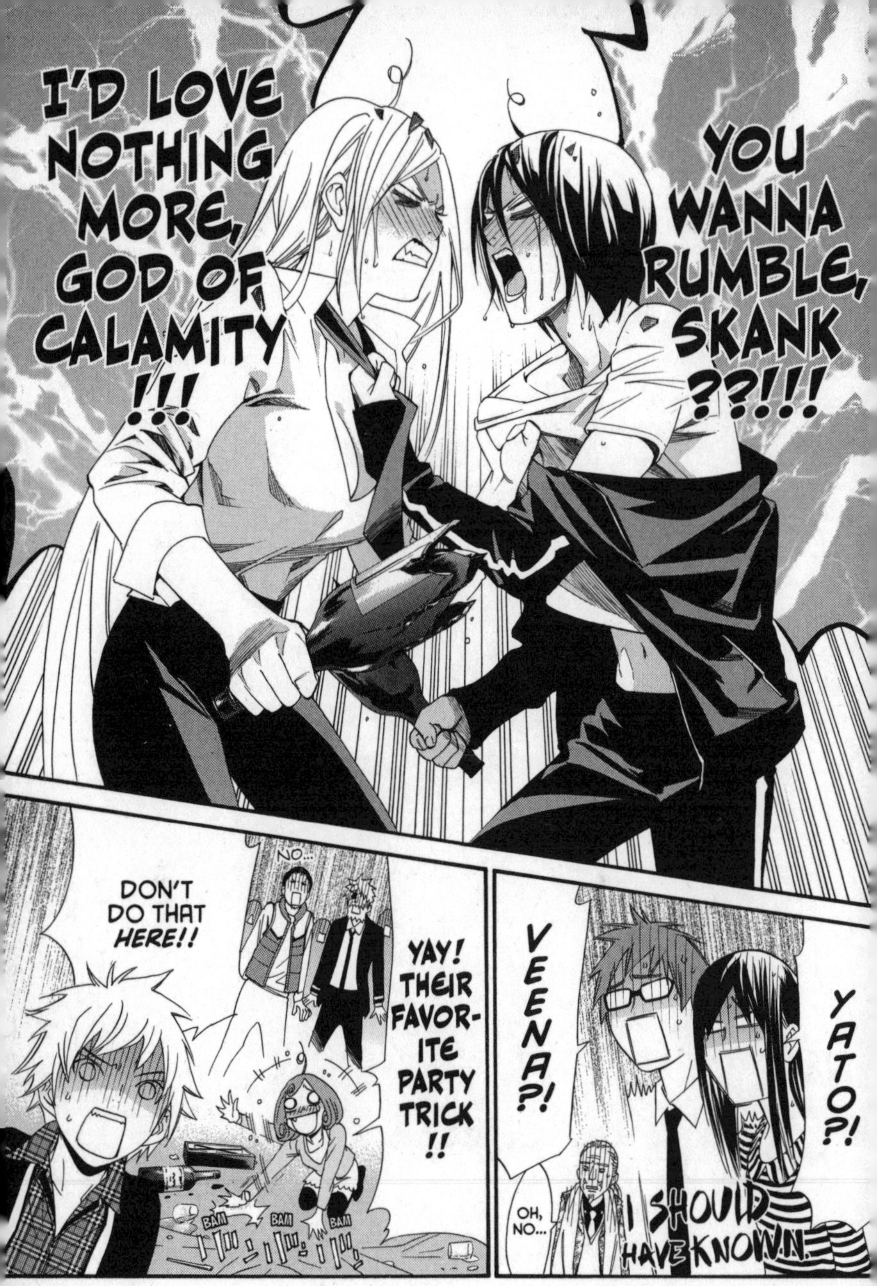
YOU WANNA RUMBLE, SKANK??!!!
I'D LOVE NOTHING MORE, GOD OF CALAMITY!!!
YATO?!
VEENA?!
I SHOULD HAVE KNOWN.
OH, NO...
NO...
YAY! THEIR FAVOR-ITE PARTY TRICK!!
DON'T DO THAT HERE!!
BAM
BAM
BAM

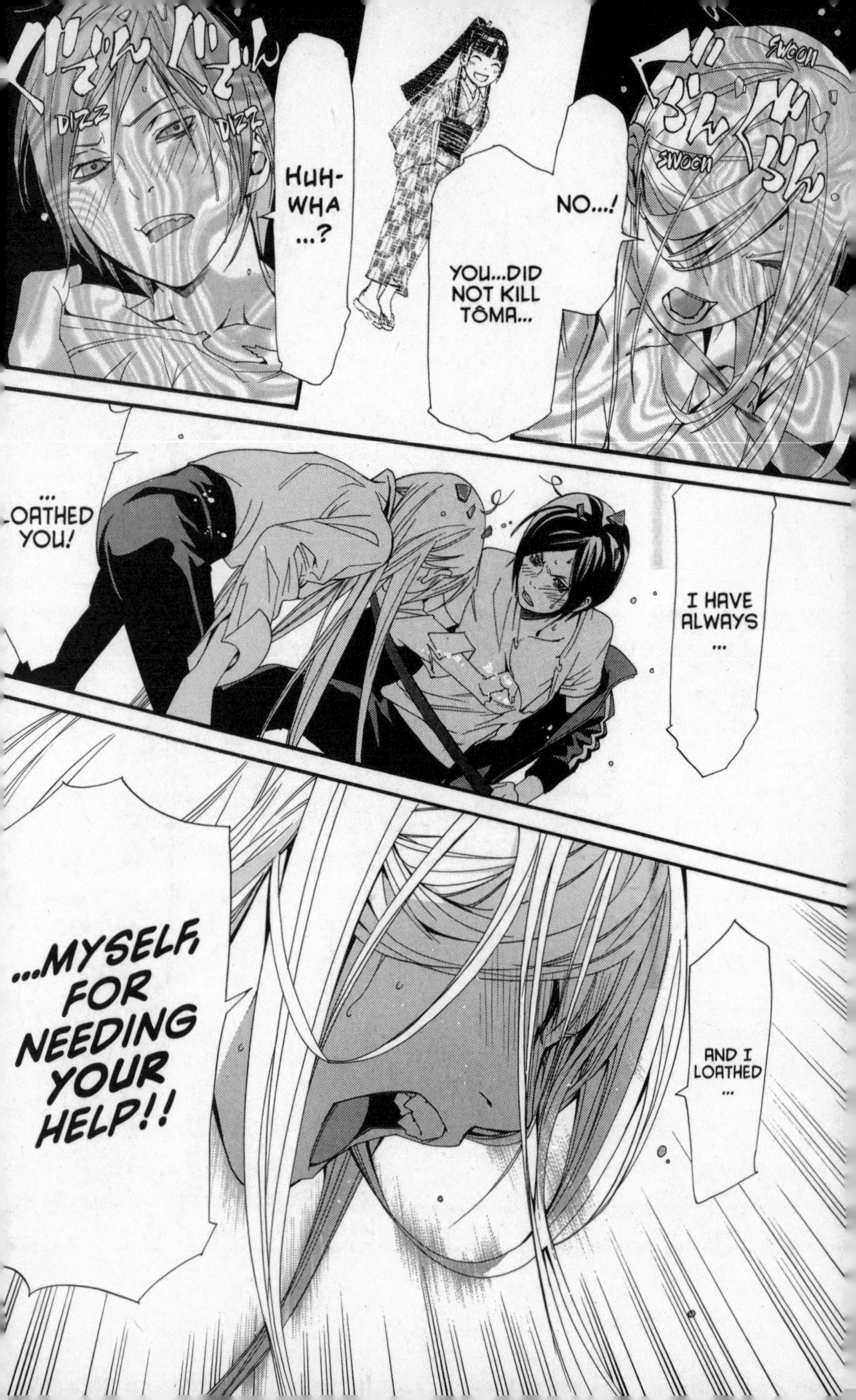
SWOON
SWOON
NO...!
YOU...DID NOT KILL TÔMA...
DIZZ
DIZZ
HUH-WHA ...?
I HAVE ALWAYS ...
... LOATHED YOU!
AND I LOATHED ...
...MYSELF, FOR NEEDING YOUR HELP!!

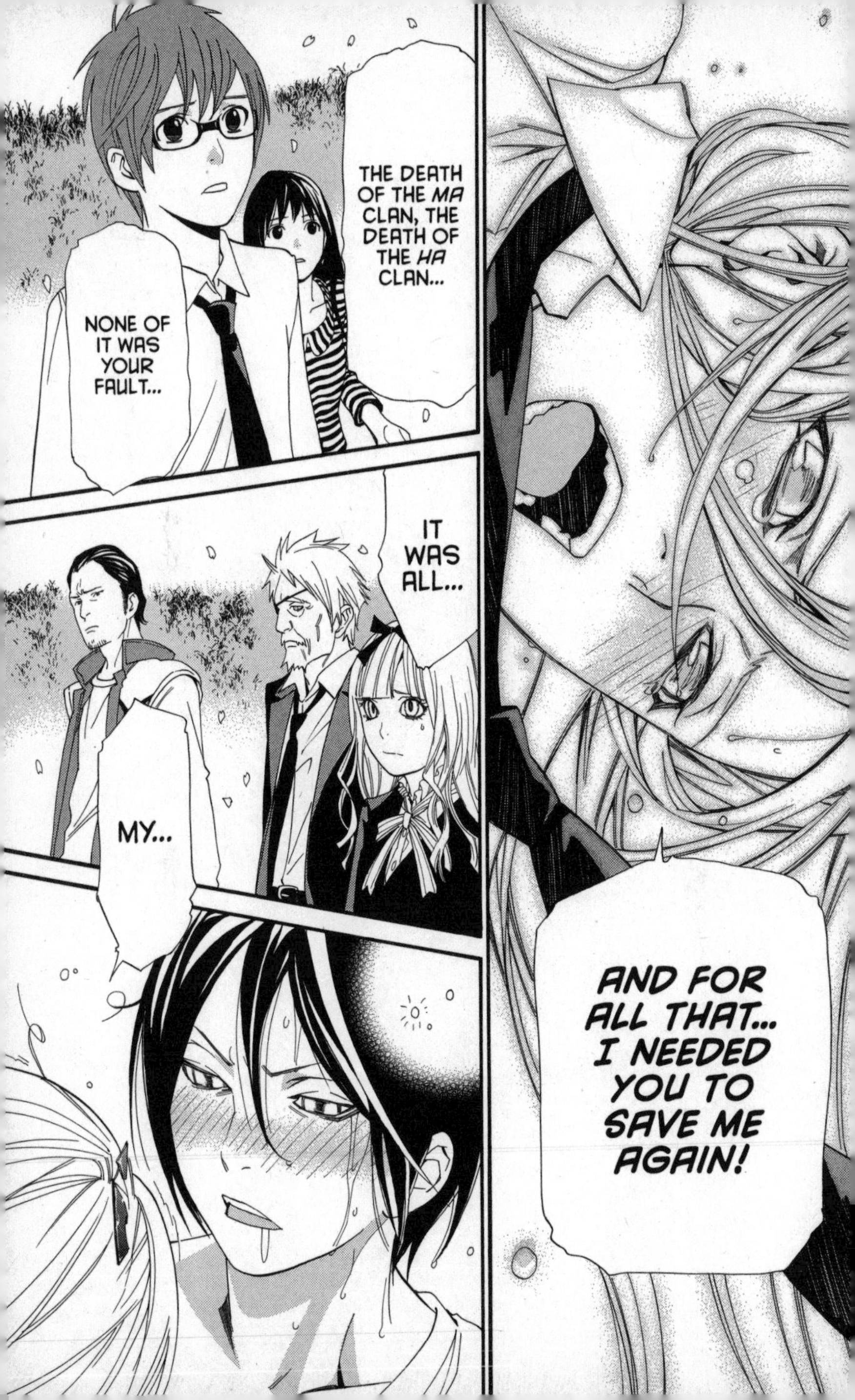
THE DEATH OF THE *MA* CLAN, THE DEATH OF THE *HA* CLAN...
NONE OF IT WAS YOUR FAULT...
IT WAS ALL...
MY...
AND FOR ALL THAT... I NEEDED YOU TO SAVE ME AGAIN!

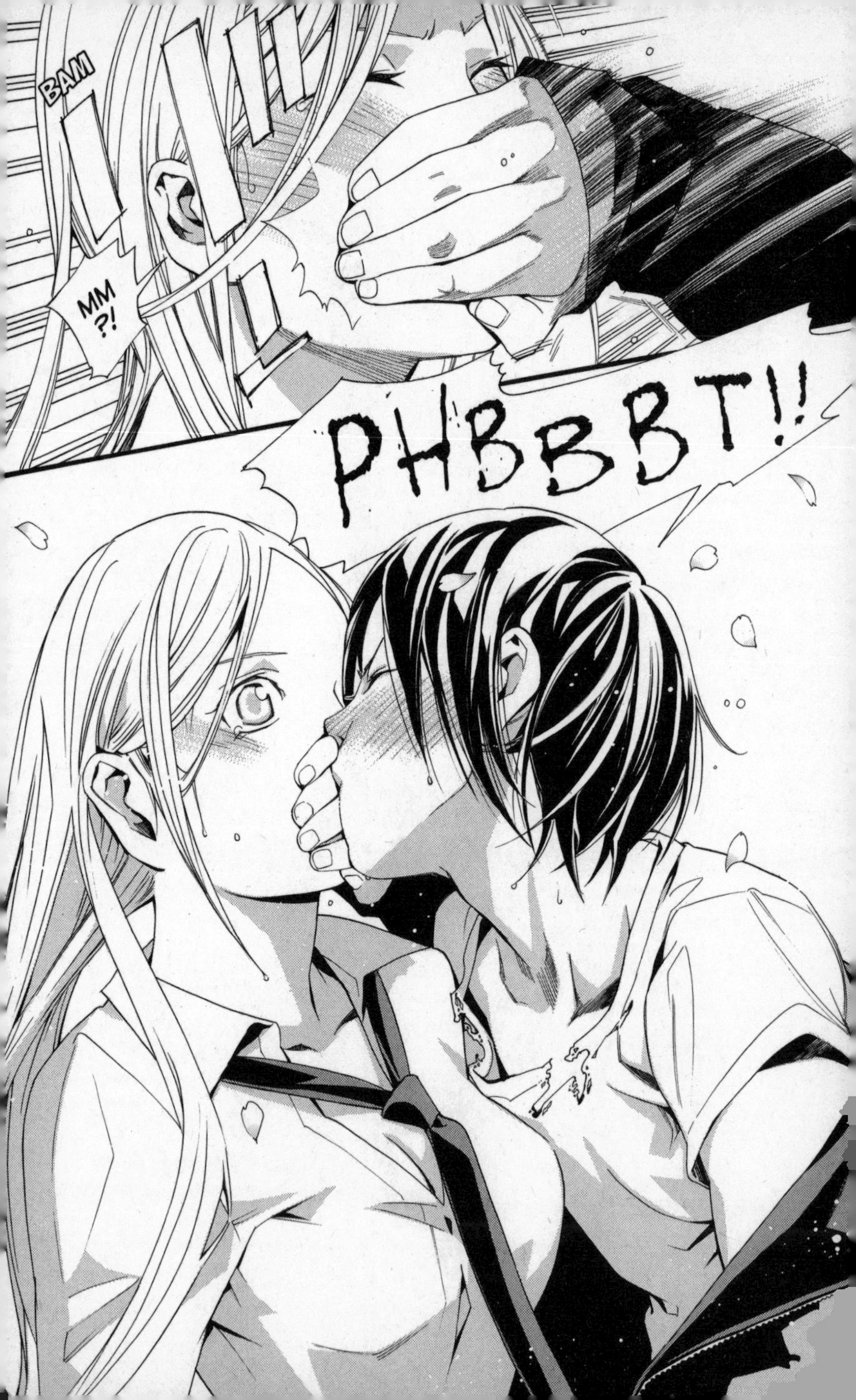
BAM
MM ?!
PHBBBT!!

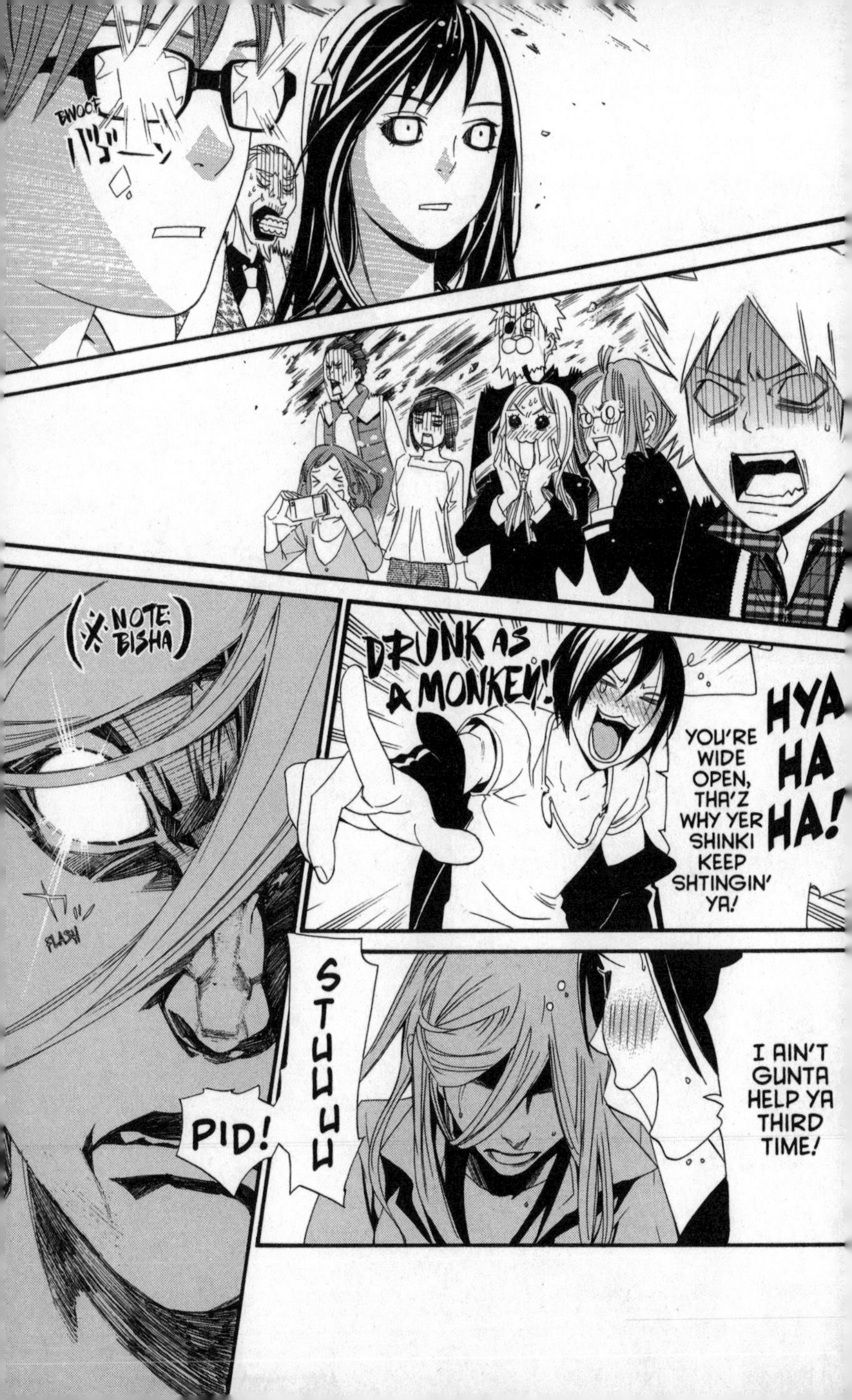
BWOOF
バゴーン
HYA HA HA!
YOU'RE WIDE OPEN, THA'Z WHY YER SHINKI KEEP SHTINGIN' YA!
DRUNK AS A MONKEY!
I AIN'T GUNTA HELP YA THIRD TIME!
STUUUUU
PID!
(※NOTE: BISHA)
FLASH

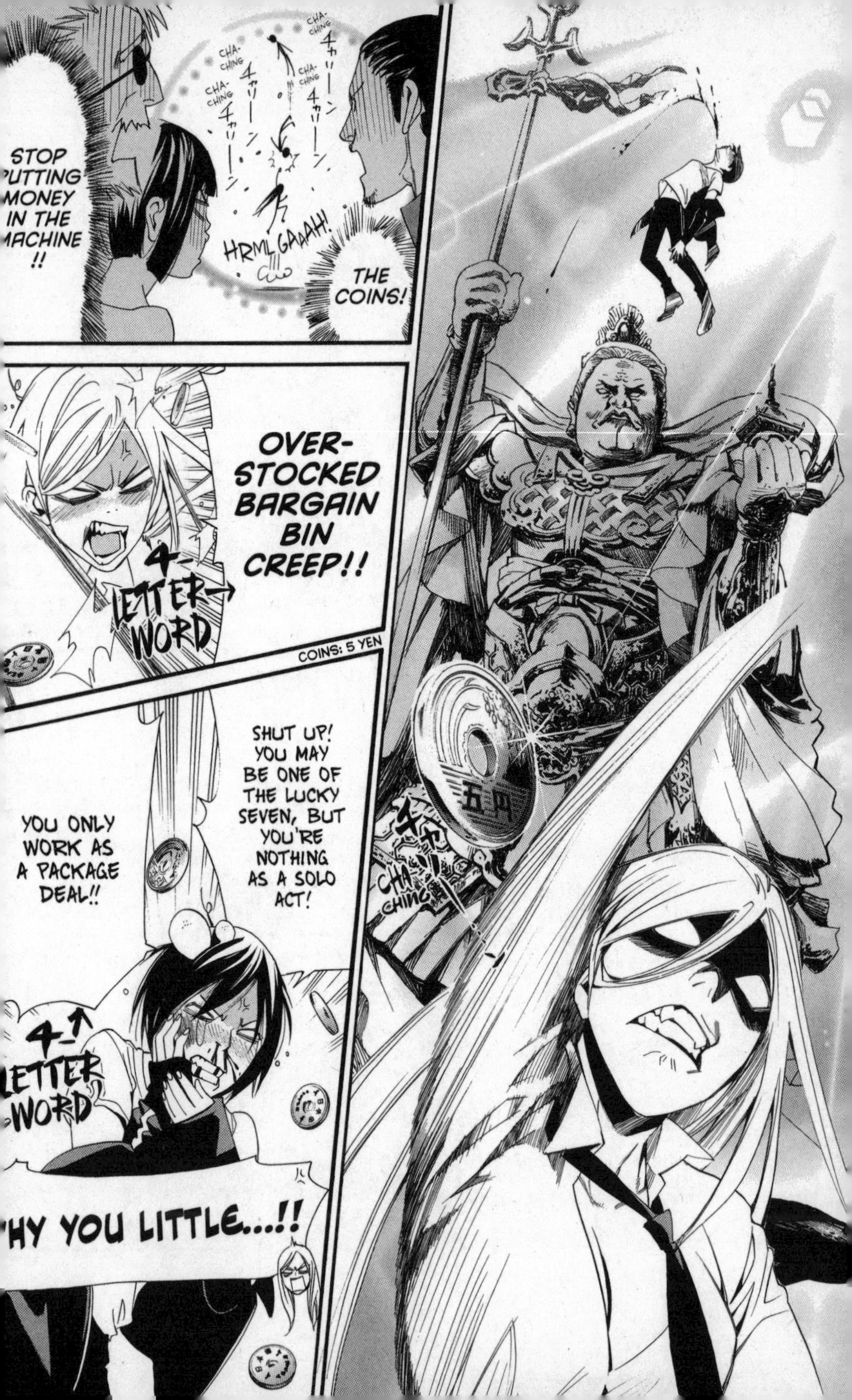

CHA-CHING
THE COINS!
HRML GAAAH!
CHA-CHING
CHA-CHING
CHA-CHING
STOP PUTTING MONEY IN THE MACHINE!!
OVER-STOCKED BARGAIN BIN CREEP!!
4-LETTER WORD
COINS: 5 YEN
SHUT UP! YOU MAY BE ONE OF THE LUCKY SEVEN, BUT YOU'RE NOTHING AS A SOLO ACT!
YOU ONLY WORK AS A PACKAGE DEAL!!
4-LETTER WORD
HY YOU LITTLE...!!

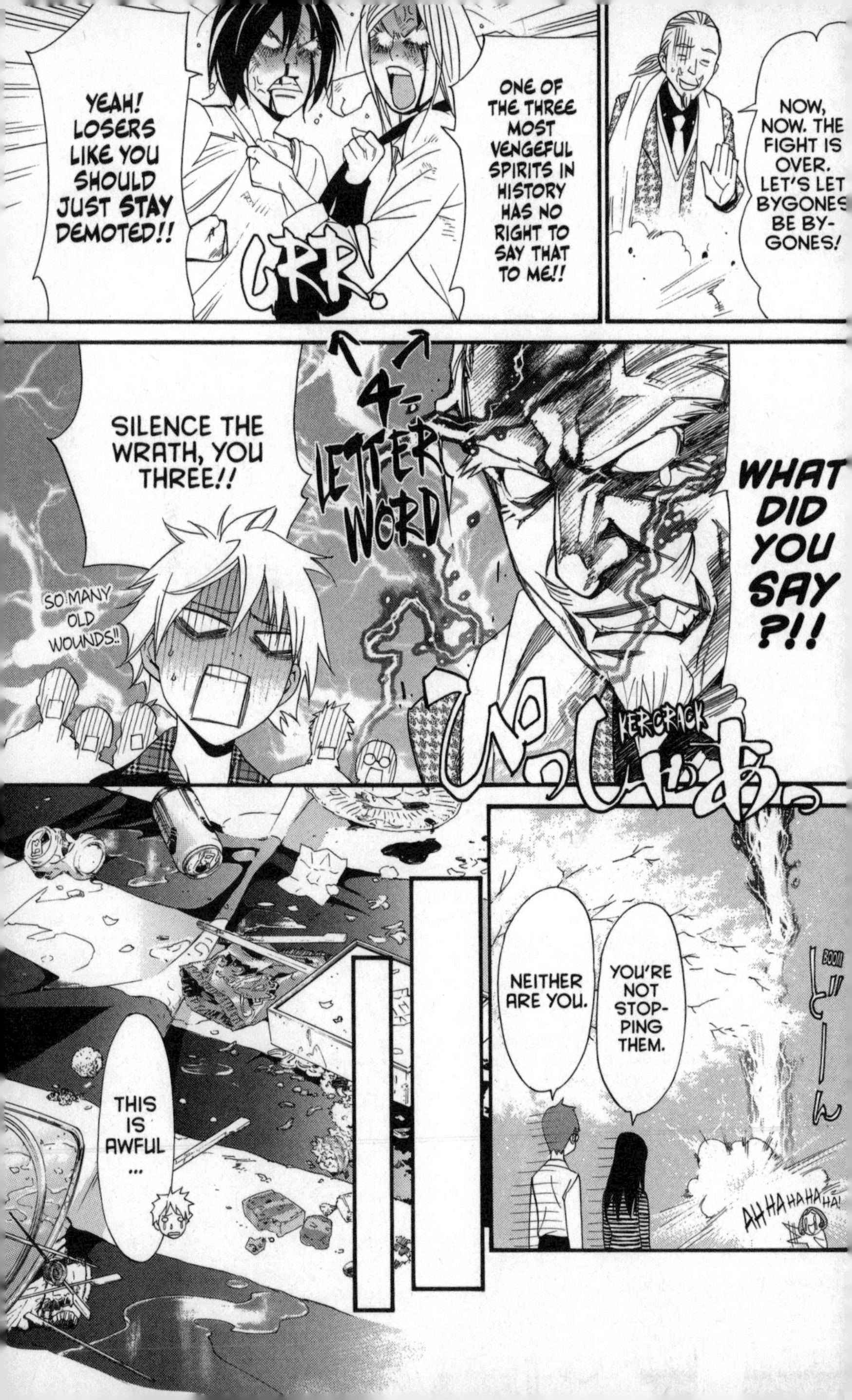
NOW, NOW. THE FIGHT IS OVER. LET'S LET BYGONES BE BY-GONES!
ONE OF THE THREE MOST VENGEFUL SPIRITS IN HISTORY HAS NO RIGHT TO SAY THAT TO ME!!
YEAH! LOSERS LIKE YOU SHOULD JUST STAY DEMOTED!!
GRR!
WHAT DID YOU SAY?!!
4-LETTER WORD
KERCRACK
SILENCE THE WRATH, YOU THREE!!
SO MANY OLD WOUNDS!!
BOOM
YOU'RE NOT STOP-PING THEM.
NEITHER ARE YOU.
AHHAHAHAHA!
THIS IS AWFUL...

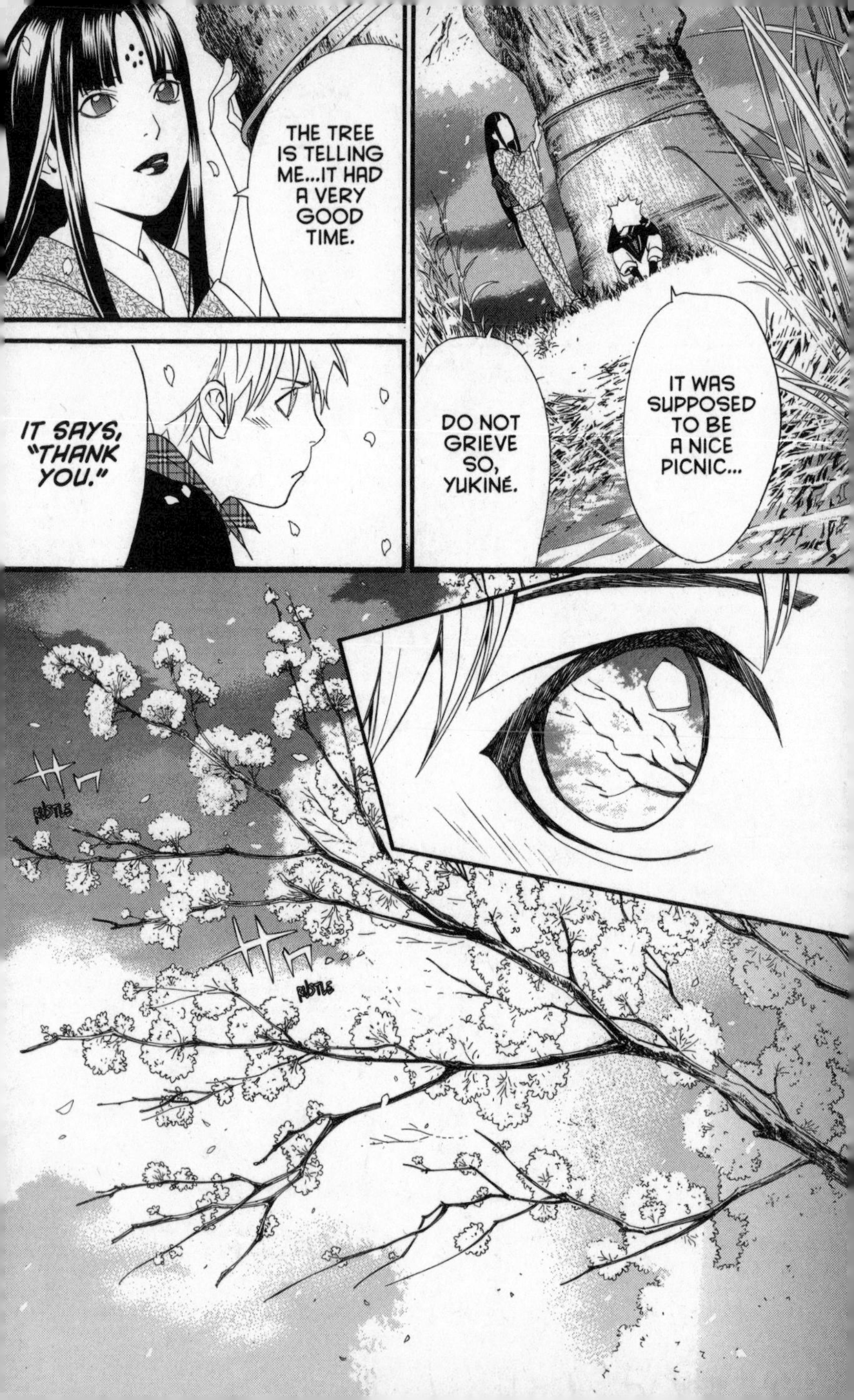
IT WAS SUPPOSED TO BE A NICE PICNIC...
DO NOT GRIEVE SO, YUKINÉ.
THE TREE IS TELLING ME...IT HAD A VERY GOOD TIME.
IT SAYS, "THANK YOU."
RUSTLE
RUSTLE

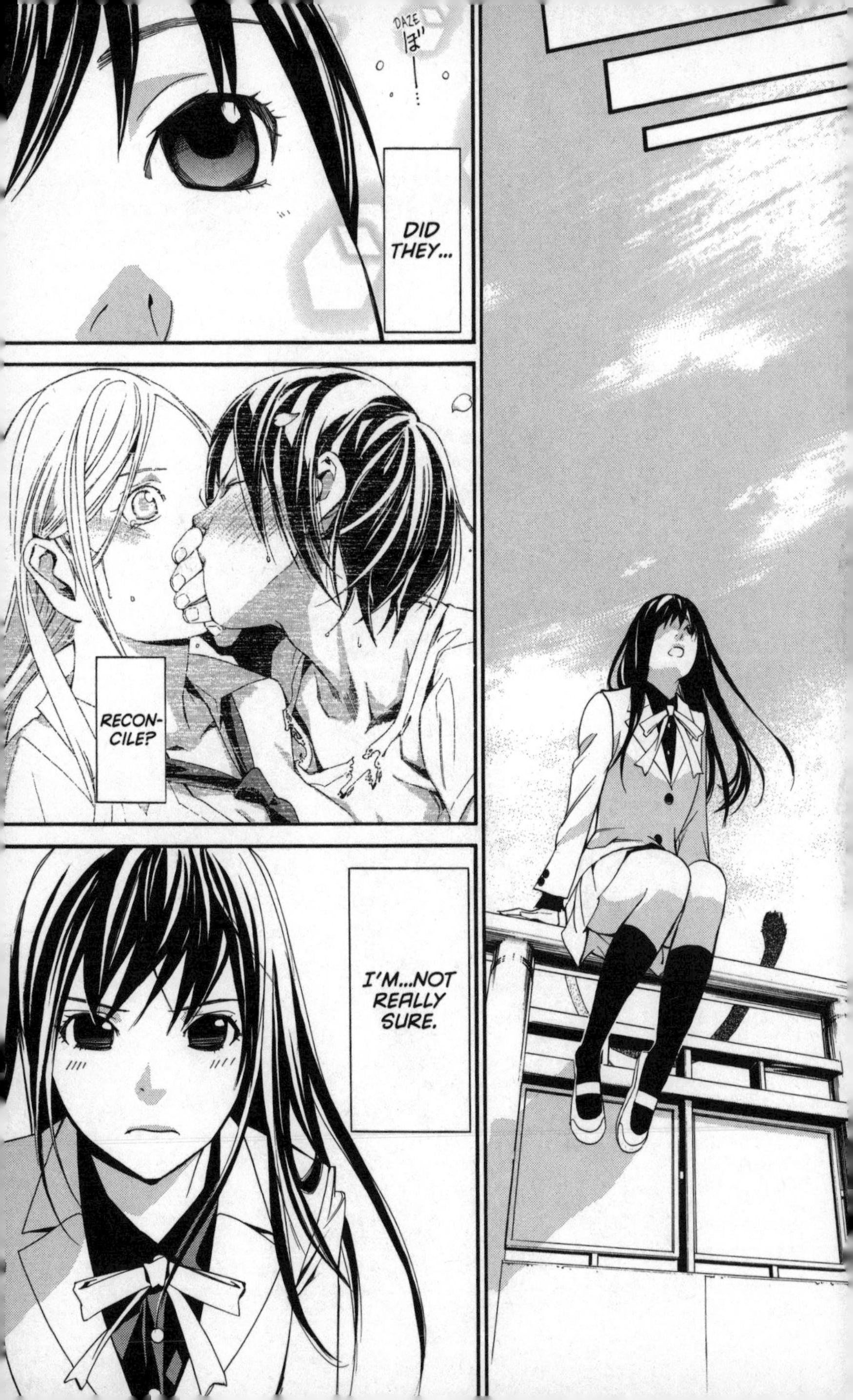
DAZE
ぼー…
DID THEY...
RECON-CILE?
I'M...NOT REALLY SURE.

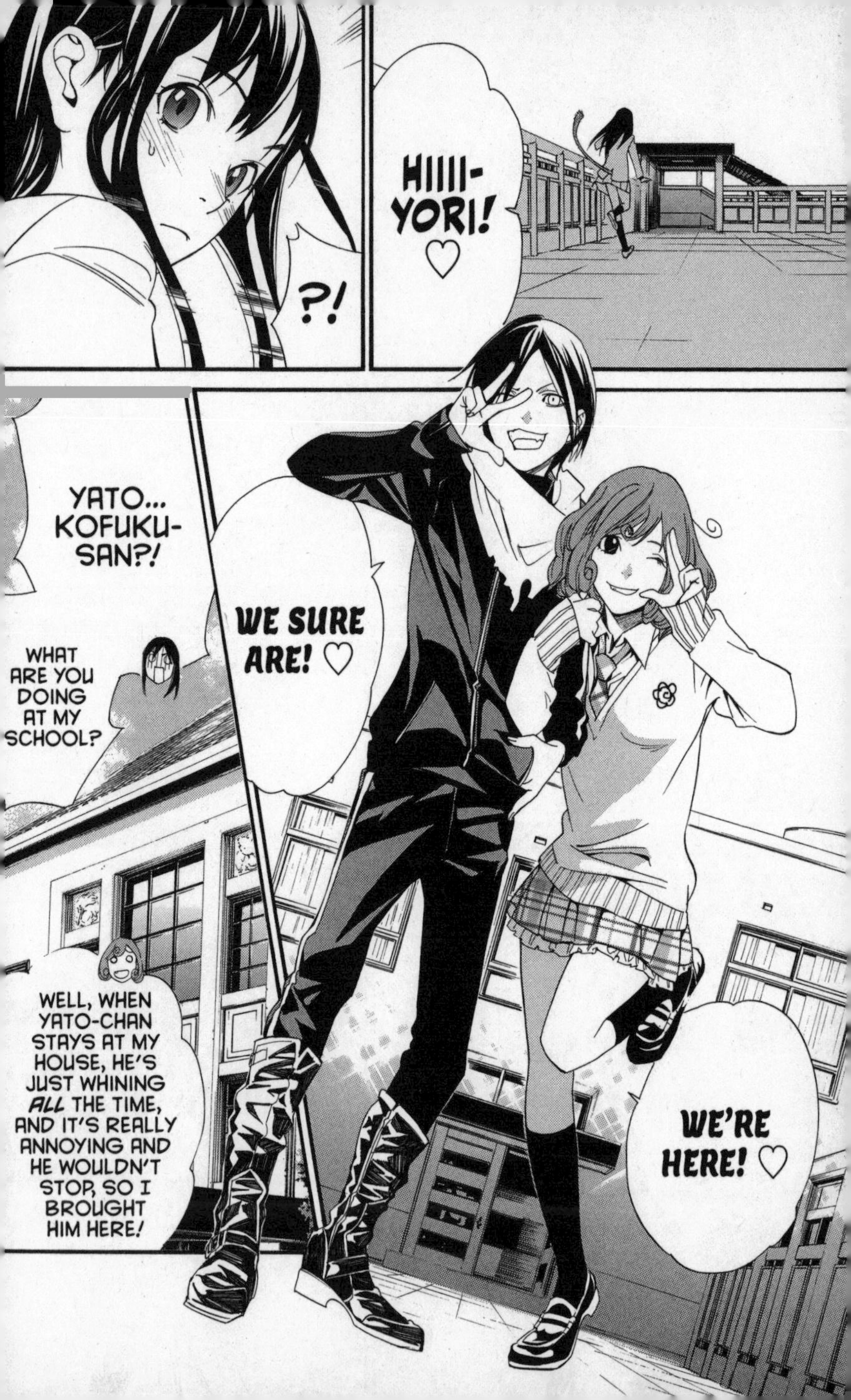
HIIII-YORI! ♡
?!
WE SURE ARE! ♡
WE'RE HERE! ♡
YATO... KOFUKU-SAN?!
WHAT ARE YOU DOING AT MY SCHOOL?
WELL, WHEN YATO-CHAN STAYS AT MY HOUSE, HE'S JUST WHINING ALL THE TIME, AND IT'S REALLY ANNOYING AND HE WOULDN'T STOP, SO I BROUGHT HIM HERE!

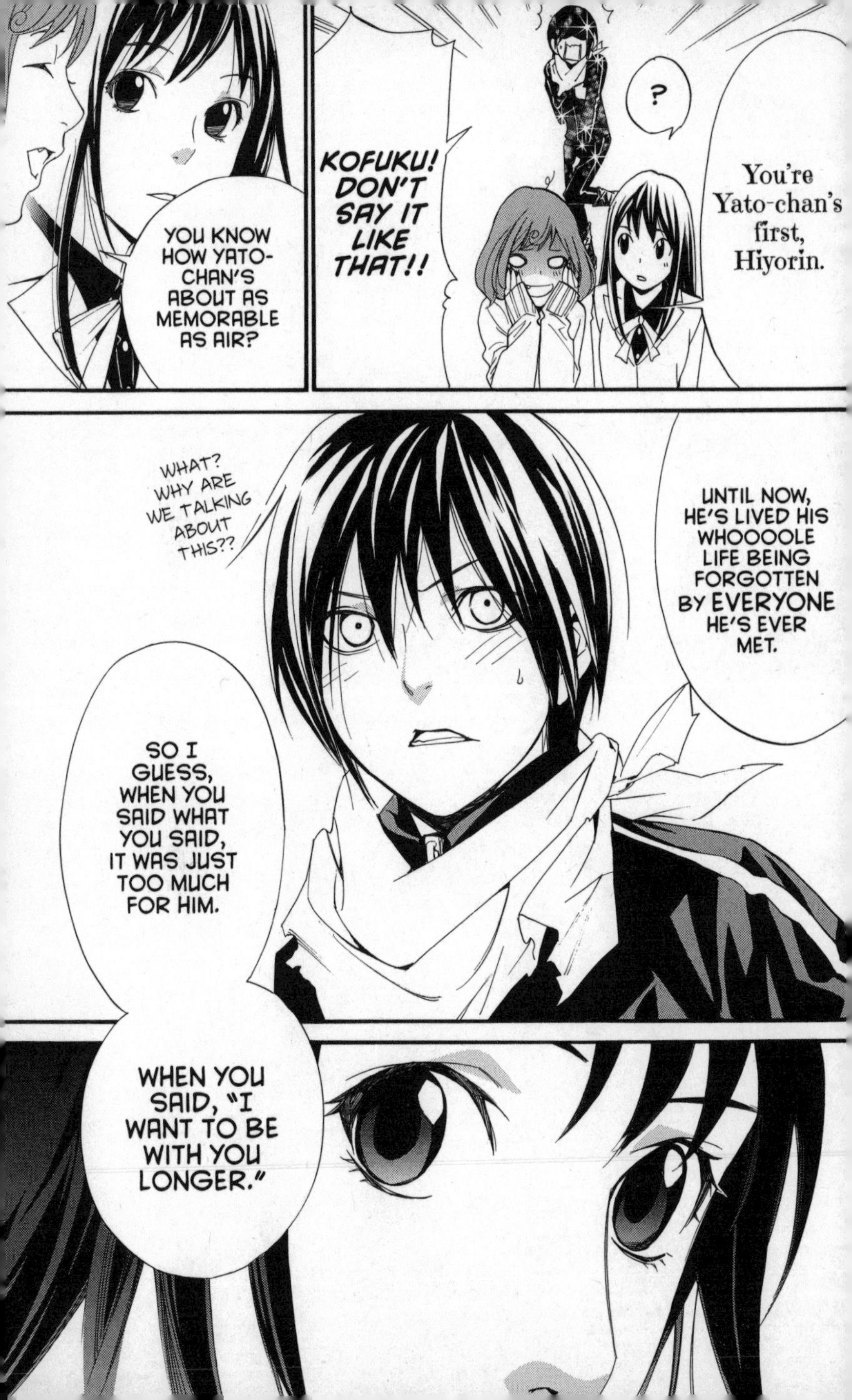
You're Yato-chan's first, Hiyorin.
?
KOFUKU! DON'T SAY IT LIKE THAT!!
YOU KNOW HOW YATO-CHAN'S ABOUT AS MEMORABLE AS AIR?
UNTIL NOW, HE'S LIVED HIS WHOOOOLE LIFE BEING FORGOTTEN BY EVERYONE HE'S EVER MET.
WHAT? WHY ARE WE TALKING ABOUT THIS??
SO I GUESS, WHEN YOU SAID WHAT YOU SAID, IT WAS JUST TOO MUCH FOR HIM.
WHEN YOU SAID, "I WANT TO BE WITH YOU LONGER."

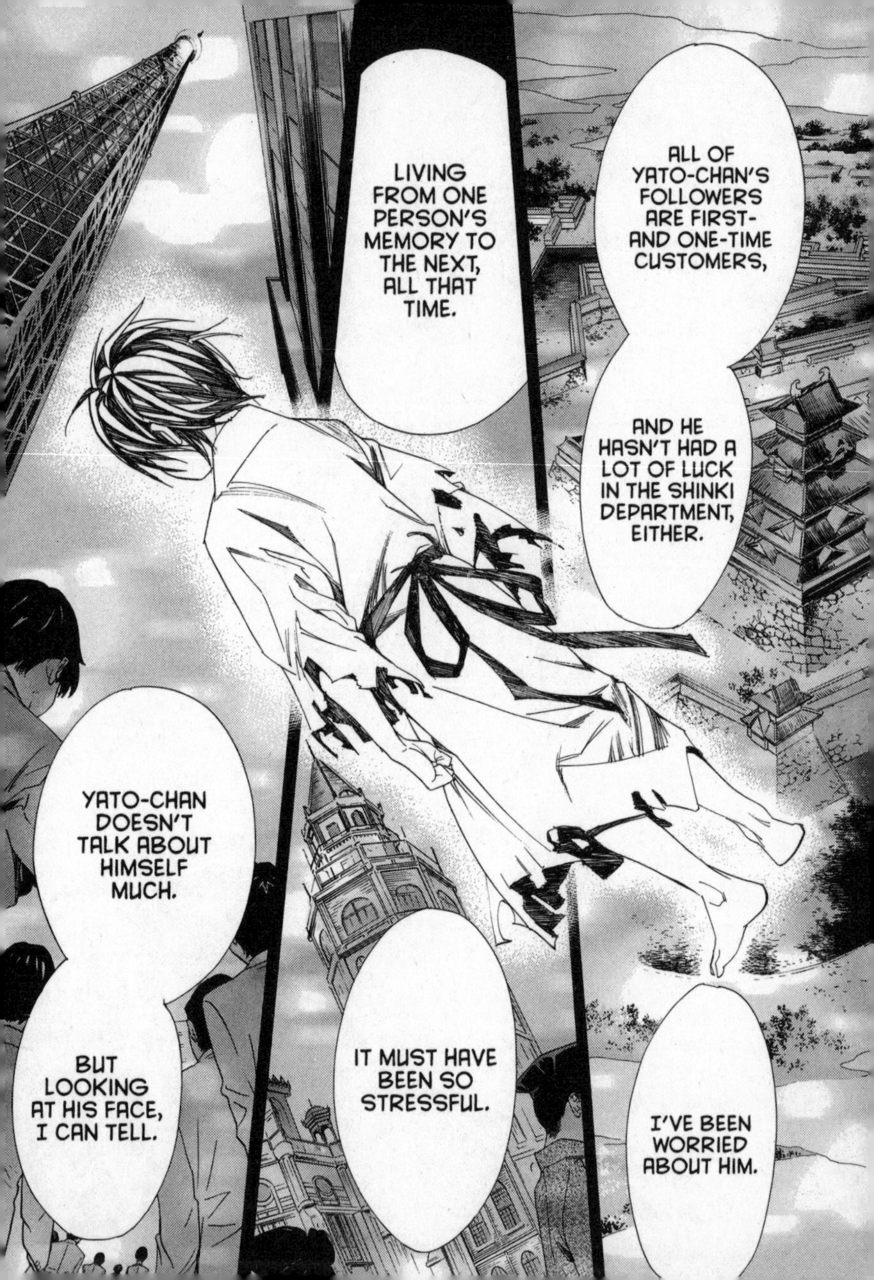
ALL OF YATO-CHAN'S FOLLOWERS ARE FIRST- AND ONE-TIME CUSTOMERS,
AND HE HASN'T HAD A LOT OF LUCK IN THE SHINKI DEPARTMENT, EITHER.
I'VE BEEN WORRIED ABOUT HIM.
LIVING FROM ONE PERSON'S MEMORY TO THE NEXT, ALL THAT TIME.
IT MUST HAVE BEEN SO STRESSFUL.
YATO-CHAN DOESN'T TALK ABOUT HIMSELF MUCH.
BUT LOOKING AT HIS FACE, I CAN TELL.

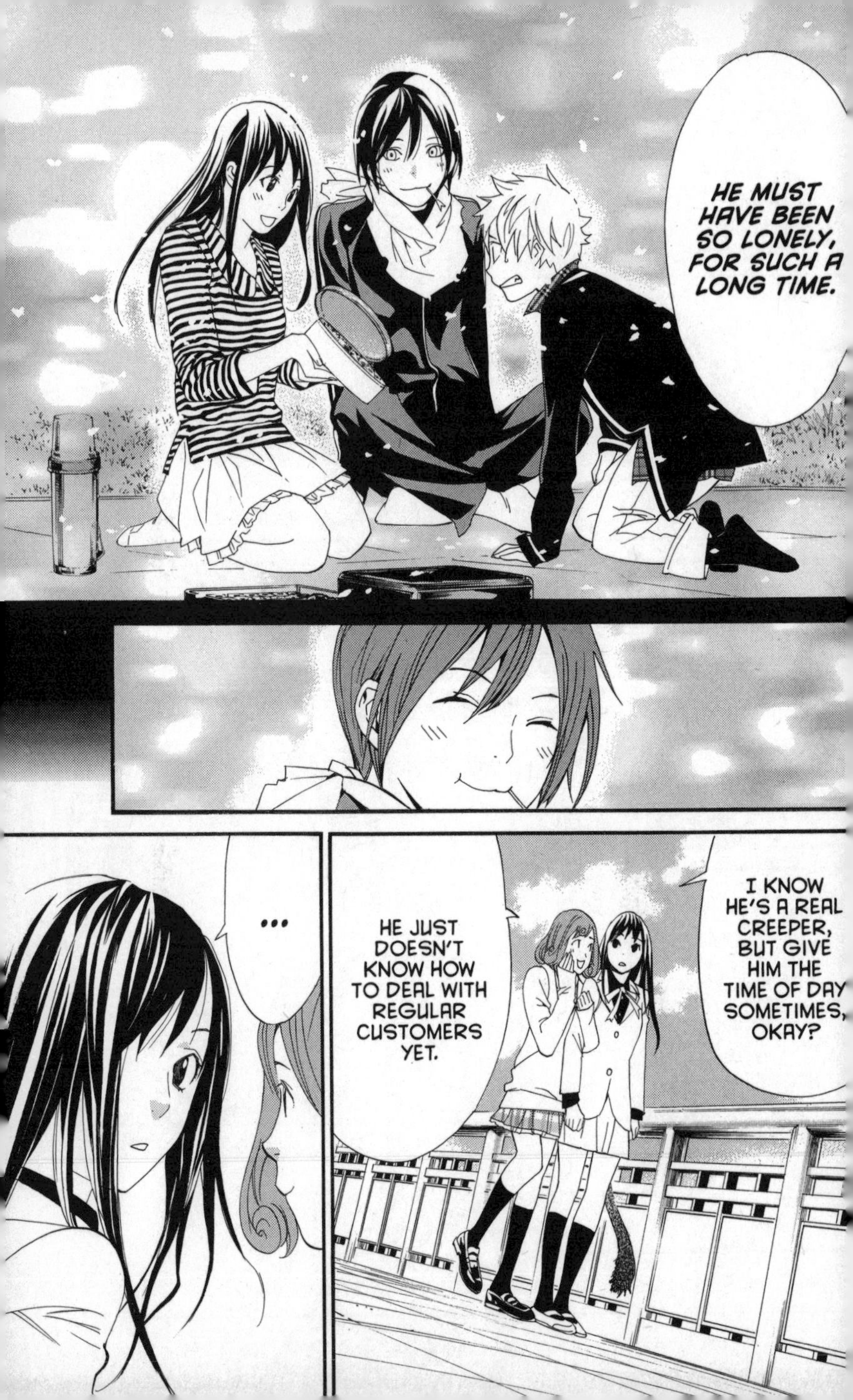
HE MUST HAVE BEEN SO LONELY, FOR SUCH A LONG TIME.
I KNOW HE'S A REAL CREEPER, BUT GIVE HIM THE TIME OF DAY SOMETIMES, OKAY?
HE JUST DOESN'T KNOW HOW TO DEAL WITH REGULAR CUSTOMERS YET.
...

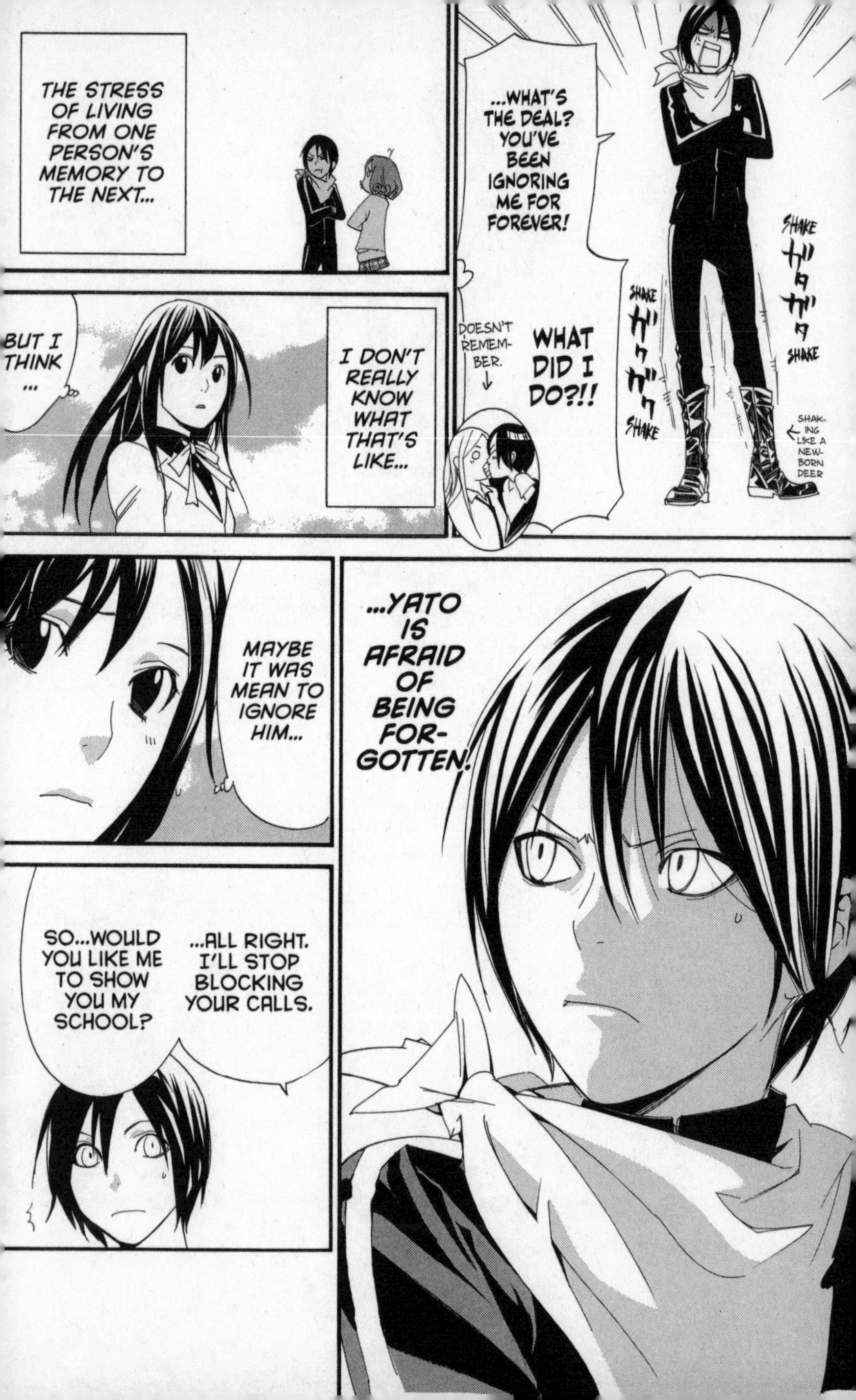

...WHAT'S THE DEAL? YOU'VE BEEN IGNORING ME FOR FOREVER!
SHAKE
SHAKE
SHAKE
SHAKE
SHAKING LIKE A NEWBORN DEER
WHAT DID I DO?!!
DOESN'T REMEMBER.
THE STRESS OF LIVING FROM ONE PERSON'S MEMORY TO THE NEXT...
I DON'T REALLY KNOW WHAT THAT'S LIKE...
BUT I THINK...
...YATO IS AFRAID OF BEING FORGOTTEN!
MAYBE IT WAS MEAN TO IGNORE HIM...
...ALL RIGHT. I'LL STOP BLOCKING YOUR CALLS.
SO...WOULD YOU LIKE ME TO SHOW YOU MY SCHOOL?

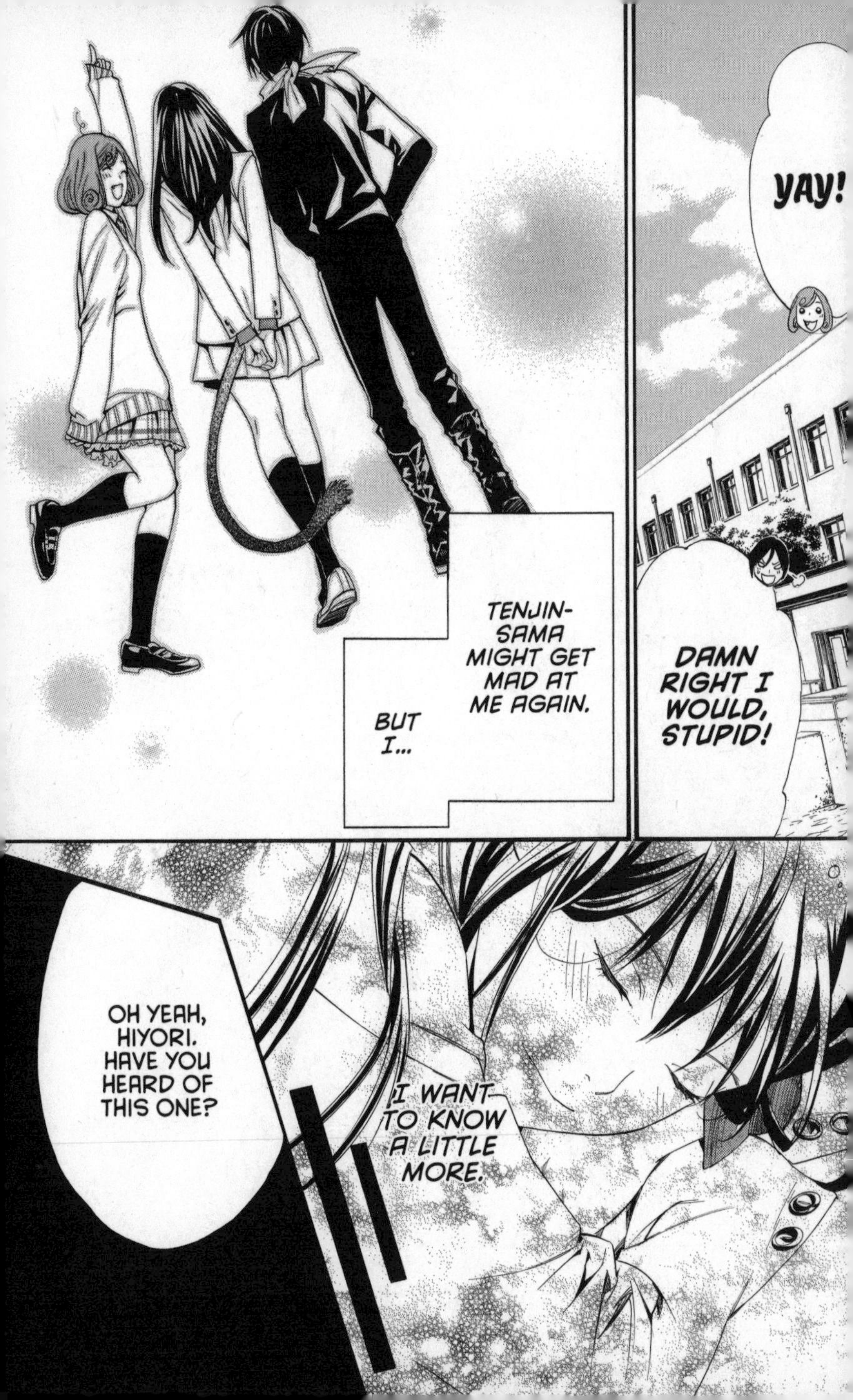
YAY!
DAMN RIGHT I WOULD, STUPID!
TENJIN-SAMA MIGHT GET MAD AT ME AGAIN.
BUT I...
I WANT TO KNOW A LITTLE MORE.
OH YEAH, HIYORI. HAVE YOU HEARD OF THIS ONE?

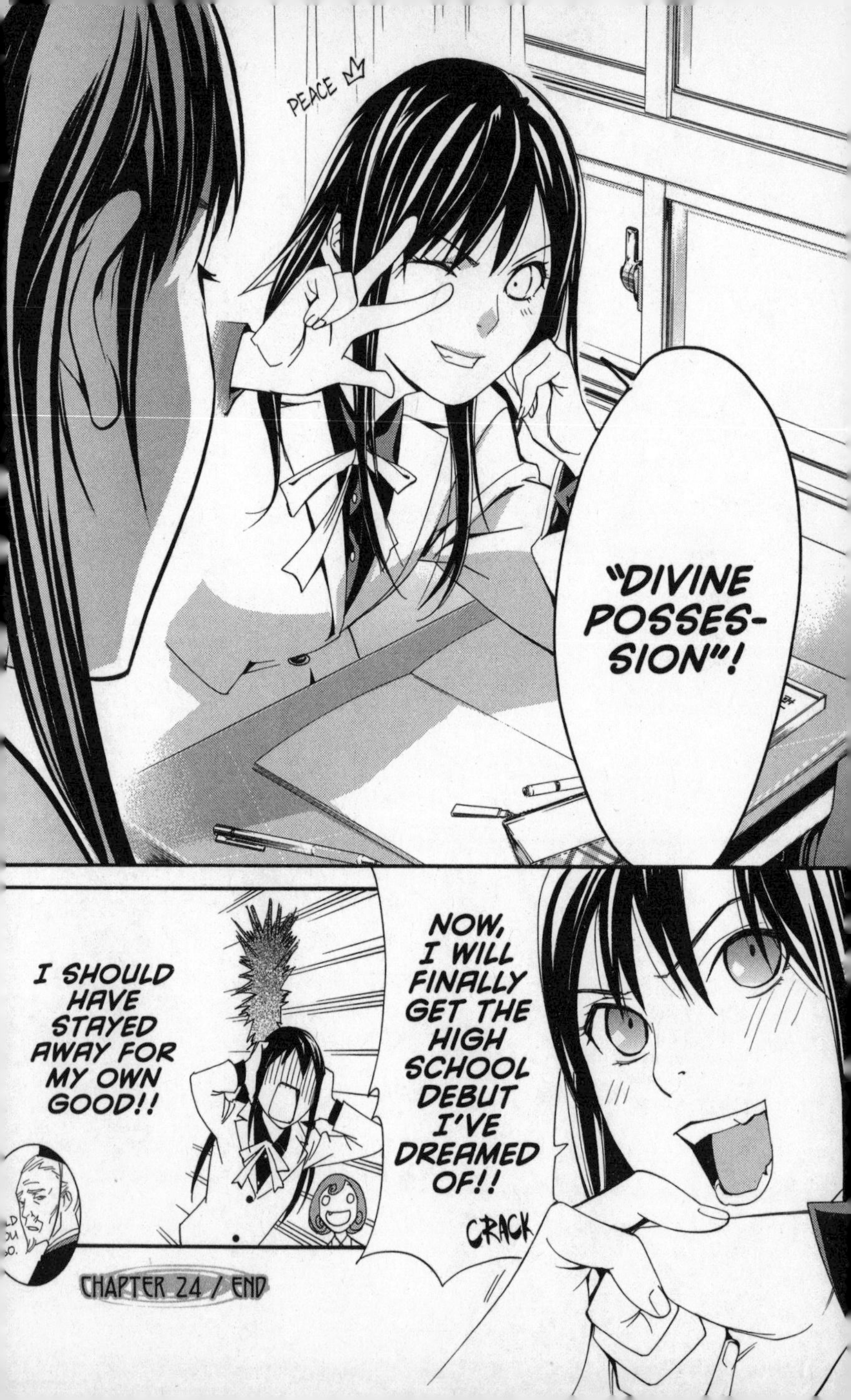
PEACE
"DIVINE POSSES-SION"!
NOW, I WILL FINALLY GET THE HIGH SCHOOL DEBUT I'VE DREAMED OF!!
CRACK
I SHOULD HAVE STAYED AWAY FOR MY OWN GOOD!!
CHAPTER 24 / END

野

兒

神

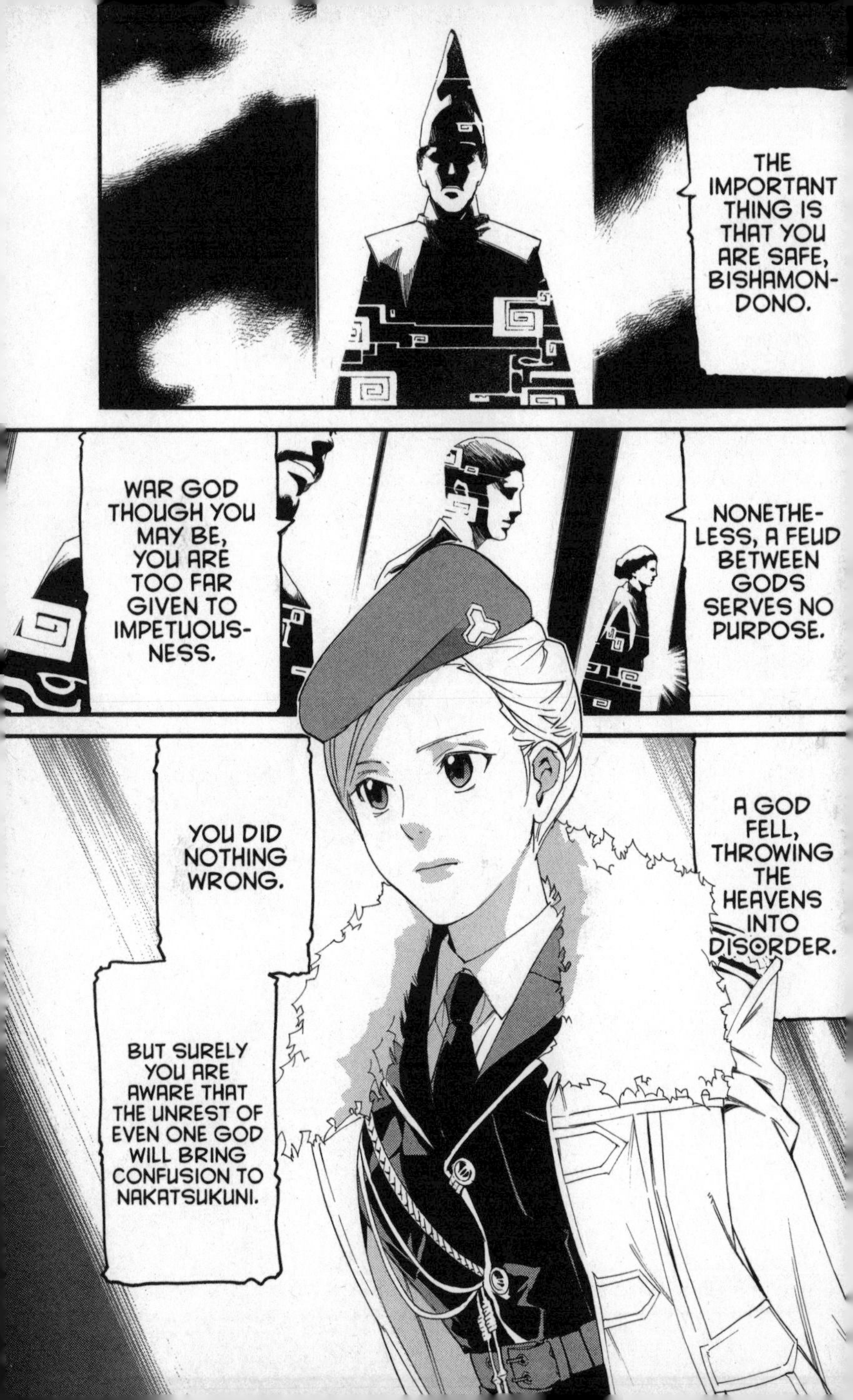
THE IMPORTANT THING IS THAT YOU ARE SAFE, BISHAMON-DONO.
NONETHELESS, A FEUD BETWEEN GODS SERVES NO PURPOSE.
WAR GOD THOUGH YOU MAY BE, YOU ARE TOO FAR GIVEN TO IMPETUOUSNESS.
A GOD FELL, THROWING THE HEAVENS INTO DISORDER.
YOU DID NOTHING WRONG.
BUT SURELY YOU ARE AWARE THAT THE UNREST OF EVEN ONE GOD WILL BRING CONFUSION TO NAKATSUKUNI.

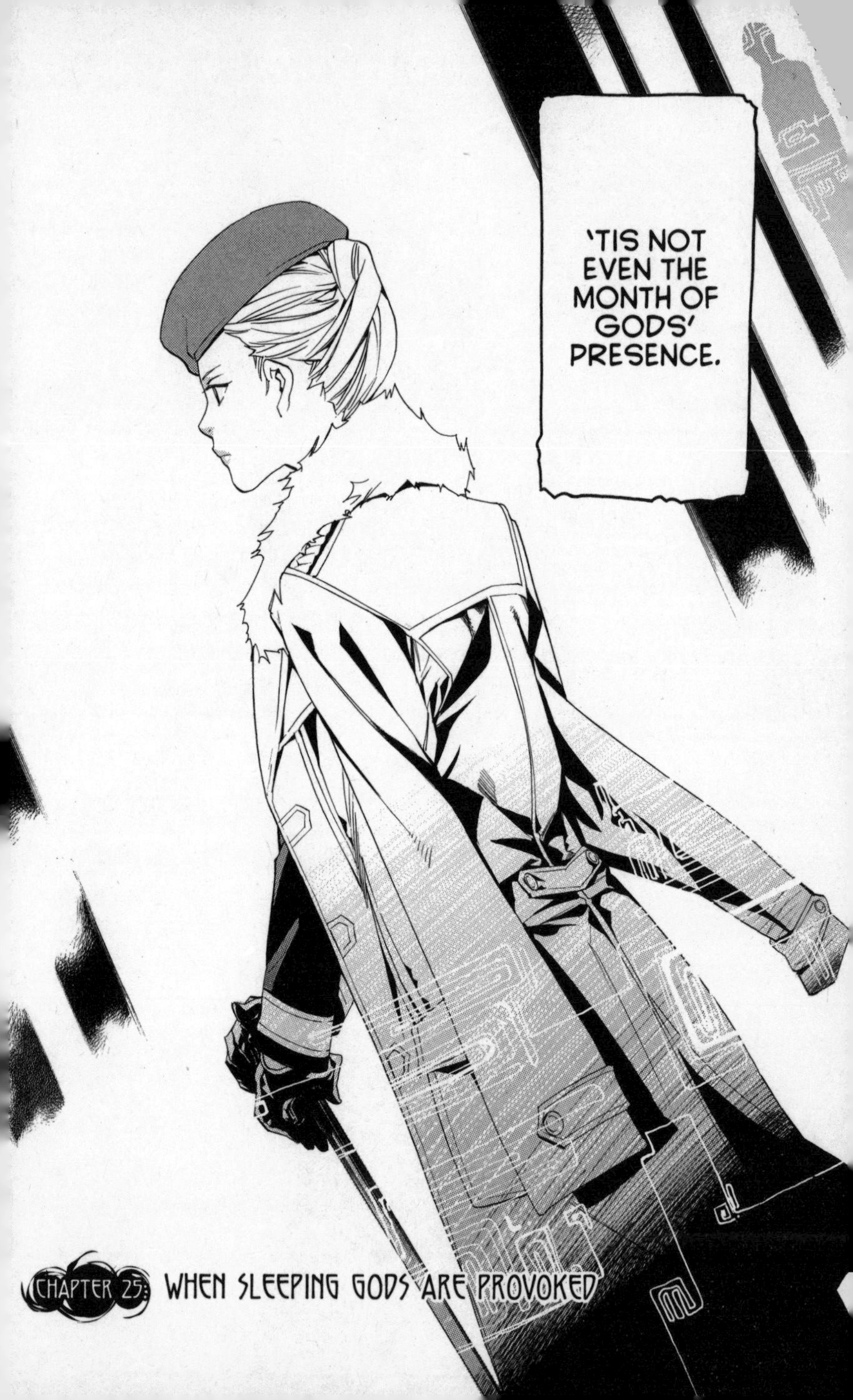
'TIS NOT EVEN THE MONTH OF GODS' PRESENCE.
CHAPTER 25: WHEN SLEEPING GODS ARE PROVOKED

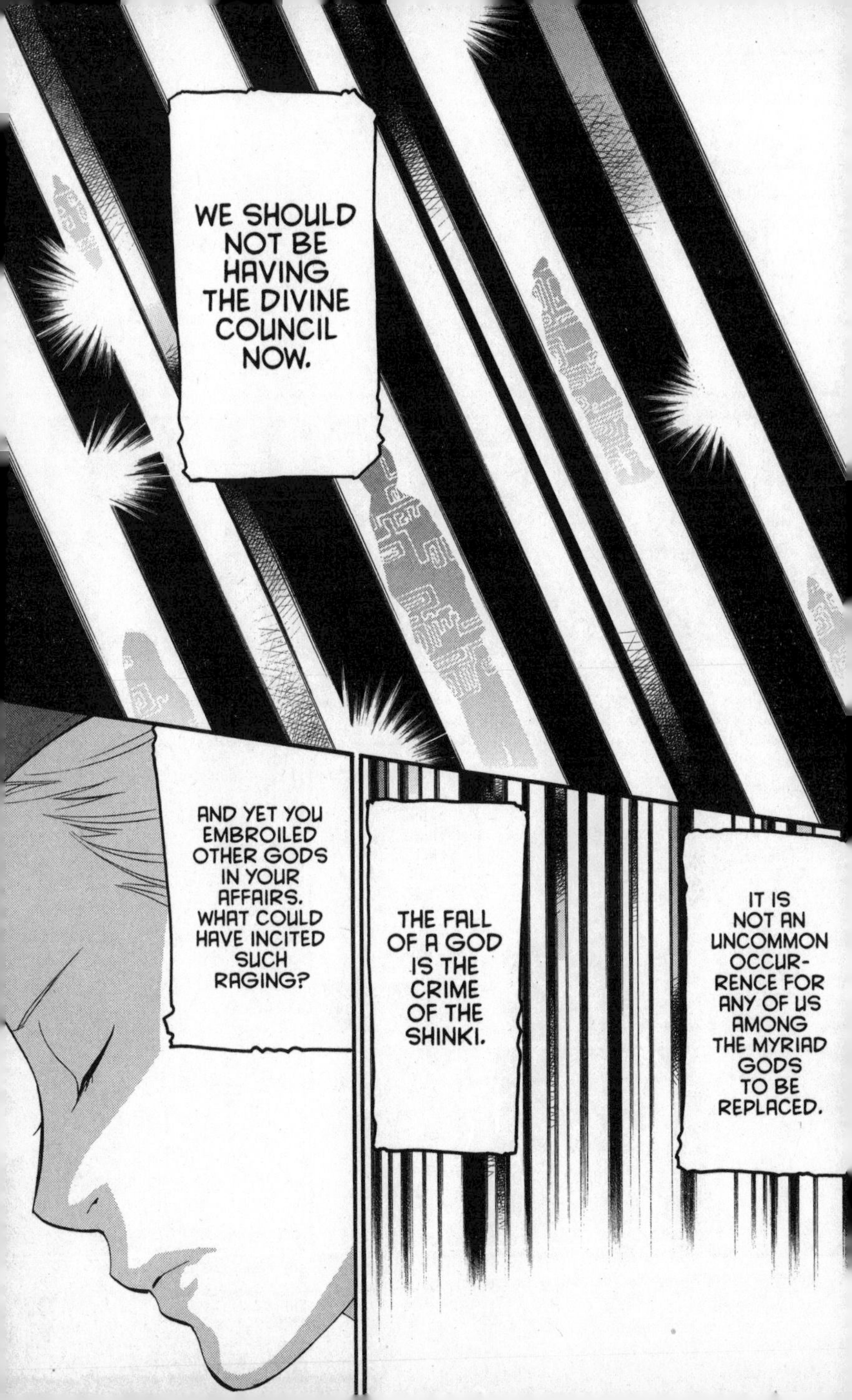
WE SHOULD NOT BE HAVING THE DIVINE COUNCIL NOW.
IT IS NOT AN UNCOMMON OCCUR-RENCE FOR ANY OF US AMONG THE MYRIAD GODS TO BE REPLACED.
THE FALL OF A GOD IS THE CRIME OF THE SHINKI.
AND YET YOU EMBROILED OTHER GODS IN YOUR AFFAIRS. WHAT COULD HAVE INCITED SUCH RAGING?

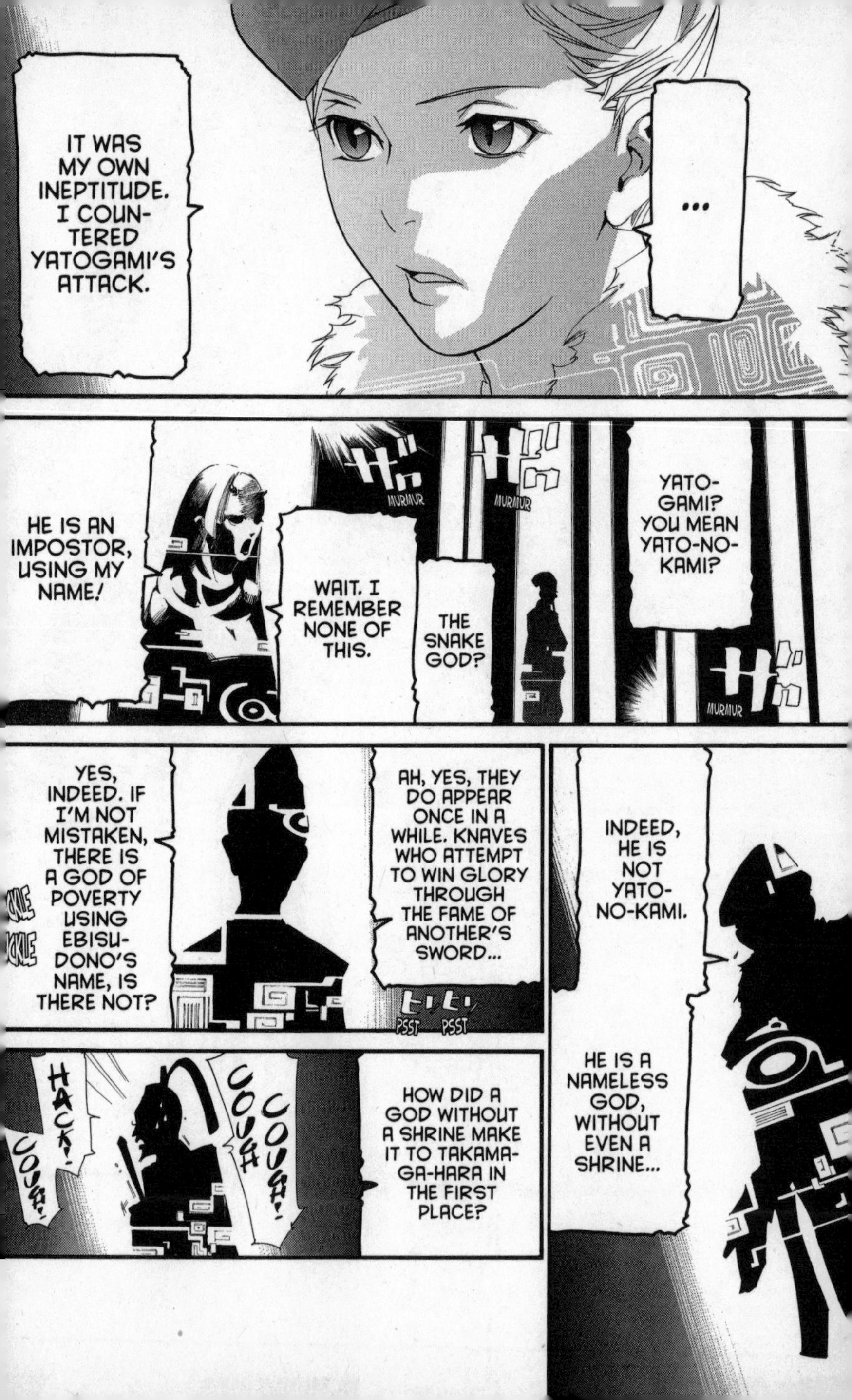
...
IT WAS MY OWN INEPTITUDE. I COUNTERED YATOGAMI'S ATTACK.
MURMUR
YATO-GAMI? YOU MEAN YATO-NO-KAMI?
MURMUR
MURMUR
THE SNAKE GOD?
WAIT. I REMEMBER NONE OF THIS.
HE IS AN IMPOSTOR, USING MY NAME!
INDEED, HE IS NOT YATO-NO-KAMI.
HE IS A NAMELESS GOD, WITHOUT EVEN A SHRINE...
AH, YES, THEY DO APPEAR ONCE IN A WHILE. KNAVES WHO ATTEMPT TO WIN GLORY THROUGH THE FAME OF ANOTHER'S SWORD...
PSST PSST
YES, INDEED. IF I'M NOT MISTAKEN, THERE IS A GOD OF POVERTY USING EBISU-DONO'S NAME, IS THERE NOT?
HOW DID A GOD WITHOUT A SHRINE MAKE IT TO TAKAMA-GA-HARA IN THE FIRST PLACE?
COUGH COUGH!
HACK! COUGH!

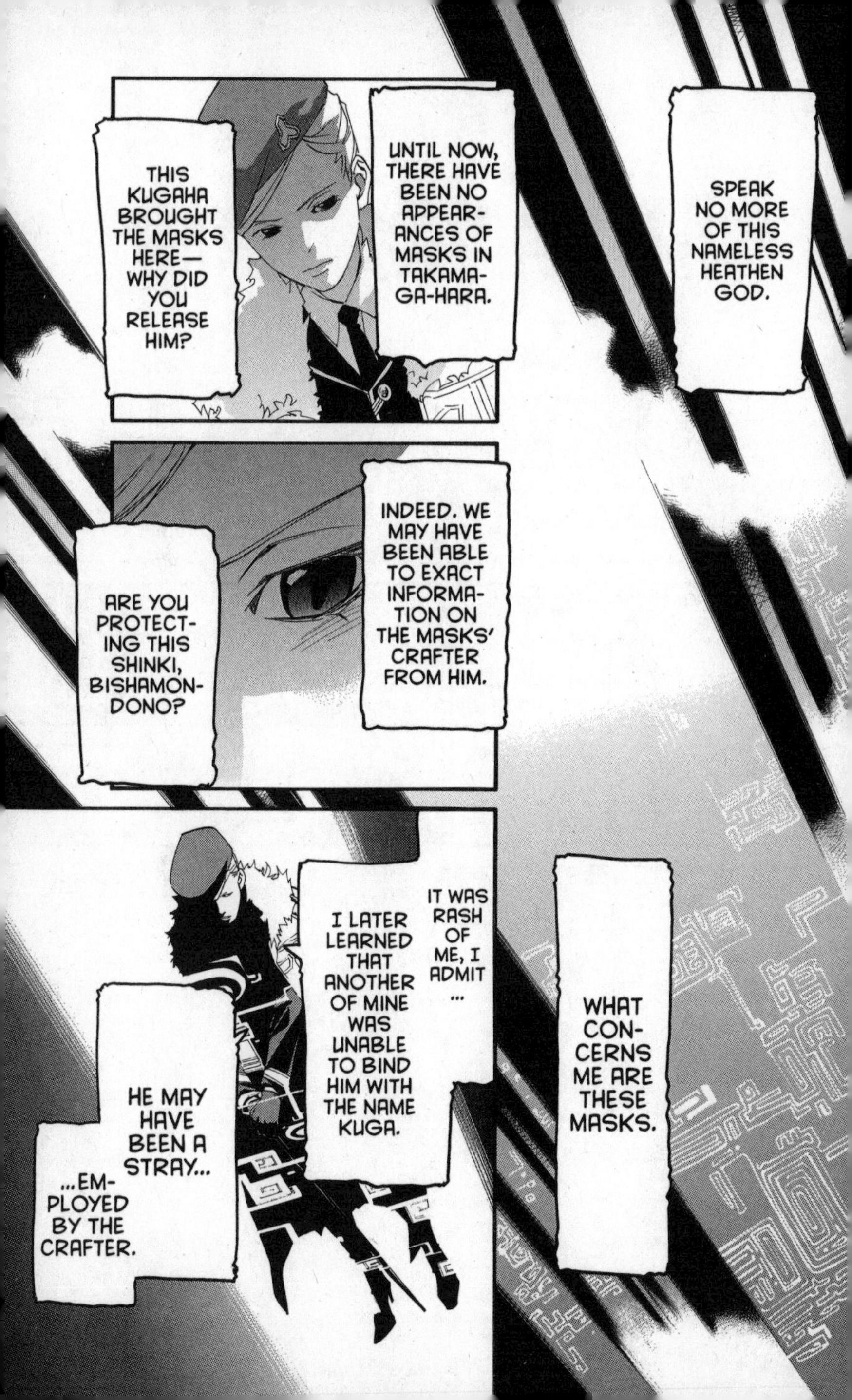

SPEAK NO MORE OF THIS NAMELESS HEATHEN GOD.
WHAT CONCERNS ME ARE THESE MASKS.
UNTIL NOW, THERE HAVE BEEN NO APPEARANCES OF MASKS IN TAKAMA-GA-HARA.
THIS KUGAHA BROUGHT THE MASKS HERE—WHY DID YOU RELEASE HIM?
INDEED. WE MAY HAVE BEEN ABLE TO EXACT INFORMATION ON THE MASKS' CRAFTER FROM HIM.
ARE YOU PROTECTING THIS SHINKI, BISHAMON-DONO?
IT WAS RASH OF ME, I ADMIT...
I LATER LEARNED THAT ANOTHER OF MINE WAS UNABLE TO BIND HIM WITH THE NAME KUGA.
HE MAY HAVE BEEN A STRAY...
...EMPLOYED BY THE CRAFTER.

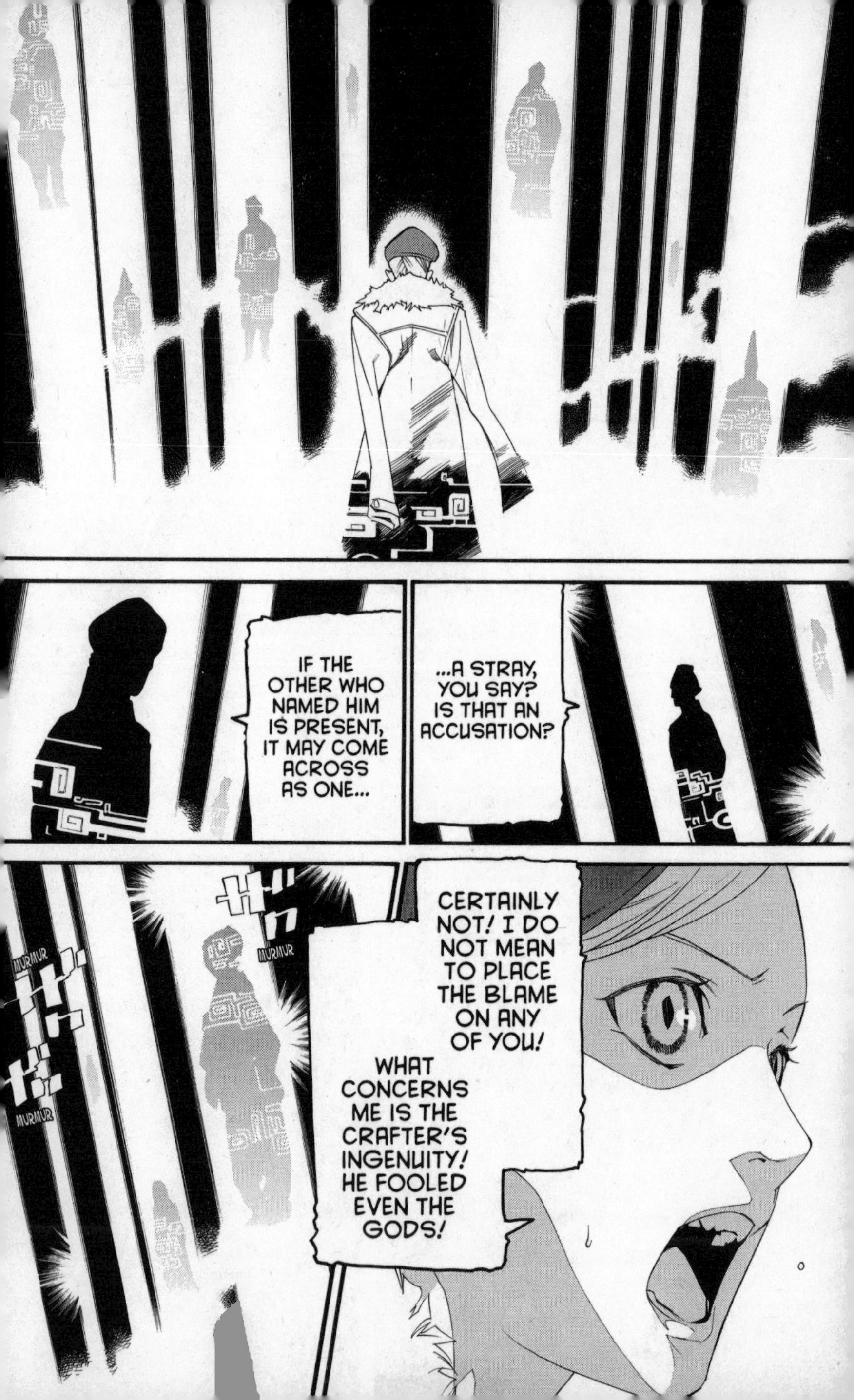

...A STRAY, YOU SAY? IS THAT AN ACCUSATION?
IF THE OTHER WHO NAMED HIM IS PRESENT, IT MAY COME ACROSS AS ONE...
CERTAINLY NOT! I DO NOT MEAN TO PLACE THE BLAME ON ANY OF YOU!
WHAT CONCERNS ME IS THE CRAFTER'S INGENUITY! HE FOOLED EVEN THE GODS!
MURMUR
MURMUR
MURMUR

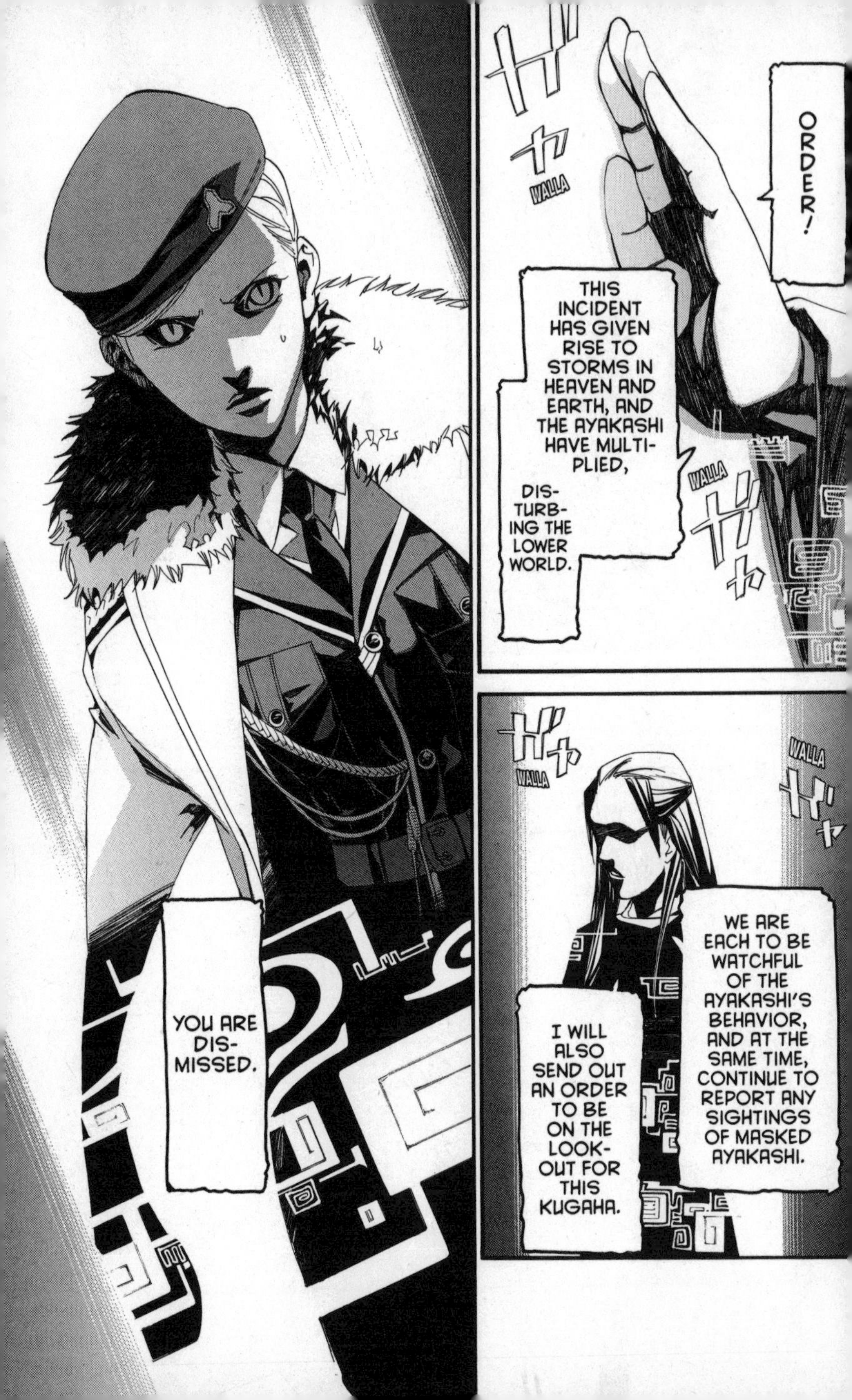
ORDER!
WALLA
THIS INCIDENT HAS GIVEN RISE TO STORMS IN HEAVEN AND EARTH, AND THE AYAKASHI HAVE MULTI-PLIED,
DIS-TURB-ING THE LOWER WORLD.
WALLA
WALLA
WALLA
WE ARE EACH TO BE WATCHFUL OF THE AYAKASHI'S BEHAVIOR, AND AT THE SAME TIME, CONTINUE TO REPORT ANY SIGHTINGS OF MASKED AYAKASHI.
I WILL ALSO SEND OUT AN ORDER TO BE ON THE LOOK-OUT FOR THIS KUGAHA.
YOU ARE DIS-MISSED.

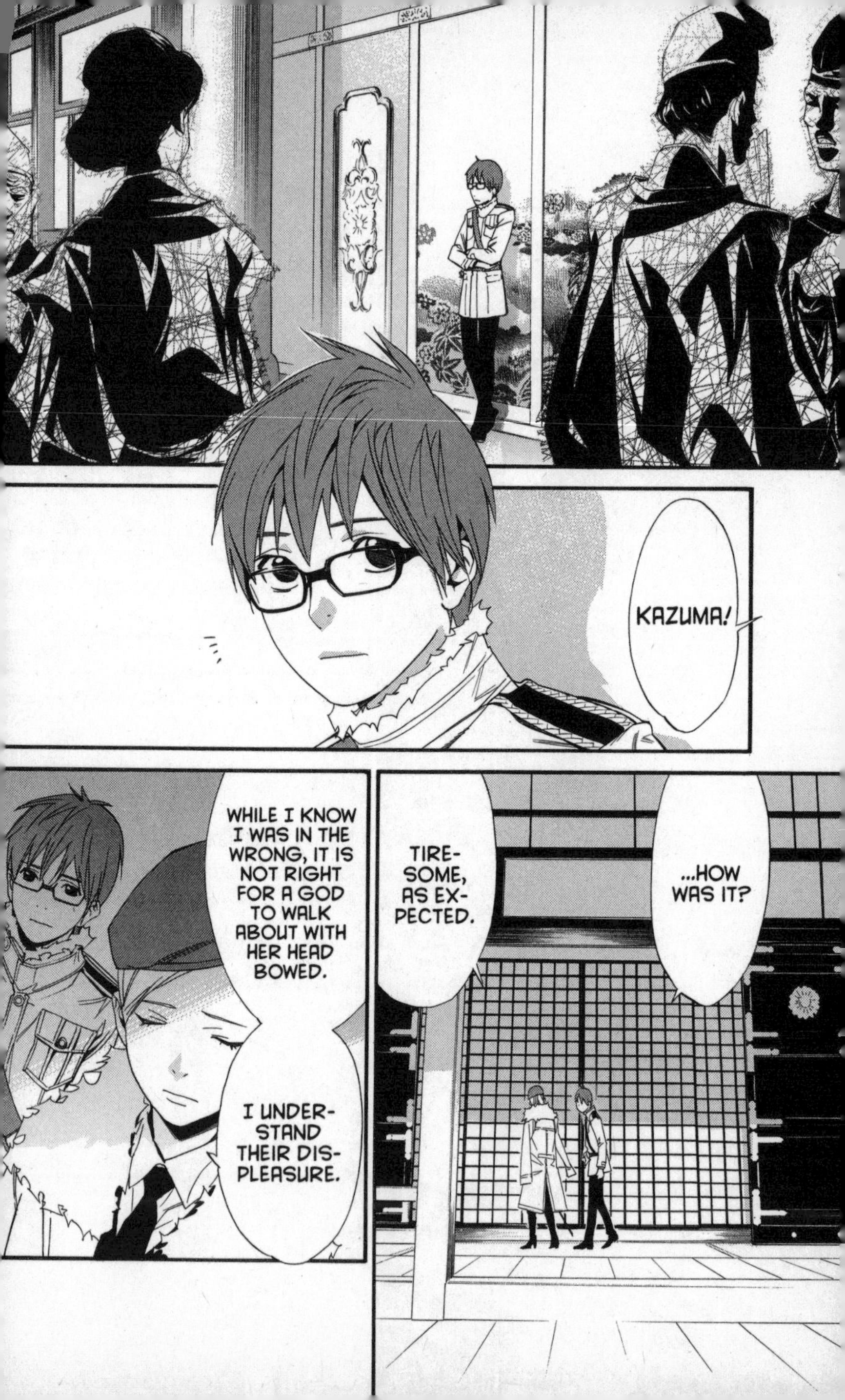
KAZUMA!
...HOW WAS IT?
TIRESOME, AS EXPECTED.
WHILE I KNOW I WAS IN THE WRONG, IT IS NOT RIGHT FOR A GOD TO WALK ABOUT WITH HER HEAD BOWED.
I UNDERSTAND THEIR DISPLEASURE.

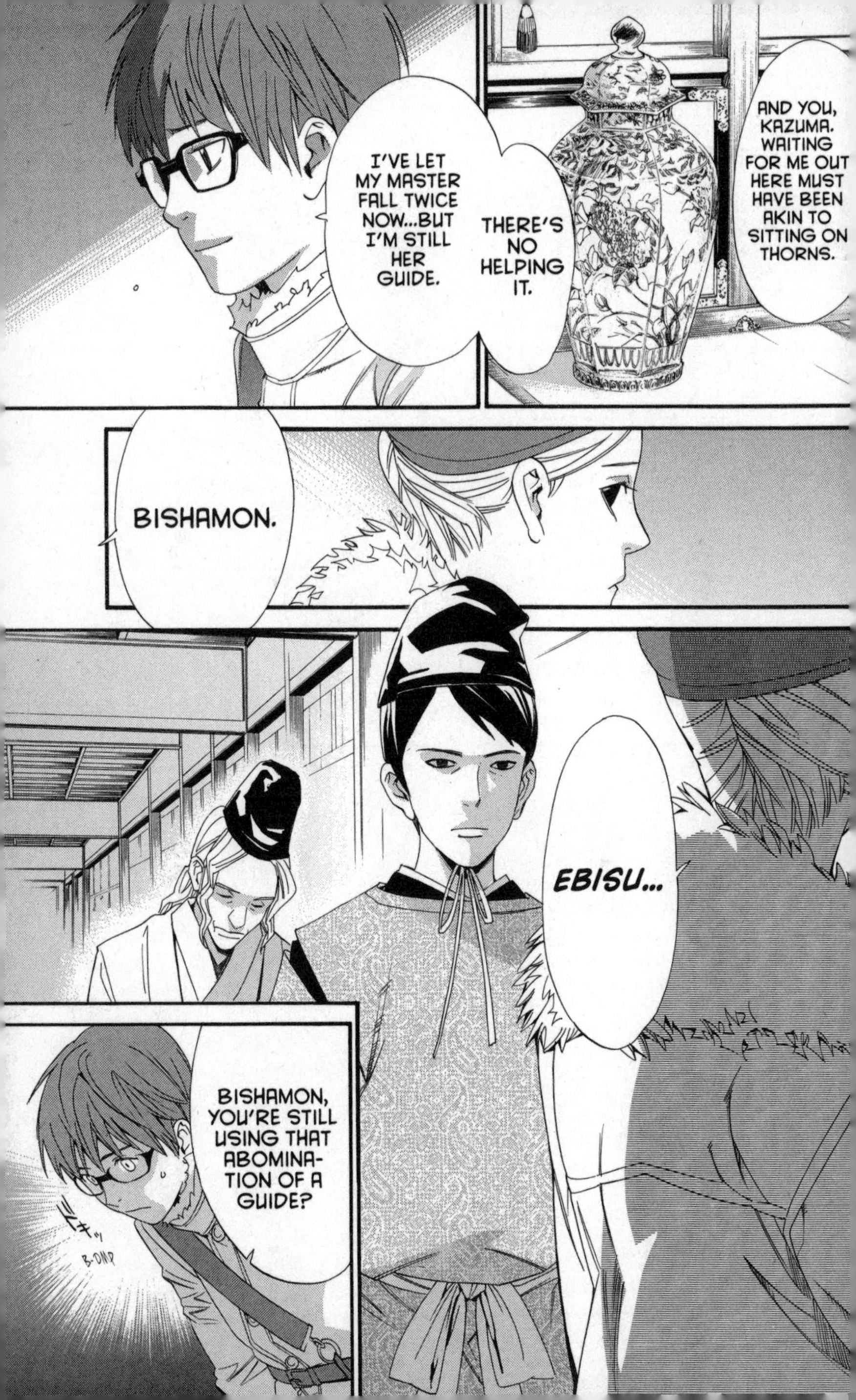

AND YOU, KAZUMA. WAITING FOR ME OUT HERE MUST HAVE BEEN AKIN TO SITTING ON THORNS.
I'VE LET MY MASTER FALL TWICE NOW...BUT I'M STILL HER GUIDE.
THERE'S NO HELPING IT.
BISHAMON.
EBISU...
BISHAMON, YOU'RE STILL USING THAT ABOMINATION OF A GUIDE?
B-DMP

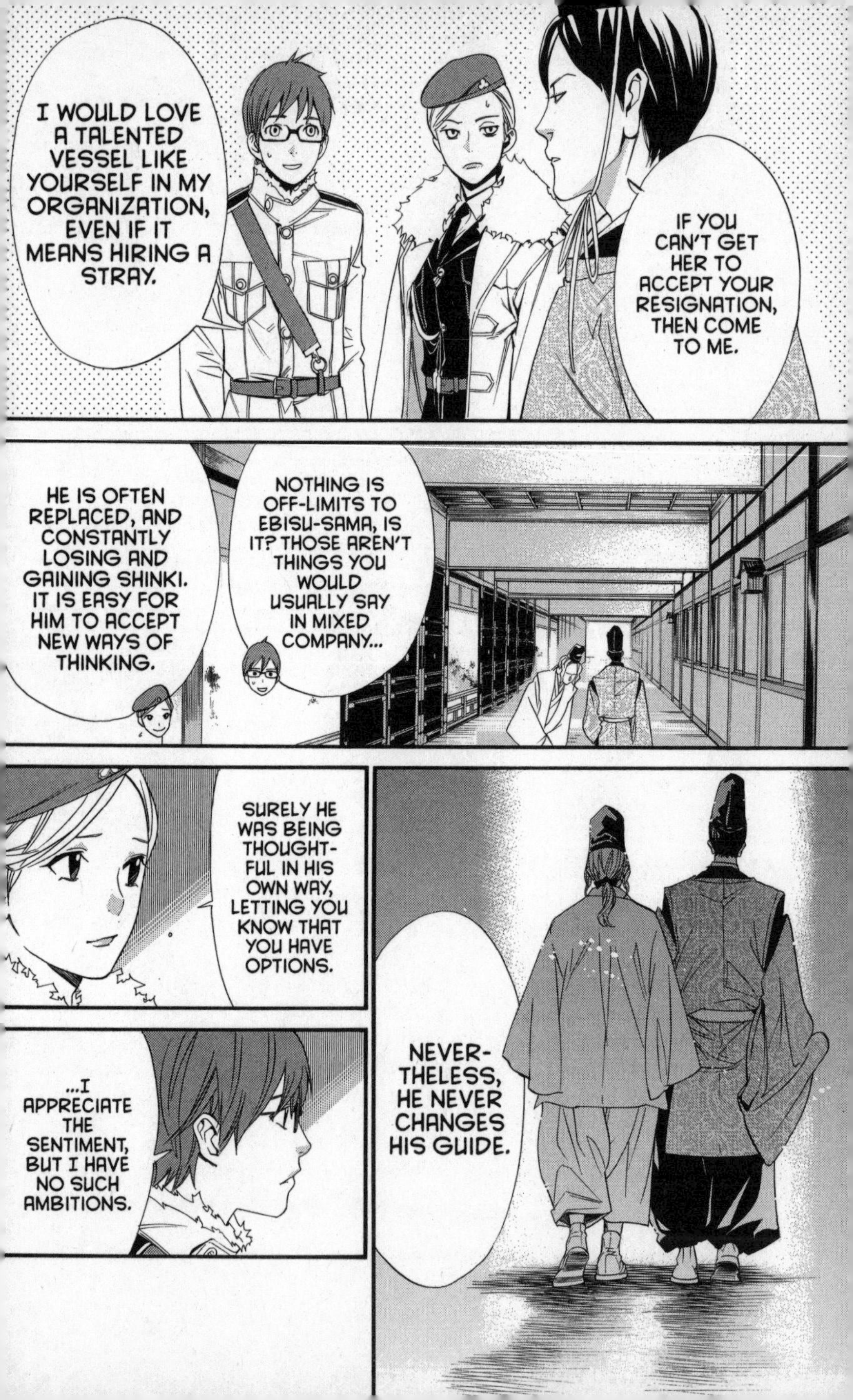
IF YOU CAN'T GET HER TO ACCEPT YOUR RESIGNATION, THEN COME TO ME.
I WOULD LOVE A TALENTED VESSEL LIKE YOURSELF IN MY ORGANIZATION, EVEN IF IT MEANS HIRING A STRAY.
NOTHING IS OFF-LIMITS TO EBISU-SAMA, IS IT? THOSE AREN'T THINGS YOU WOULD USUALLY SAY IN MIXED COMPANY...
HE IS OFTEN REPLACED, AND CONSTANTLY LOSING AND GAINING SHINKI. IT IS EASY FOR HIM TO ACCEPT NEW WAYS OF THINKING.
NEVER-THELESS, HE NEVER CHANGES HIS GUIDE.
SURELY HE WAS BEING THOUGHT-FUL IN HIS OWN WAY, LETTING YOU KNOW THAT YOU HAVE OPTIONS.
...I APPRECIATE THE SENTIMENT, BUT I HAVE NO SUCH AMBITIONS.

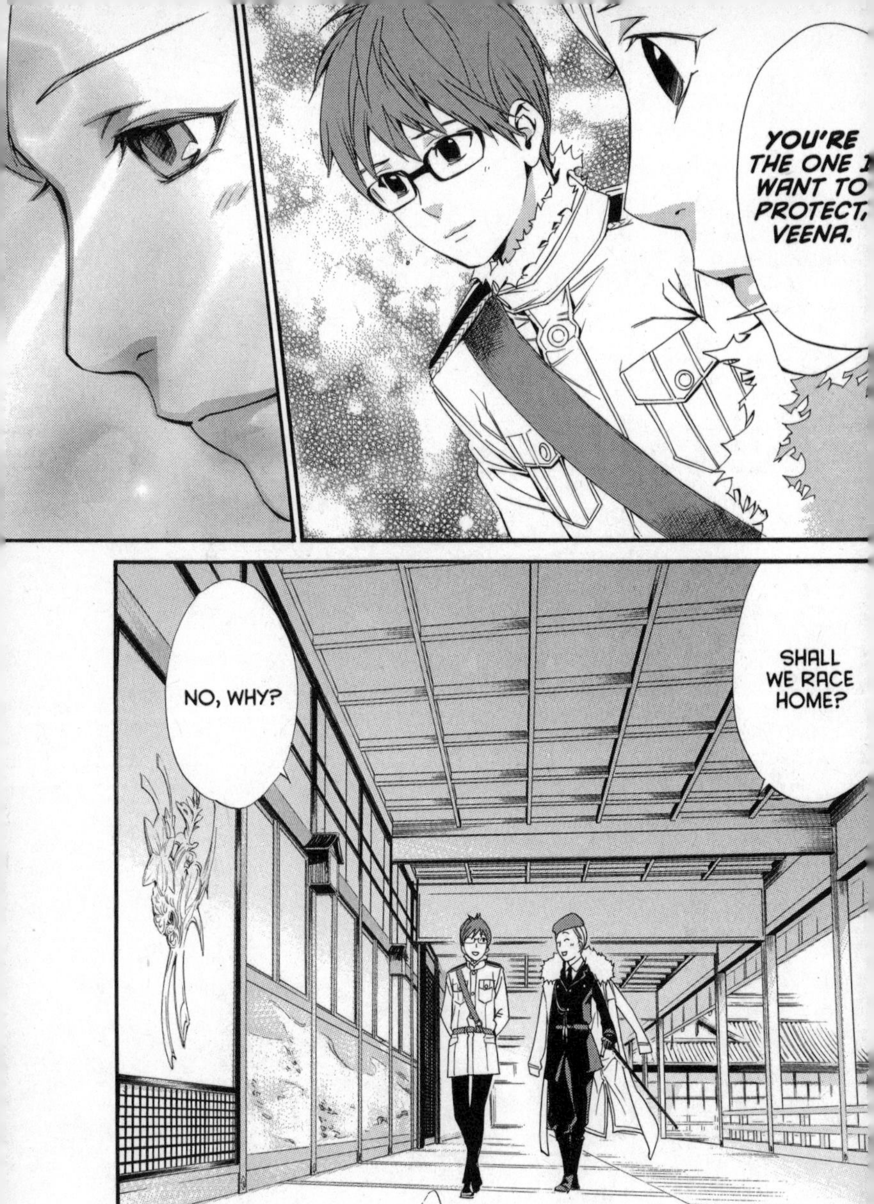
YOU'RE THE ONE I WANT TO PROTECT, VEENA.
SHALL WE RACE HOME?
NO, WHY?
...

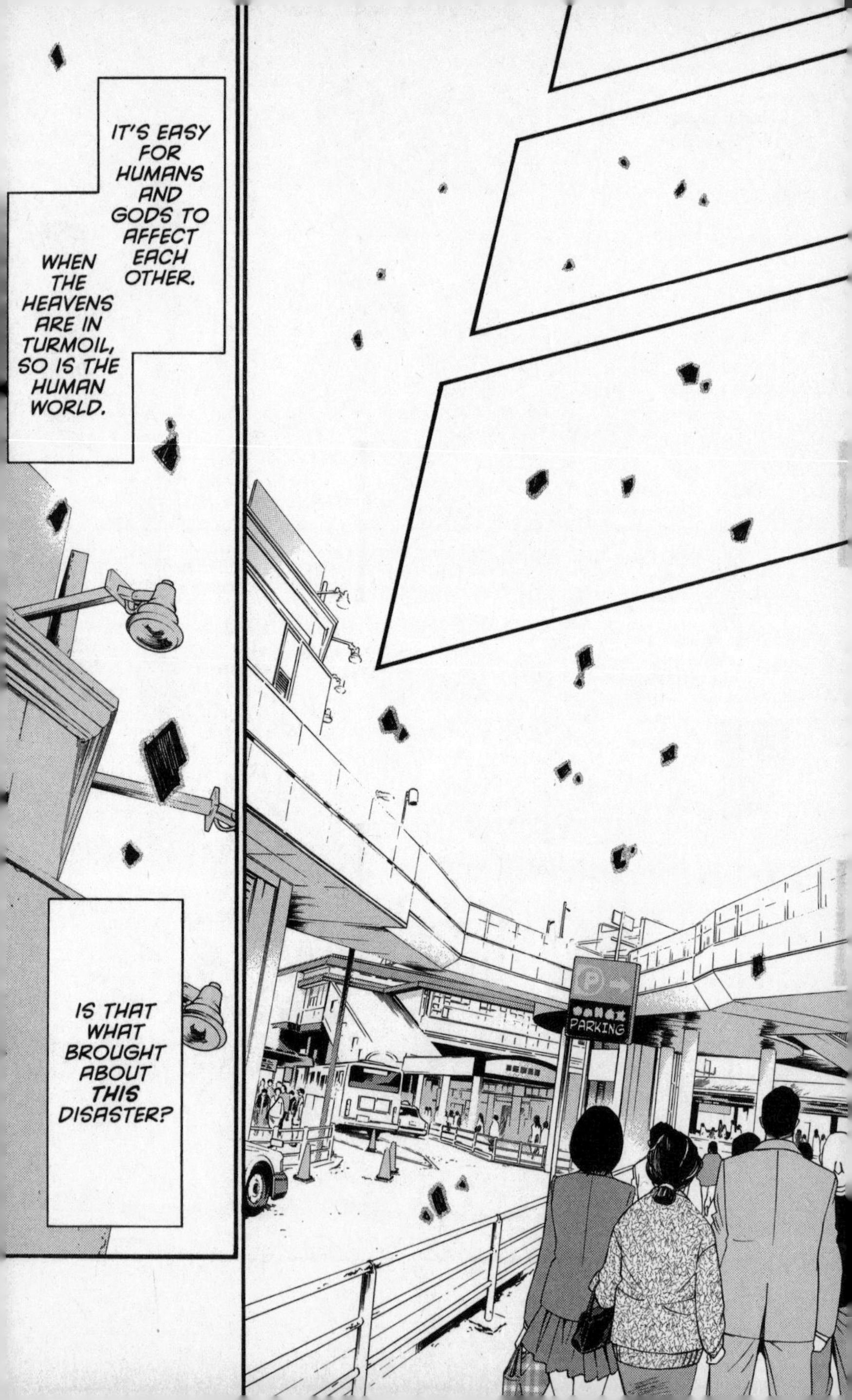
PARKING
IT'S EASY FOR HUMANS AND GODS TO AFFECT EACH OTHER.
WHEN THE HEAVENS ARE IN TURMOIL, SO IS THE HUMAN WORLD.
IS THAT WHAT BROUGHT ABOUT THIS DISASTER?

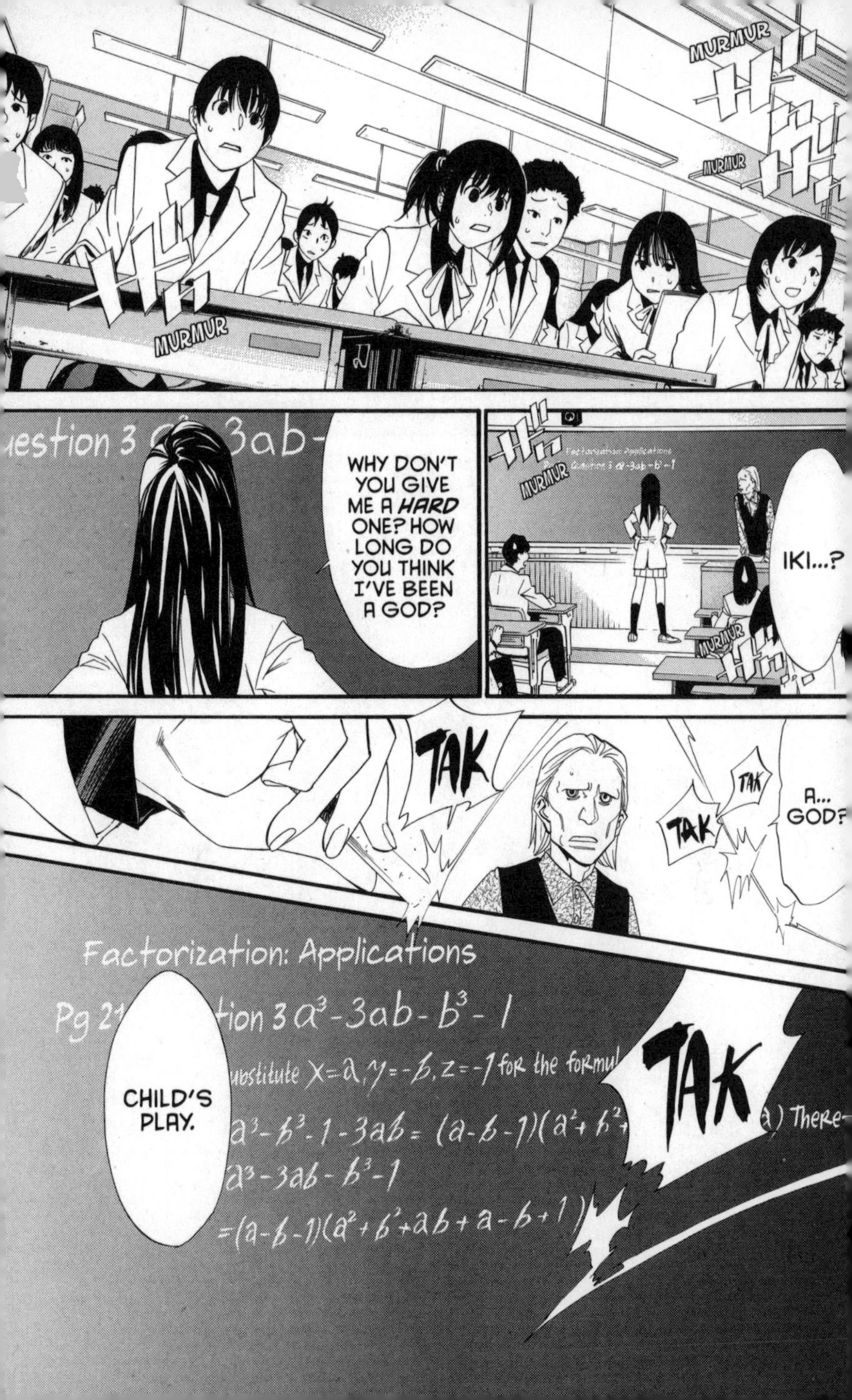
MURMUR
MURMUR
MURMUR
MURMUR
IKI...?
MURMUR
WHY DON'T YOU GIVE ME A *HARD* ONE? HOW LONG DO YOU THINK I'VE BEEN A GOD?
A... GOD?
TAK
TAK
TAK
Factorization: Applications
TAK
CHILD'S PLAY.

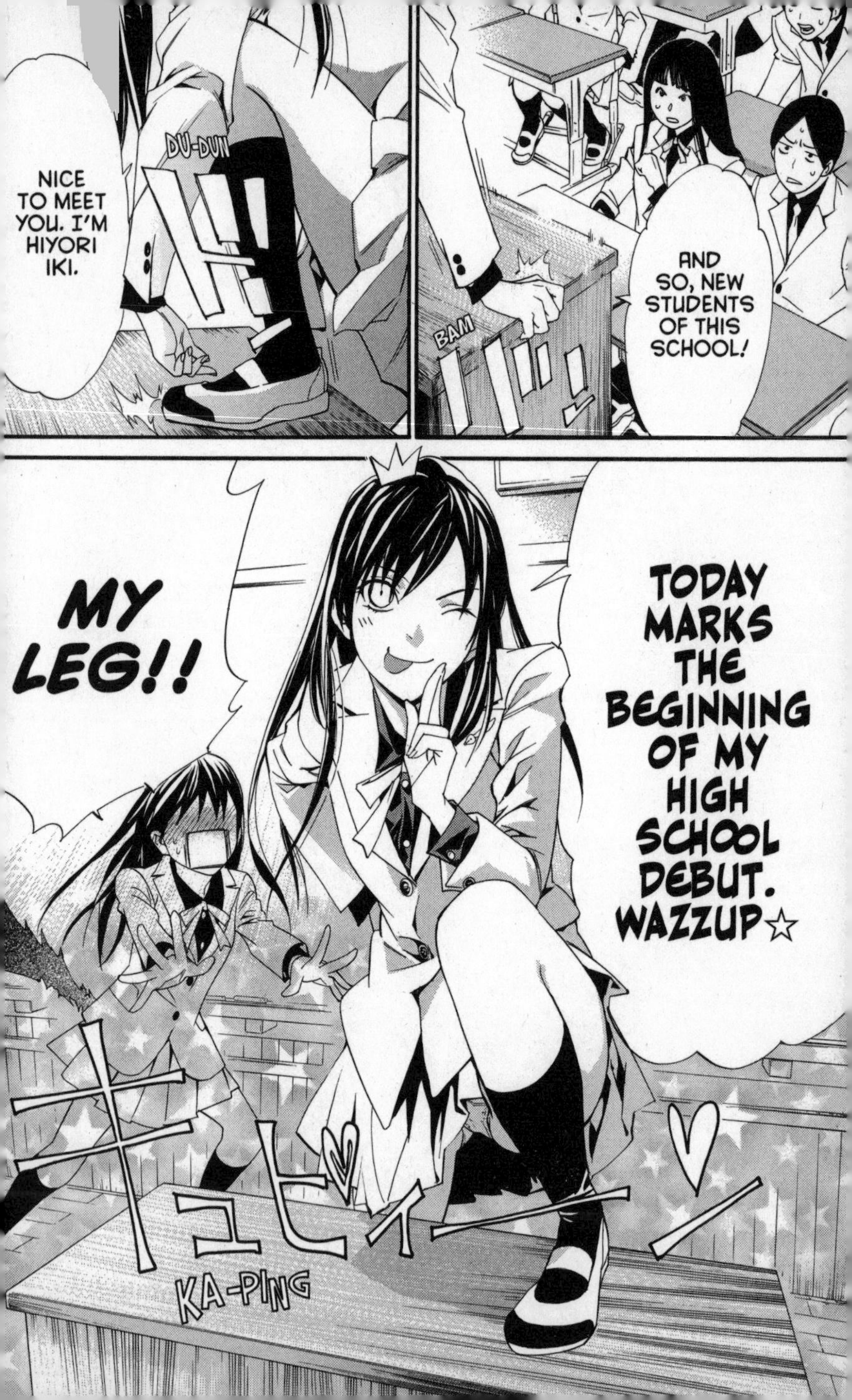
AND SO, NEW STUDENTS OF THIS SCHOOL!
BAM
NICE TO MEET YOU. I'M HIYORI IKI.
DU-DUN
TODAY MARKS THE BEGINNING OF MY HIGH SCHOOL DEBUT. WAZZUP☆
MY LEG!!
KA-PING

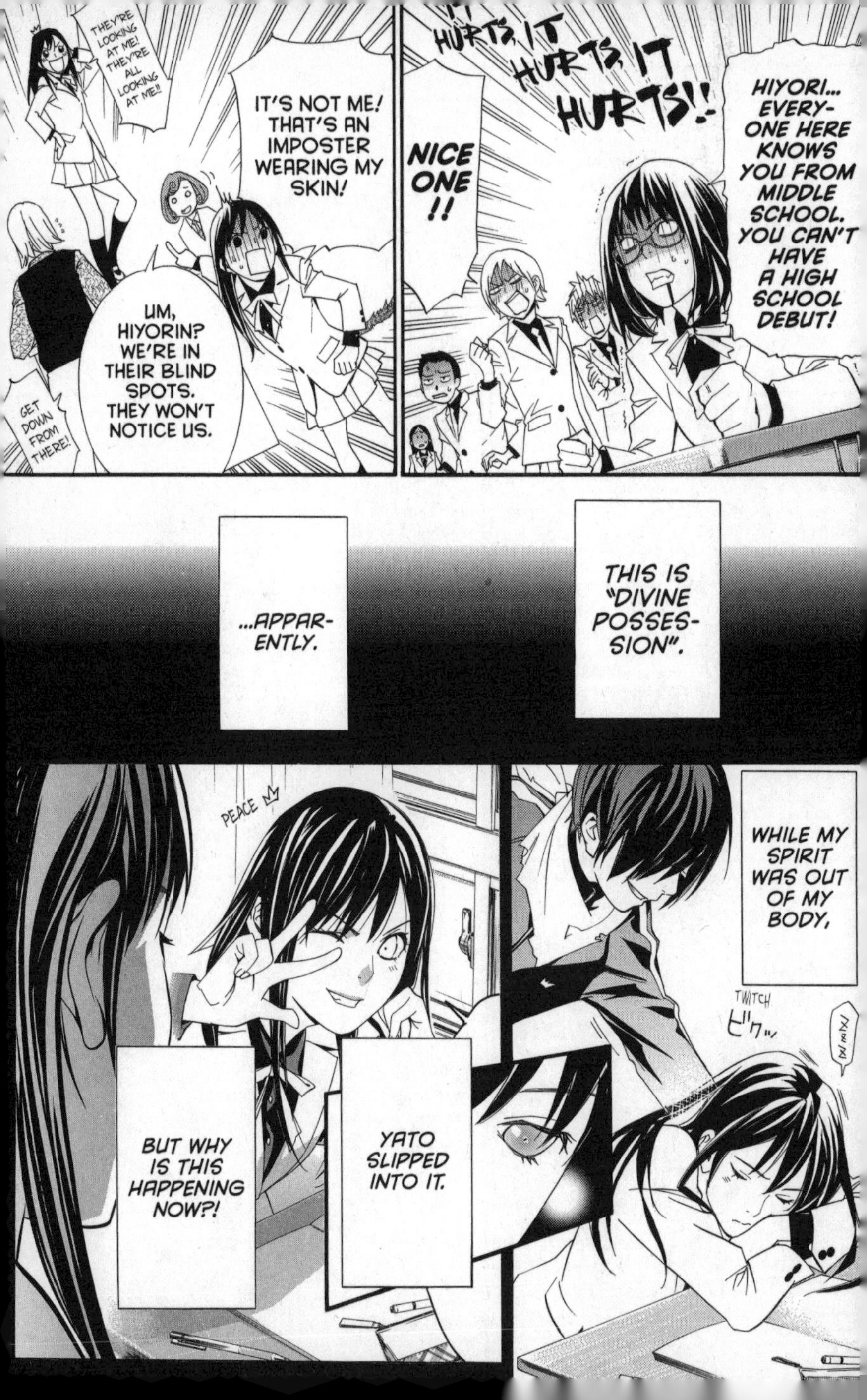
HIYORI... EVERY-ONE HERE KNOWS YOU FROM MIDDLE SCHOOL. YOU CAN'T HAVE A HIGH SCHOOL DEBUT!
IT HURTS, IT HURTS, IT HURTS!!
NICE ONE!!
IT'S NOT ME! THAT'S AN IMPOSTER WEARING MY SKIN!
THEY'RE LOOKING AT ME! THEY'RE ALL LOOKING AT ME!!
UM, HIYORIN? WE'RE IN THEIR BLIND SPOTS. THEY WON'T NOTICE US.
GET DOWN FROM THERE!
THIS IS "DIVINE POSSESSION".
...APPAR-ENTLY.
WHILE MY SPIRIT WAS OUT OF MY BODY,
TWITCH
PEACE
YATO SLIPPED INTO IT.
BUT WHY IS THIS HAPPENING NOW?!

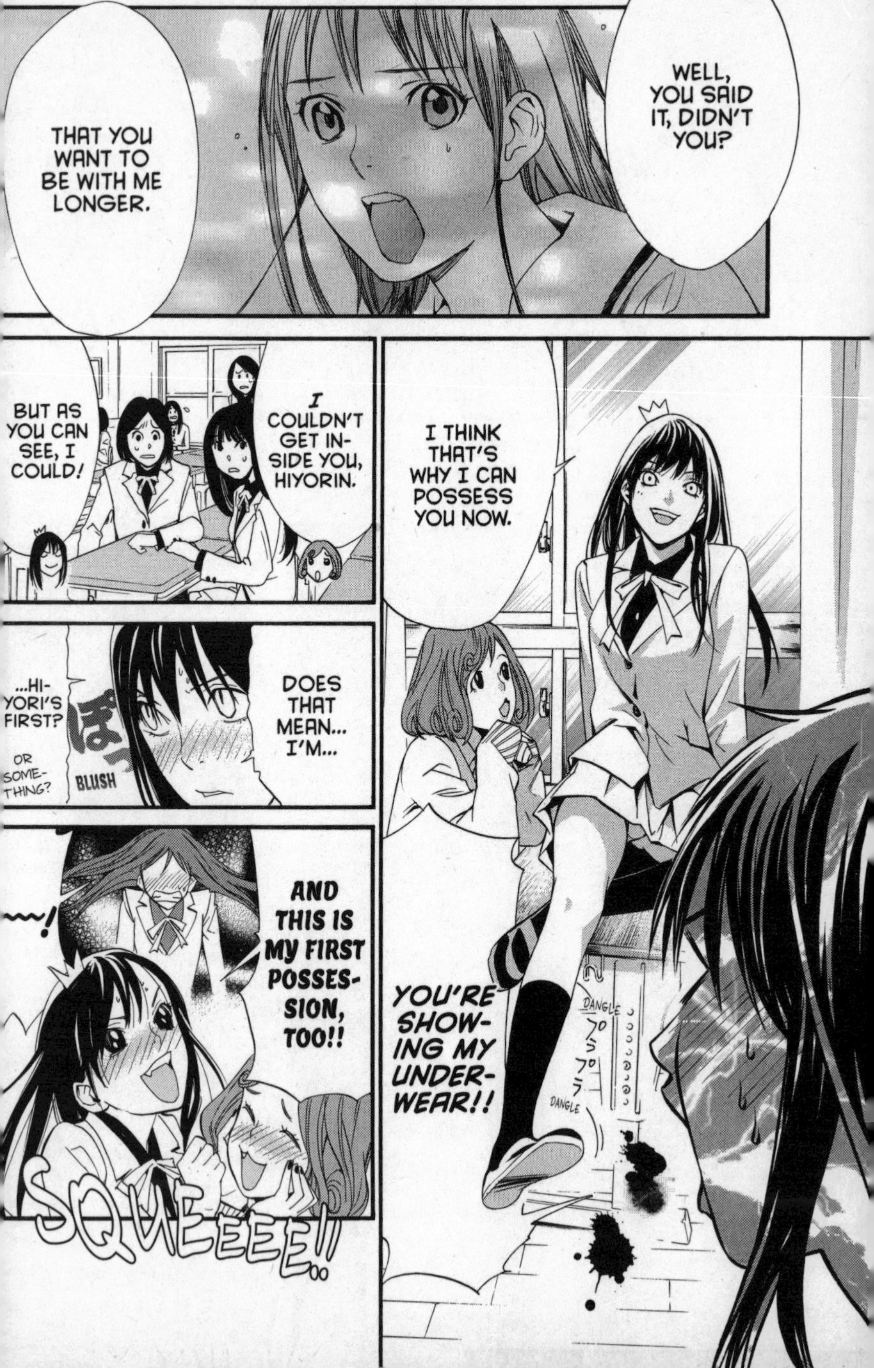
WELL, YOU SAID IT, DIDN'T YOU?
THAT YOU WANT TO BE WITH ME LONGER.
I THINK THAT'S WHY I CAN POSSESS YOU NOW.
DANGLE
ぷらぷら
DANGLE
YOU'RE SHOWING MY UNDERWEAR!!
I COULDN'T GET INSIDE YOU, HIYORIN.
BUT AS YOU CAN SEE, I COULD!
DOES THAT MEAN... I'M...
...HIYORI'S FIRST?
ぽっ
BLUSH
OR SOMETHING?
AND THIS IS MY FIRST POSSESSION, TOO!!
~~!
SQUEEEE!!

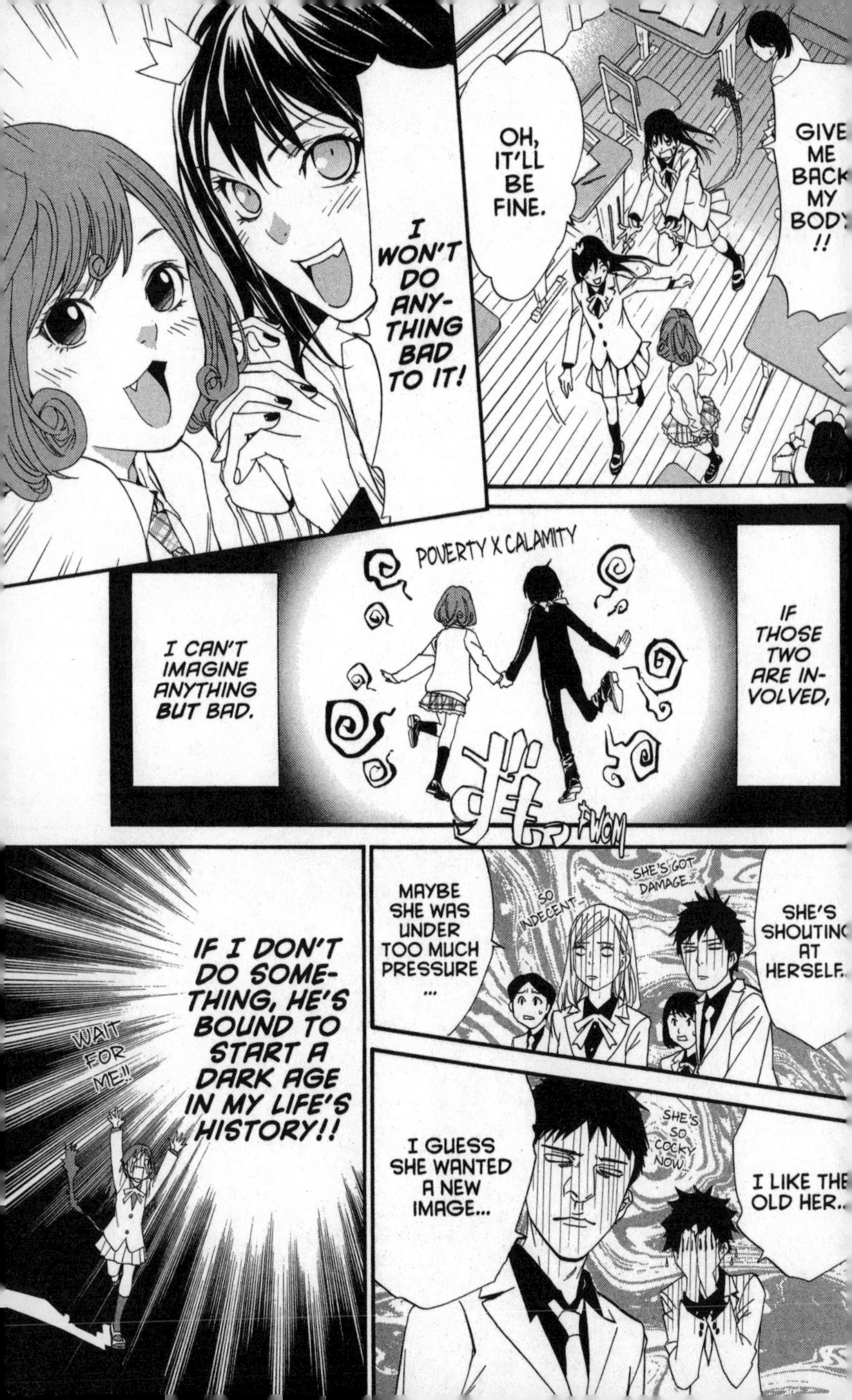
GIVE ME BACK MY BODY!!
OH, IT'LL BE FINE.
I WON'T DO ANYTHING BAD TO IT!
IF THOSE TWO ARE INVOLVED,
POVERTY X CALAMITY
FWOM
I CAN'T IMAGINE ANYTHING BUT BAD.
SHE'S SHOUTING AT HERSELF...
SHE'S GOT DAMAGE...
SO INDECENT...
MAYBE SHE WAS UNDER TOO MUCH PRESSURE ...
I LIKE THE OLD HER...
SHE'S SO COCKY NOW...
I GUESS SHE WANTED A NEW IMAGE...
IF I DON'T DO SOMETHING, HE'S BOUND TO START A DARK AGE IN MY LIFE'S HISTORY!!
WAIT FOR ME!!

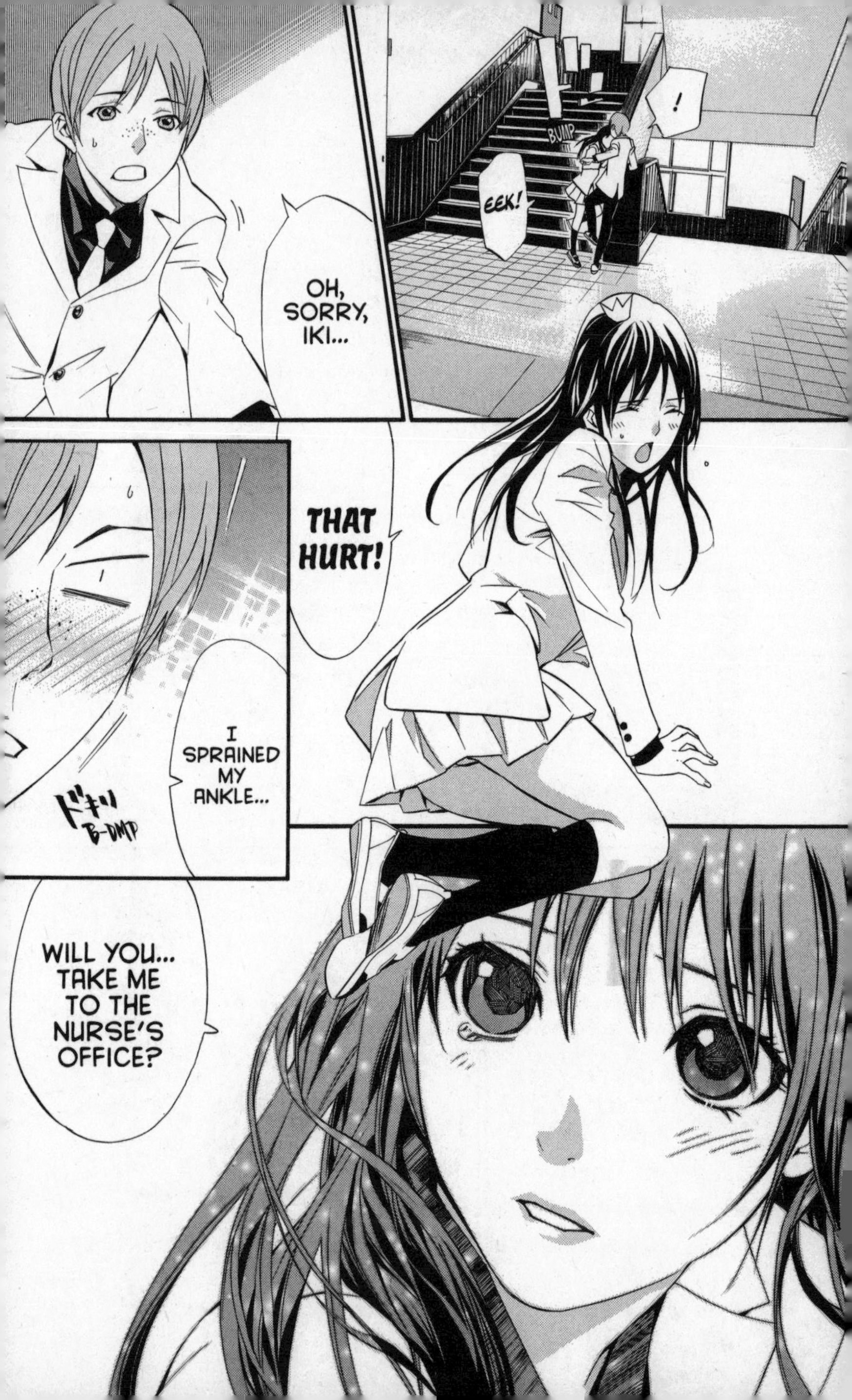
!
BUMP
EEK!
OH, SORRY, IKI...
THAT HURT!
I SPRAINED MY ANKLE...
ドキッ
B-DMP
WILL YOU... TAKE ME TO THE NURSE'S OFFICE?

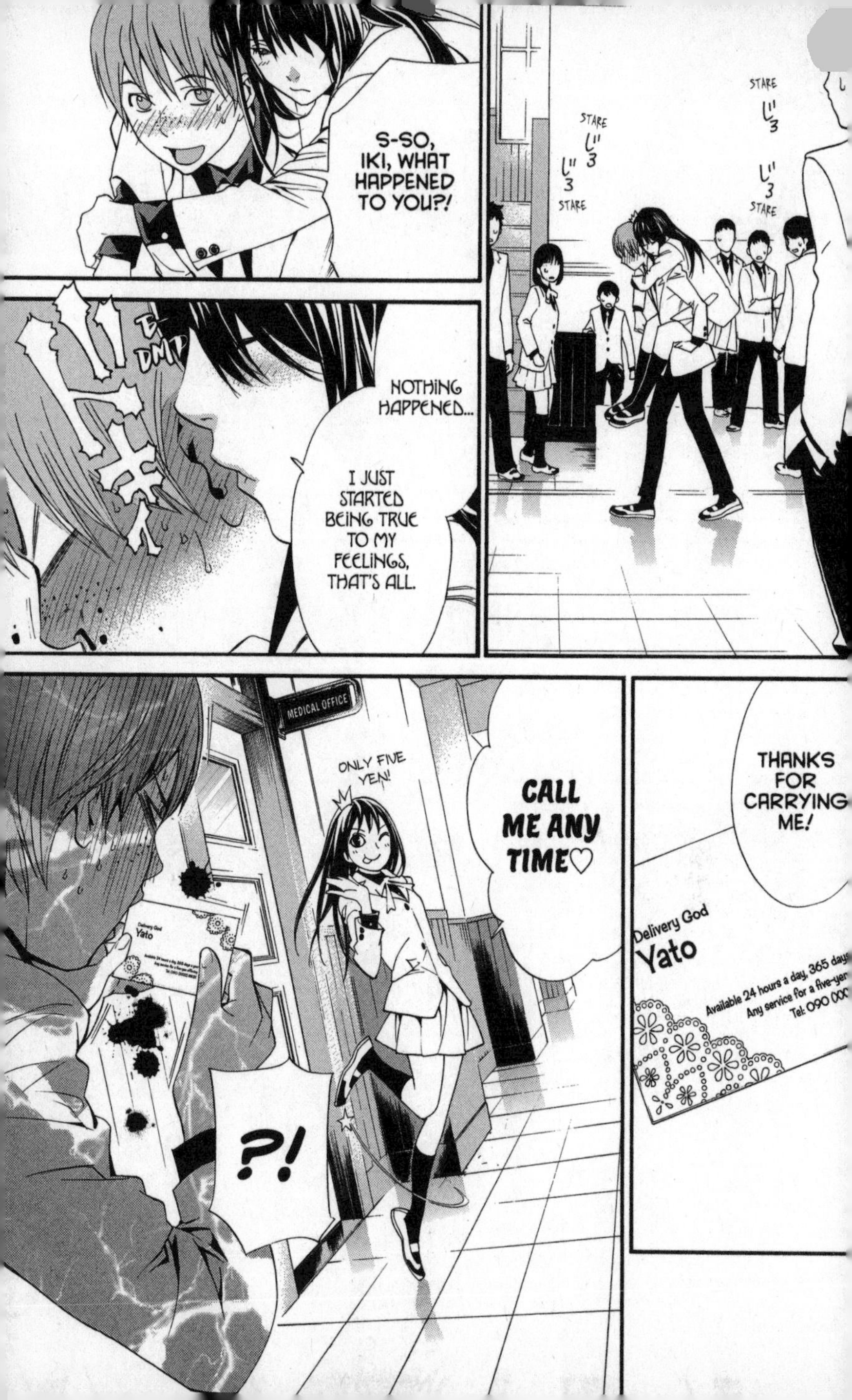

STARE
STARE
STARE
STARE
S-SO, IKI, WHAT HAPPENED TO YOU?!
NOTHING HAPPENED...
I JUST STARTED BEING TRUE TO MY FEELINGS, THAT'S ALL.
THANKS FOR CARRYING ME!
Delivery God
Yato
Available 24 hours a day, 365 days
Any service for a five-yen
Tel: 090 000
MEDICAL OFFICE
ONLY FIVE YEN!
CALL ME ANY TIME♡
?!

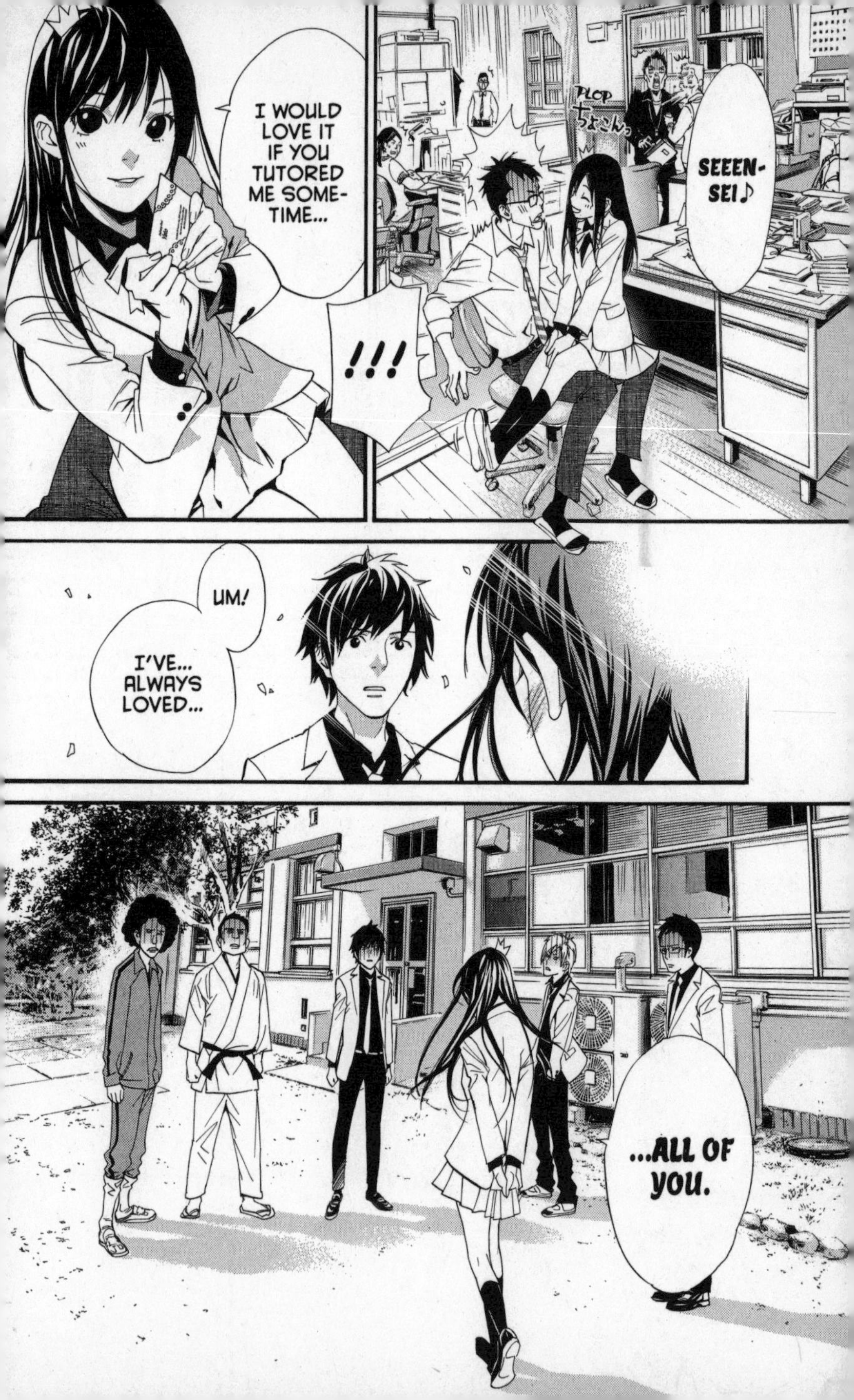

SEEEN-SEI♪
PLOP
ちょこんっ
!!!
I WOULD LOVE IT IF YOU TUTORED ME SOME-TIME...
UM!
I'VE... ALWAYS LOVED...
...ALL OF YOU.

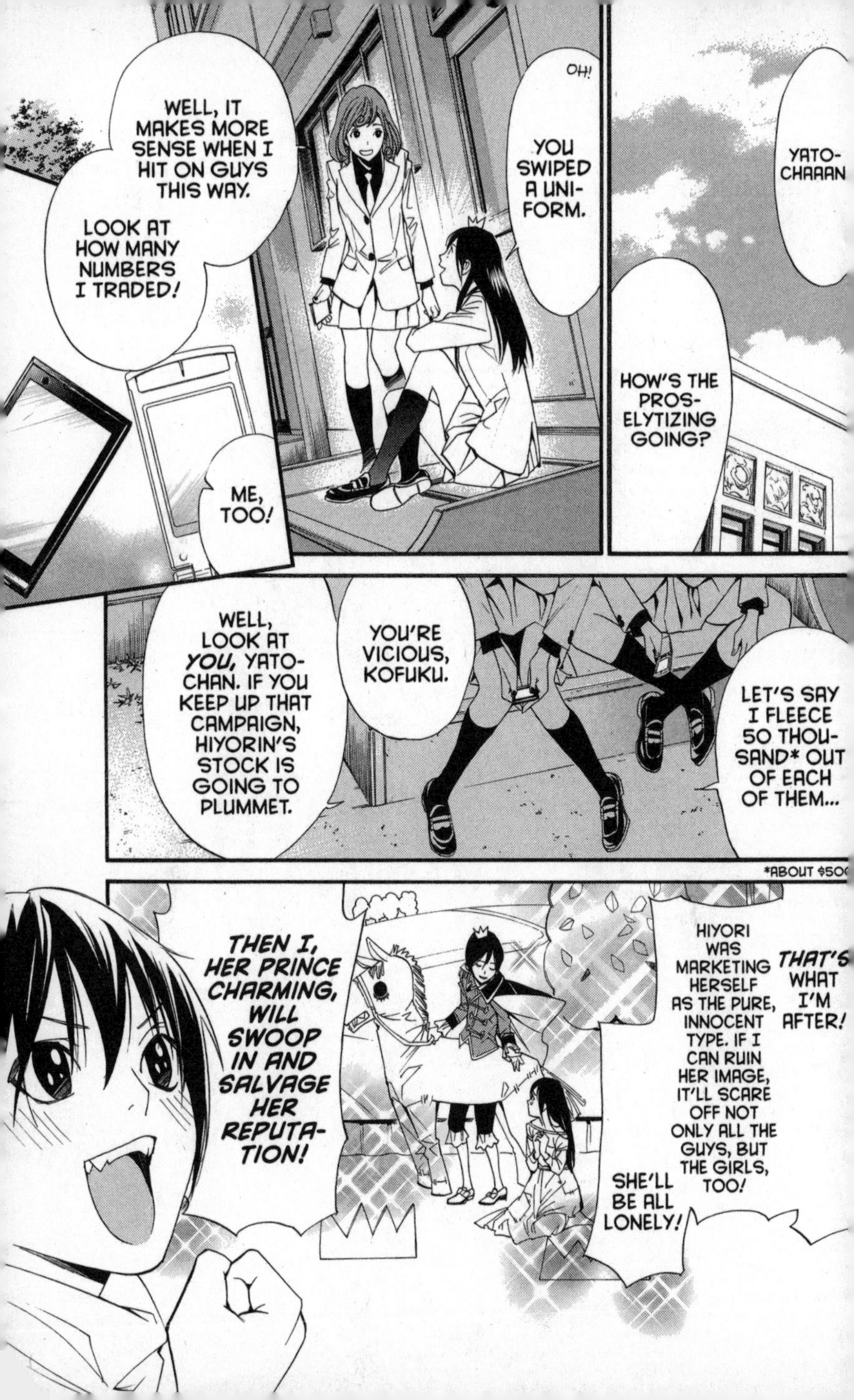
YATO-CHAAAN
HOW'S THE PROS-ELYTIZING GOING?
OH!
YOU SWIPED A UNI-FORM.
WELL, IT MAKES MORE SENSE WHEN I HIT ON GUYS THIS WAY.
LOOK AT HOW MANY NUMBERS I TRADED!
ME, TOO!
LET'S SAY I FLEECE 50 THOU-SAND* OUT OF EACH OF THEM...
YOU'RE VICIOUS, KOFUKU.
WELL, LOOK AT *YOU*, YATO-CHAN. IF YOU KEEP UP THAT CAMPAIGN, HIYORIN'S STOCK IS GOING TO PLUMMET.
*ABOUT $50
THAT'S WHAT I'M AFTER!
HIYORI WAS MARKETING HERSELF AS THE PURE, INNOCENT TYPE. IF I CAN RUIN HER IMAGE, IT'LL SCARE OFF NOT ONLY ALL THE GUYS, BUT THE GIRLS, TOO!
SHE'LL BE ALL LONELY!
THEN I, HER PRINCE CHARMING, WILL SWOOP IN AND SALVAGE HER REPUTA-TION!

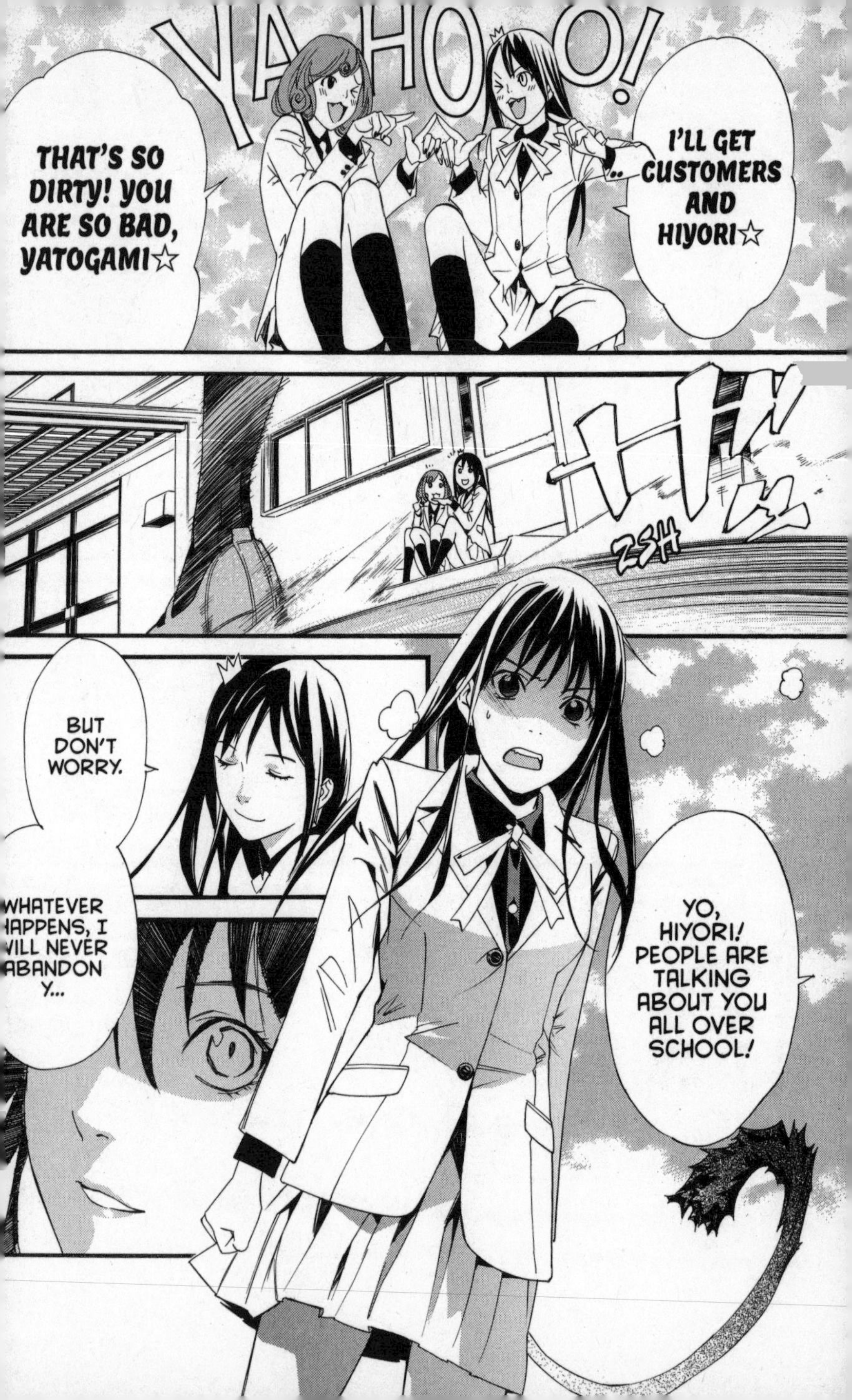
YAHOOO!
I'LL GET CUSTOMERS AND HIYORI☆
THAT'S SO DIRTY! YOU ARE SO BAD, YATOGAMI☆
ZSH
YO, HIYORI! PEOPLE ARE TALKING ABOUT YOU ALL OVER SCHOOL!
BUT DON'T WORRY.
WHATEVER HAPPENS, I WILL NEVER ABANDON Y...

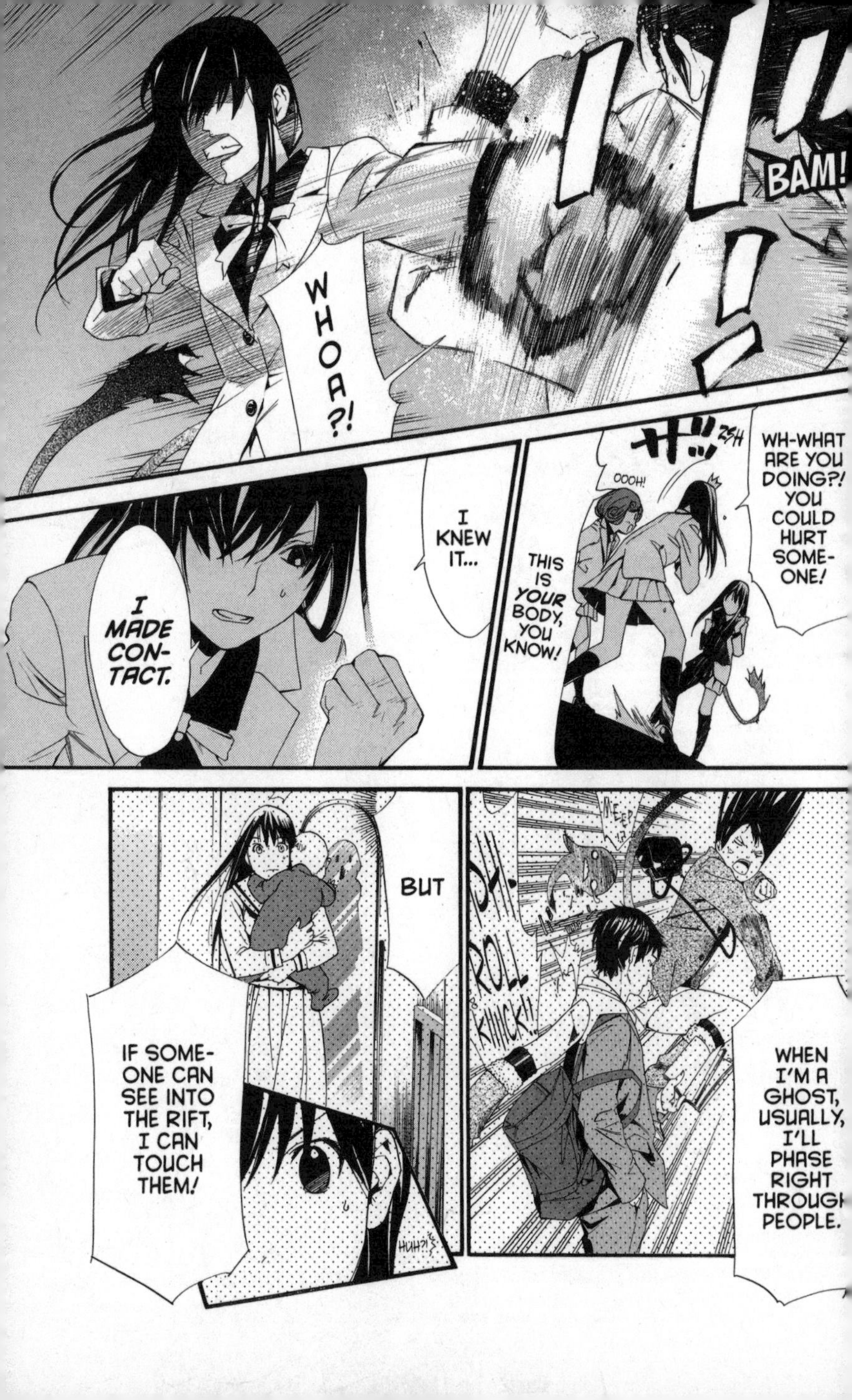
BAM!
WHOA?!
WH-WHAT ARE YOU DOING?! YOU COULD HURT SOMEONE!
ZSH
OOOH!
THIS IS *YOUR* BODY, YOU KNOW!
I KNEW IT...
I MADE CONTACT.
WHEN I'M A GHOST, USUALLY, I'LL PHASE RIGHT THROUGH PEOPLE.
ROLL
KHICK!!
BUT
IF SOMEONE CAN SEE INTO THE RIFT, I CAN TOUCH THEM!
HUH?!

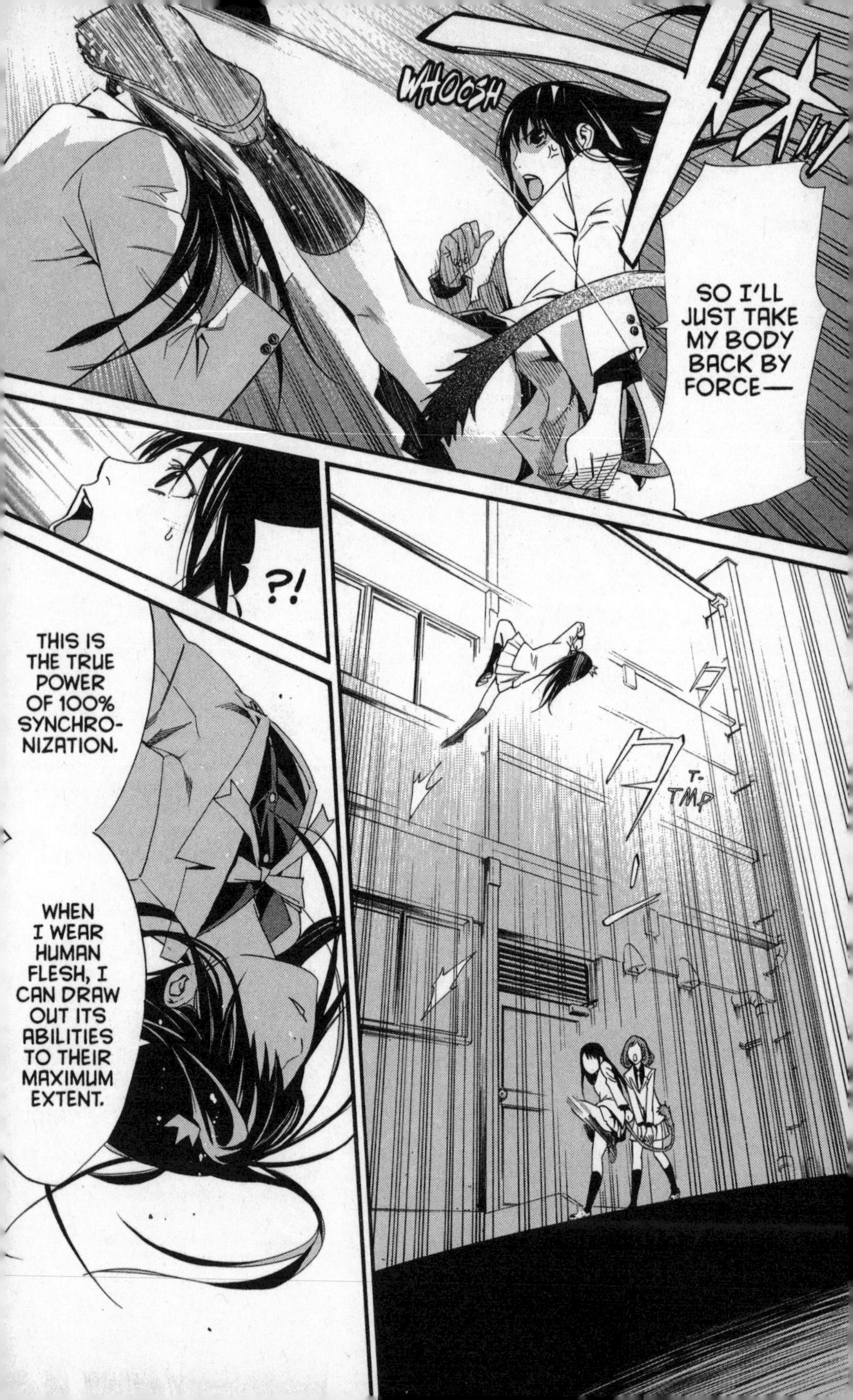
SO I'LL JUST TAKE MY BODY BACK BY FORCE—
WHOOSH
?!
T-TMP
THIS IS THE TRUE POWER OF 100% SYNCHRONIZATION.
WHEN I WEAR HUMAN FLESH, I CAN DRAW OUT ITS ABILITIES TO THEIR MAXIMUM EXTENT.

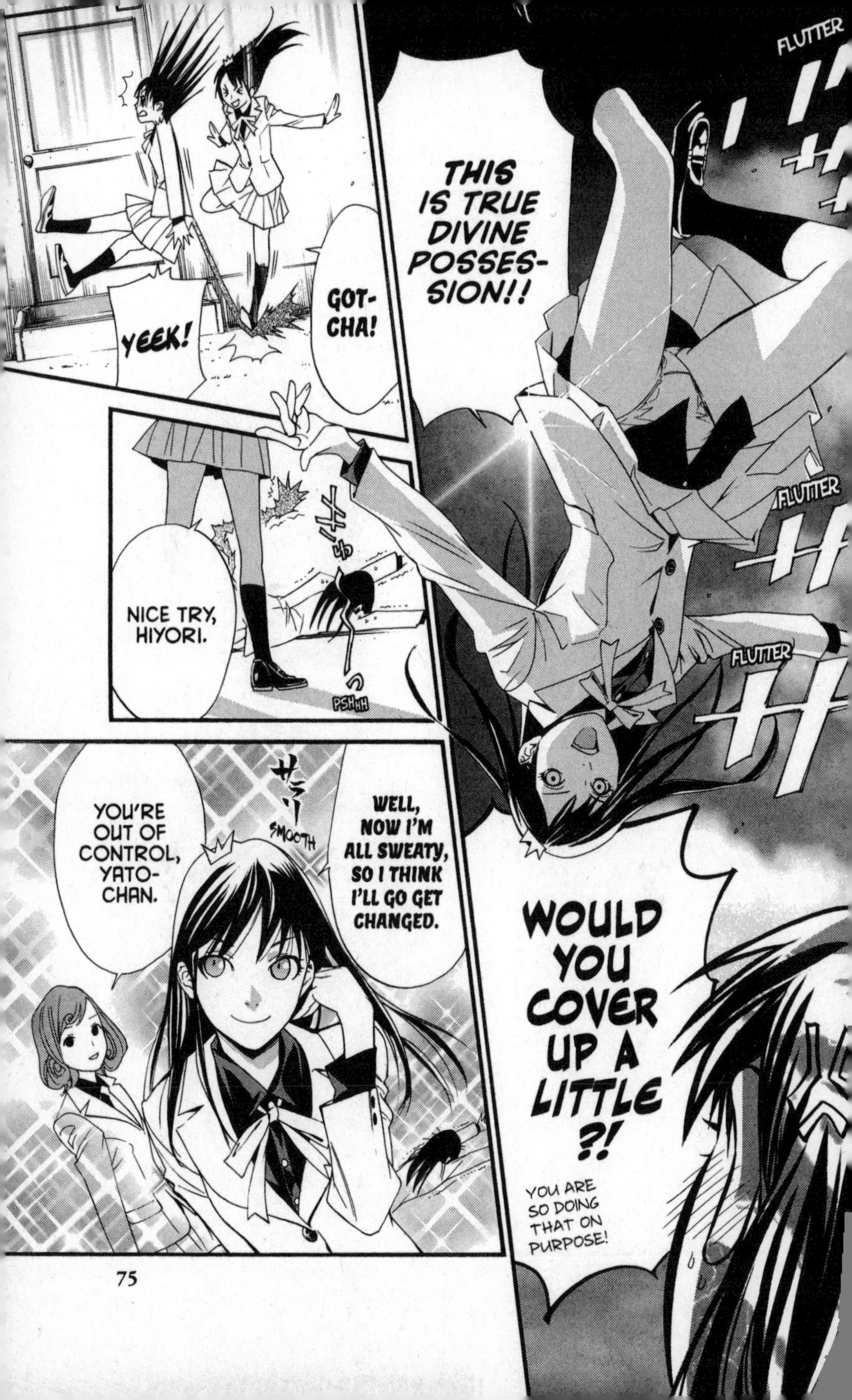
FLUTTER
THIS IS TRUE DIVINE POSSES-SION!!
FLUTTER
FLUTTER
WOULD YOU COVER UP A LITTLE?!
YOU ARE SO DOING THAT ON PURPOSE!
GOT-CHA!
YEEK!
NICE TRY, HIYORI.
PSHHH
WELL, NOW I'M ALL SWEATY, SO I THINK I'LL GO GET CHANGED.
SMOOTH
YOU'RE OUT OF CONTROL, YATO-CHAN.

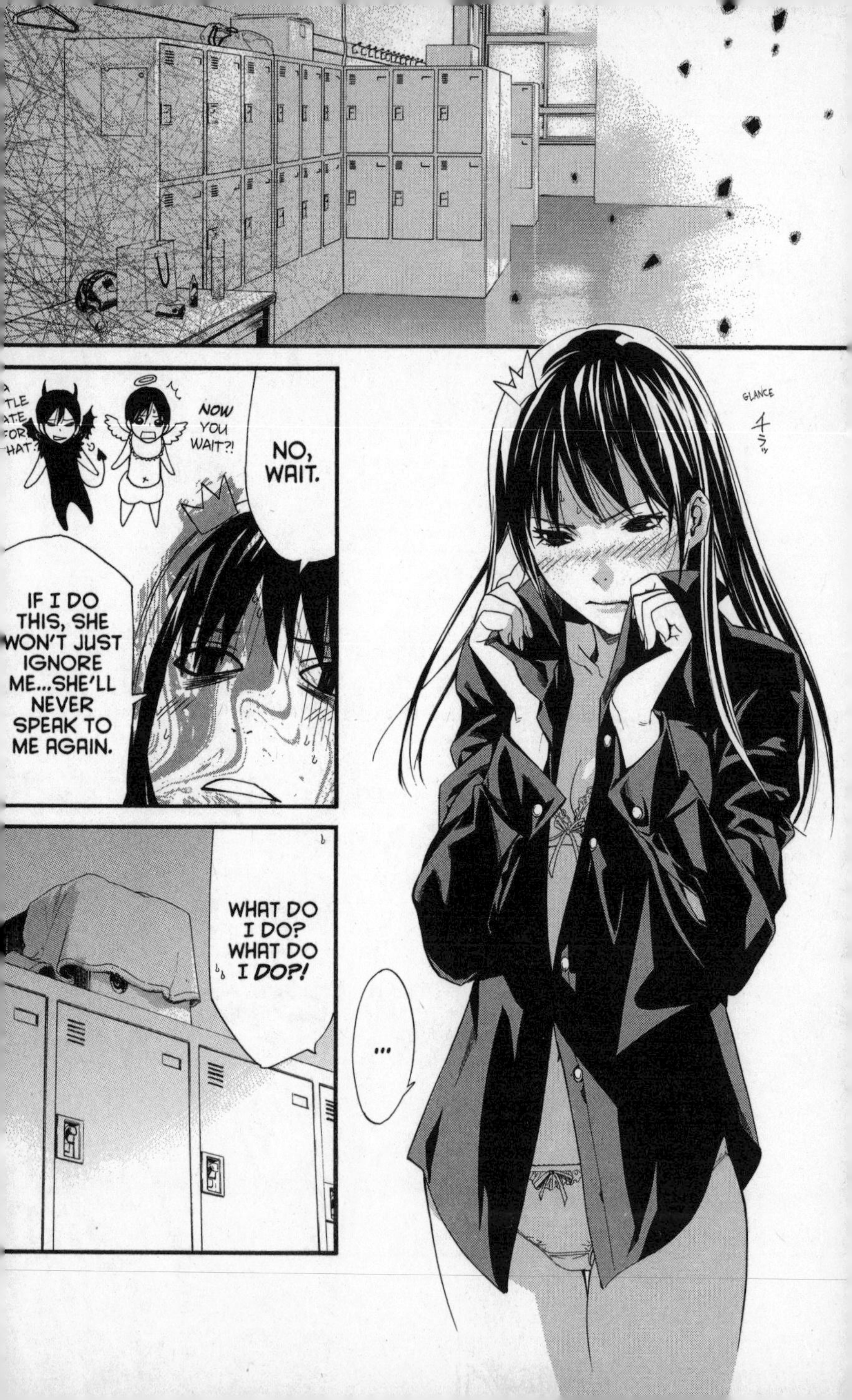

GLANCE
...
NO, WAIT.
NOW YOU WAIT?!
IF I DO THIS, SHE WON'T JUST IGNORE ME...SHE'LL NEVER SPEAK TO ME AGAIN.
WHAT DO I DO? WHAT DO I DO?!

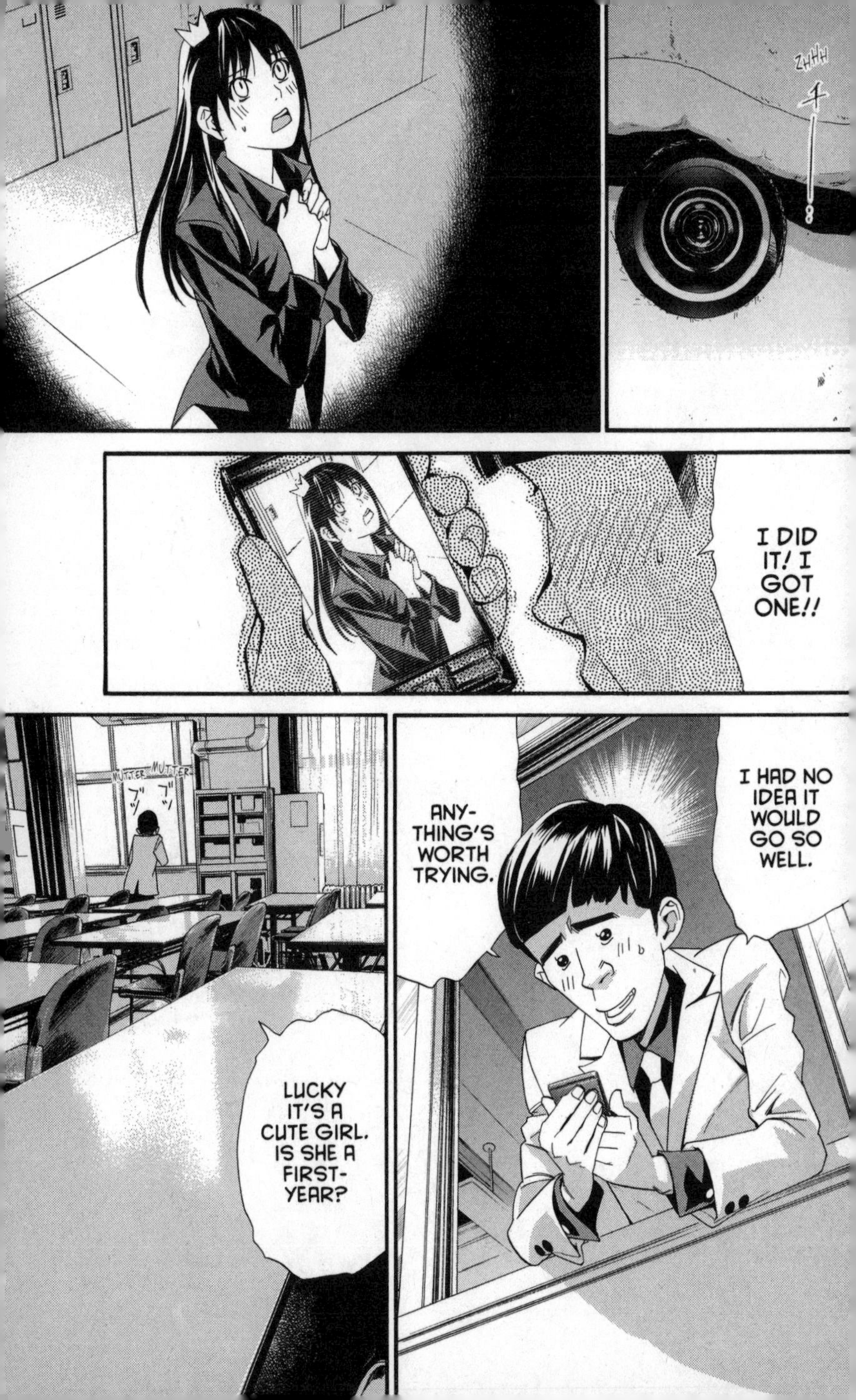
ZHHH
I DID IT! I GOT ONE!!
I HAD NO IDEA IT WOULD GO SO WELL.
ANY-THING'S WORTH TRYING.
MUTTER MUTTER
ブツ ブツ
LUCKY IT'S A CUTE GIRL. IS SHE A FIRST-YEAR?

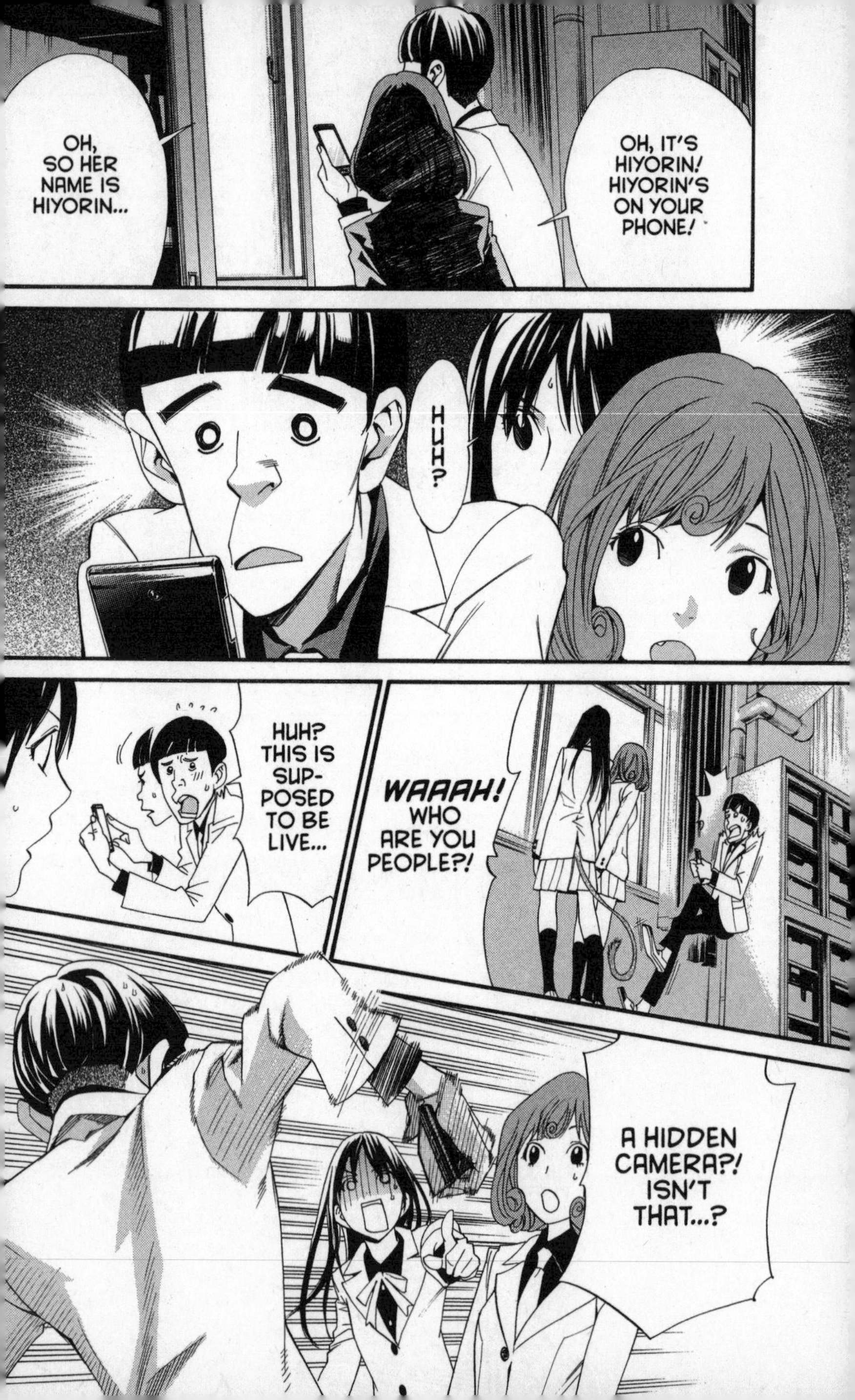
OH, IT'S HIYORIN! HIYORIN'S ON YOUR PHONE!
OH, SO HER NAME IS HIYORIN...
HUH?
WAAAH! WHO ARE YOU PEOPLE?!
HUH? THIS IS SUP-POSED TO BE LIVE...
A HIDDEN CAMERA?! ISN'T THAT...?

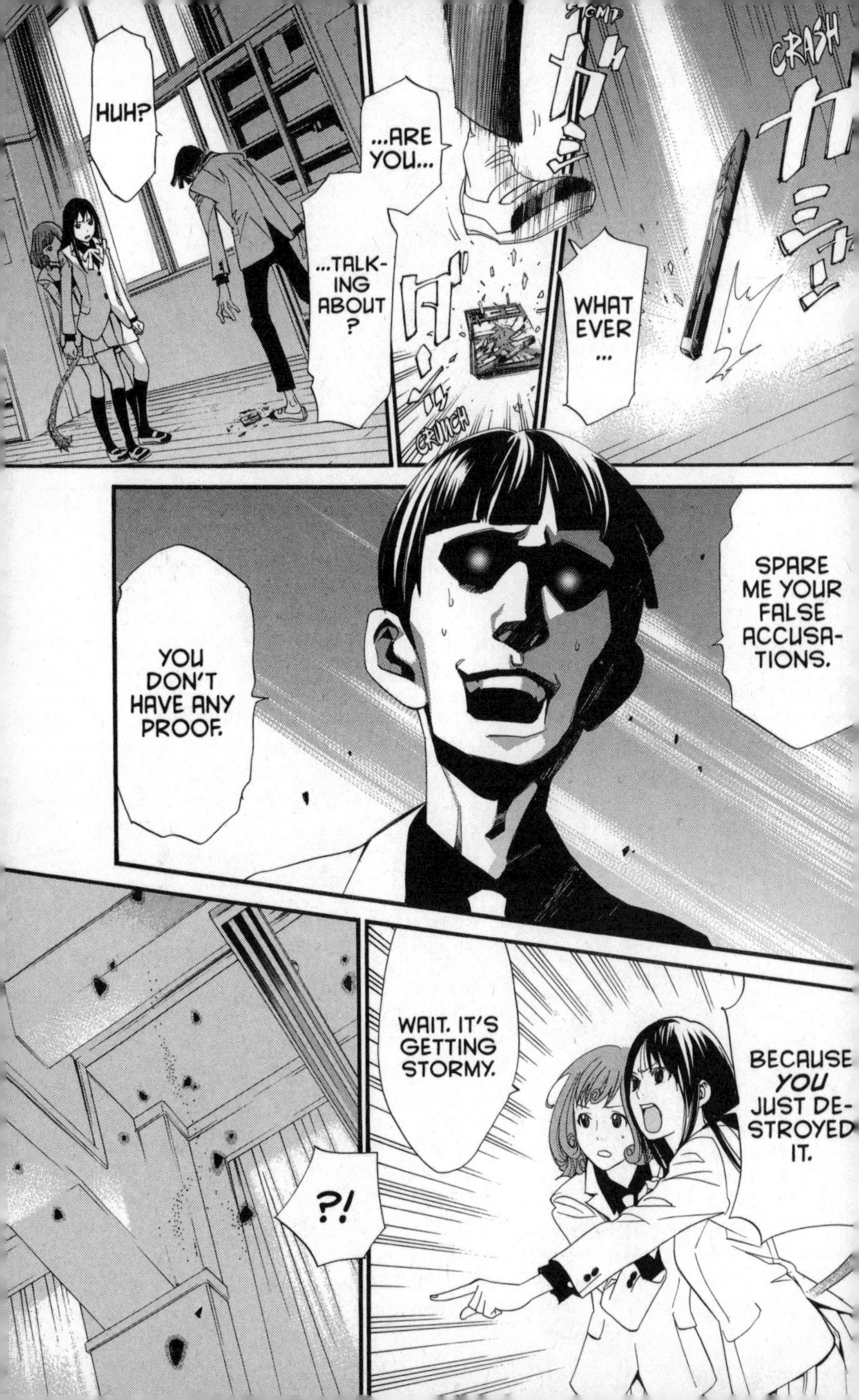
CRASH
WHAT EVER ...
STOMP
...ARE YOU...
...TALKING ABOUT ?
CRUNCH
HUH?
SPARE ME YOUR FALSE ACCUSATIONS.
YOU DON'T HAVE ANY PROOF.
BECAUSE *YOU* JUST DESTROYED IT.
WAIT. IT'S GETTING STORMY.
?!

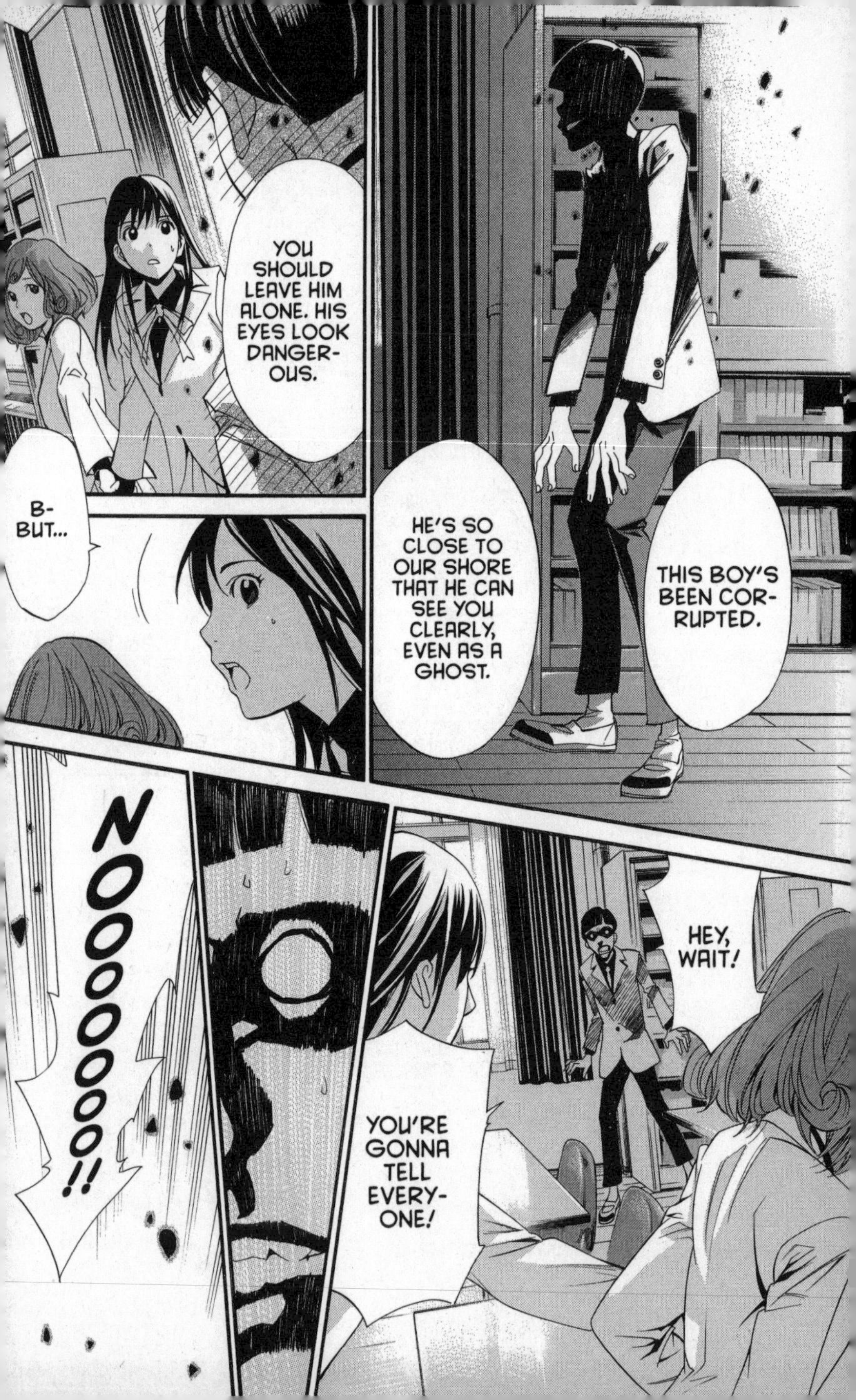
THIS BOY'S BEEN COR-RUPTED.
HE'S SO CLOSE TO OUR SHORE THAT HE CAN SEE YOU CLEARLY, EVEN AS A GHOST.
YOU SHOULD LEAVE HIM ALONE. HIS EYES LOOK DANGER-OUS.
B-BUT...
HEY, WAIT!
YOU'RE GONNA TELL EVERY-ONE!
NOOOOOOOOO!!

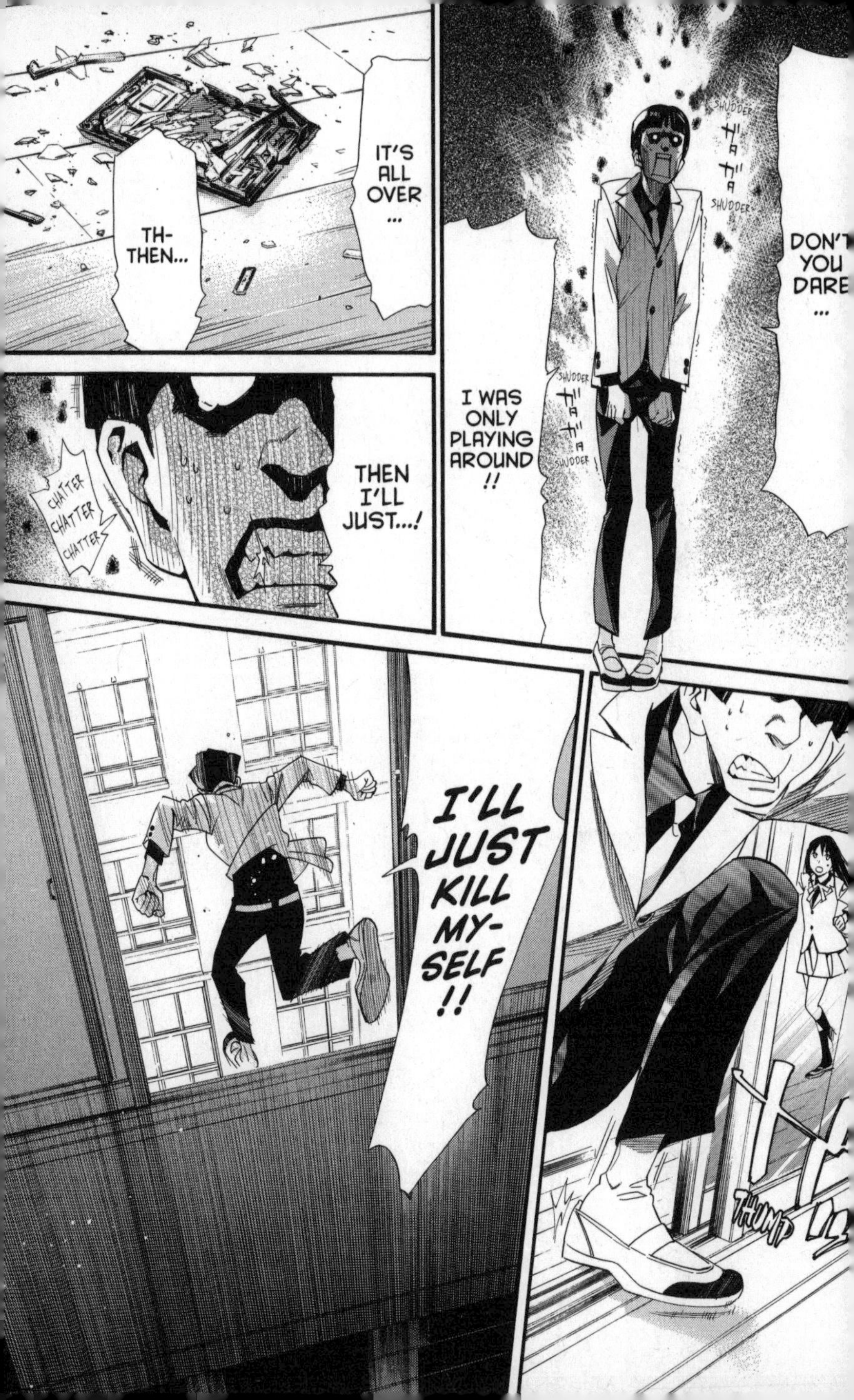
DON'T YOU DARE...
SHUDDER SHUDDER
SHUDDER SHUDDER
I WAS ONLY PLAYING AROUND!!
IT'S ALL OVER...
TH-THEN...
CHATTER CHATTER CHATTER
THEN I'LL JUST...!
THUMP
I'LL JUST KILL MY-SELF!!

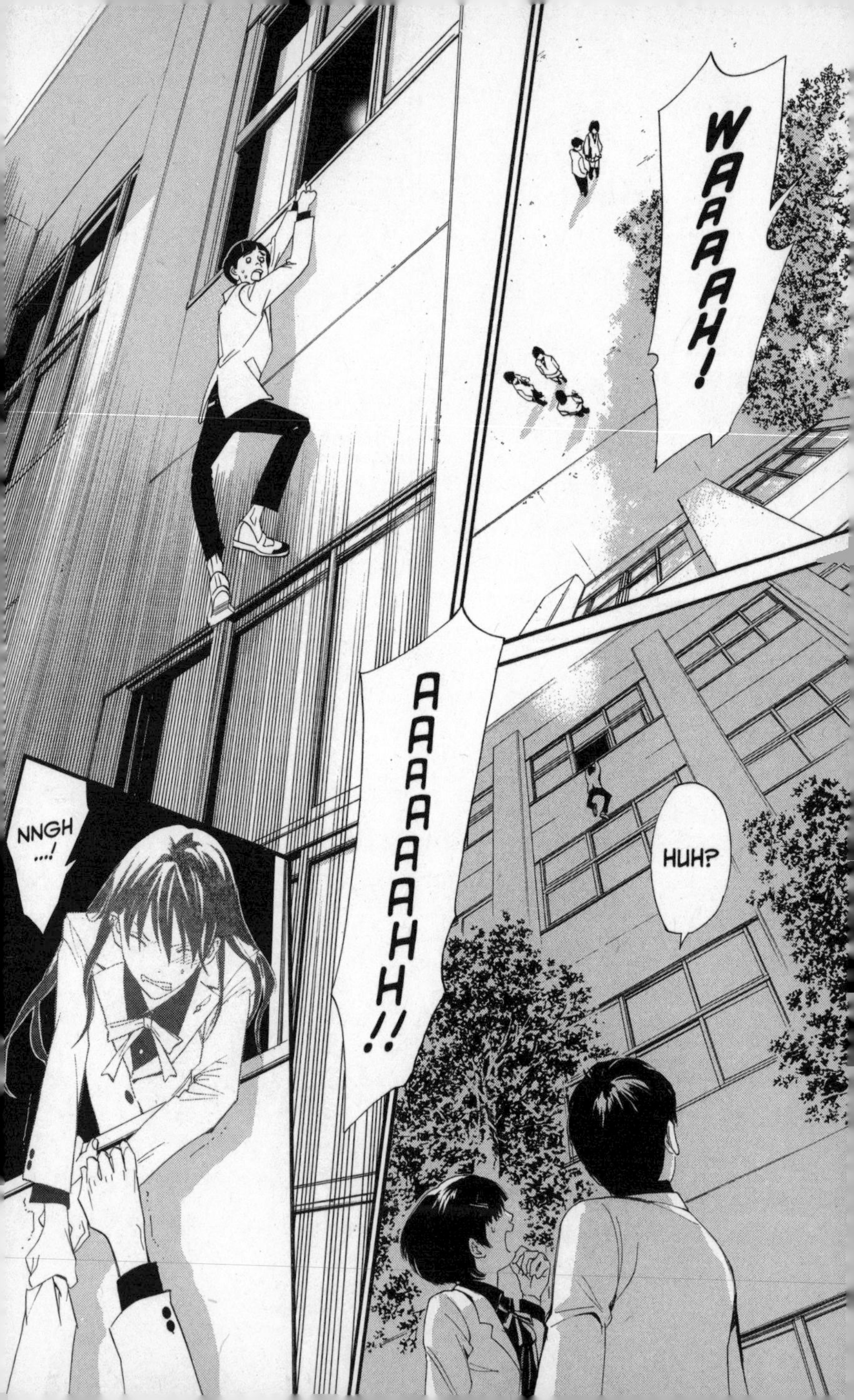
WAAAAAH!
AAAAAAAHH!!
HUH?
NNGH ...!

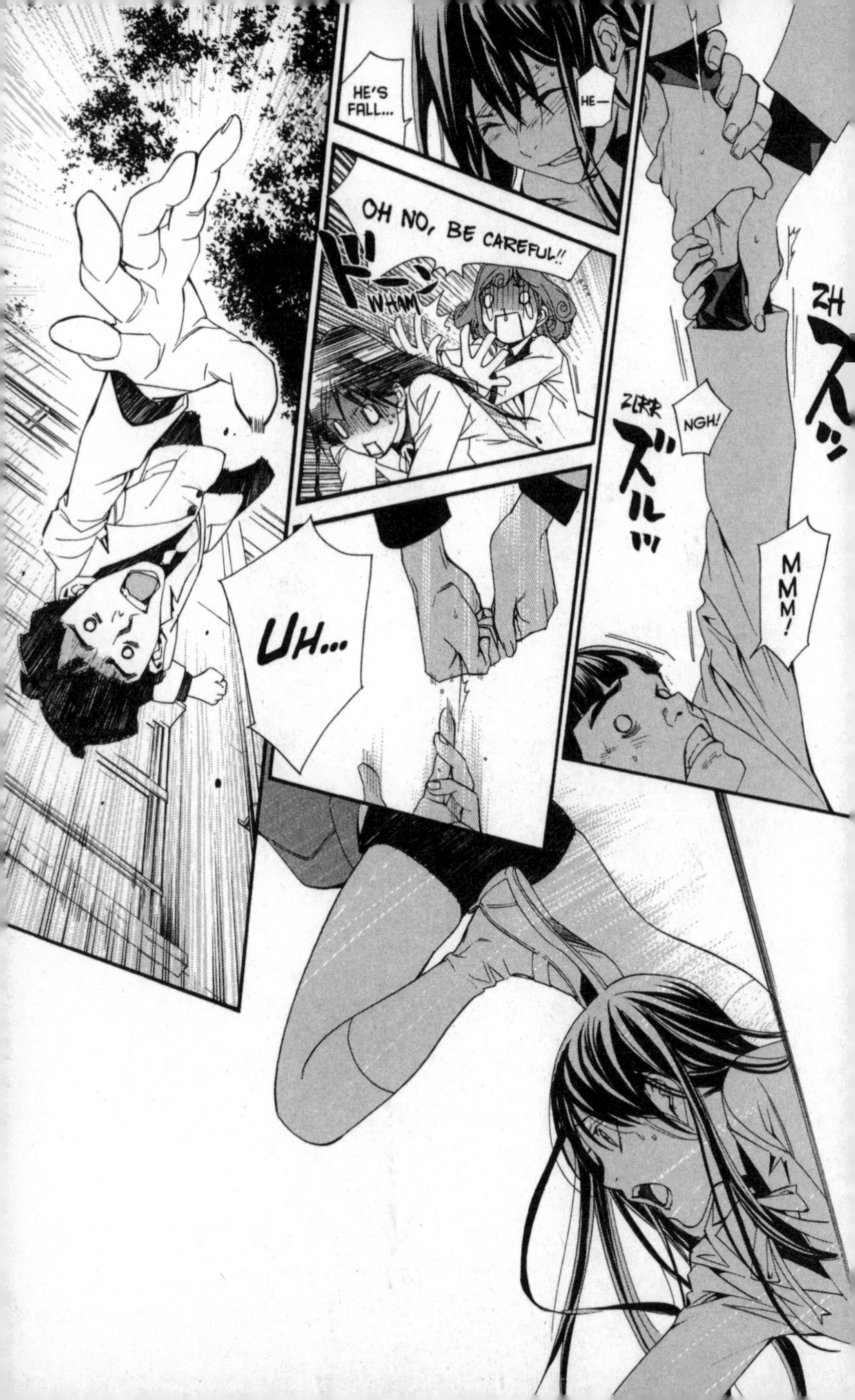
ZH
スッ
NGH!
ZLRR
ズルッ
MMM!
HE—
HE'S FALL...
OH NO, BE CAREFUL!!
WHAM
UH...

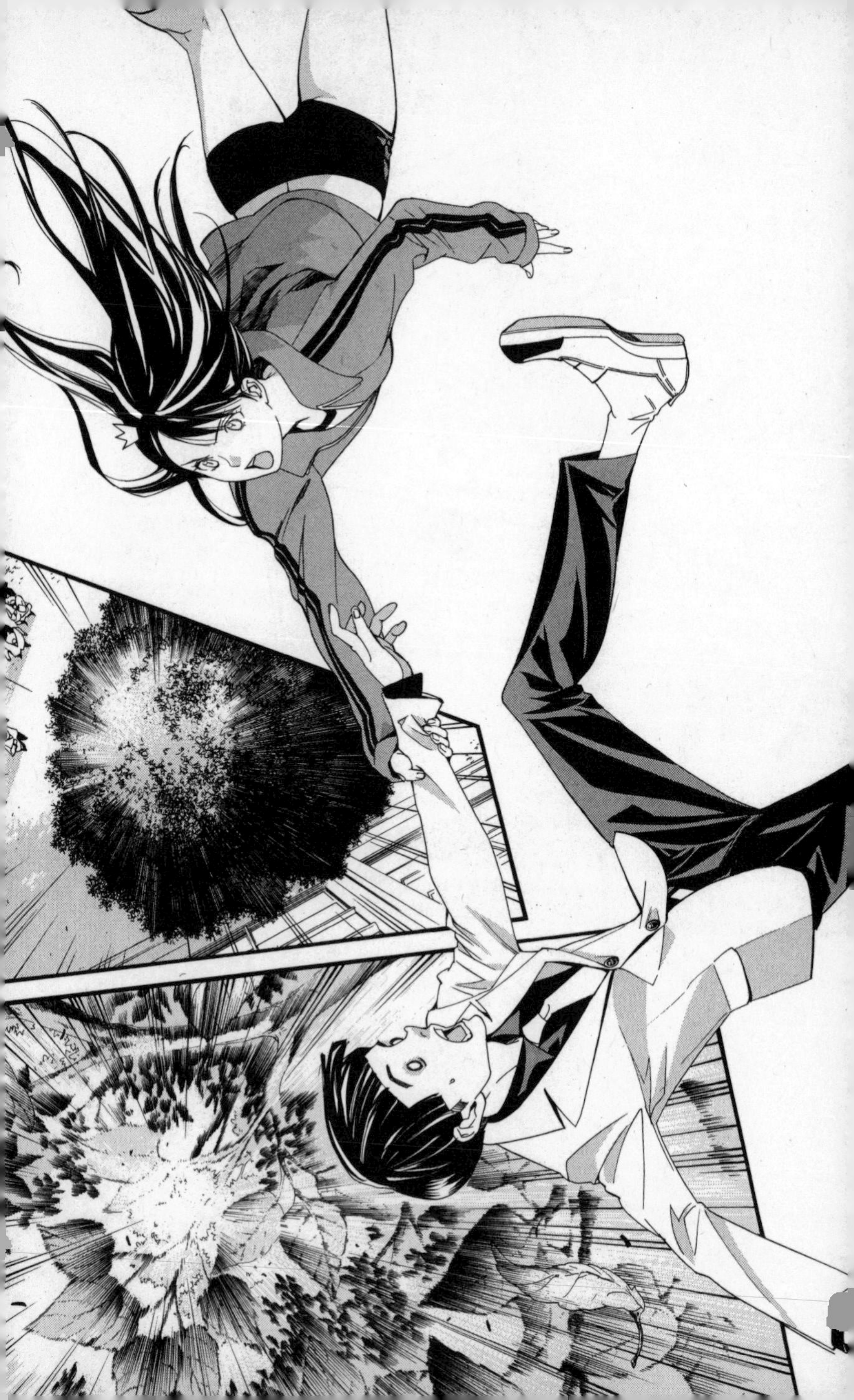

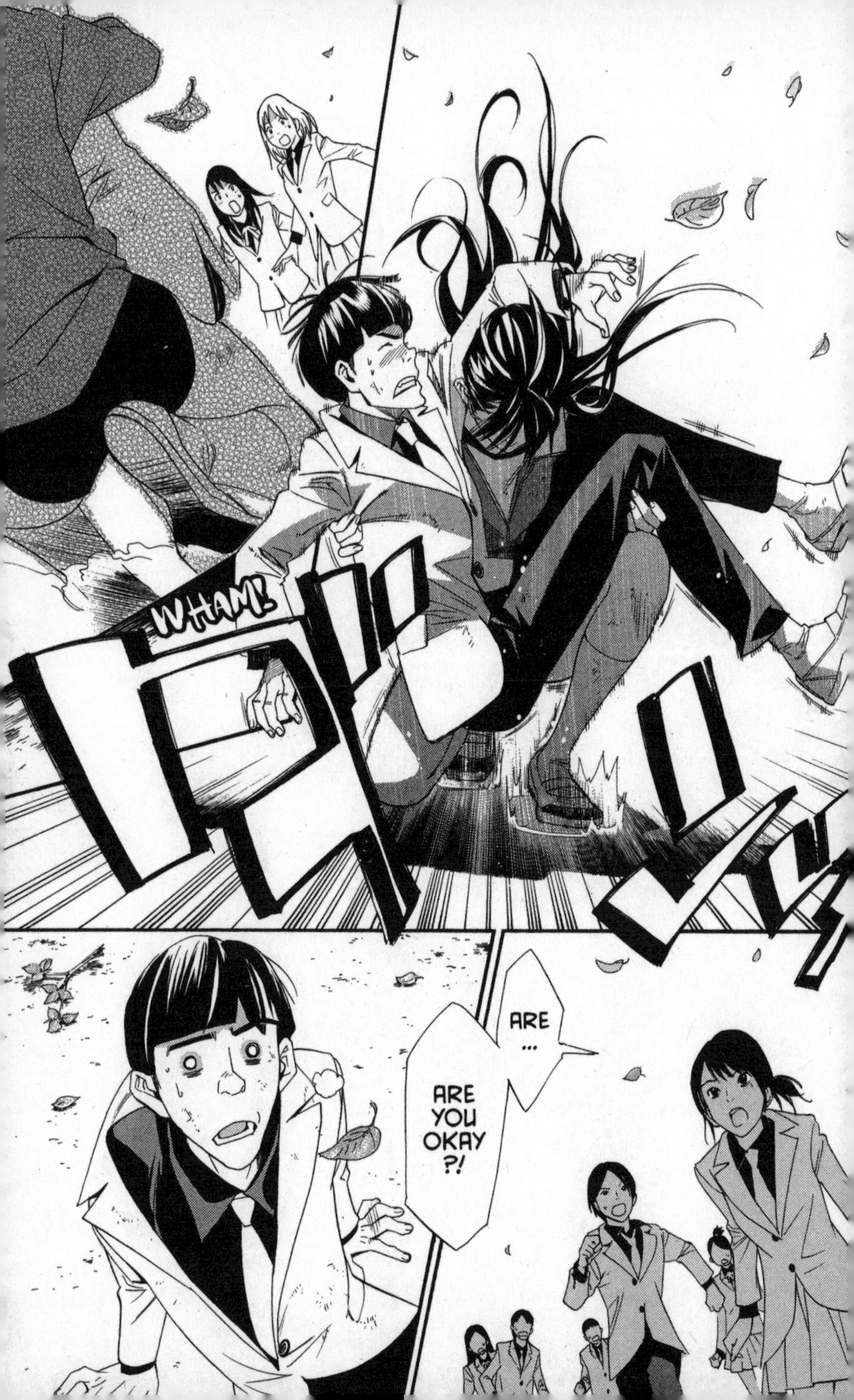
WHAM!
ARE ...
ARE YOU OKAY ?!

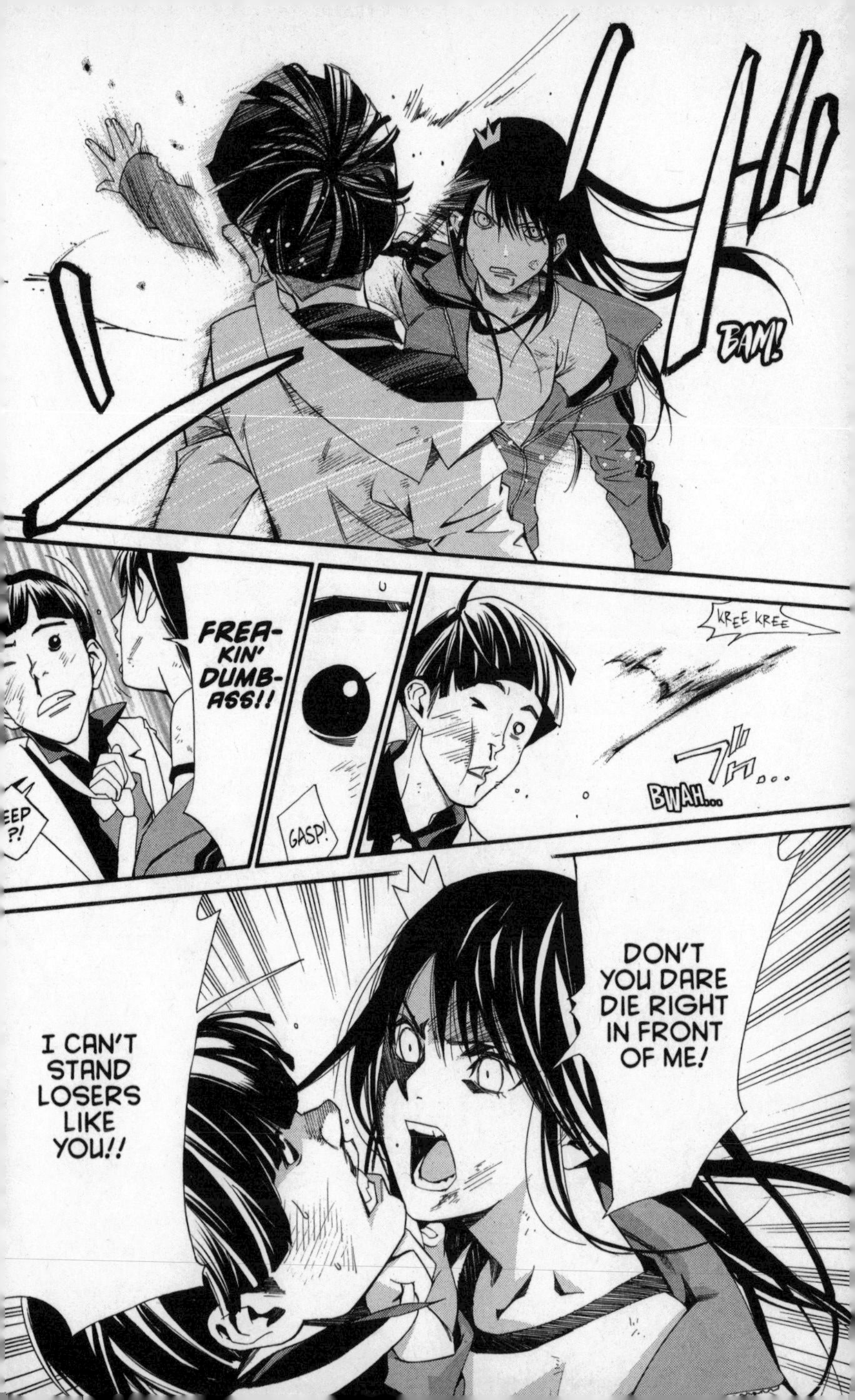
BAM!
KREE KREE
BWAH...
GASP!
FREA-KIN' DUMB-ASS!!
DON'T YOU DARE DIE RIGHT IN FRONT OF ME!
I CAN'T STAND LOSERS LIKE YOU!!

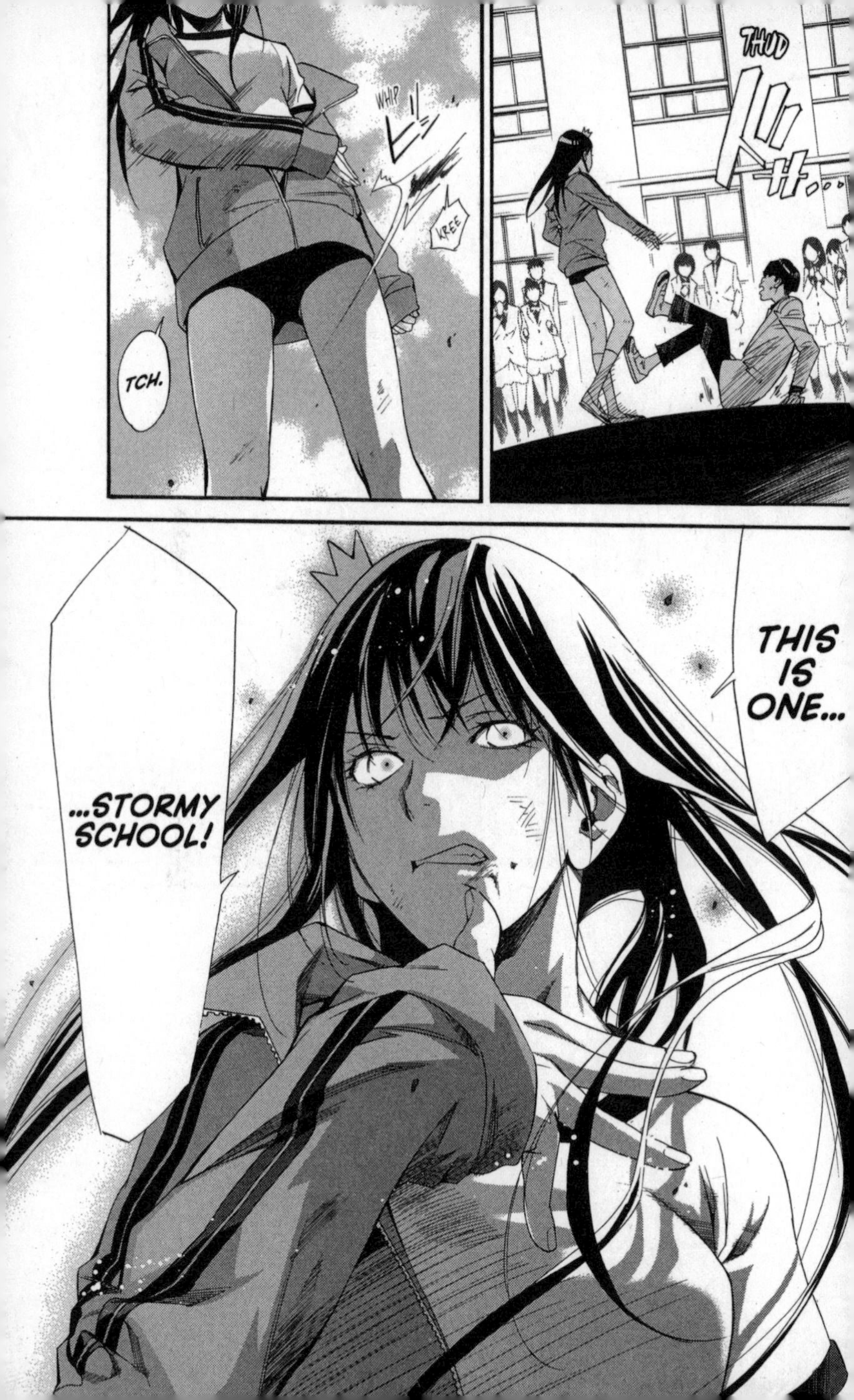
THUD
WHIP
KREE
TCH.
THIS IS ONE...
...STORMY SCHOOL!

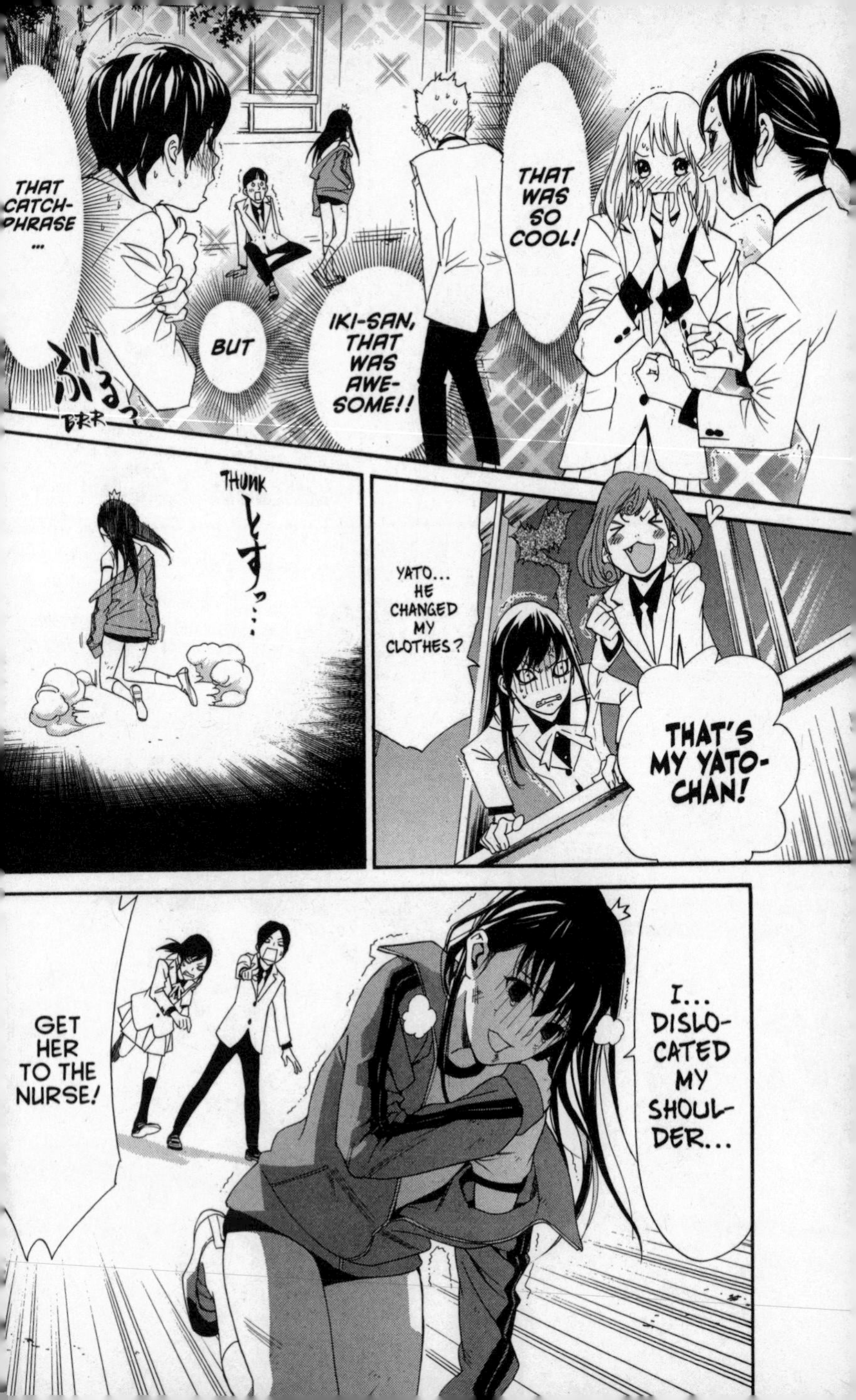
THAT WAS SO COOL!
IKI-SAN, THAT WAS AWESOME!!
BUT
THAT CATCH-PHRASE ...
ぶるっ
BRR
THAT'S MY YATO-CHAN!
YATO... HE CHANGED MY CLOTHES?
THUNK
とすっ...
I... DISLOCATED MY SHOULDER...
GET HER TO THE NURSE!

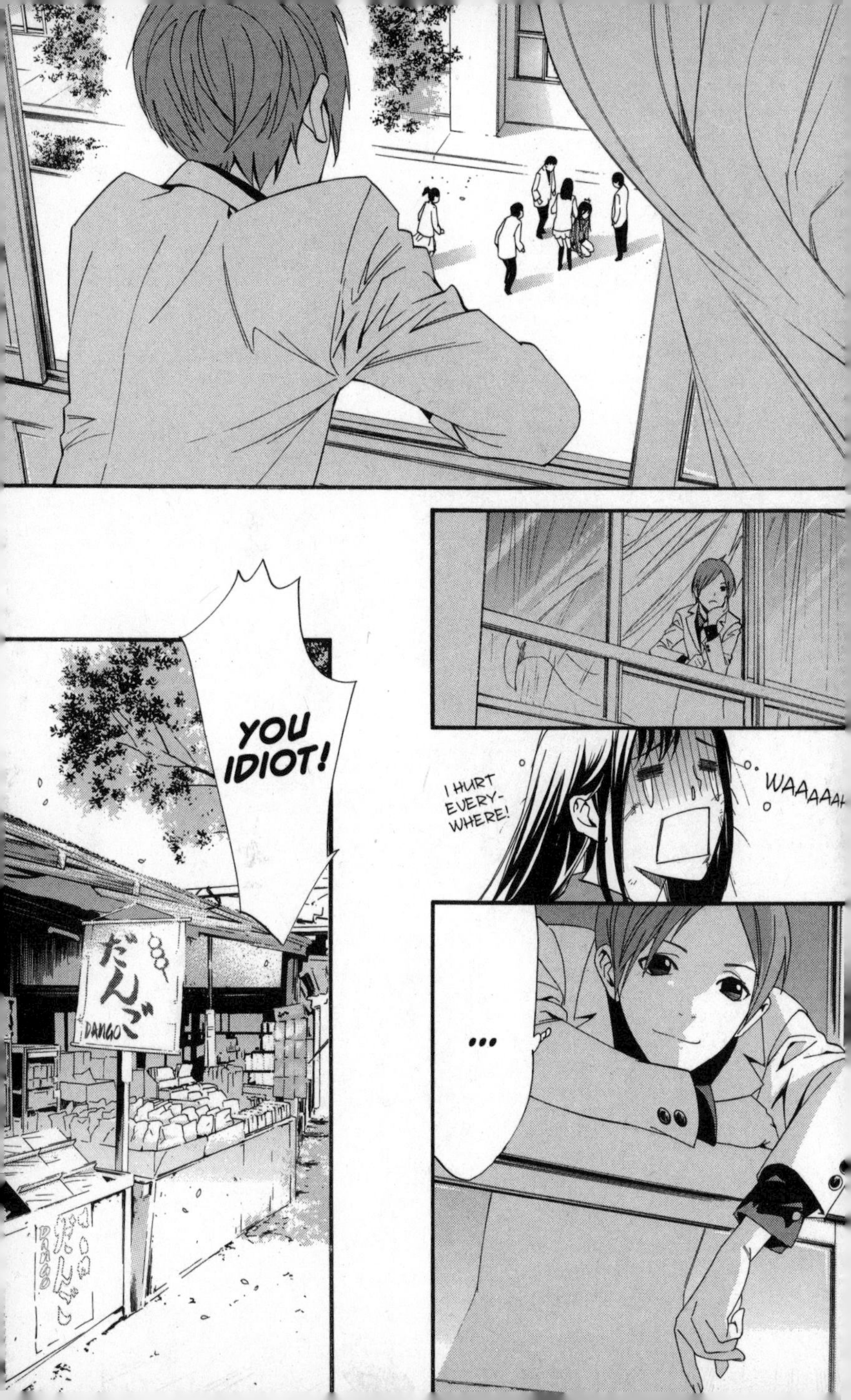
WAAAAAH
I HURT EVERY-WHERE!
...
YOU IDIOT!
だんご
DANGO
だんご
DANGO

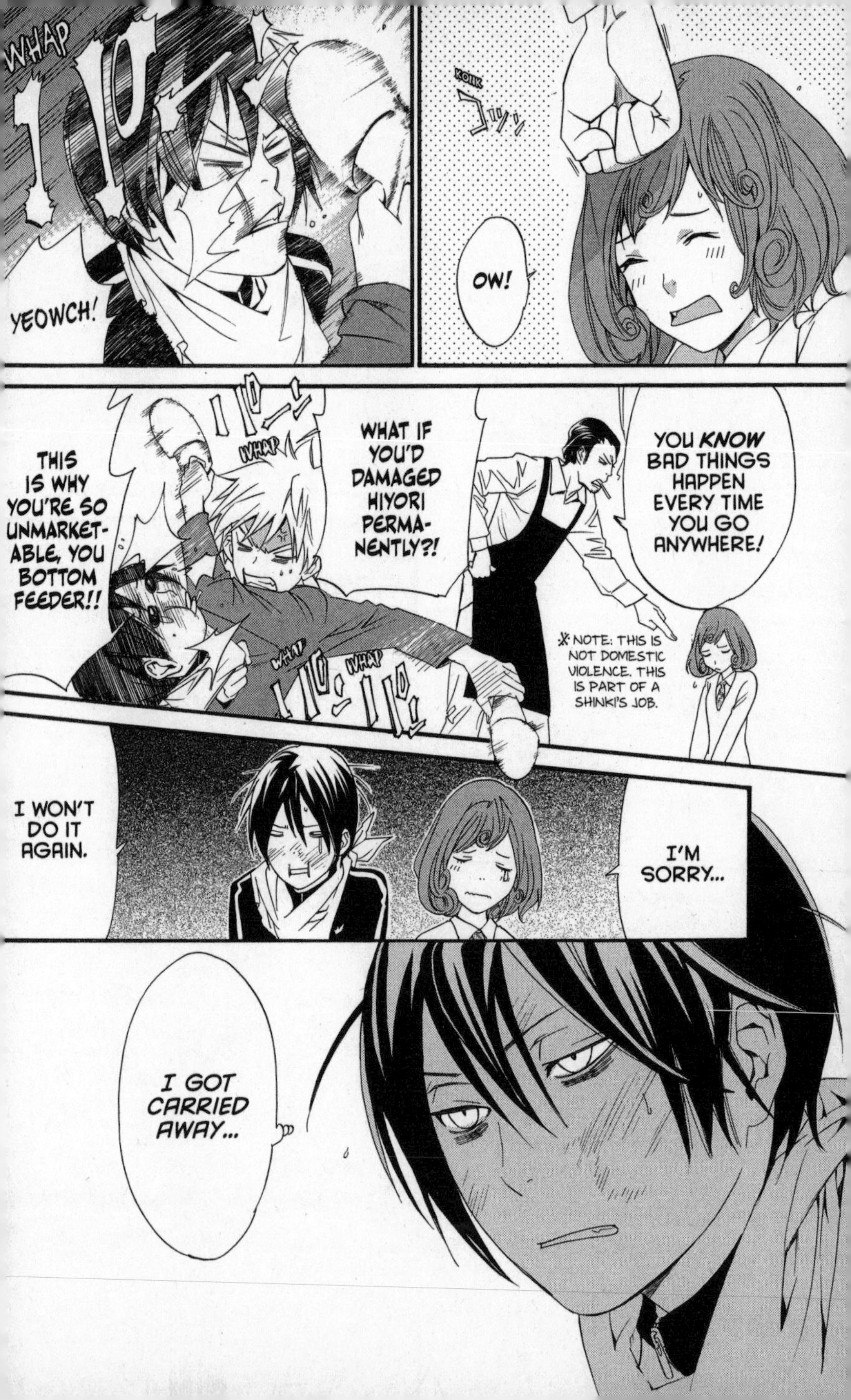
KONK
OW!
WHAP
YEOWCH!
YOU KNOW BAD THINGS HAPPEN EVERY TIME YOU GO ANYWHERE!
※NOTE: THIS IS NOT DOMESTIC VIOLENCE. THIS IS PART OF A SHINKI'S JOB.
WHAT IF YOU'D DAMAGED HIYORI PERMA-NENTLY?!
WHAP
THIS IS WHY YOU'RE SO UNMARKET-ABLE, YOU BOTTOM FEEDER!!
WHAP WHAP
I'M SORRY...
I WON'T DO IT AGAIN.
I GOT CARRIED AWAY...

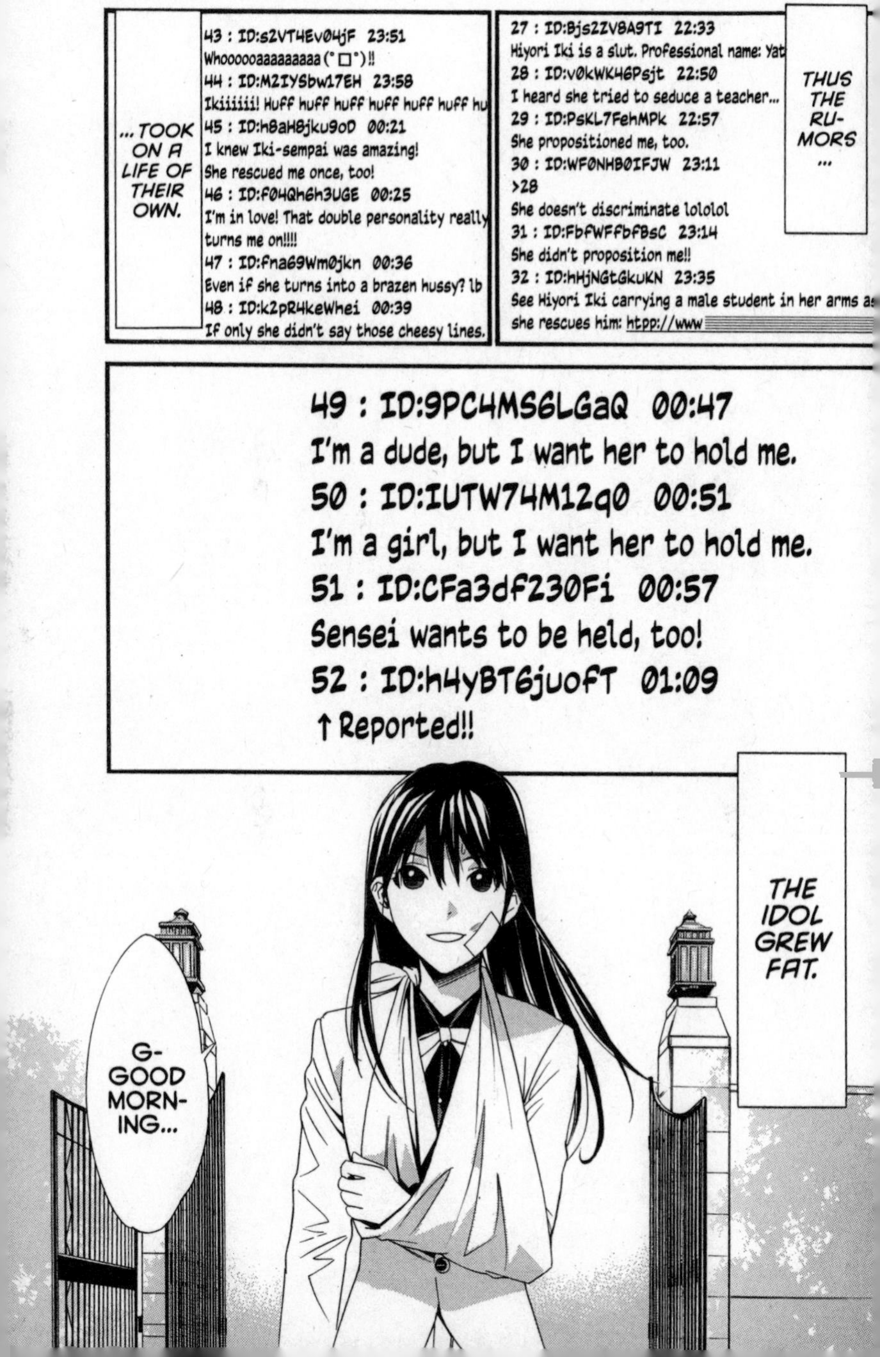
THUS THE RUMORS...
27 : ID:Bjs2ZV8A9TI 22:33
Hiyori Iki is a slut. Professional name: Yat
28 : ID:v0kWK46Psjt 22:50
I heard she tried to seduce a teacher...
29 : ID:PsKL7FehMPk 22:57
She propositioned me, too.
30 : ID:WF0NHB0IFJW 23:11
>28
She doesn't discriminate lololol
31 : ID:FbFWFfbFBsC 23:14
She didn't proposition me!!
32 : ID:hHjNGtGkuKN 23:35
See Hiyori Iki carrying a male student in her arms as
she rescues him: htpp://www
43 : ID:s2VT4Ev04jF 23:51
Whoooooaaaaaaaaa (°□°)!!
44 : ID:M2IYSbw17EH 23:58
Ikiiiiii! Huff huff huff huff huff huff hu
45 : ID:h8aH8jku9oD 00:21
I knew Iki-sempai was amazing!
She rescued me once, too!
46 : ID:f04Qh6h3UGE 00:25
I'm in love! That double personality really
turns me on!!!!
47 : ID:fna69Wm0jkn 00:36
Even if she turns into a brazen hussy? lb
48 : ID:k2pR4keWhei 00:39
If only she didn't say those cheesy lines.
...TOOK ON A LIFE OF THEIR OWN.
49 : ID:9PC4MS6LGaQ 00:47
I'm a dude, but I want her to hold me.
50 : ID:IUTW74M12q0 00:51
I'm a girl, but I want her to hold me.
51 : ID:CFa3df230Fi 00:57
Sensei wants to be held, too!
52 : ID:h4yBT6juofT 01:09
↑Reported!!
THE IDOL GREW FAT.
G-GOOD MORNING...

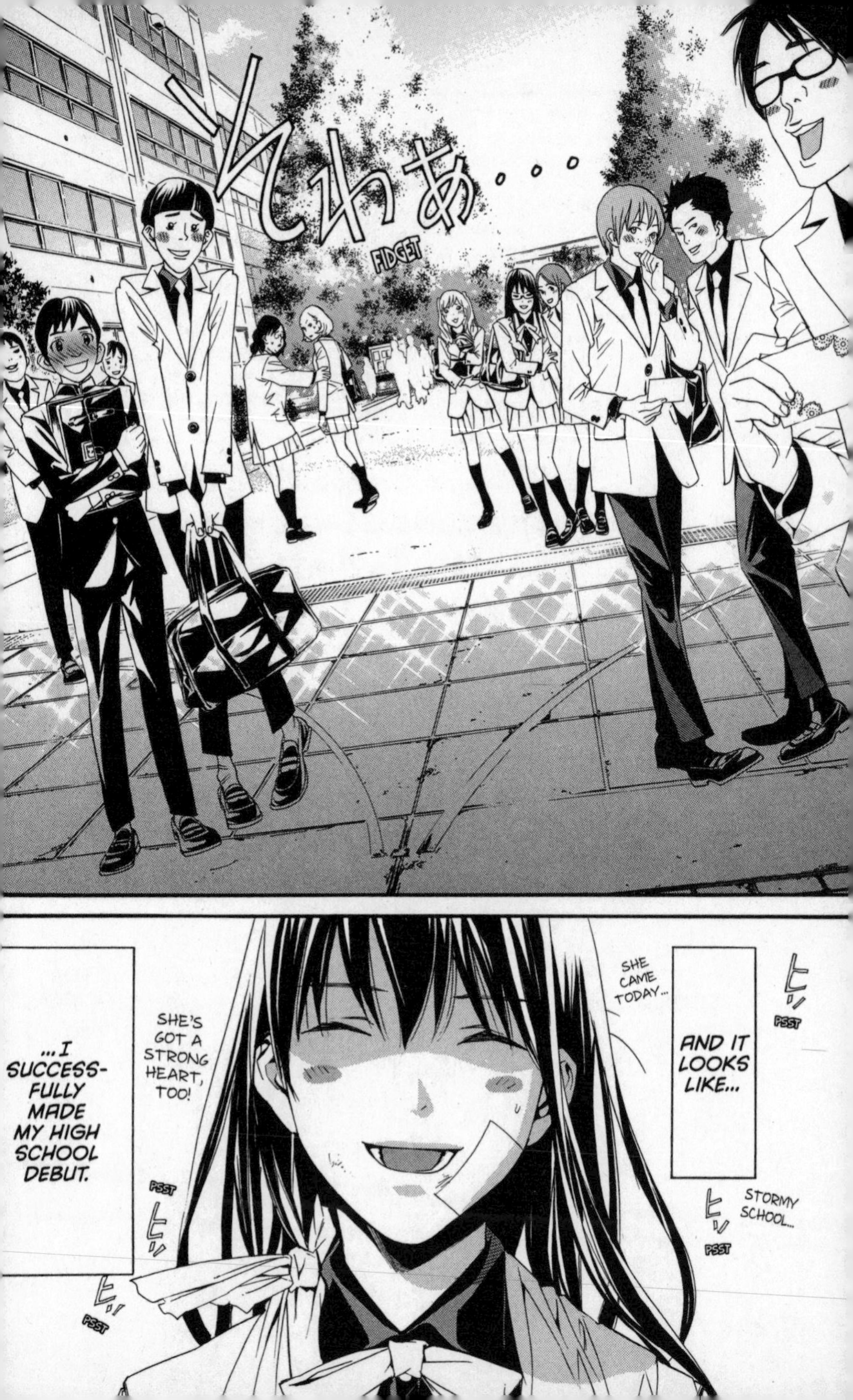

んわあ。。。
FIDGET
ヒソ
PSST
SHE CAME TODAY...
AND IT LOOKS LIKE...
STORMY SCHOOL...
ヒソ
PSST
SHE'S GOT A STRONG HEART, TOO!
...I SUCCESS-FULLY MADE MY HIGH SCHOOL DEBUT.
PSST
ヒソ
ヒソ
PSST

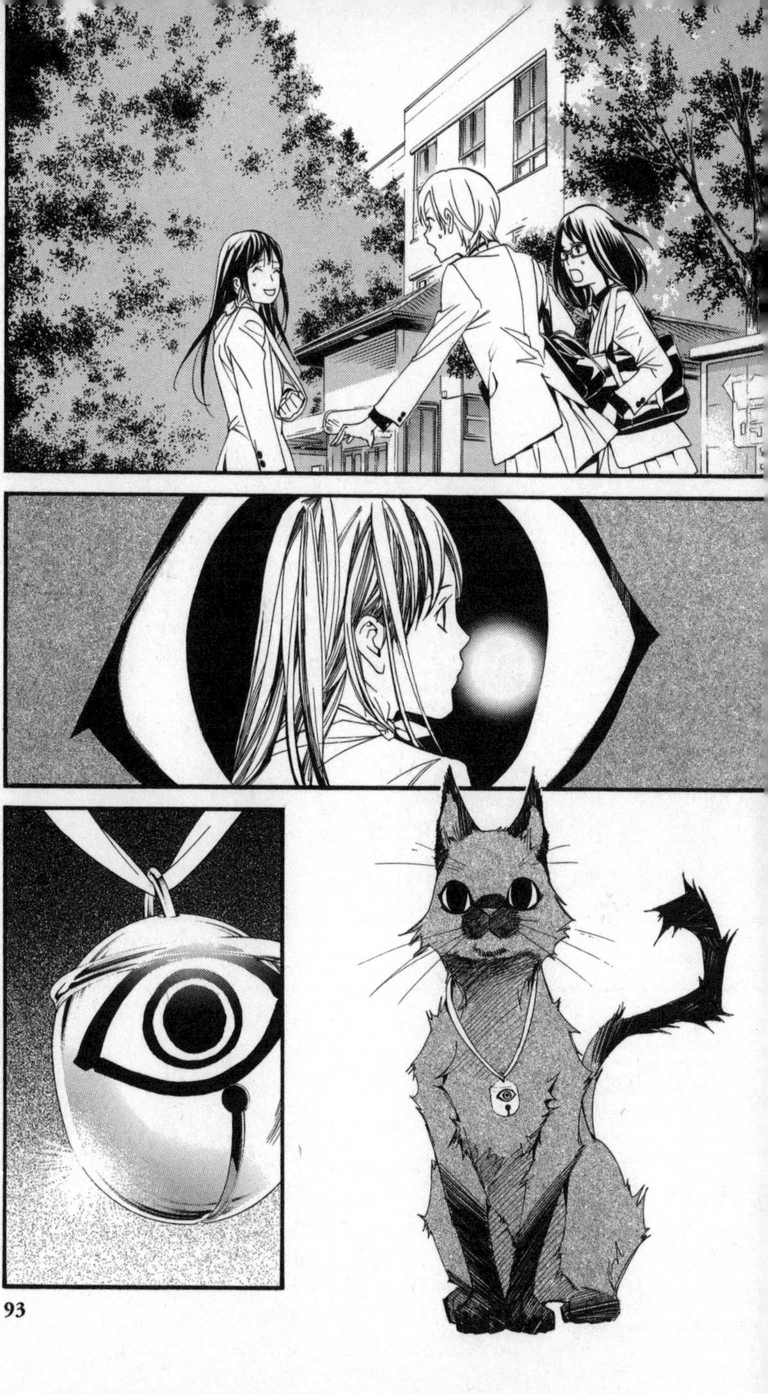

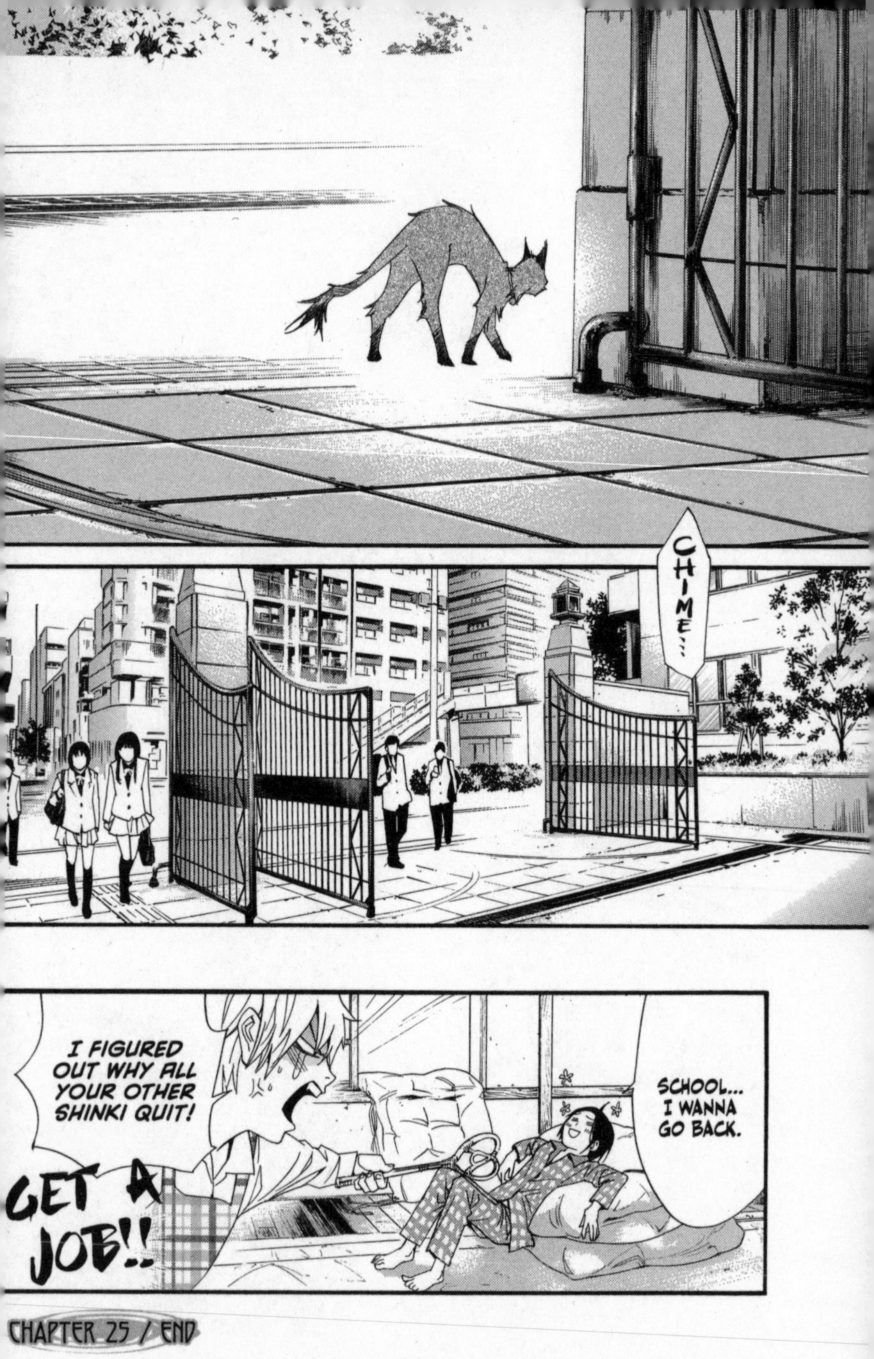
CHIME...
SCHOOL... I WANNA GO BACK.
I FIGURED OUT WHY ALL YOUR OTHER SHINKI QUIT!
GET A JOB!!

CHAPTER 25 / END

封

皀

神

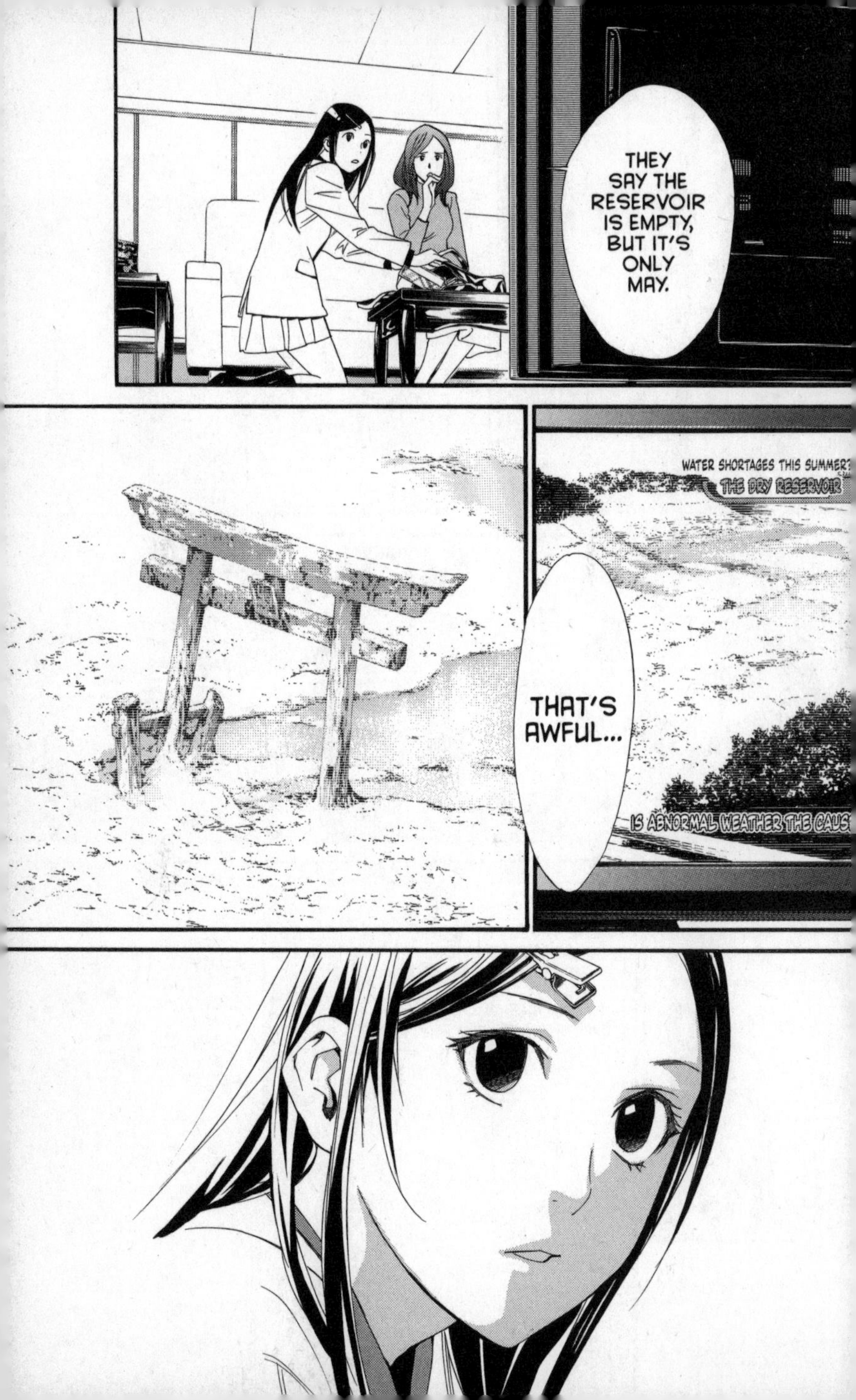
THEY SAY THE RESERVOIR IS EMPTY, BUT IT'S ONLY MAY.
WATER SHORTAGES THIS SUMMER?
THE DRY RESERVOIR
IS ABNORMAL WEATHER THE CAUS
THAT'S AWFUL...

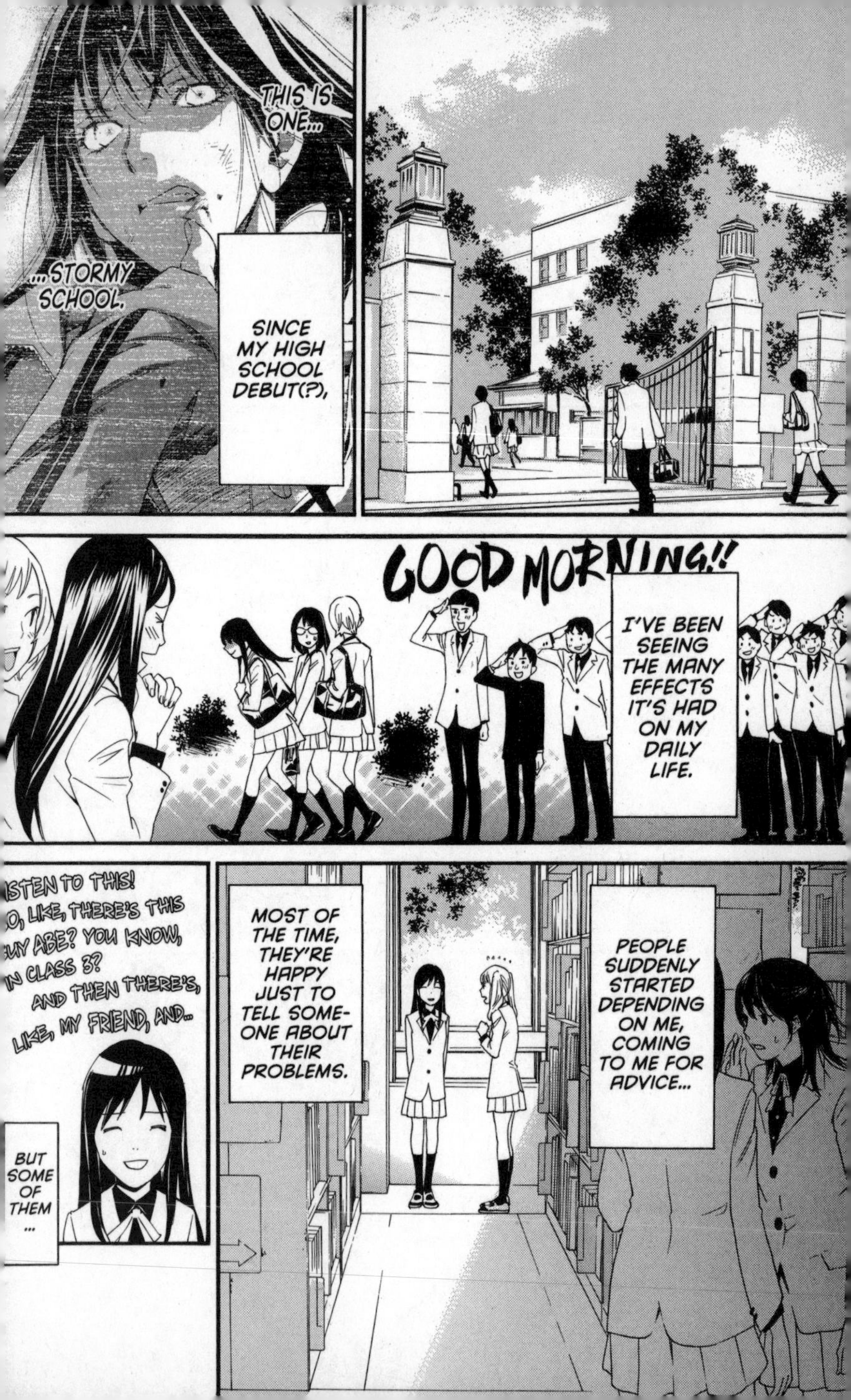
THIS IS ONE...
...STORMY SCHOOL.
SINCE MY HIGH SCHOOL DEBUT(?),
I'VE BEEN SEEING THE MANY EFFECTS IT'S HAD ON MY DAILY LIFE.
GOOD MORNING!!
PEOPLE SUDDENLY STARTED DEPENDING ON ME, COMING TO ME FOR ADVICE...
MOST OF THE TIME, THEY'RE HAPPY JUST TO TELL SOME-ONE ABOUT THEIR PROBLEMS.
ISTEN TO THIS! O, LIKE, THERE'S THIS UY ABE? YOU KNOW, IN CLASS 3? AND THEN THERE'S, LIKE, MY FRIEND, AND...
BUT SOME OF THEM ...

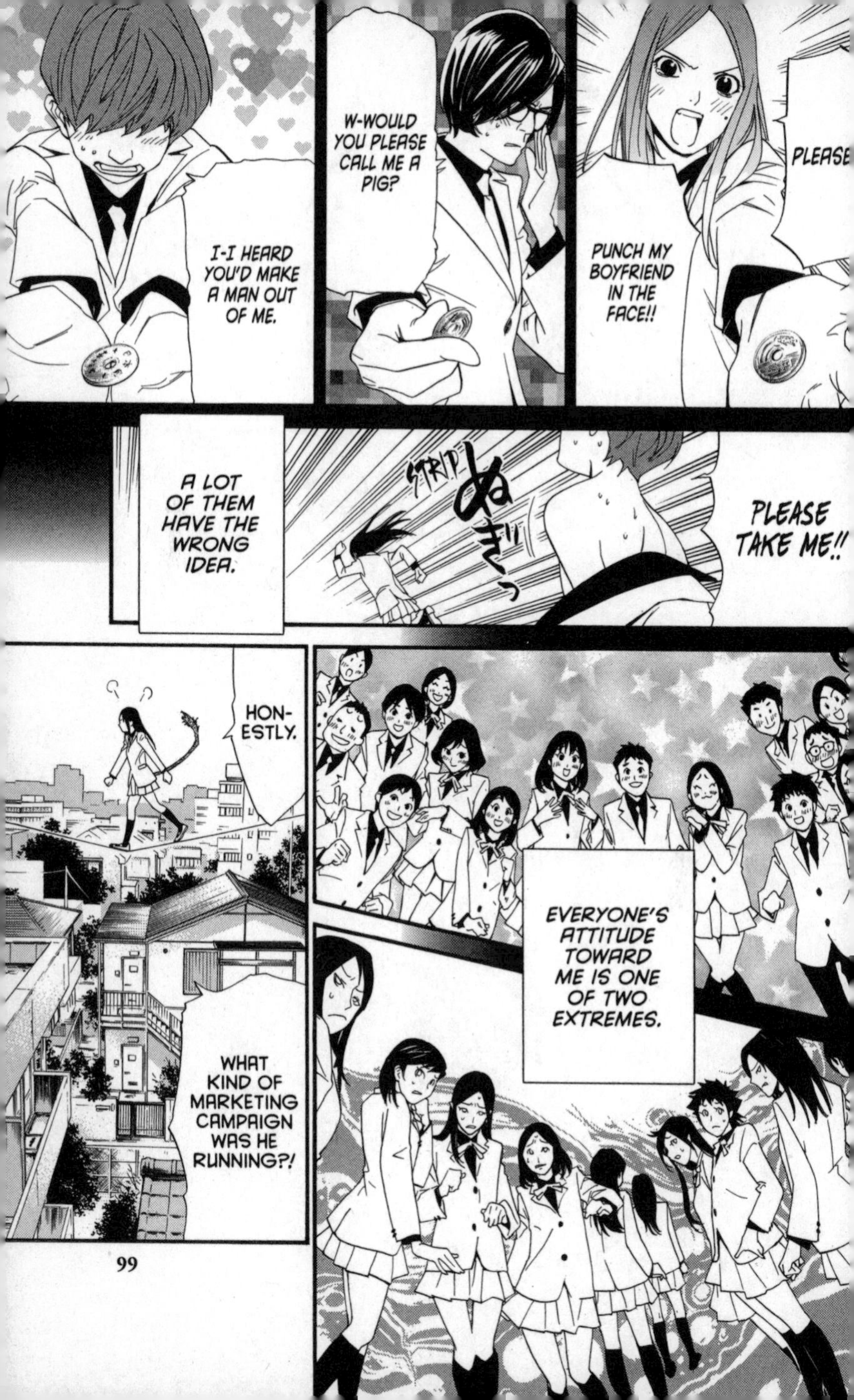
PLEASE
PUNCH MY BOYFRIEND IN THE FACE!!
W-WOULD YOU PLEASE CALL ME A PIG?
I-I HEARD YOU'D MAKE A MAN OUT OF ME.
PLEASE TAKE ME!!
STRIP
A LOT OF THEM HAVE THE WRONG IDEA.
EVERYONE'S ATTITUDE TOWARD ME IS ONE OF TWO EXTREMES.
HON-ESTLY.
WHAT KIND OF MARKETING CAMPAIGN WAS HE RUNNING?!

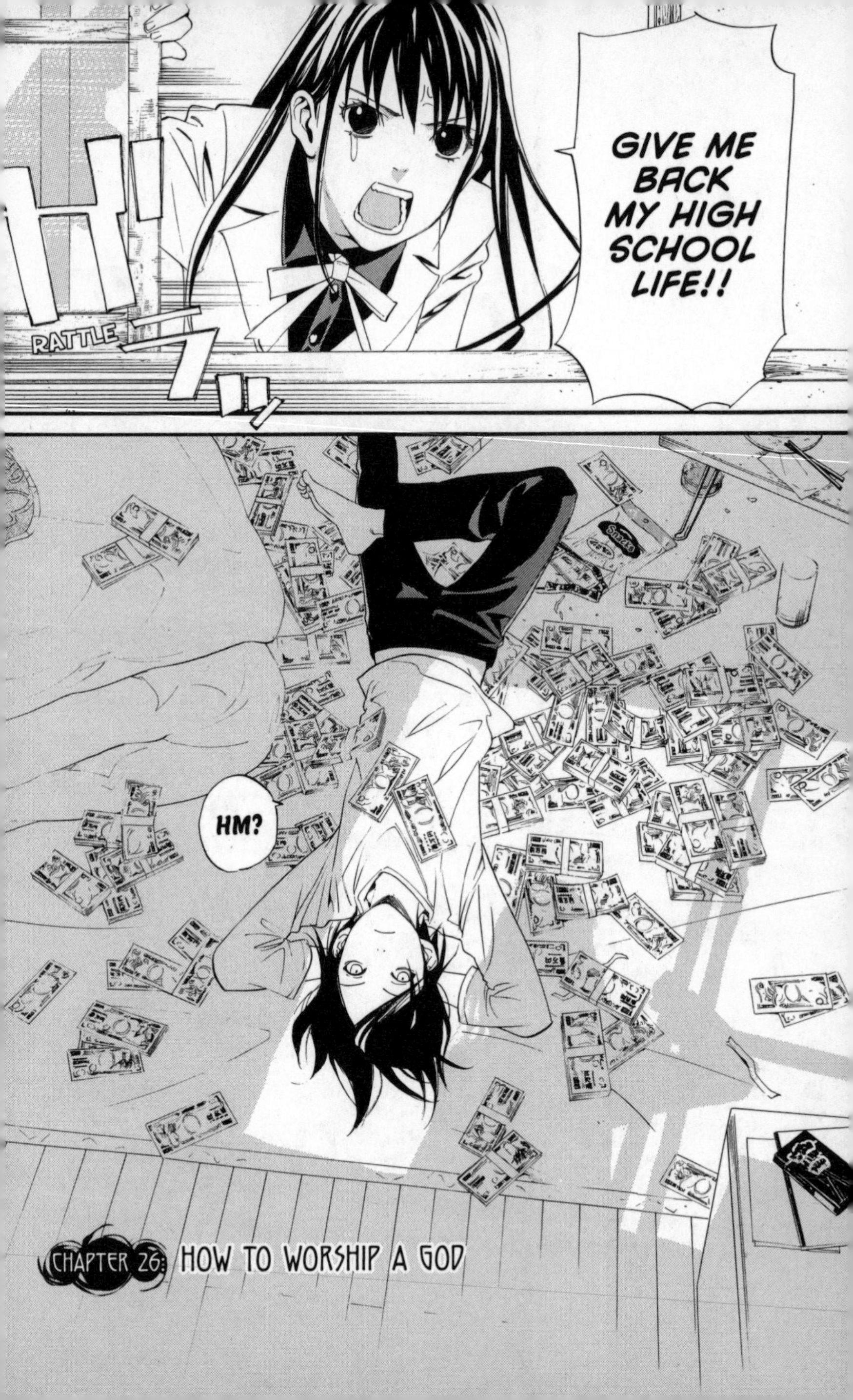
GIVE ME BACK MY HIGH SCHOOL LIFE!!
RATTLE
HM?
Snacks
CHAPTER 26: HOW TO WORSHIP A GOD

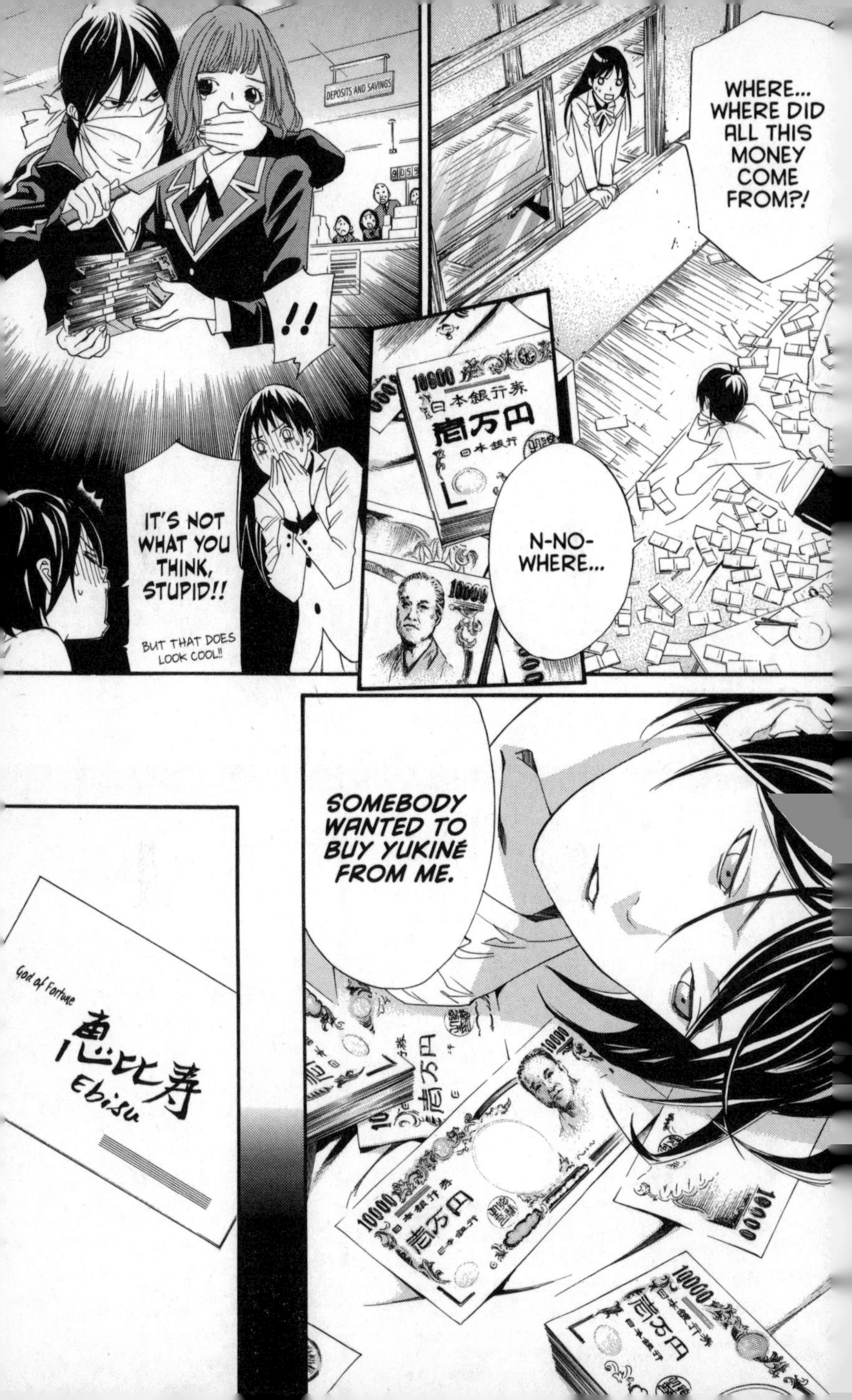
WHERE... WHERE DID ALL THIS MONEY COME FROM?!
N-NO-WHERE...
DEPOSITS AND SAVINGS
!!
IT'S NOT WHAT YOU THINK, STUPID!!
BUT THAT DOES LOOK COOL!!
SOMEBODY WANTED TO BUY YUKINE FROM ME.
God of Fortune
恵比寿
Ebisu

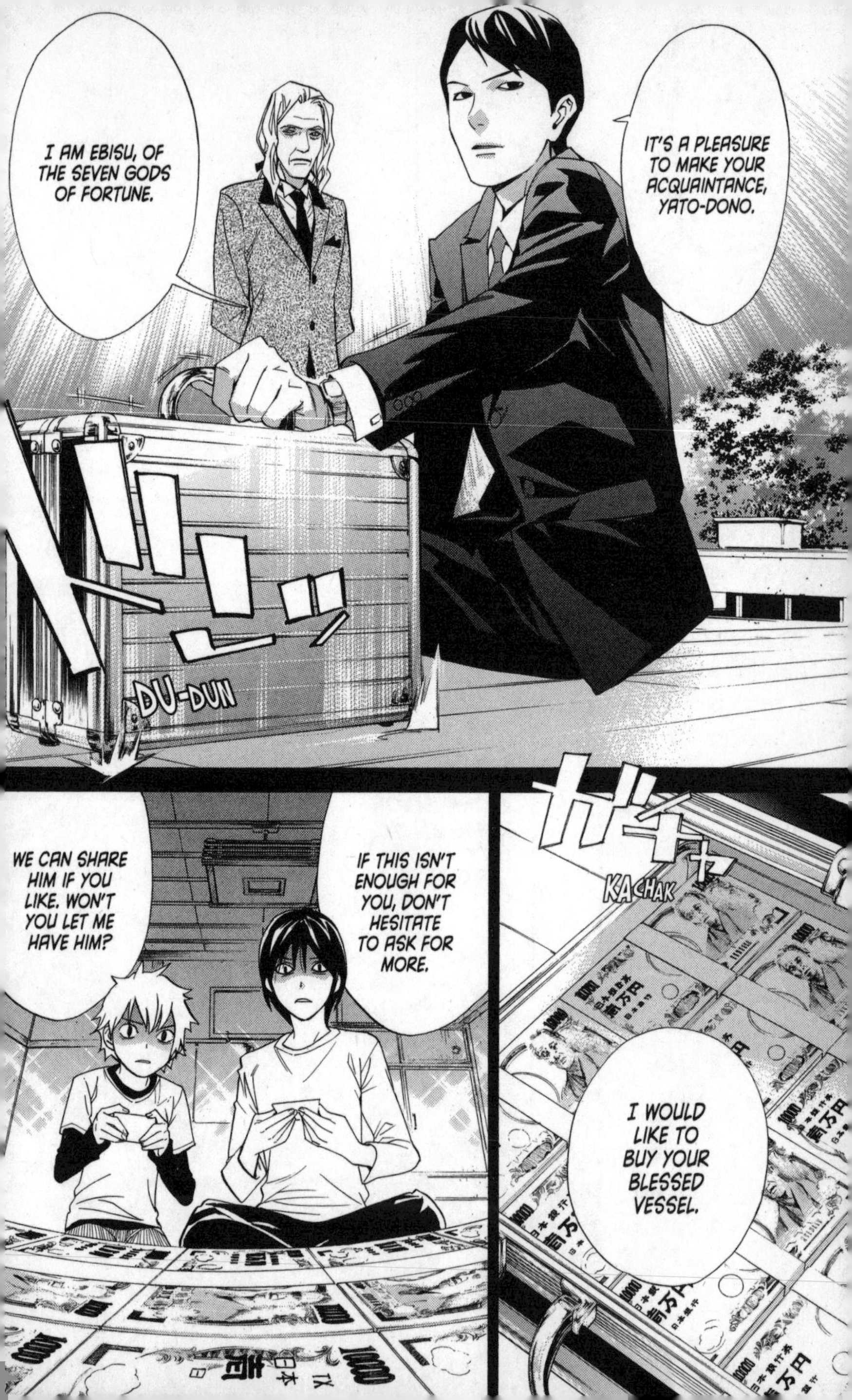
IT'S A PLEASURE TO MAKE YOUR ACQUAINTANCE, YATO-DONO.
I AM EBISU, OF THE SEVEN GODS OF FORTUNE.
DU-DUN
KACHAK
I WOULD LIKE TO BUY YOUR BLESSED VESSEL.
IF THIS ISN'T ENOUGH FOR YOU, DON'T HESITATE TO ASK FOR MORE.
WE CAN SHARE HIM IF YOU LIKE. WON'T YOU LET ME HAVE HIM?

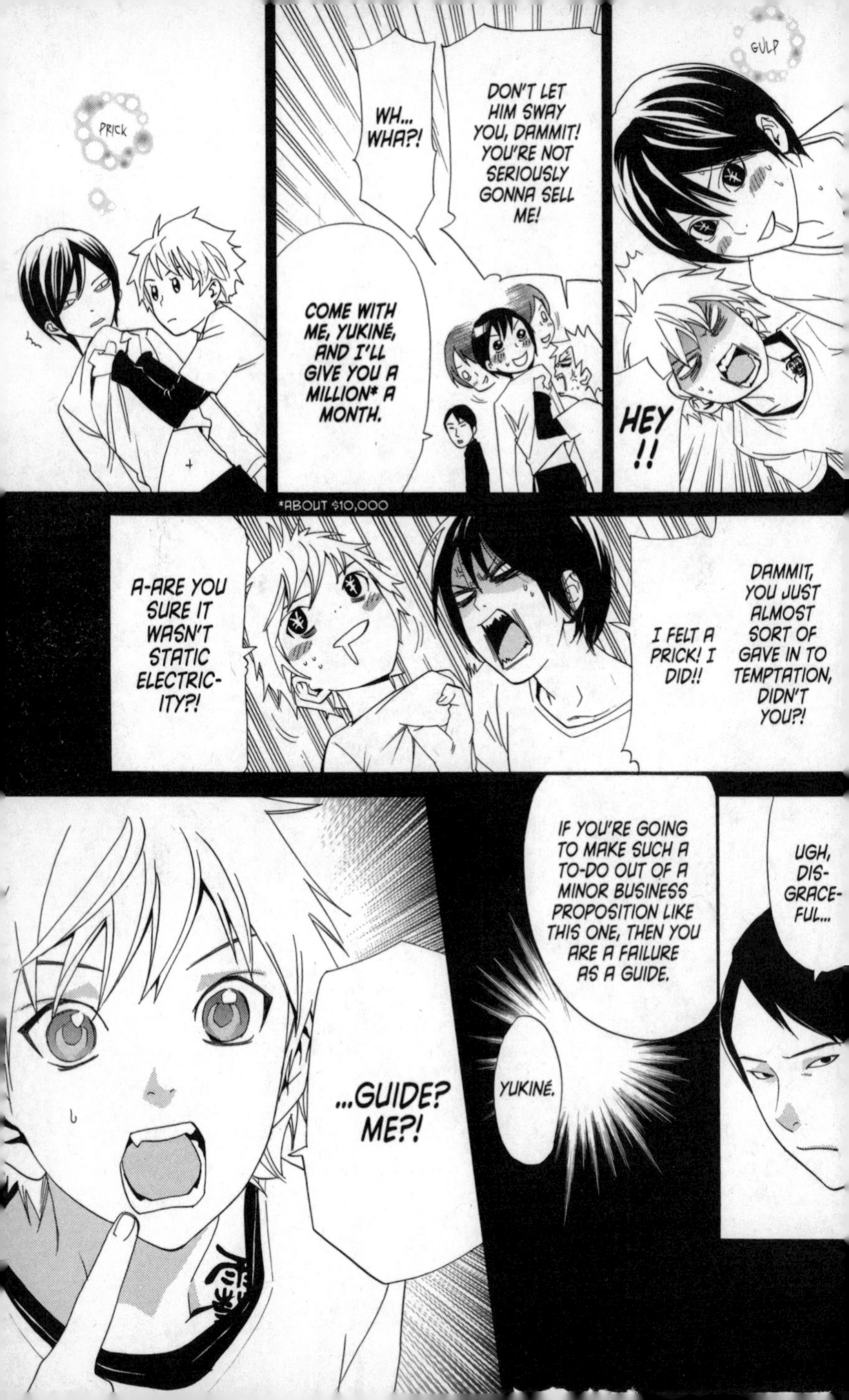
GULP
HEY!!
DON'T LET HIM SWAY YOU, DAMMIT! YOU'RE NOT SERIOUSLY GONNA SELL ME!
WH... WHA?!
COME WITH ME, YUKINÉ, AND I'LL GIVE YOU A MILLION* A MONTH.
PRICK
DAMMIT, YOU JUST ALMOST SORT OF GAVE IN TO TEMPTATION, DIDN'T YOU?!
I FELT A PRICK! I DID!!
A-ARE YOU SURE IT WASN'T STATIC ELECTRIC-ITY?!
UGH, DIS-GRACE-FUL...
IF YOU'RE GOING TO MAKE SUCH A TO-DO OUT OF A MINOR BUSINESS PROPOSITION LIKE THIS ONE, THEN YOU ARE A FAILURE AS A GUIDE.
YUKINÉ.
...GUIDE? ME?!
*ABOUT $10,000

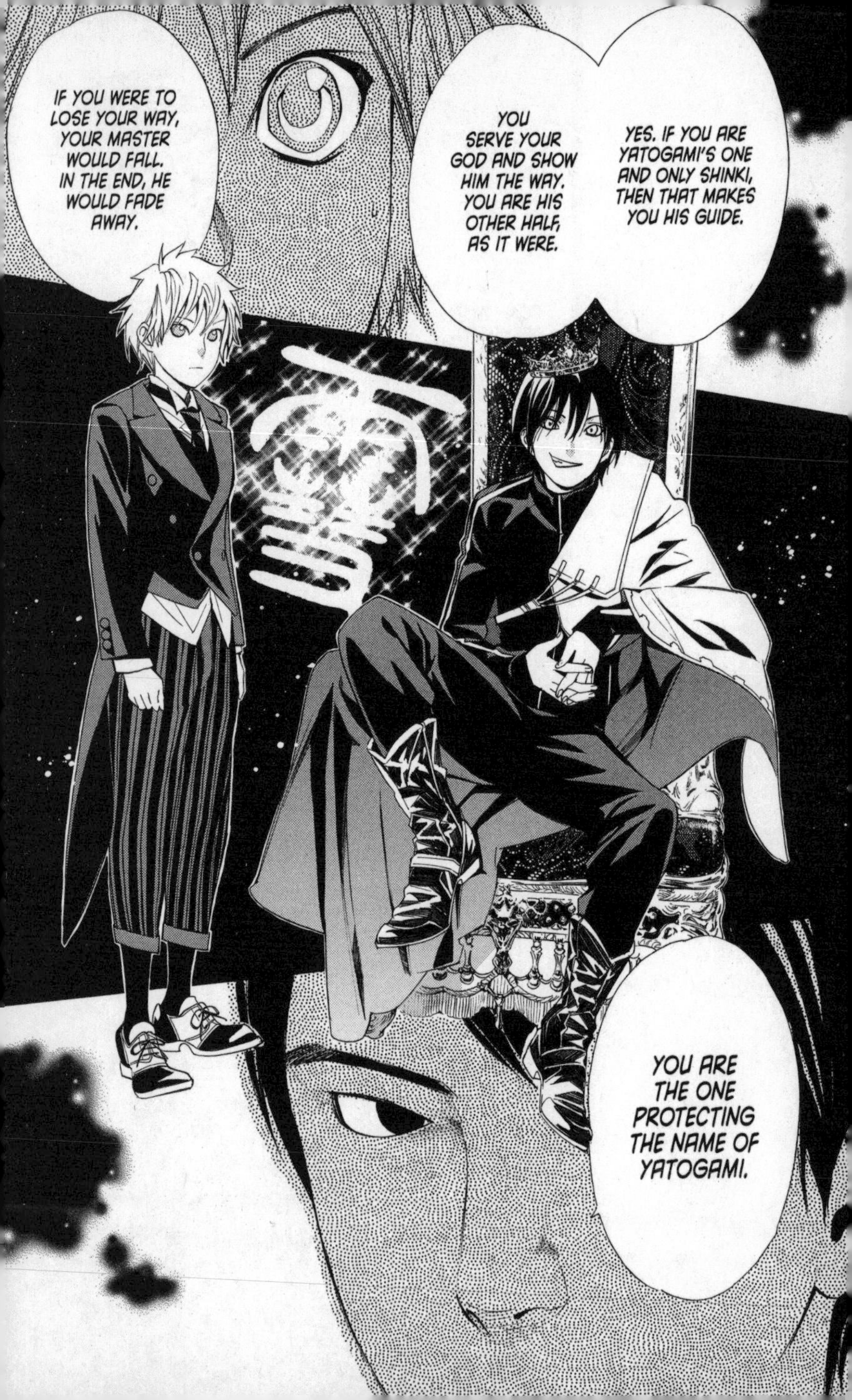
YES. IF YOU ARE YATOGAMI'S ONE AND ONLY SHINKI, THEN THAT MAKES YOU HIS GUIDE.
YOU SERVE YOUR GOD AND SHOW HIM THE WAY. YOU ARE HIS OTHER HALF, AS IT WERE.
IF YOU WERE TO LOSE YOUR WAY, YOUR MASTER WOULD FALL. IN THE END, HE WOULD FADE AWAY.
YOU ARE THE ONE PROTECTING THE NAME OF YATOGAMI.

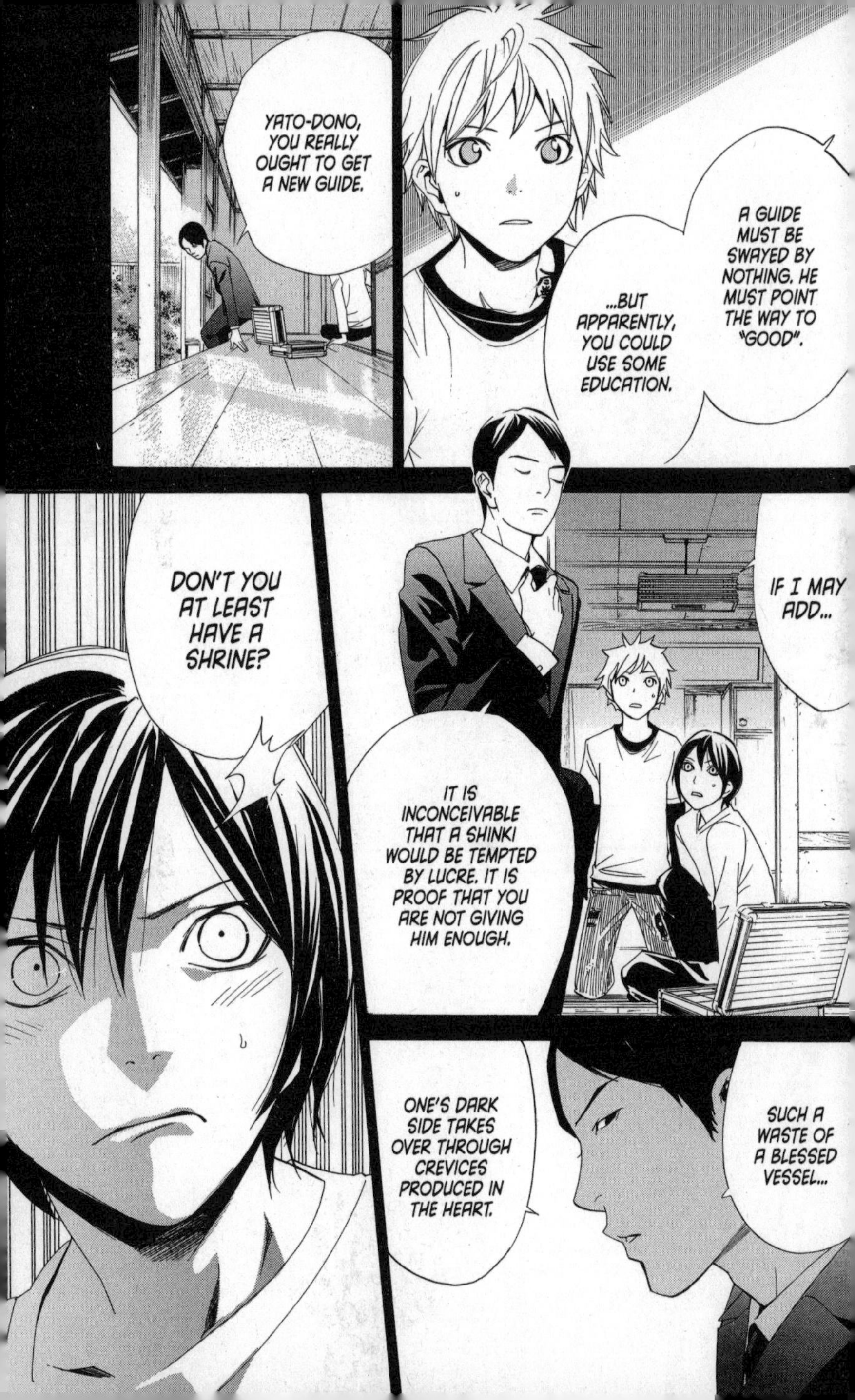
A GUIDE MUST BE SWAYED BY NOTHING. HE MUST POINT THE WAY TO "GOOD".
...BUT APPARENTLY, YOU COULD USE SOME EDUCATION.
YATO-DONO, YOU REALLY OUGHT TO GET A NEW GUIDE.
IF I MAY ADD...
IT IS INCONCEIVABLE THAT A SHINKI WOULD BE TEMPTED BY LUCRE. IT IS PROOF THAT YOU ARE NOT GIVING HIM ENOUGH.
SUCH A WASTE OF A BLESSED VESSEL...
ONE'S DARK SIDE TAKES OVER THROUGH CREVICES PRODUCED IN THE HEART.
DON'T YOU AT LEAST HAVE A SHRINE?

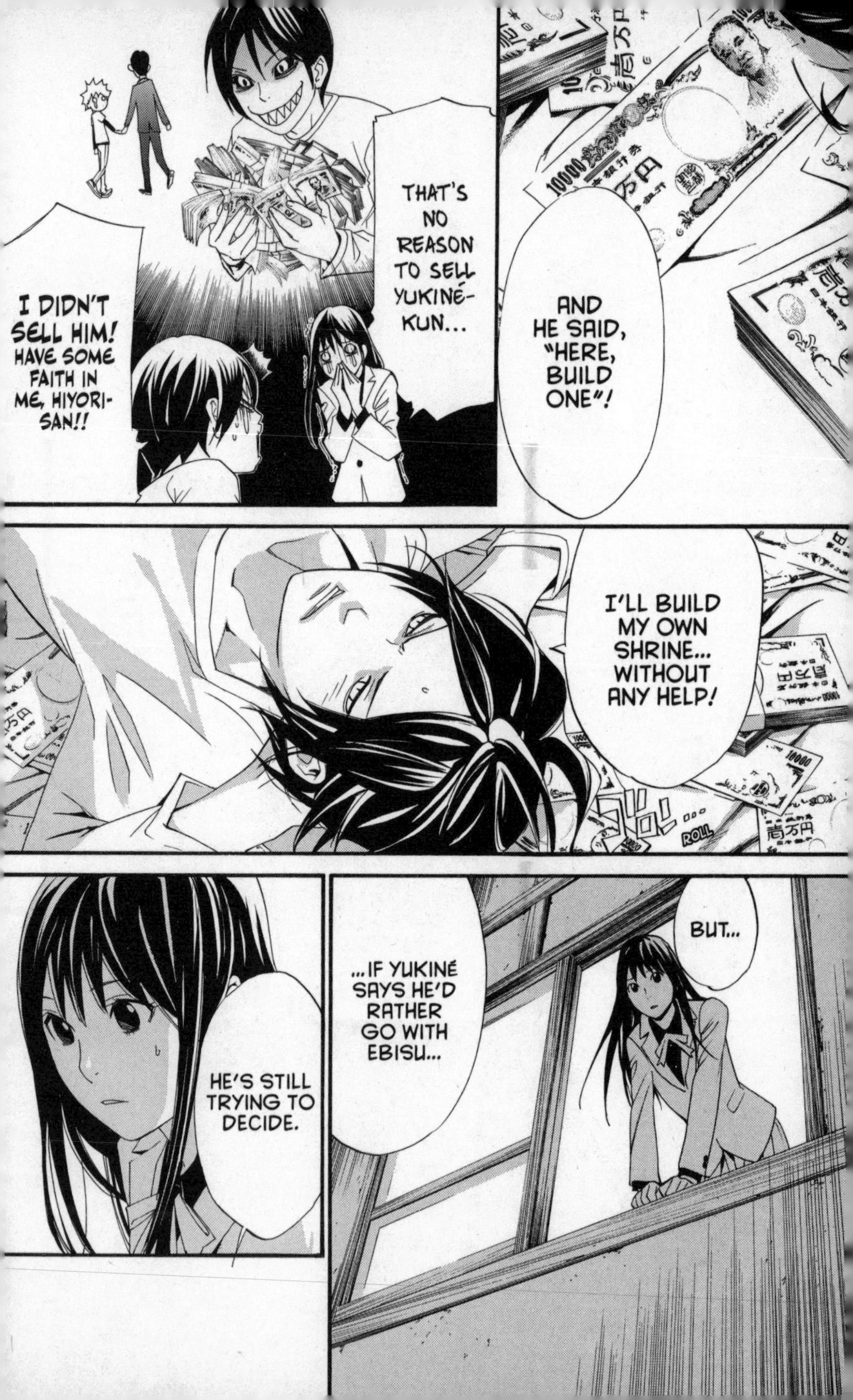
AND HE SAID, "HERE, BUILD ONE"!
THAT'S NO REASON TO SELL YUKINÉ-KUN...
I DIDN'T SELL HIM! HAVE SOME FAITH IN ME, HIYORI-SAN!!
I'LL BUILD MY OWN SHRINE... WITHOUT ANY HELP!
ROLL
BUT...
...IF YUKINÉ SAYS HE'D RATHER GO WITH EBISU...
HE'S STILL TRYING TO DECIDE.

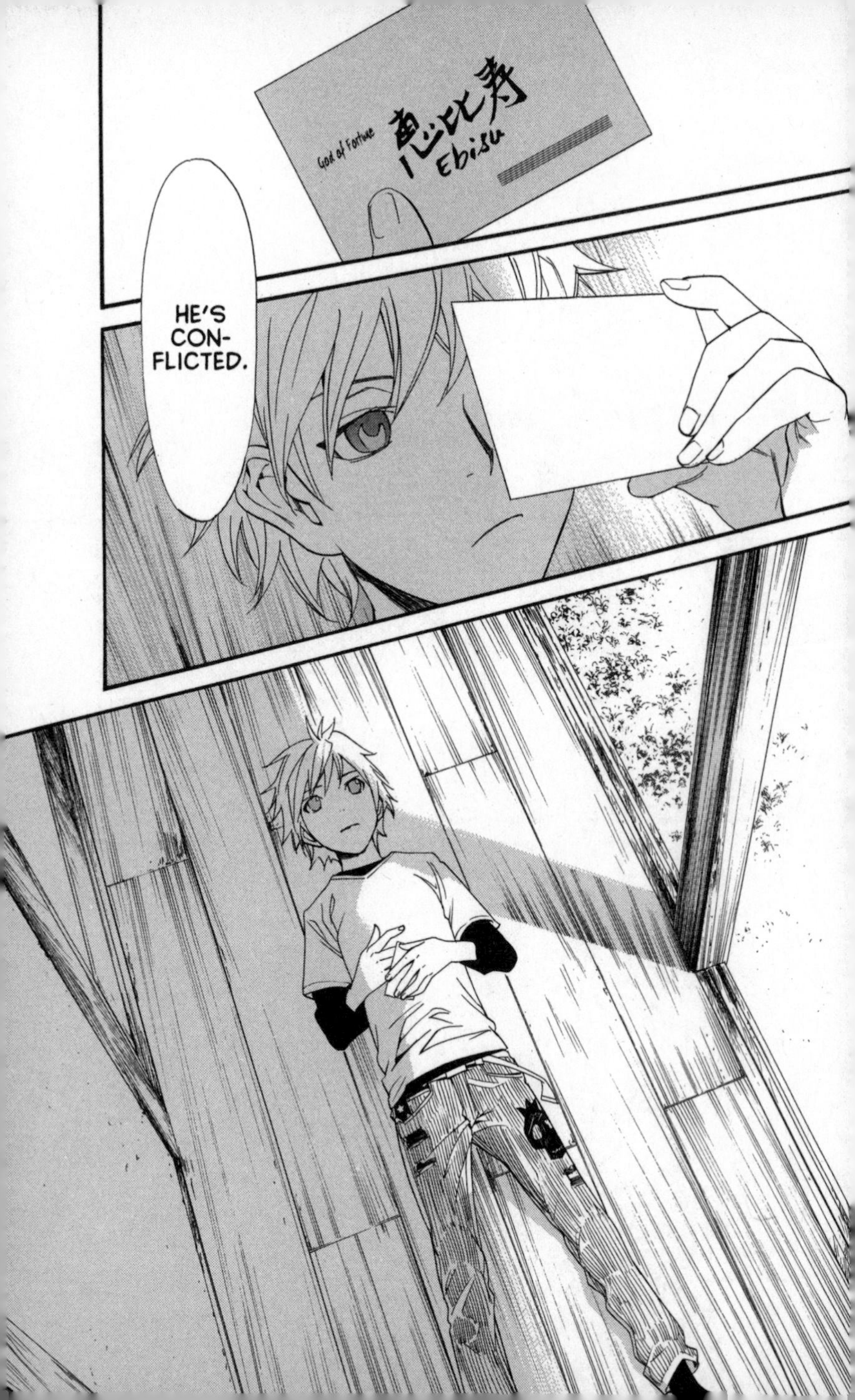
God of Fortune
恵比寿
Ebisu
HE'S CON-FLICTED.

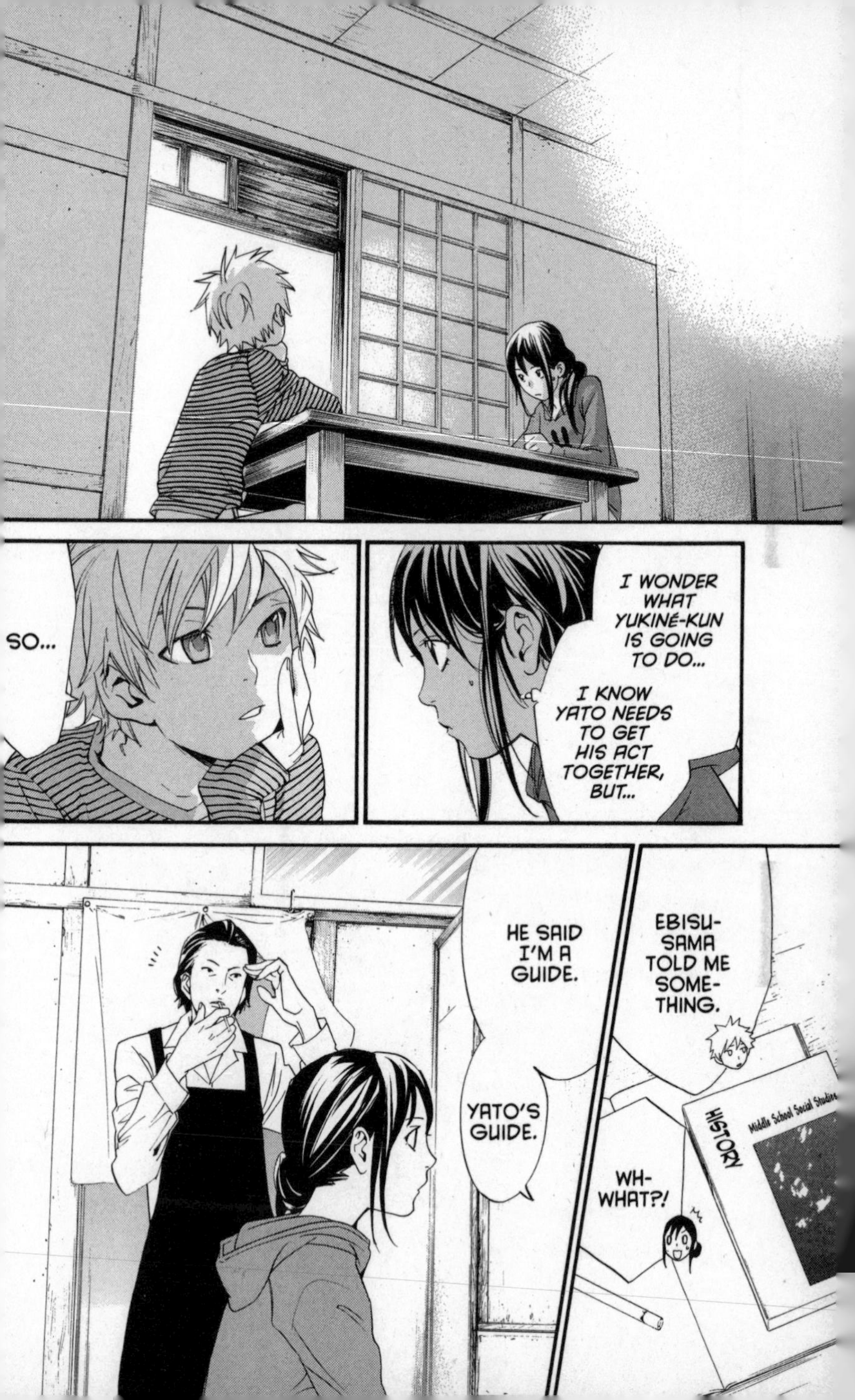
I WONDER WHAT YUKINÉ-KUN IS GOING TO DO...
I KNOW YATO NEEDS TO GET HIS ACT TOGETHER, BUT...
SO...
EBISU-SAMA TOLD ME SOME-THING.
WH-WHAT?!
HISTORY
HE SAID I'M A GUIDE.
YATO'S GUIDE.

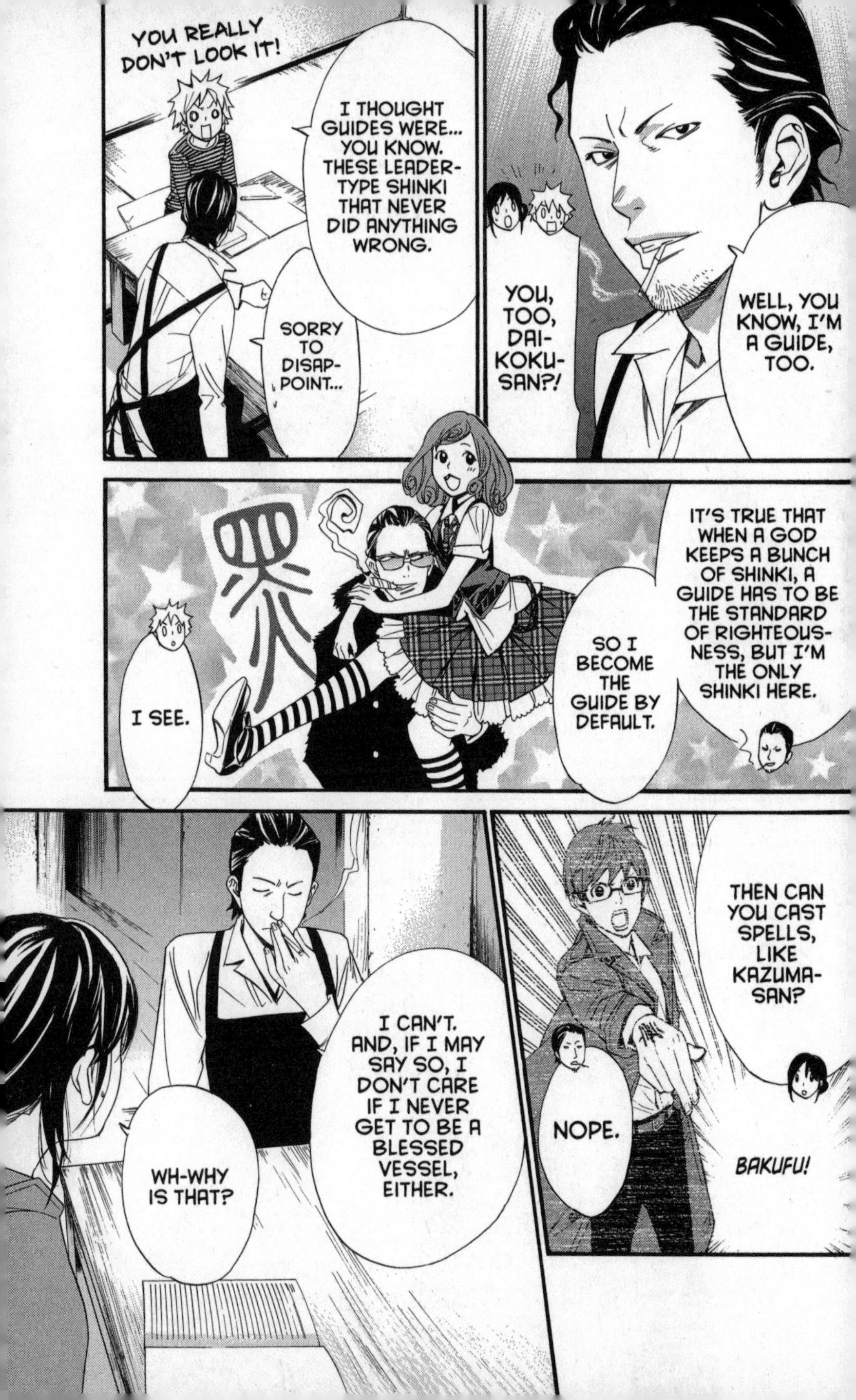
WELL, YOU KNOW, I'M A GUIDE, TOO.
YOU, TOO, DAI-KOKU-SAN?!
YOU REALLY DON'T LOOK IT!
I THOUGHT GUIDES WERE... YOU KNOW. THESE LEADER-TYPE SHINKI THAT NEVER DID ANYTHING WRONG.
SORRY TO DISAP-POINT...
IT'S TRUE THAT WHEN A GOD KEEPS A BUNCH OF SHINKI, A GUIDE HAS TO BE THE STANDARD OF RIGHTEOUS-NESS, BUT I'M THE ONLY SHINKI HERE.
SO I BECOME THE GUIDE BY DEFAULT.
I SEE.
THEN CAN YOU CAST SPELLS, LIKE KAZUMA-SAN?
BAKUFU!
NOPE.
I CAN'T. AND, IF I MAY SAY SO, I DON'T CARE IF I NEVER GET TO BE A BLESSED VESSEL, EITHER.
WH-WHY IS THAT?

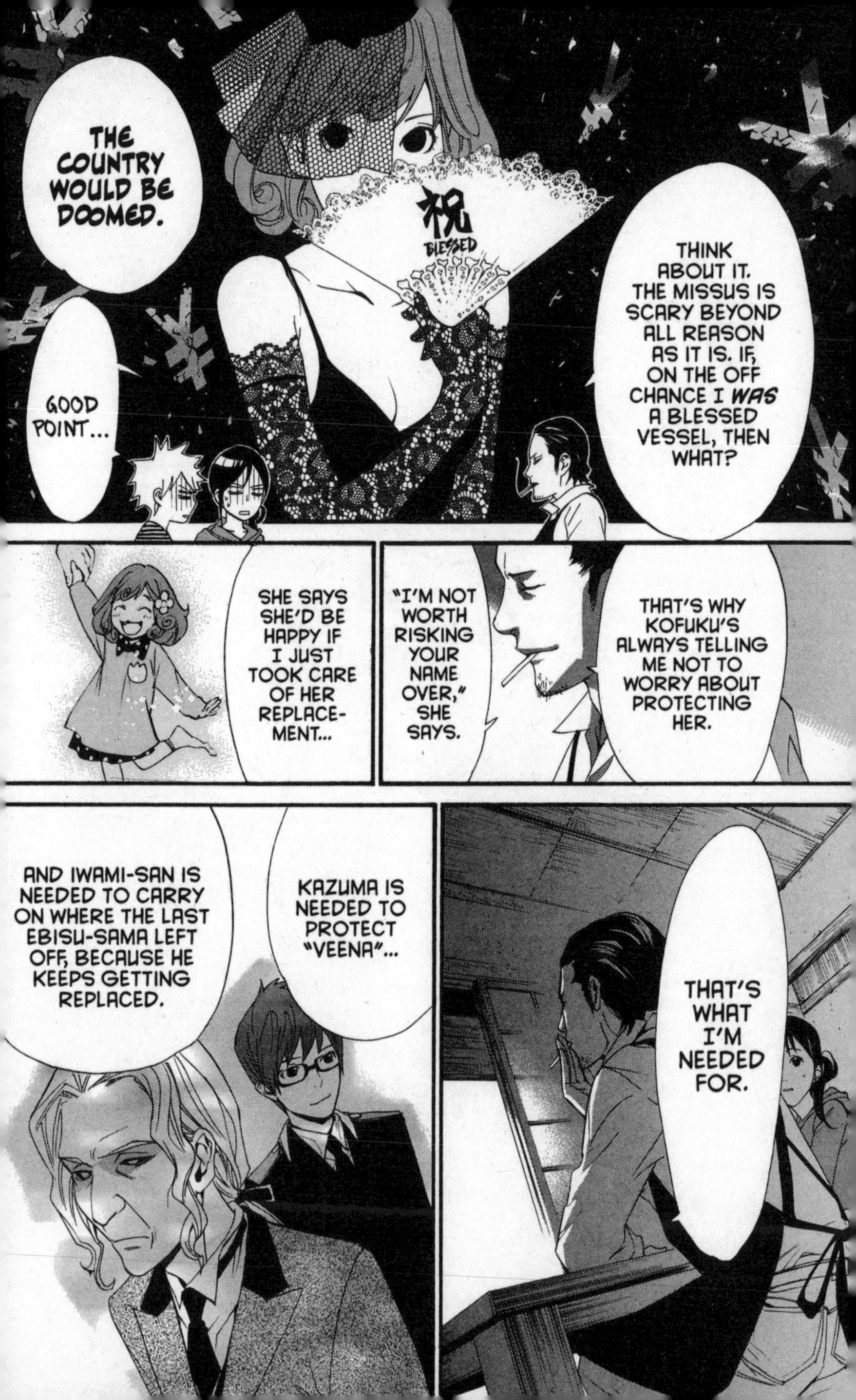
THINK ABOUT IT. THE MISSUS IS SCARY BEYOND ALL REASON AS IT IS. IF, ON THE OFF CHANCE I *WAS* A BLESSED VESSEL, THEN WHAT?
祝
BLESSED
THE COUNTRY WOULD BE DOOMED.
GOOD POINT...
THAT'S WHY KOFUKU'S ALWAYS TELLING ME NOT TO WORRY ABOUT PROTECTING HER.
"I'M NOT WORTH RISKING YOUR NAME OVER," SHE SAYS.
SHE SAYS SHE'D BE HAPPY IF I JUST TOOK CARE OF HER REPLACE-MENT...
THAT'S WHAT I'M NEEDED FOR.
KAZUMA IS NEEDED TO PROTECT "VEENA"...
AND IWAMI-SAN IS NEEDED TO CARRY ON WHERE THE LAST EBISU-SAMA LEFT OFF, BECAUSE HE KEEPS GETTING REPLACED.

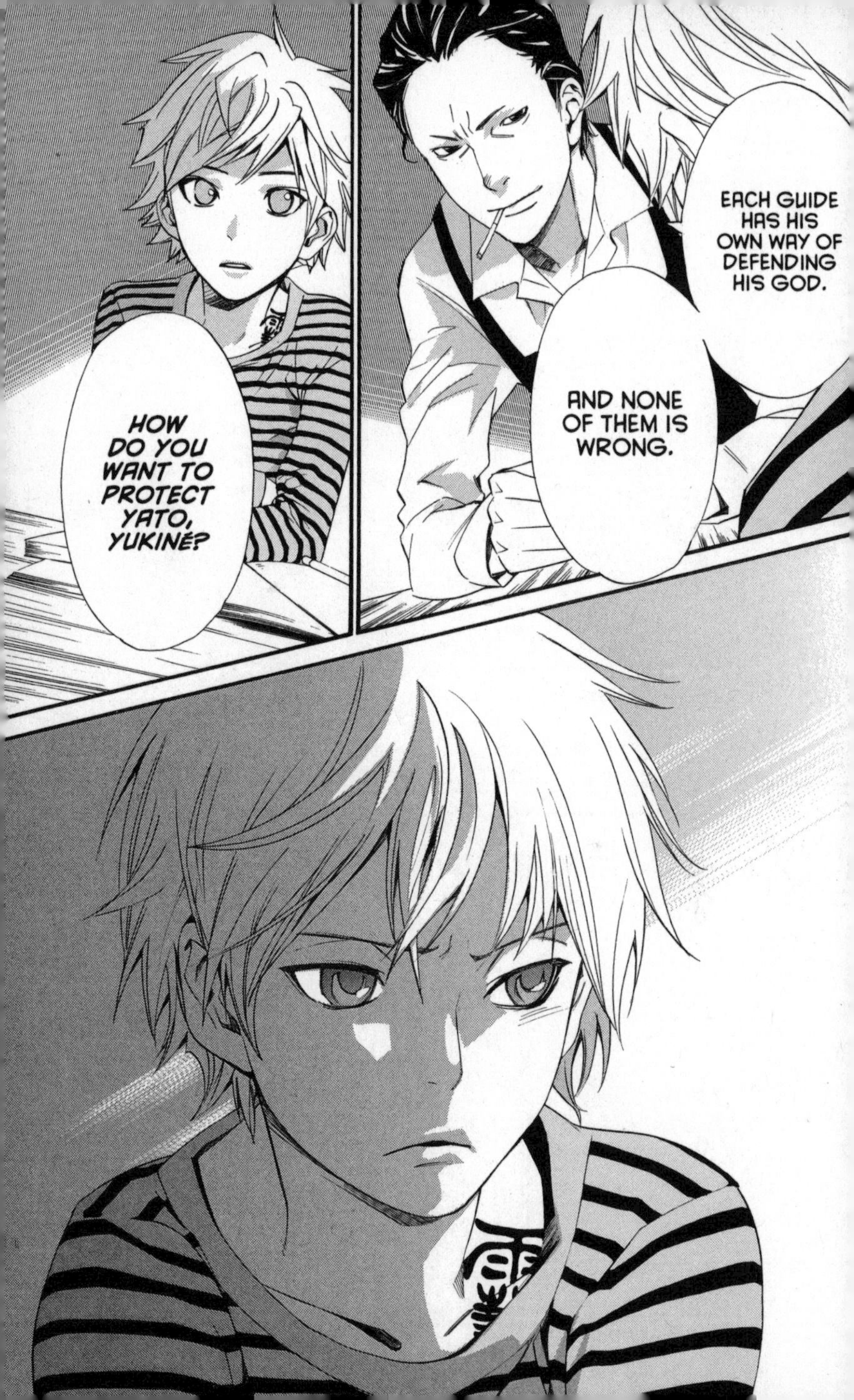
EACH GUIDE HAS HIS OWN WAY OF DEFENDING HIS GOD.
AND NONE OF THEM IS WRONG.
HOW DO YOU WANT TO PROTECT YATO, YUKINÉ?

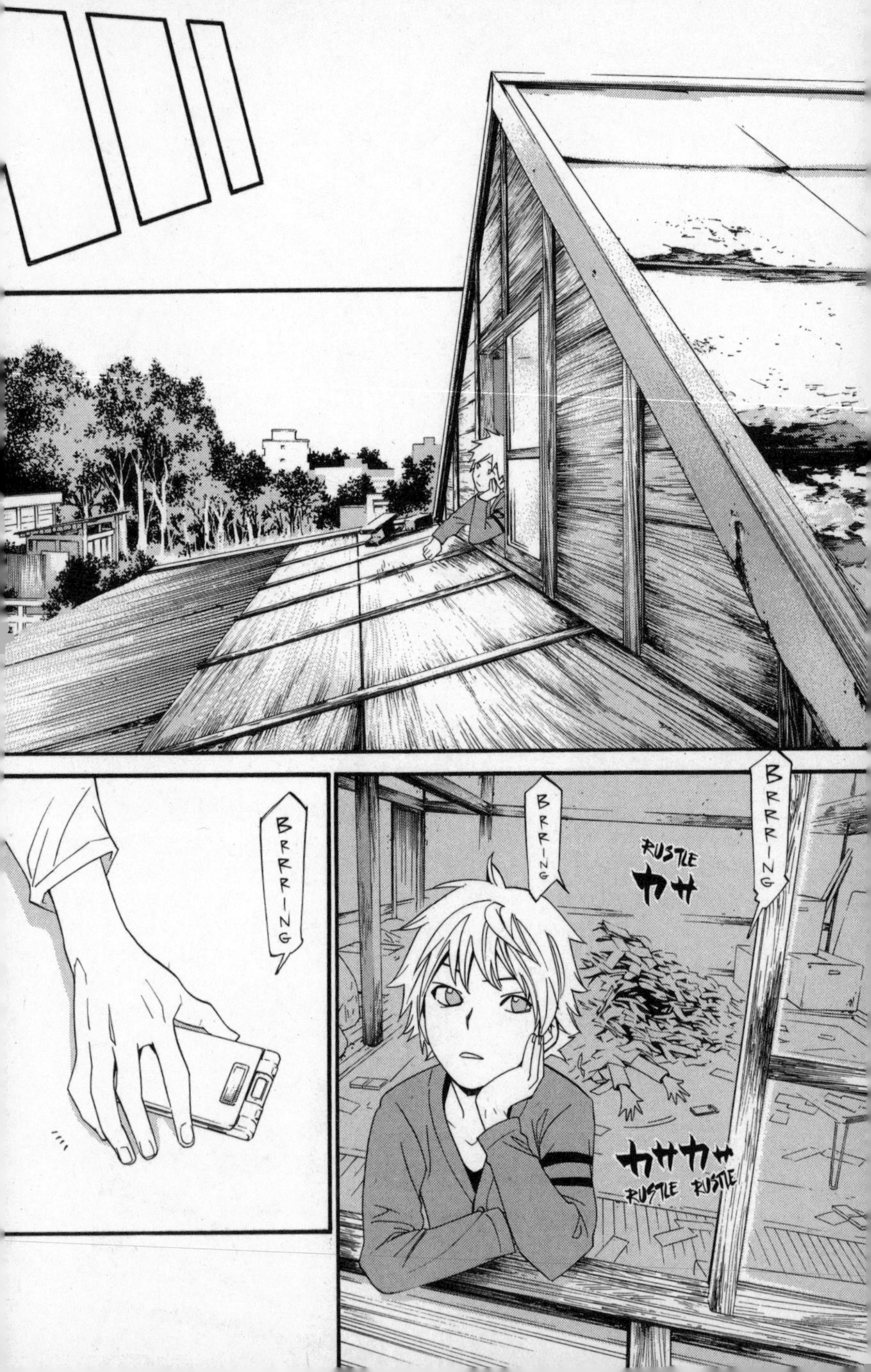
BRRRING
BRRING
カサ
RUSTLE
カサカサ
RUSTLE RUSTLE
BRRRING

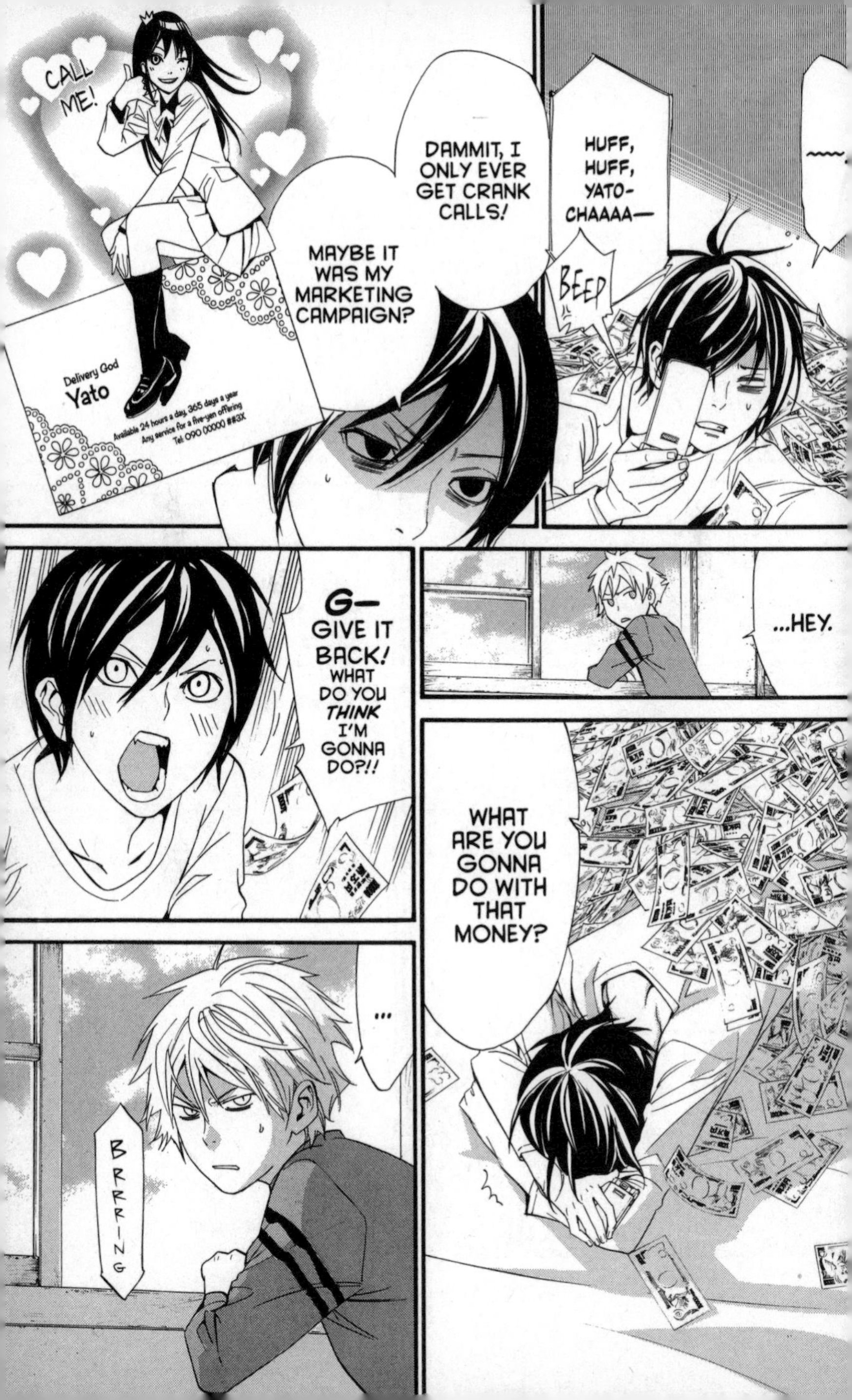

HUFF, HUFF, YATO-CHAAAA—
BEEP
DAMMIT, I ONLY EVER GET CRANK CALLS!
MAYBE IT WAS MY MARKETING CAMPAIGN?
CALL ME!
Delivery God
Yato
Available 24 hours a day, 365 days a year
Any service for a five-yen offering
Tel: 090 00000 ##3X
...HEY.
WHAT ARE YOU GONNA DO WITH THAT MONEY?
G— GIVE IT BACK! WHAT DO YOU *THINK* I'M GONNA DO?!!
...
BRRRING

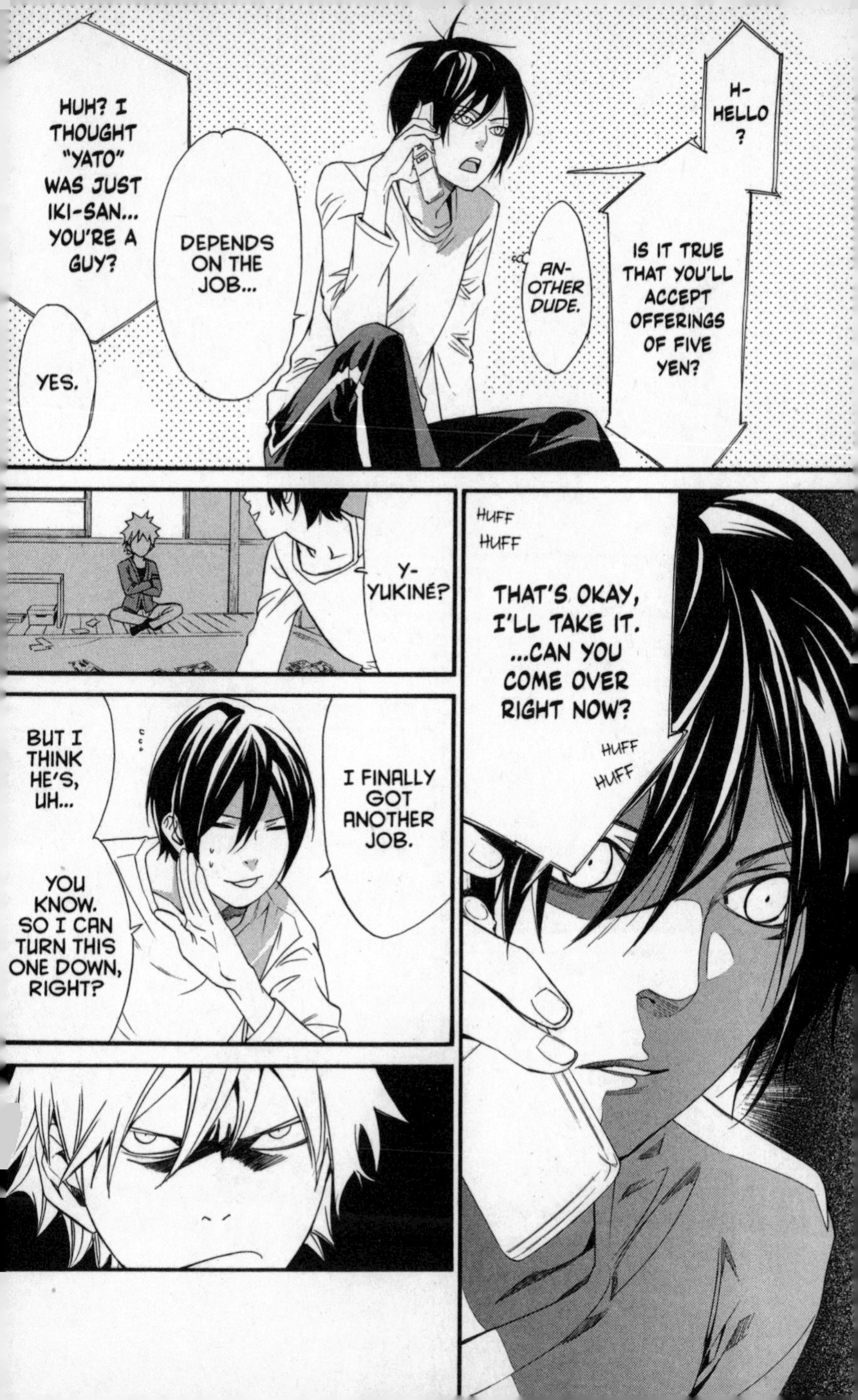
H-HELLO?
IS IT TRUE THAT YOU'LL ACCEPT OFFERINGS OF FIVE YEN?
AN-OTHER DUDE.
DEPENDS ON THE JOB...
HUH? I THOUGHT "YATO" WAS JUST IKI-SAN... YOU'RE A GUY?
YES.
HUFF HUFF
THAT'S OKAY, I'LL TAKE IT. ...CAN YOU COME OVER RIGHT NOW?
HUFF HUFF
Y-YUKINE?
I FINALLY GOT ANOTHER JOB.
BUT I THINK HE'S, UH...
YOU KNOW. SO I CAN TURN THIS ONE DOWN, RIGHT?

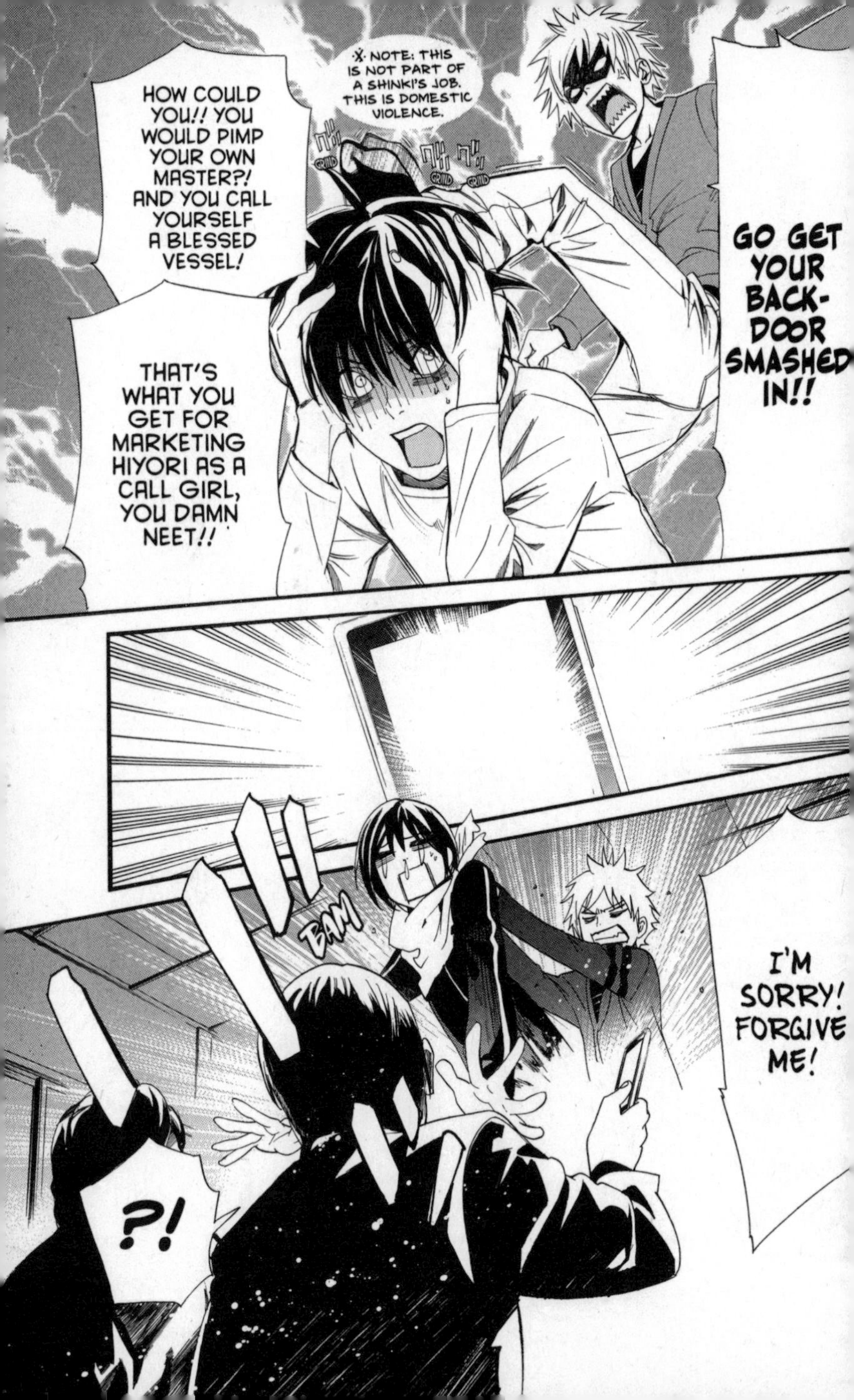
GO GET YOUR BACK-DOOR SMASHED IN!!
※ NOTE: THIS IS NOT PART OF A SHINKI'S JOB. THIS IS DOMESTIC VIOLENCE.
GRIIND GRIIND GRIIND
HOW COULD YOU!! YOU WOULD PIMP YOUR OWN MASTER?! AND YOU CALL YOURSELF A BLESSED VESSEL!
THAT'S WHAT YOU GET FOR MARKETING HIYORI AS A CALL GIRL, YOU DAMN NEET!!
I'M SORRY! FORGIVE ME!
BAM
?!

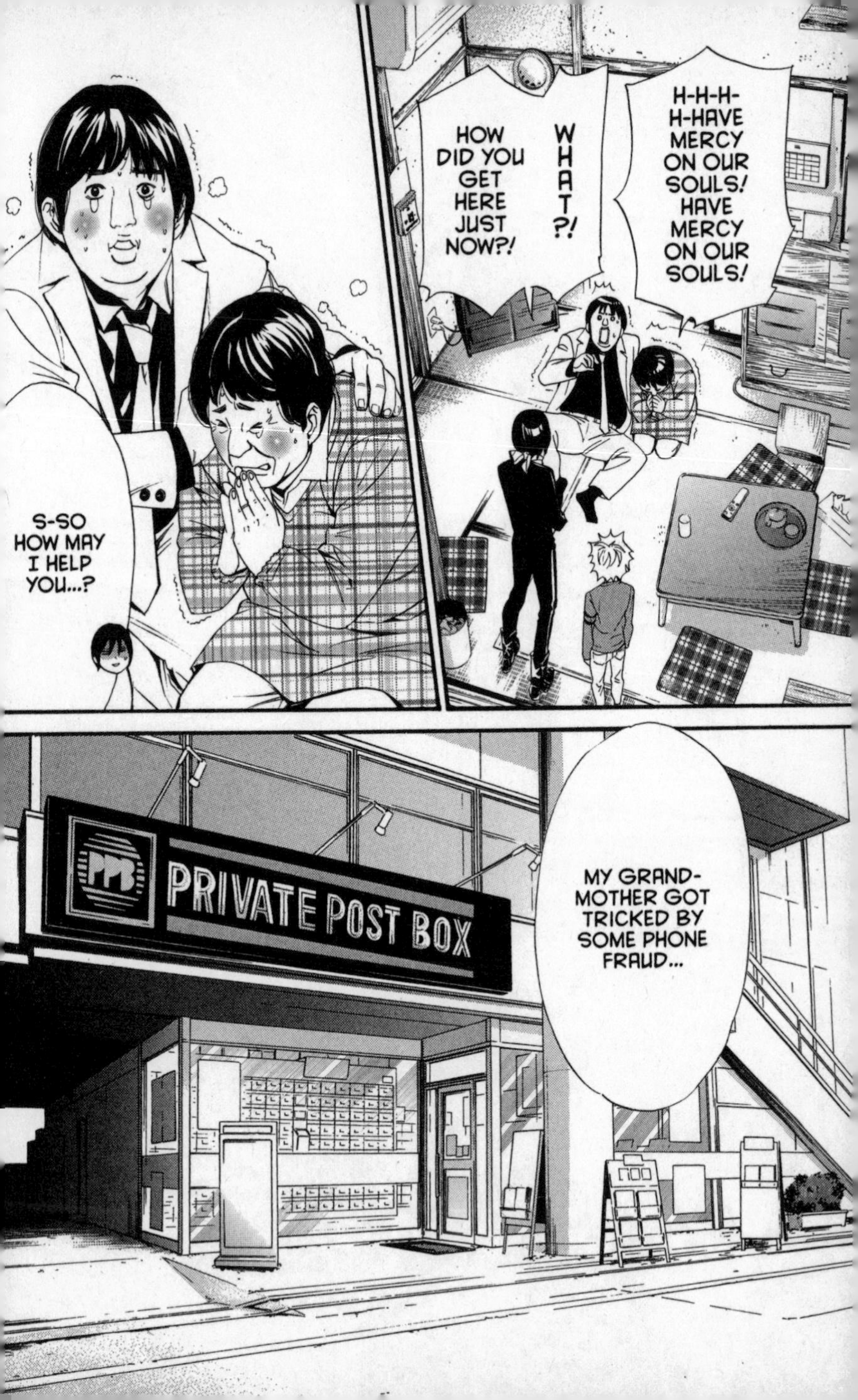
H-H-H-H-HAVE MERCY ON OUR SOULS! HAVE MERCY ON OUR SOULS!
WHAT?!
HOW DID YOU GET HERE JUST NOW?!
S-SO HOW MAY I HELP YOU...?
PPB
PRIVATE POST BOX
MY GRAND-MOTHER GOT TRICKED BY SOME PHONE FRAUD...

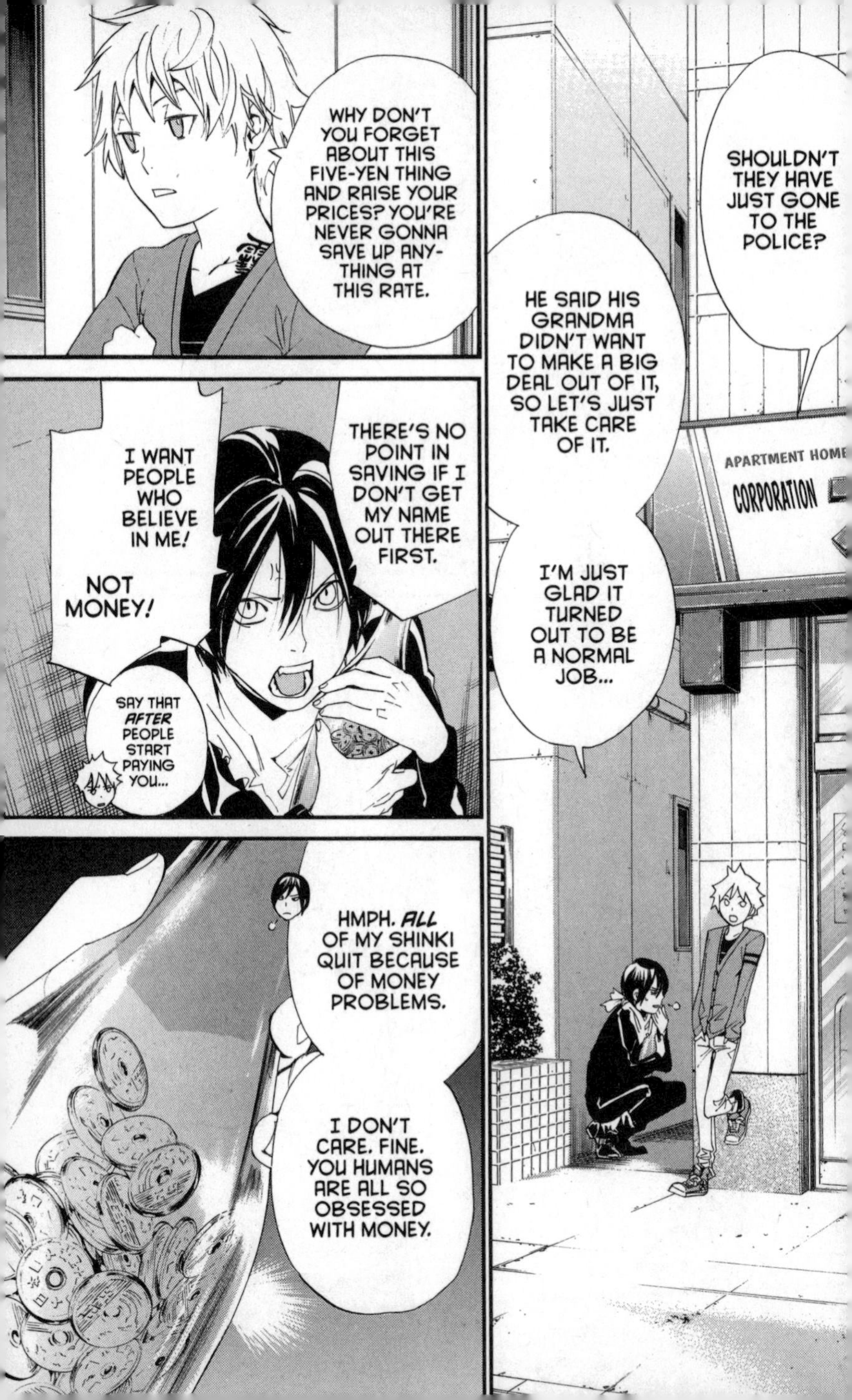
SHOULDN'T THEY HAVE JUST GONE TO THE POLICE?
HE SAID HIS GRANDMA DIDN'T WANT TO MAKE A BIG DEAL OUT OF IT, SO LET'S JUST TAKE CARE OF IT.
APARTMENT HOME
CORPORATION
I'M JUST GLAD IT TURNED OUT TO BE A NORMAL JOB...
WHY DON'T YOU FORGET ABOUT THIS FIVE-YEN THING AND RAISE YOUR PRICES? YOU'RE NEVER GONNA SAVE UP ANY-THING AT THIS RATE.
THERE'S NO POINT IN SAVING IF I DON'T GET MY NAME OUT THERE FIRST.
I WANT PEOPLE WHO BELIEVE IN ME!
NOT MONEY!
SAY THAT *AFTER* PEOPLE START PAYING YOU...
HMPH. *ALL* OF MY SHINKI QUIT BECAUSE OF MONEY PROBLEMS.
I DON'T CARE. FINE. YOU HUMANS ARE ALL SO OBSESSED WITH MONEY.

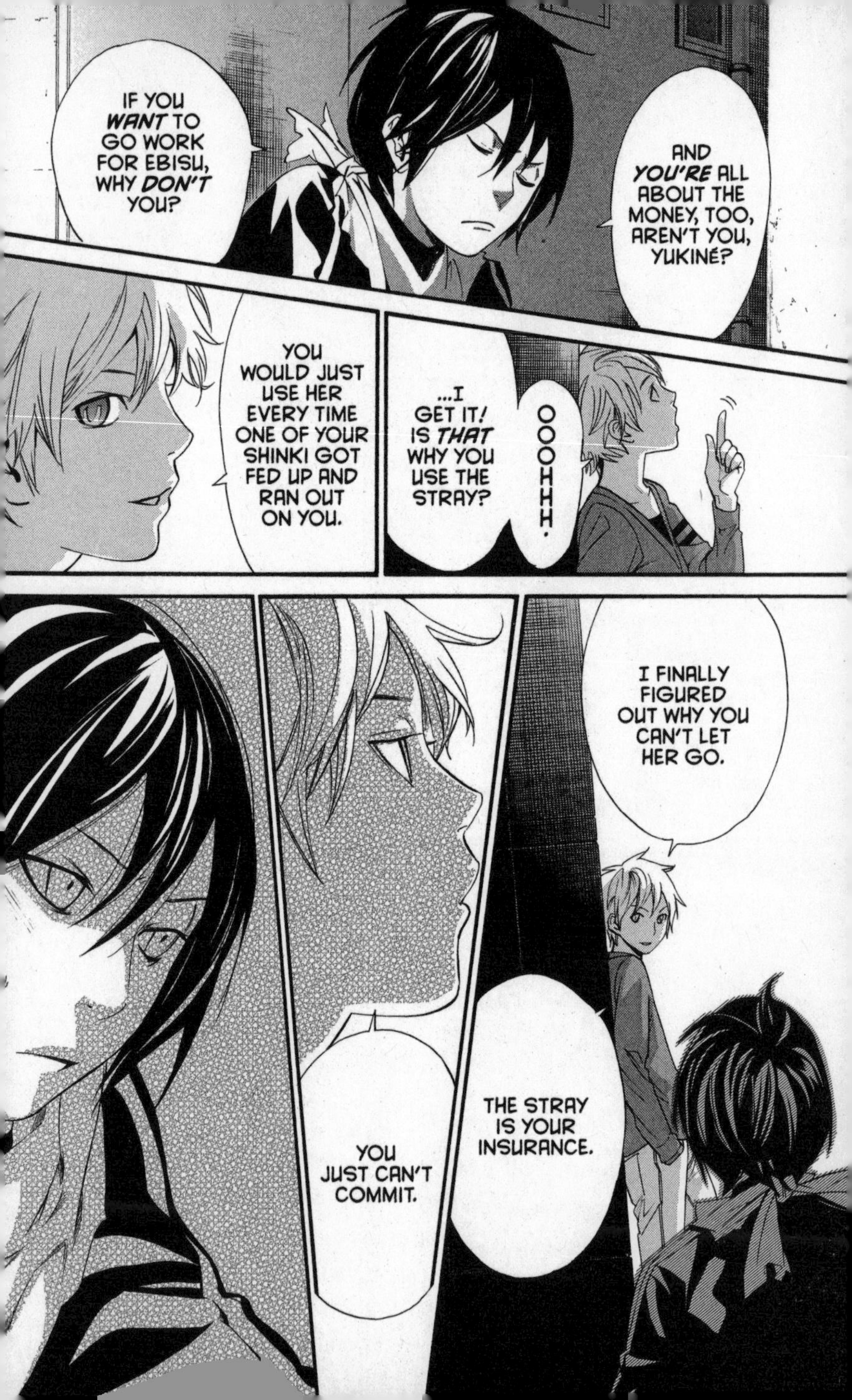
AND *YOU'RE* ALL ABOUT THE MONEY, TOO, AREN'T YOU, YUKINÉ?
IF YOU *WANT* TO GO WORK FOR EBISU, WHY *DON'T* YOU?
OOOHHH.
...I GET IT! IS *THAT* WHY YOU USE THE STRAY?
YOU WOULD JUST USE HER EVERY TIME ONE OF YOUR SHINKI GOT FED UP AND RAN OUT ON YOU.
I FINALLY FIGURED OUT WHY YOU CAN'T LET HER GO.
THE STRAY IS YOUR INSURANCE.
YOU JUST CAN'T COMMIT.

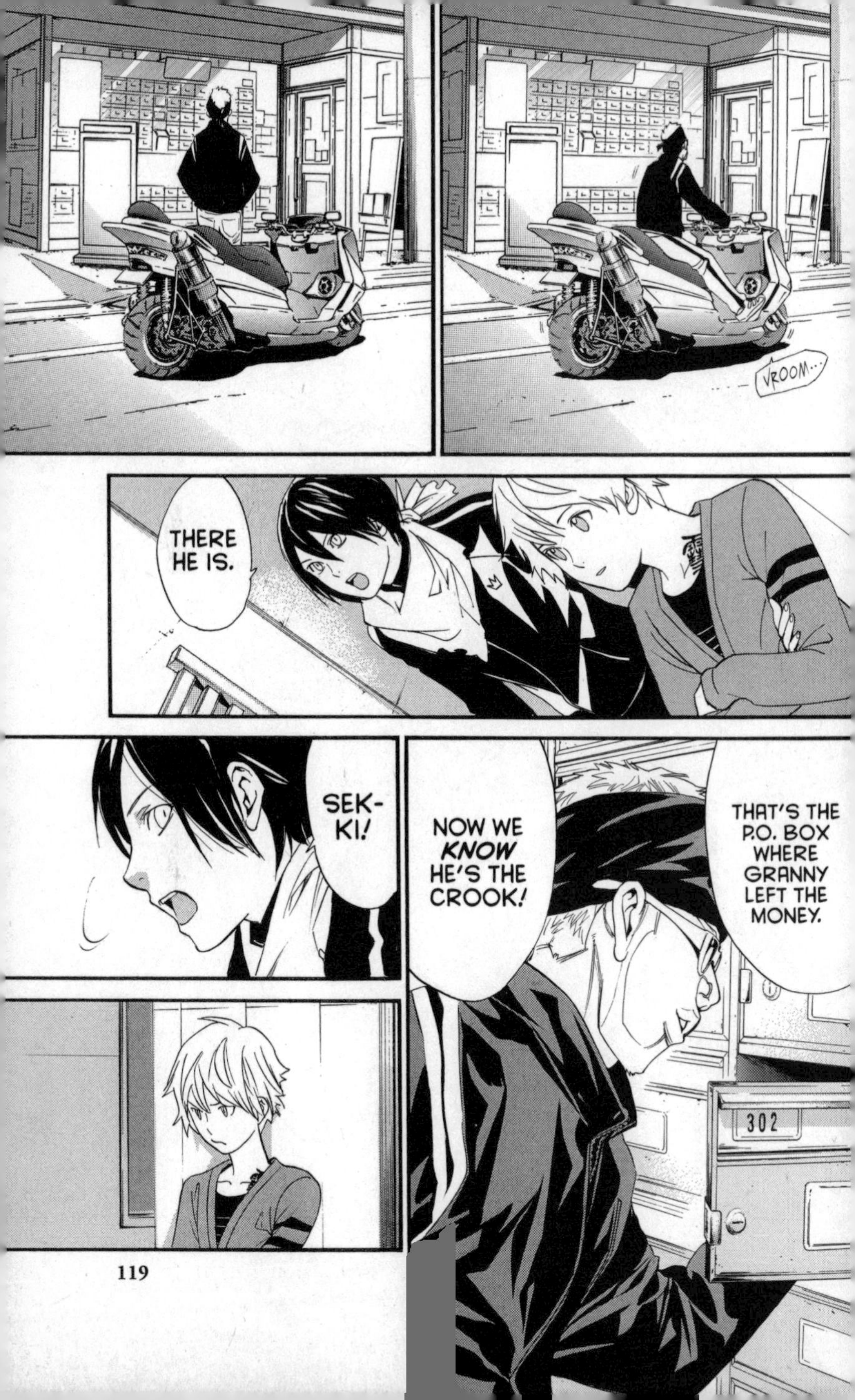
VROOM...
THERE HE IS.
THAT'S THE P.O. BOX WHERE GRANNY LEFT THE MONEY.
NOW WE *KNOW* HE'S THE CROOK!
SEK-KI!
302

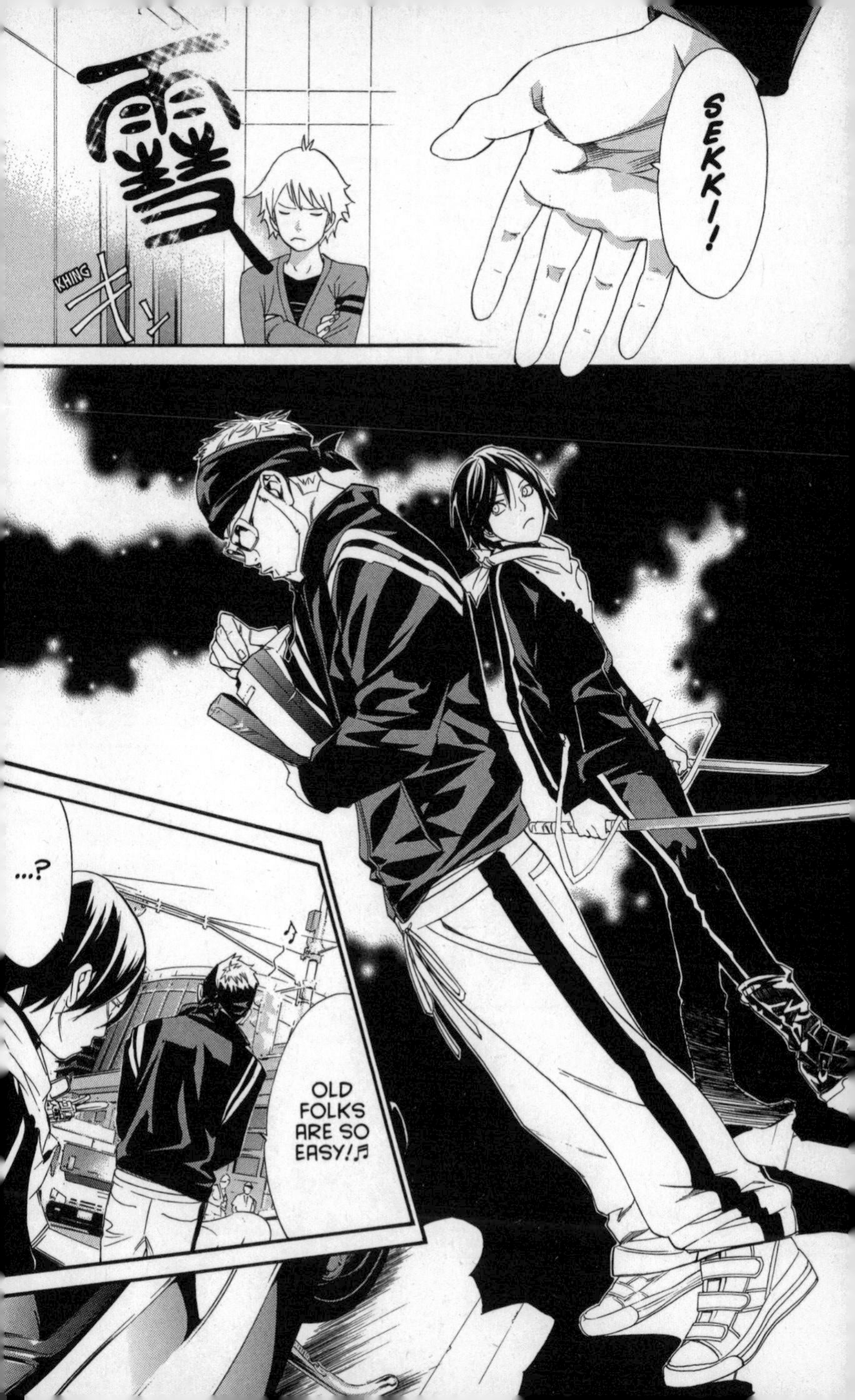
SEKKI!
雪
KHING
OLD FOLKS ARE SO EASY!♬
...?

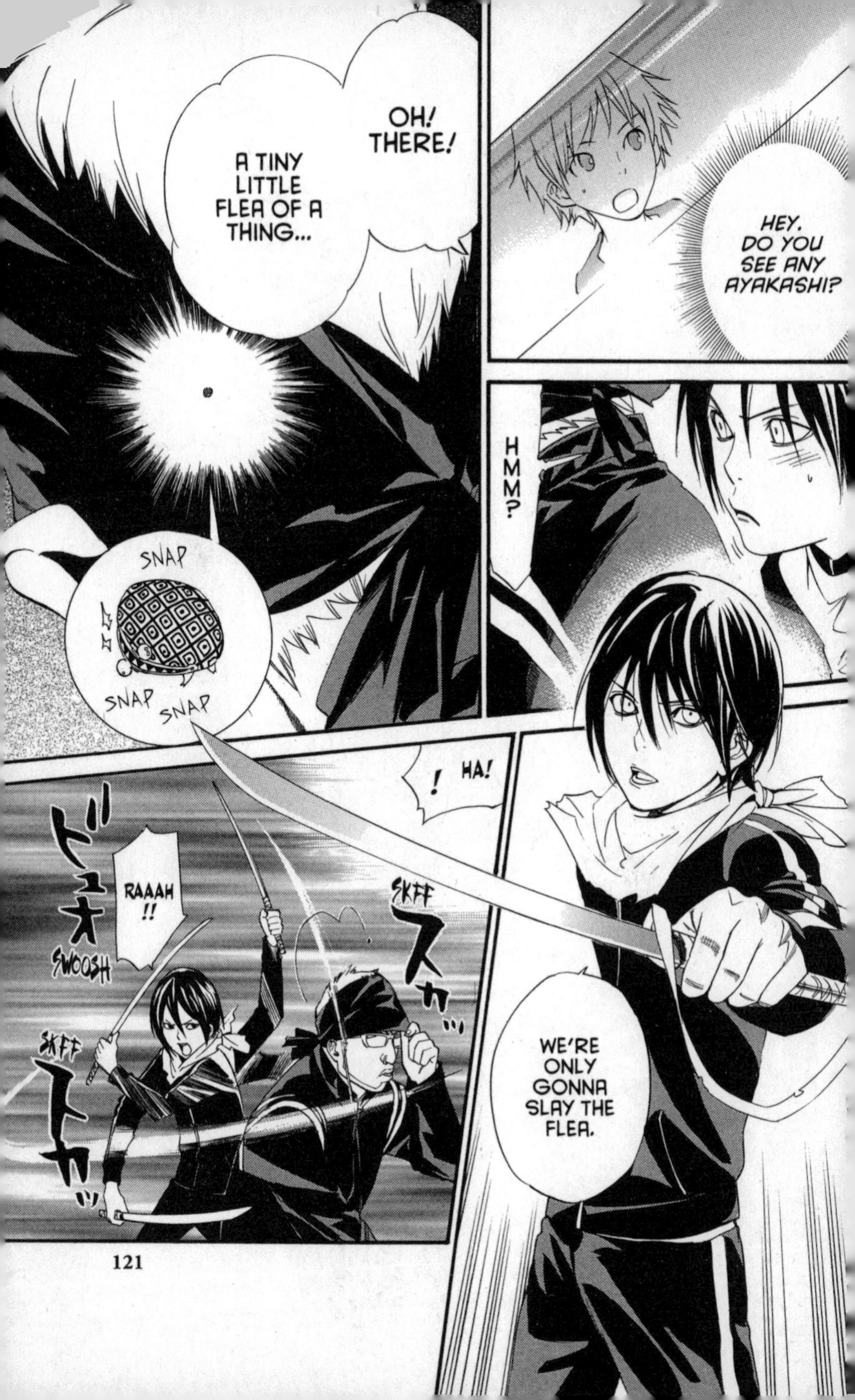
HEY. DO YOU SEE ANY AYAKASHI?
HMM?
OH! THERE!
A TINY LITTLE FLEA OF A THING...
SNAP
SNAP SNAP
! HA!
WE'RE ONLY GONNA SLAY THE FLEA.
RAAAH!!
SWOOSH
SKFF
SKFF

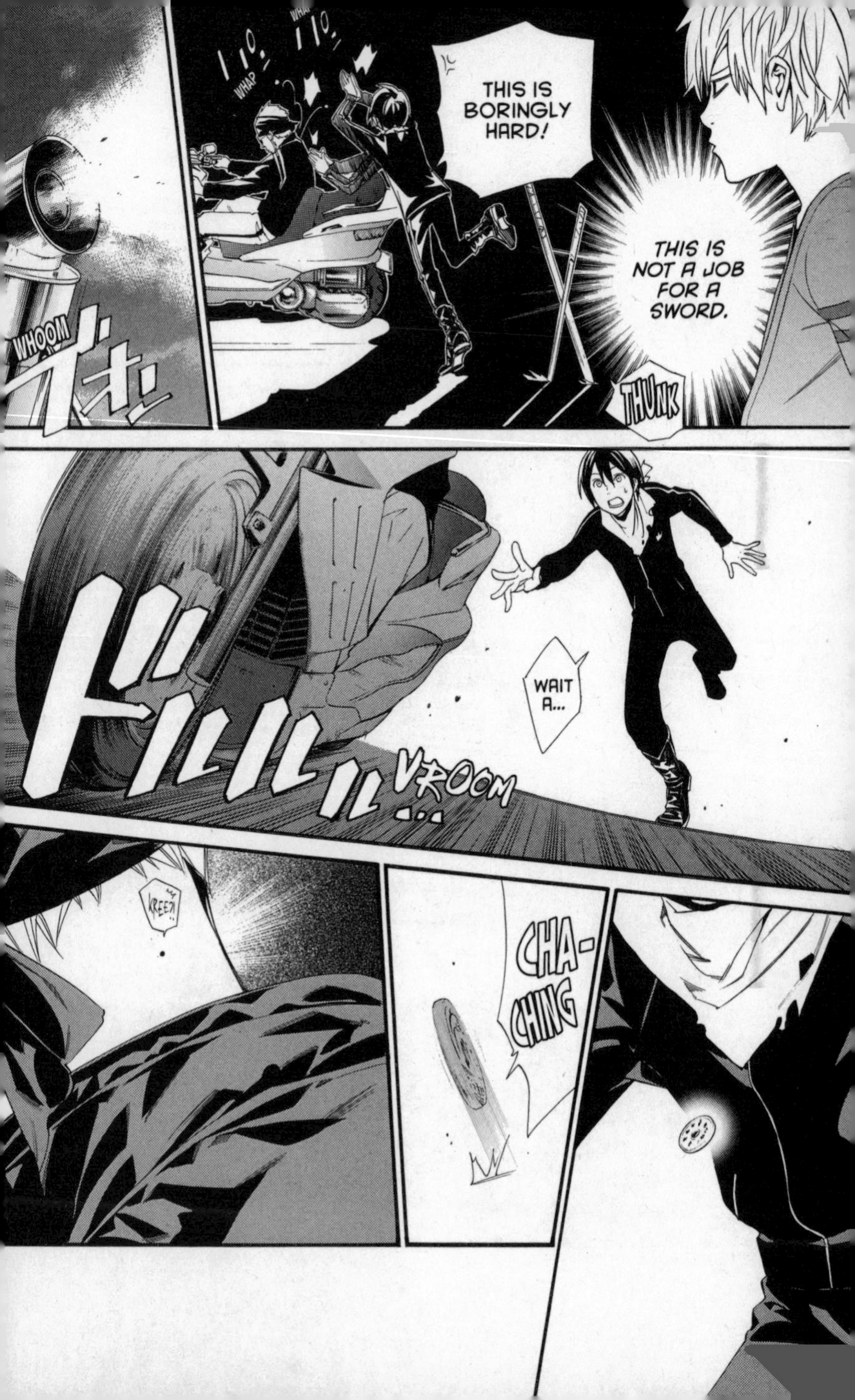
THIS IS NOT A JOB FOR A SWORD.
THUNK
THIS IS BORINGLY HARD!
WHAP
WHAP
WHOOM
WAIT A...
VROOM...
CHA-CHING
KREE?!

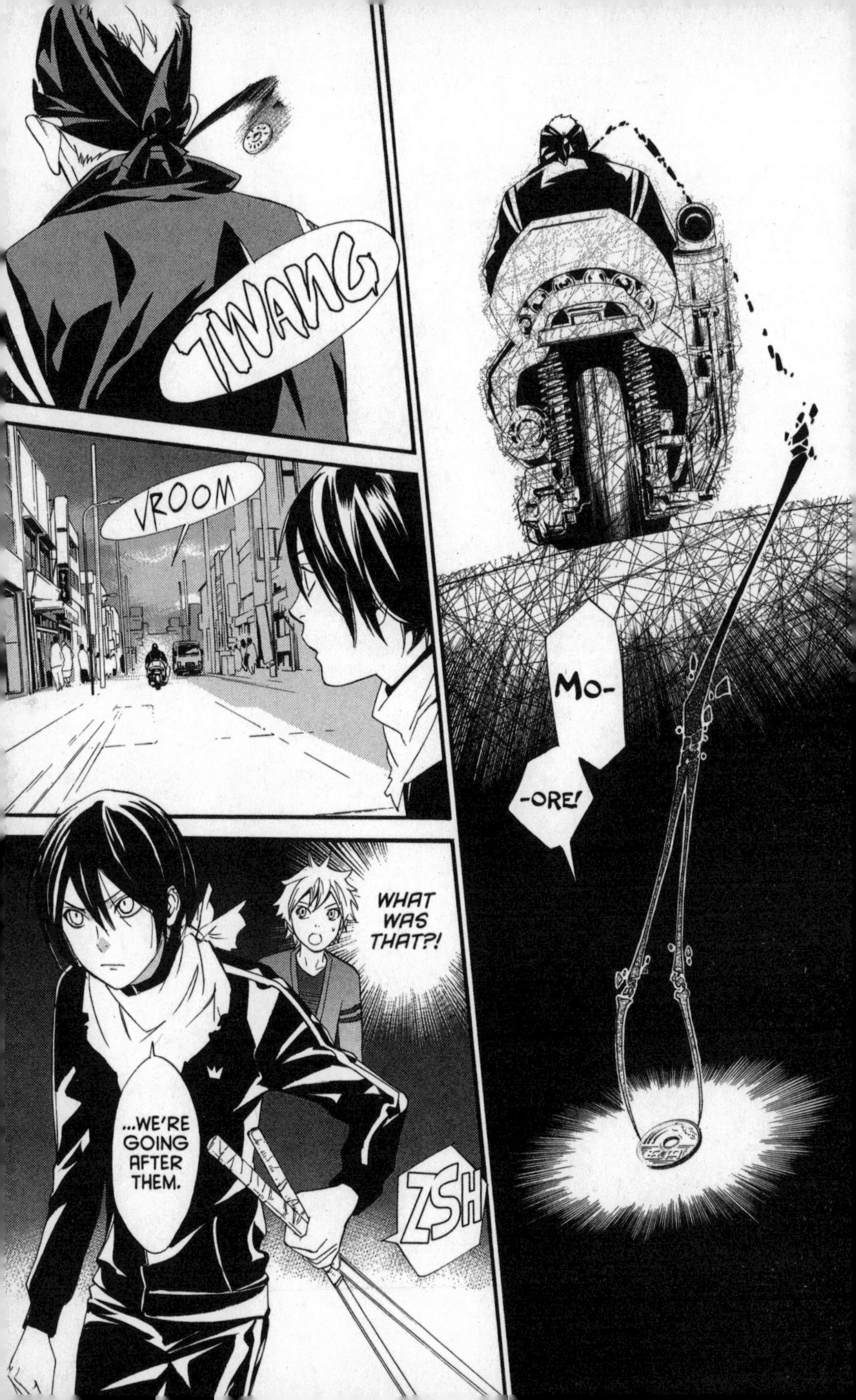
MO-
-ORE!
TWANG
VROOM
WHAT WAS THAT?!
...WE'RE GOING AFTER THEM.
ZSH

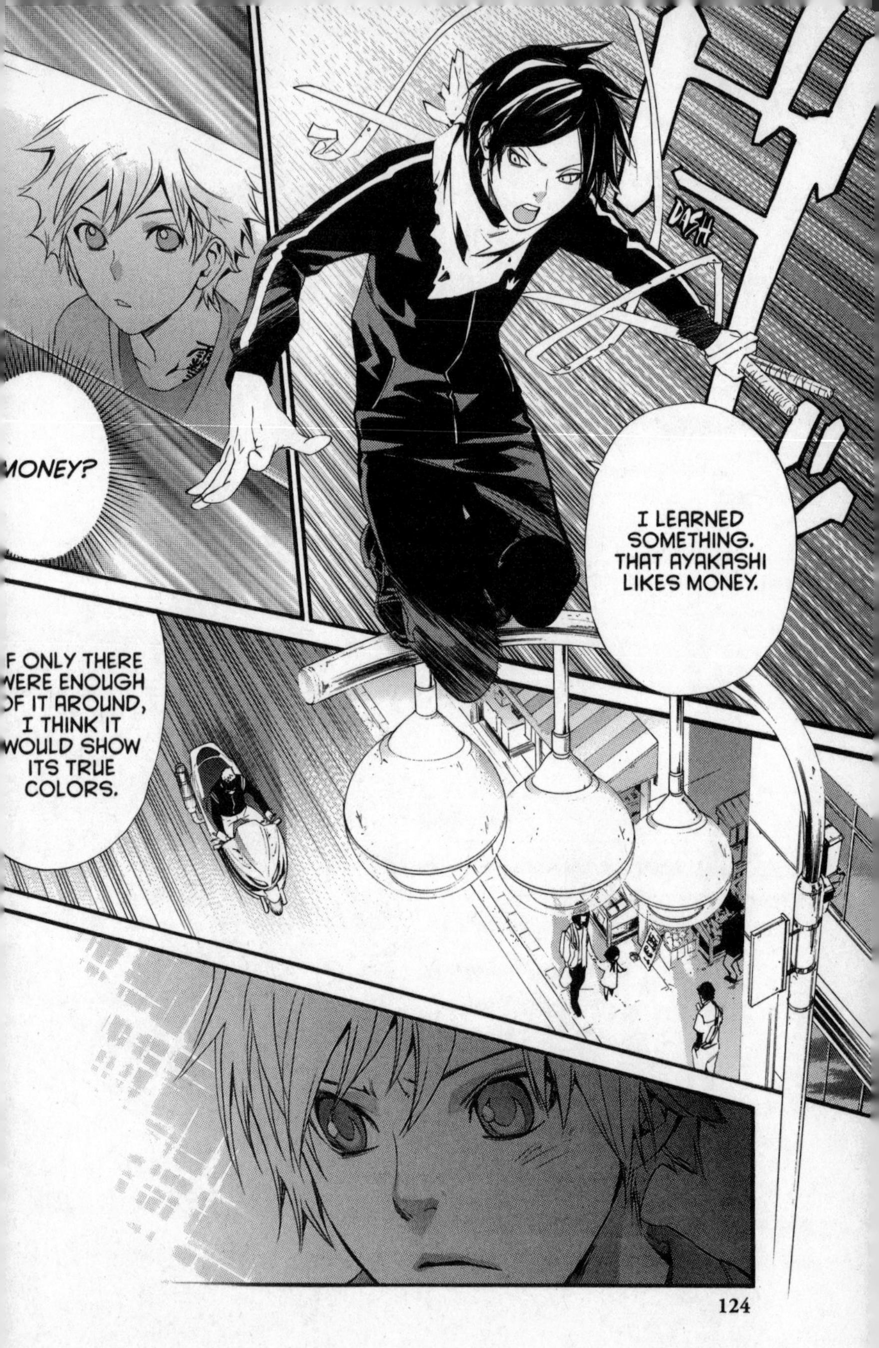
DASH
I LEARNED SOMETHING. THAT AYAKASHI LIKES MONEY.
MONEY?
F ONLY THERE WERE ENOUGH OF IT AROUND, I THINK IT WOULD SHOW ITS TRUE COLORS.

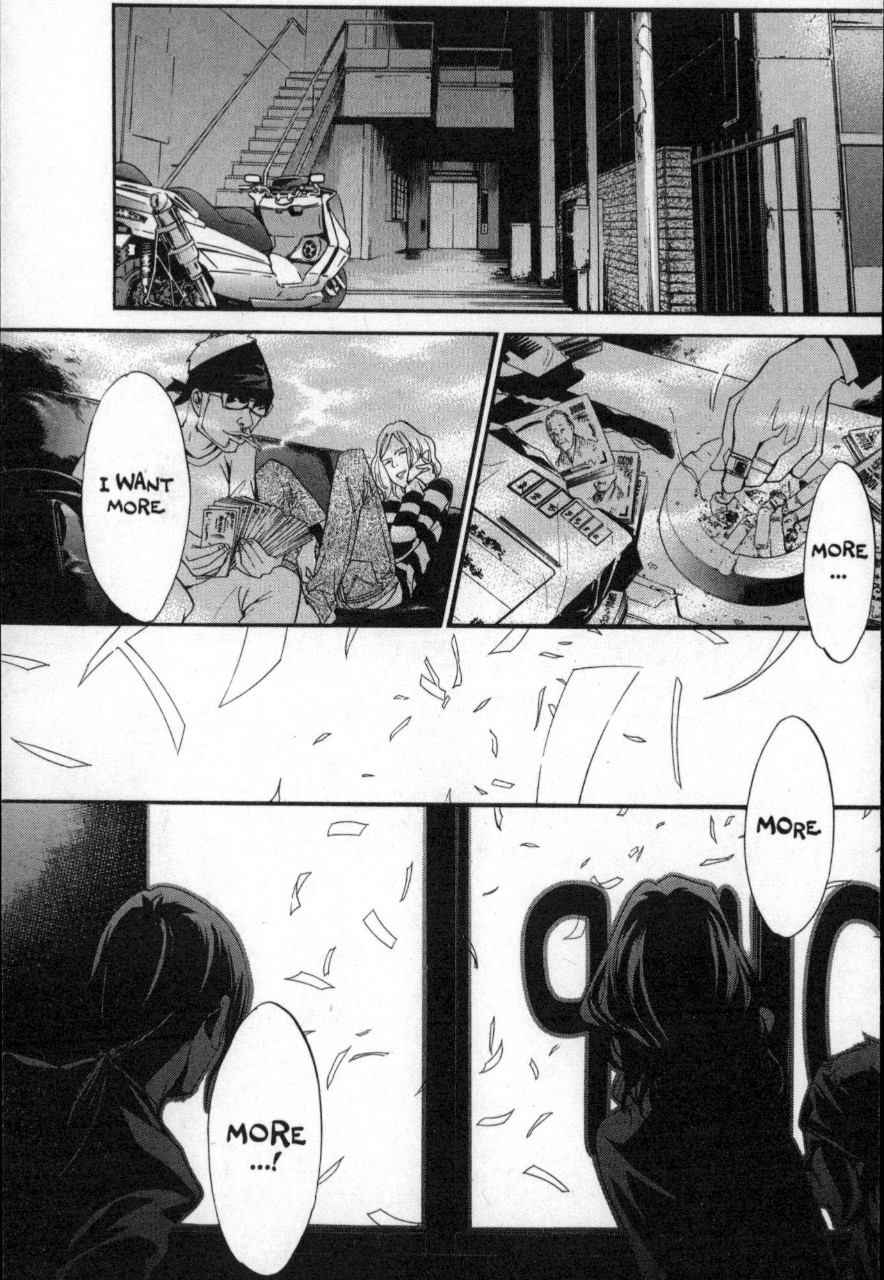
MORE ...
I WANT MORE
MORE.
MORE ...!

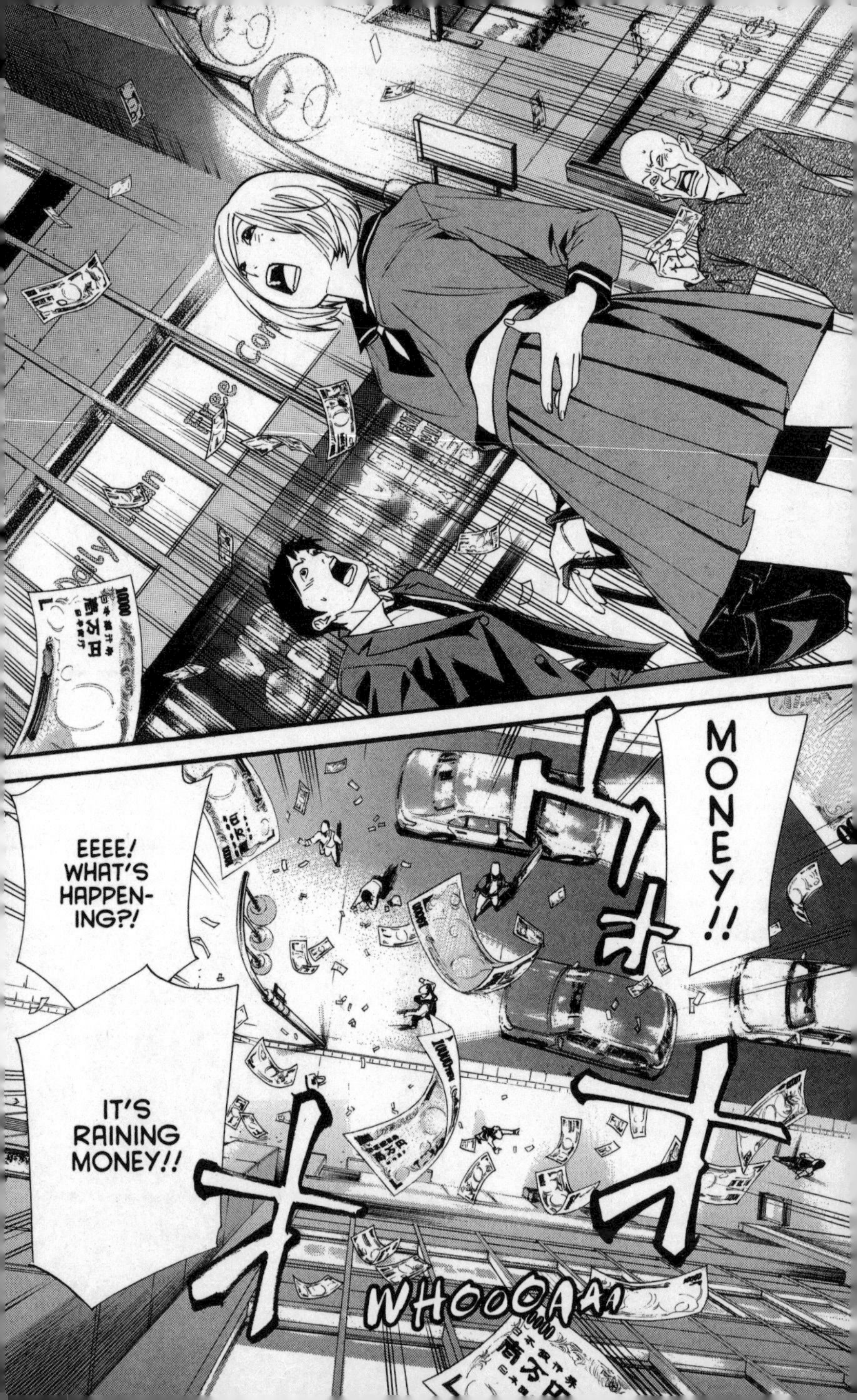
MONEY!!
EEEE! WHAT'S HAPPEN-ING?!
IT'S RAINING MONEY!!
WHOOOAAA

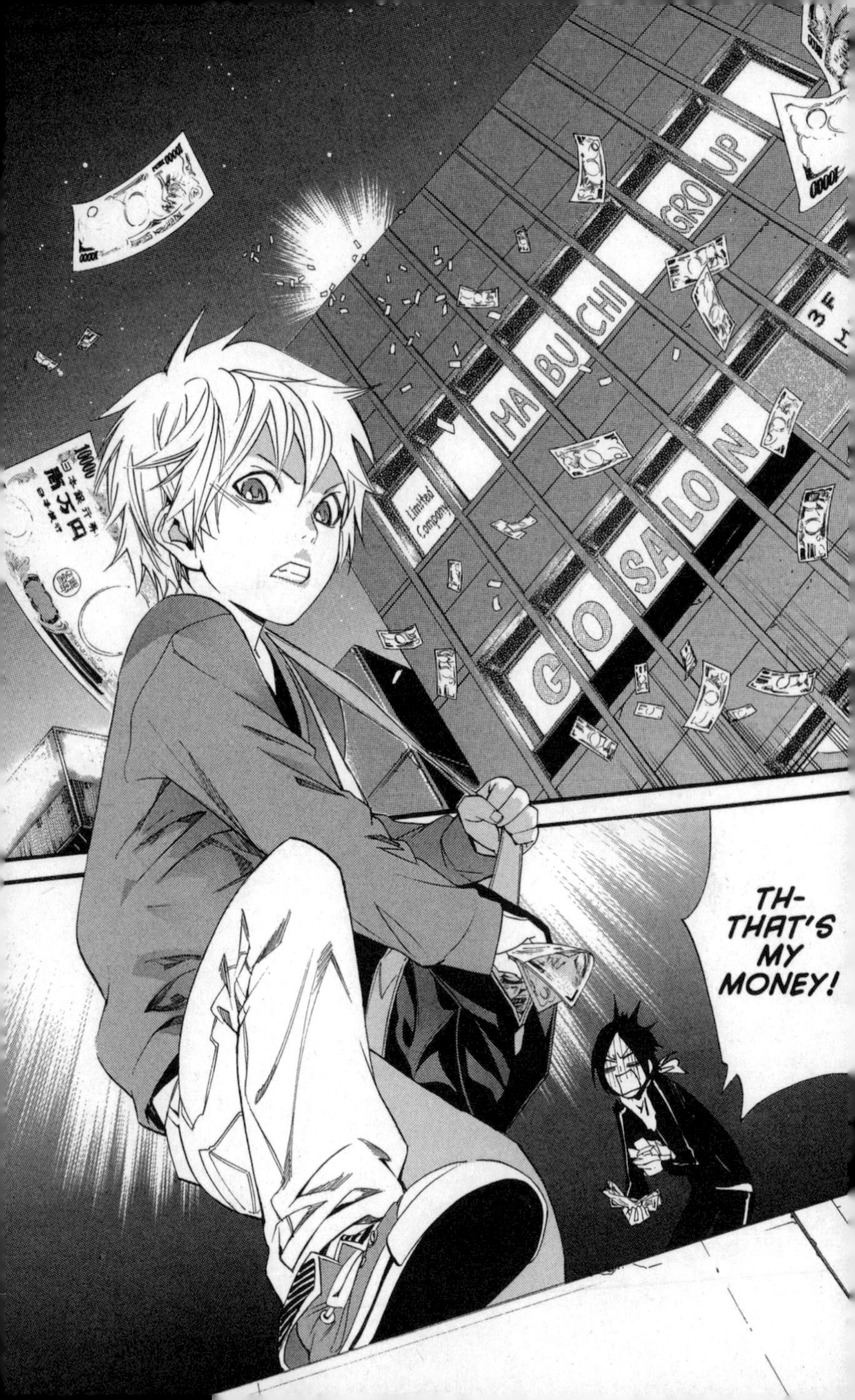
MABUCHI GROUP
3F
GO SALON
Limited Company
TH-THAT'S MY MONEY!

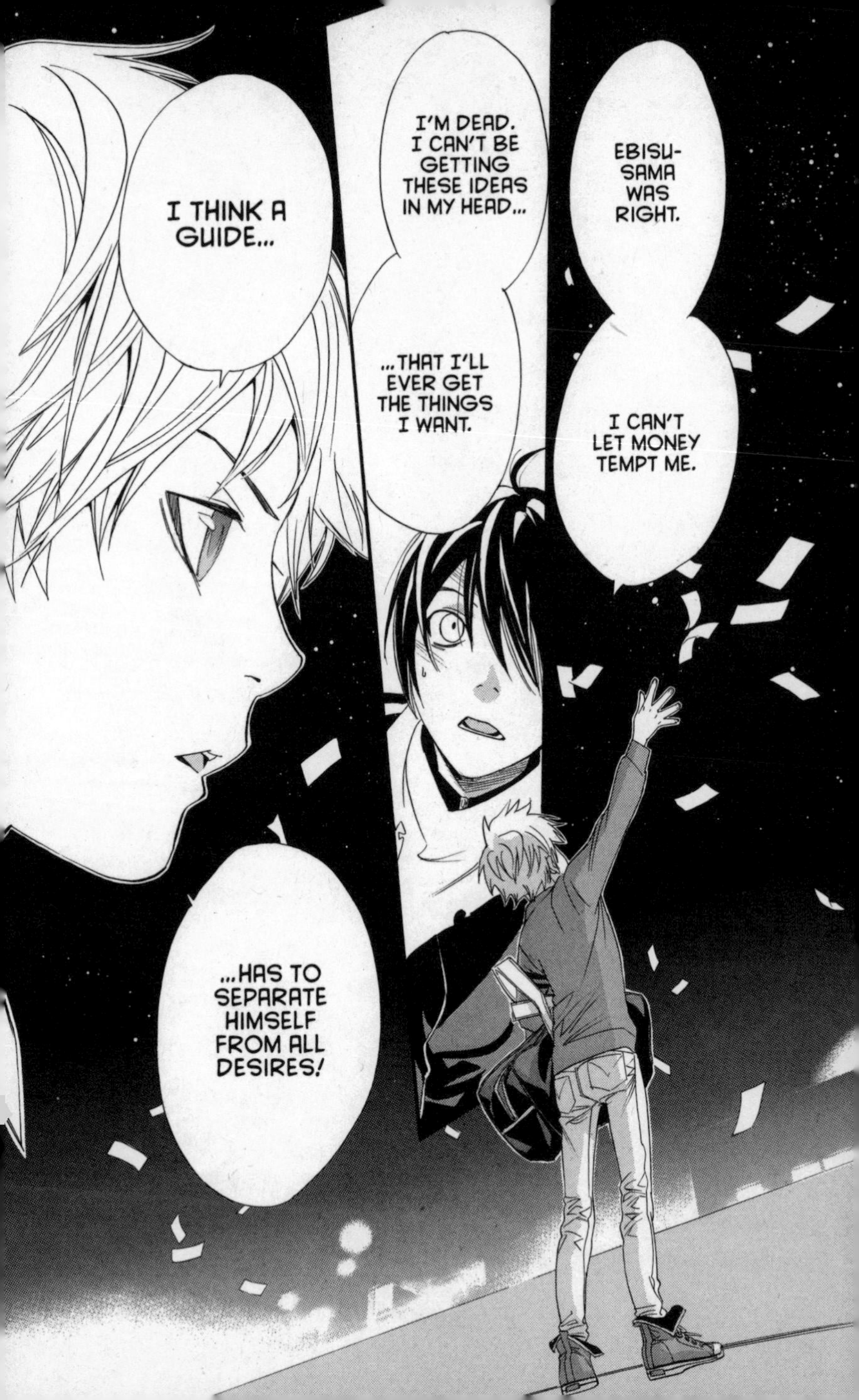
EBISU-SAMA WAS RIGHT.
I CAN'T LET MONEY TEMPT ME.
I'M DEAD. I CAN'T BE GETTING THESE IDEAS IN MY HEAD...
...THAT I'LL EVER GET THE THINGS I WANT.
I THINK A GUIDE...
...HAS TO SEPARATE HIMSELF FROM ALL DESIRES!

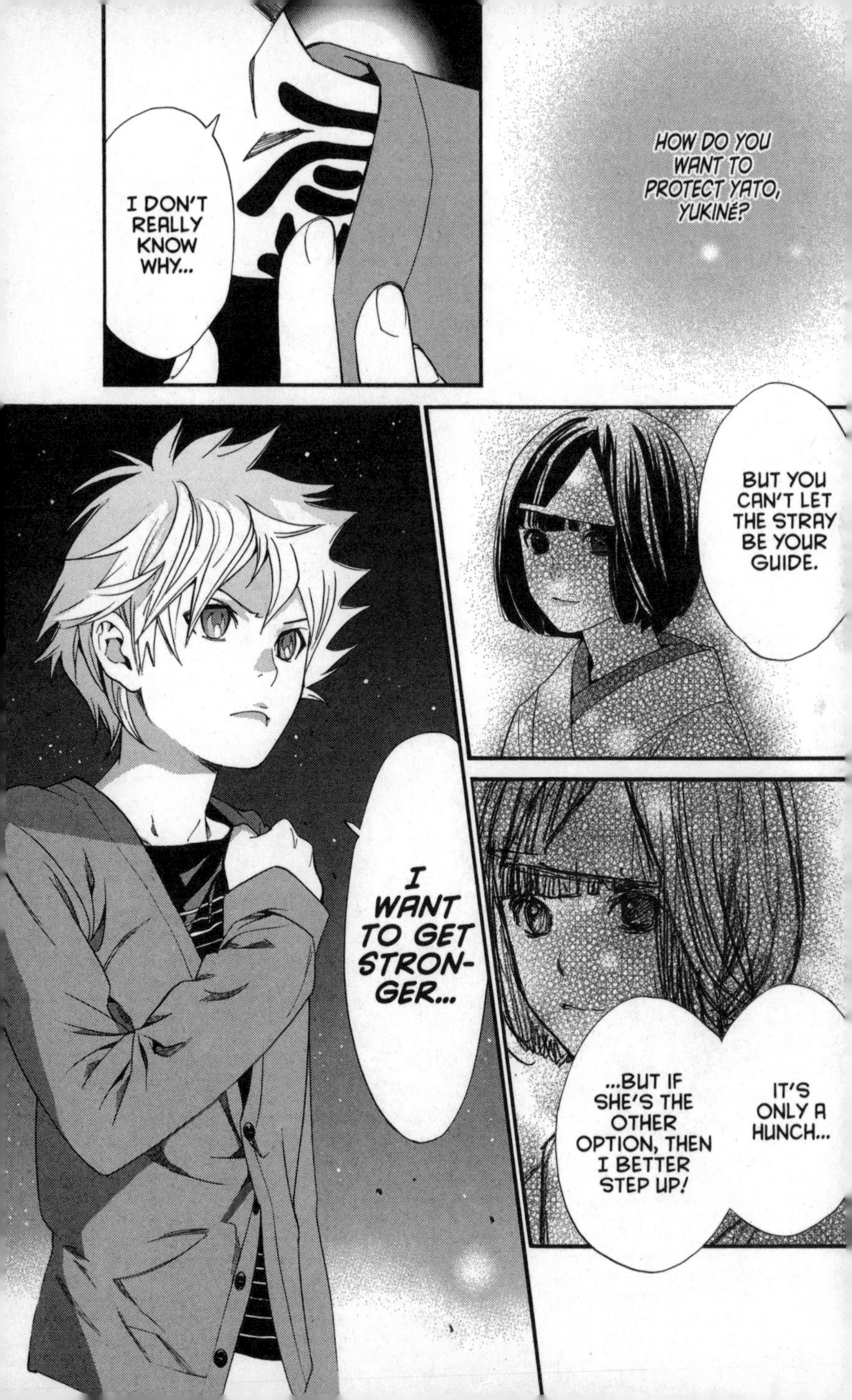
HOW DO YOU WANT TO PROTECT YATO, YUKINÉ?
I DON'T REALLY KNOW WHY...
BUT YOU CAN'T LET THE STRAY BE YOUR GUIDE.
IT'S ONLY A HUNCH...
...BUT IF SHE'S THE OTHER OPTION, THEN I BETTER STEP UP!
I WANT TO GET STRONGER...

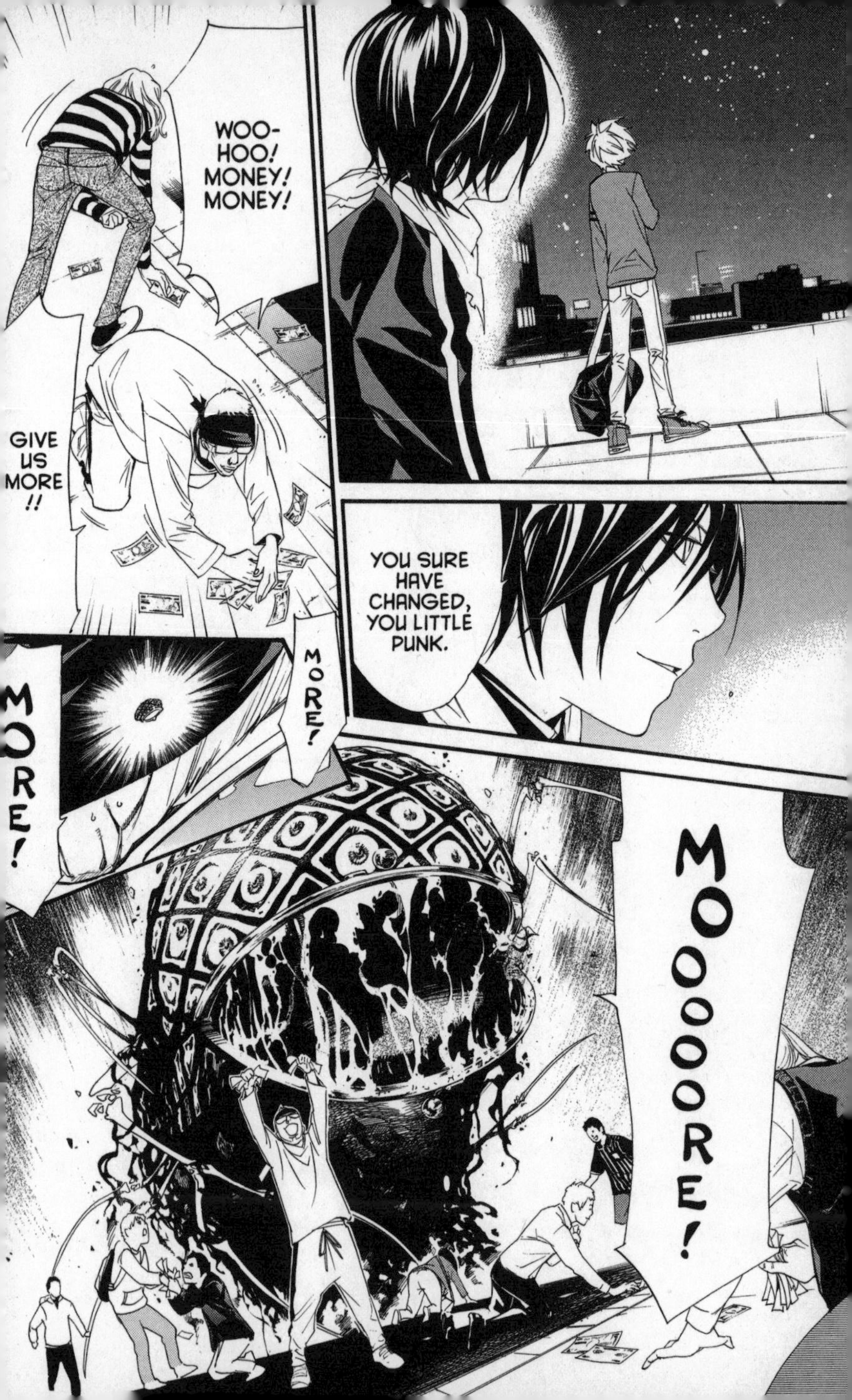
YOU SURE HAVE CHANGED, YOU LITTLE PUNK.
WOO-HOO! MONEY! MONEY!
GIVE US MORE!!
MOOOOORE!
MORE!
MORE!

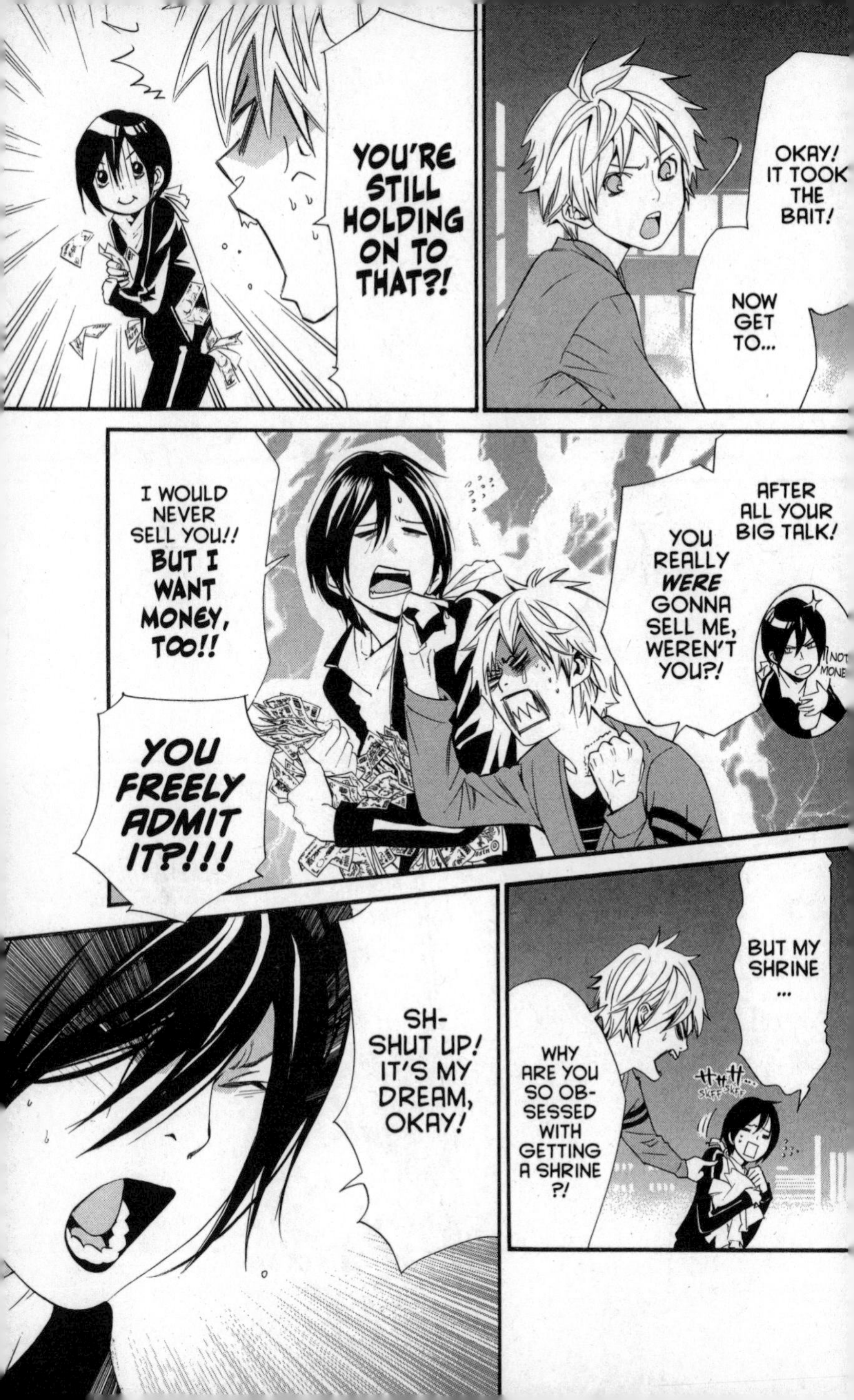
OKAY! IT TOOK THE BAIT!
NOW GET TO...
YOU'RE STILL HOLDING ON TO THAT?!
AFTER ALL YOUR BIG TALK!
YOU REALLY *WERE* GONNA SELL ME, WEREN'T YOU?!
I WOULD NEVER SELL YOU!! BUT I WANT MONEY, TOO!!
YOU FREELY ADMIT IT?!!!
BUT MY SHRINE ...
SKFF SKFF
WHY ARE YOU SO OB-SESSED WITH GETTING A SHRINE?!
SH- SHUT UP! IT'S MY DREAM, OKAY!

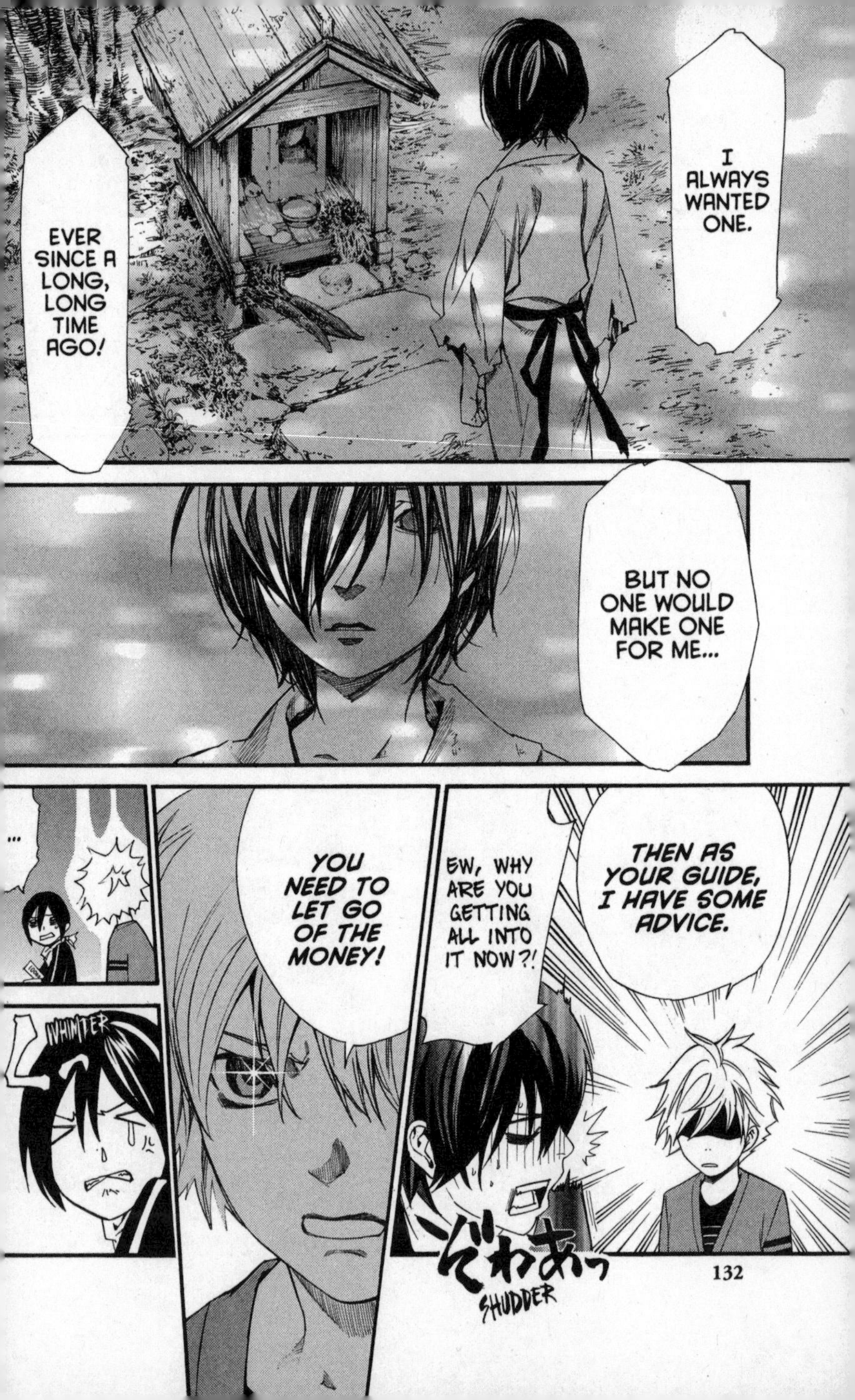
I ALWAYS WANTED ONE.
EVER SINCE A LONG, LONG TIME AGO!
BUT NO ONE WOULD MAKE ONE FOR ME...
THEN AS YOUR GUIDE, I HAVE SOME ADVICE.
EW, WHY ARE YOU GETTING ALL INTO IT NOW?!
ぞわあっ
SHUDDER
YOU NEED TO LET GO OF THE MONEY!
...
WHIMPER

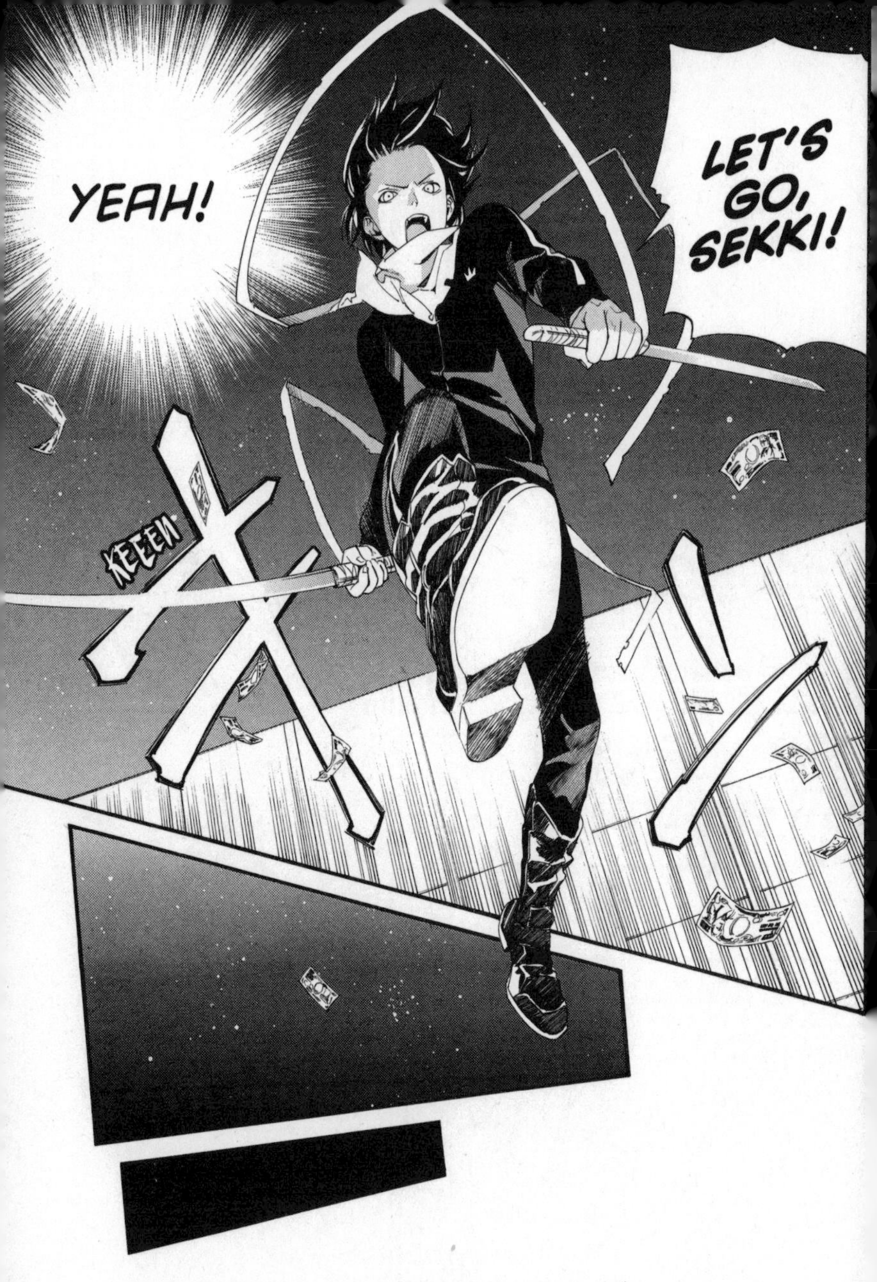
LET'S GO, SEKKI!
YEAH!
KEEEN

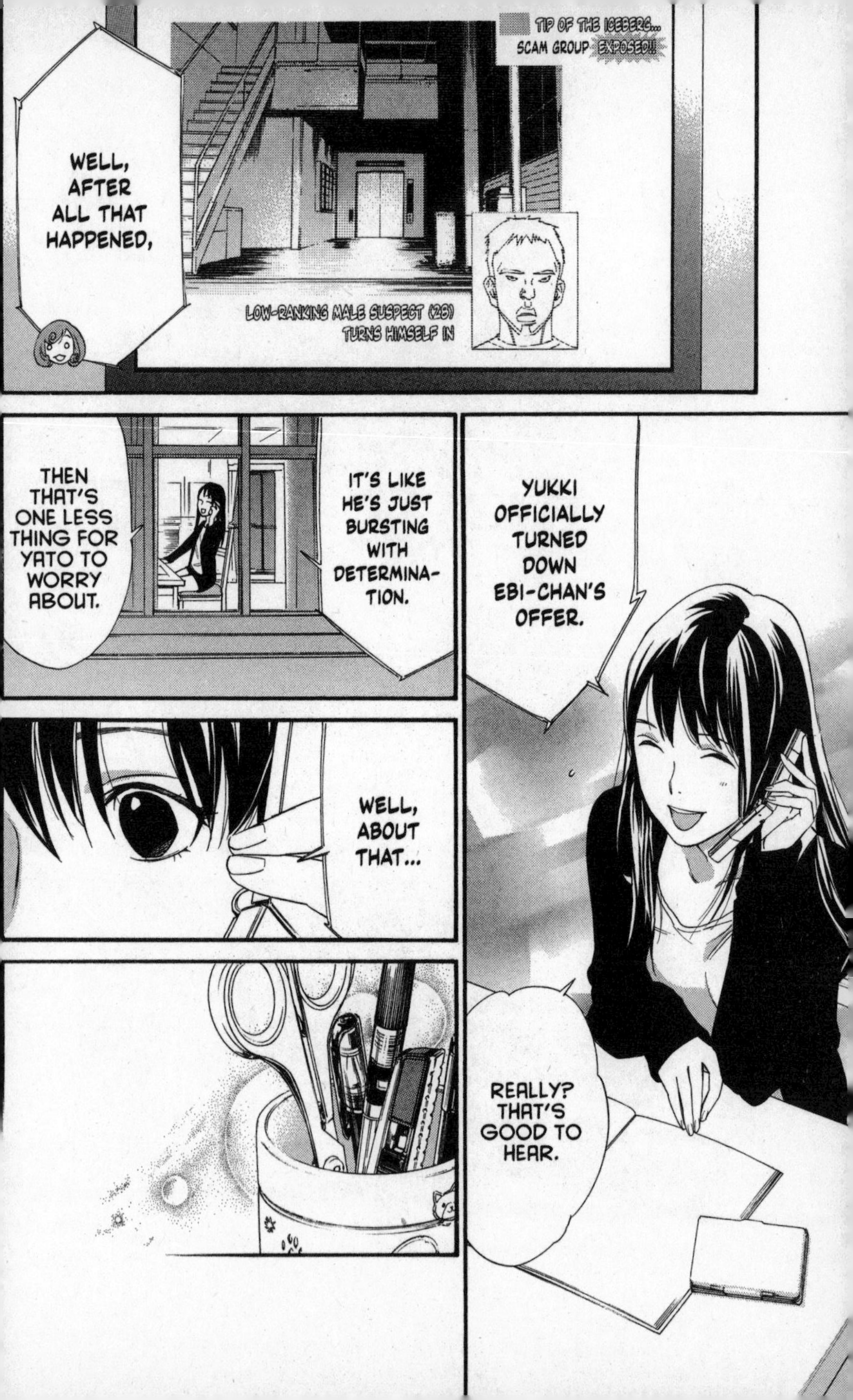
TIP OF THE ICEBERG... SCAM GROUP EXPOSED!!
WELL, AFTER ALL THAT HAPPENED,
LOW-RANKING MALE SUSPECT (28) TURNS HIMSELF IN
YUKKI OFFICIALLY TURNED DOWN EBI-CHAN'S OFFER.
REALLY? THAT'S GOOD TO HEAR.
IT'S LIKE HE'S JUST BURSTING WITH DETERMINA-TION.
THEN THAT'S ONE LESS THING FOR YATO TO WORRY ABOUT.
WELL, ABOUT THAT...

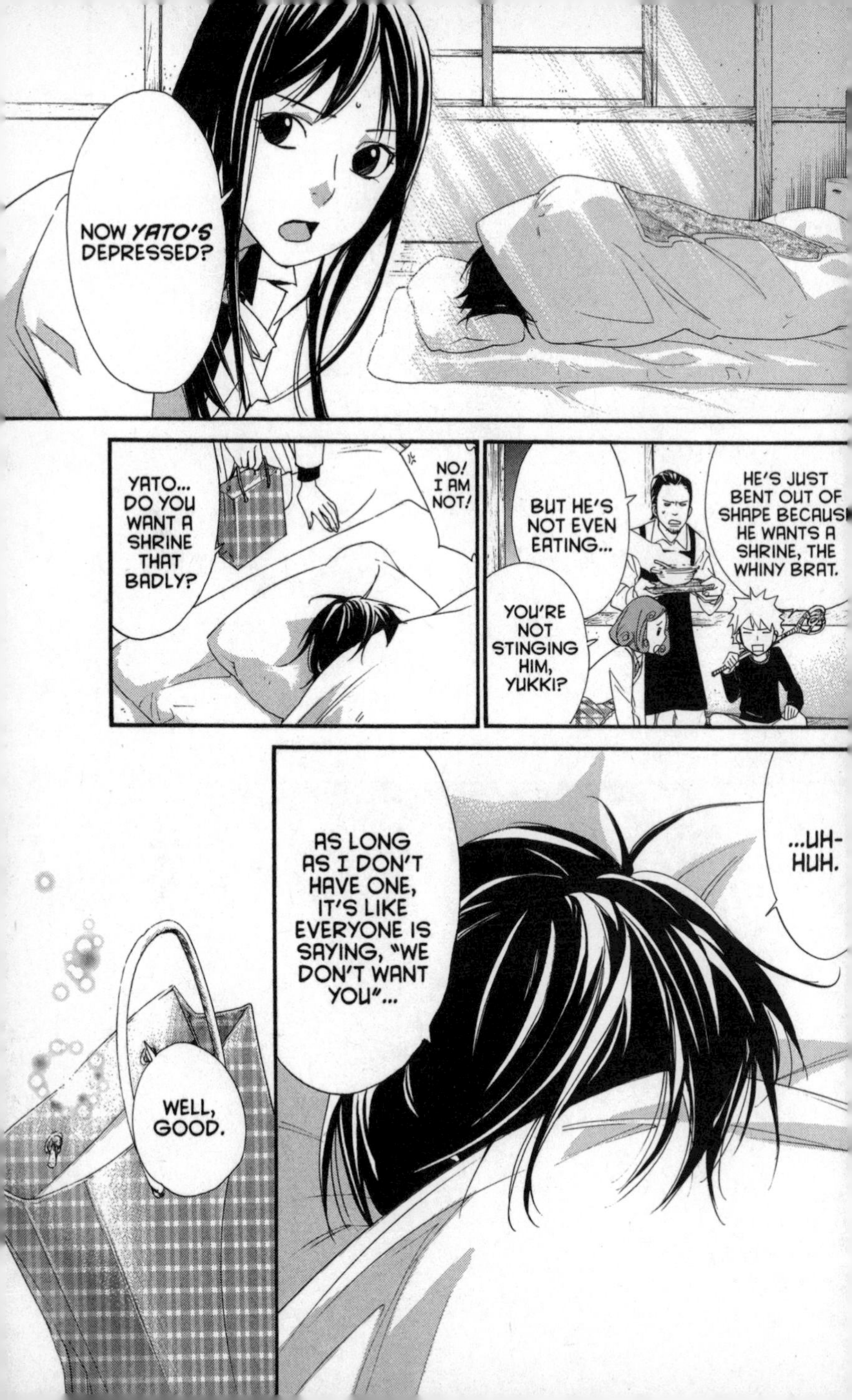
NOW YATO'S DEPRESSED?
HE'S JUST BENT OUT OF SHAPE BECAUS HE WANTS A SHRINE, THE WHINY BRAT.
BUT HE'S NOT EVEN EATING...
YOU'RE NOT STINGING HIM, YUKKI?
NO! I AM NOT!
YATO... DO YOU WANT A SHRINE THAT BADLY?
...UH-HUH.
AS LONG AS I DON'T HAVE ONE, IT'S LIKE EVERYONE IS SAYING, "WE DON'T WANT YOU"...
WELL, GOOD.

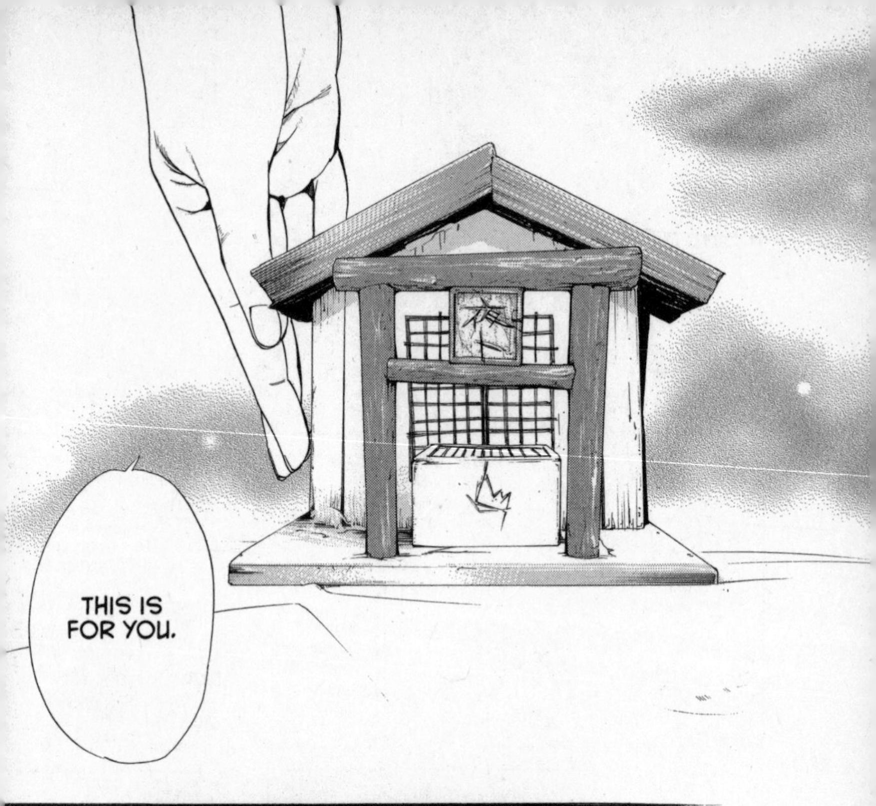
THIS IS FOR YOU.
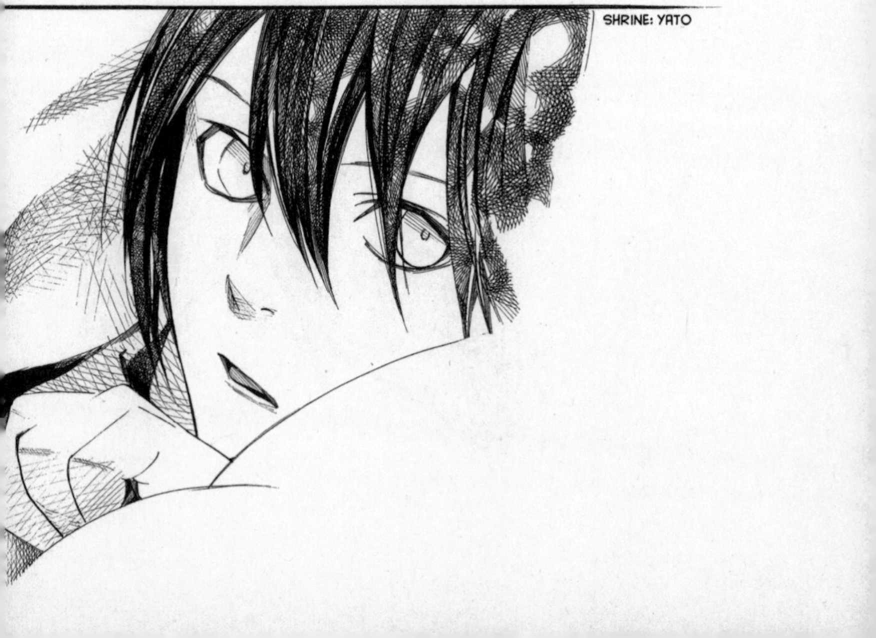
SHRINE: YATO

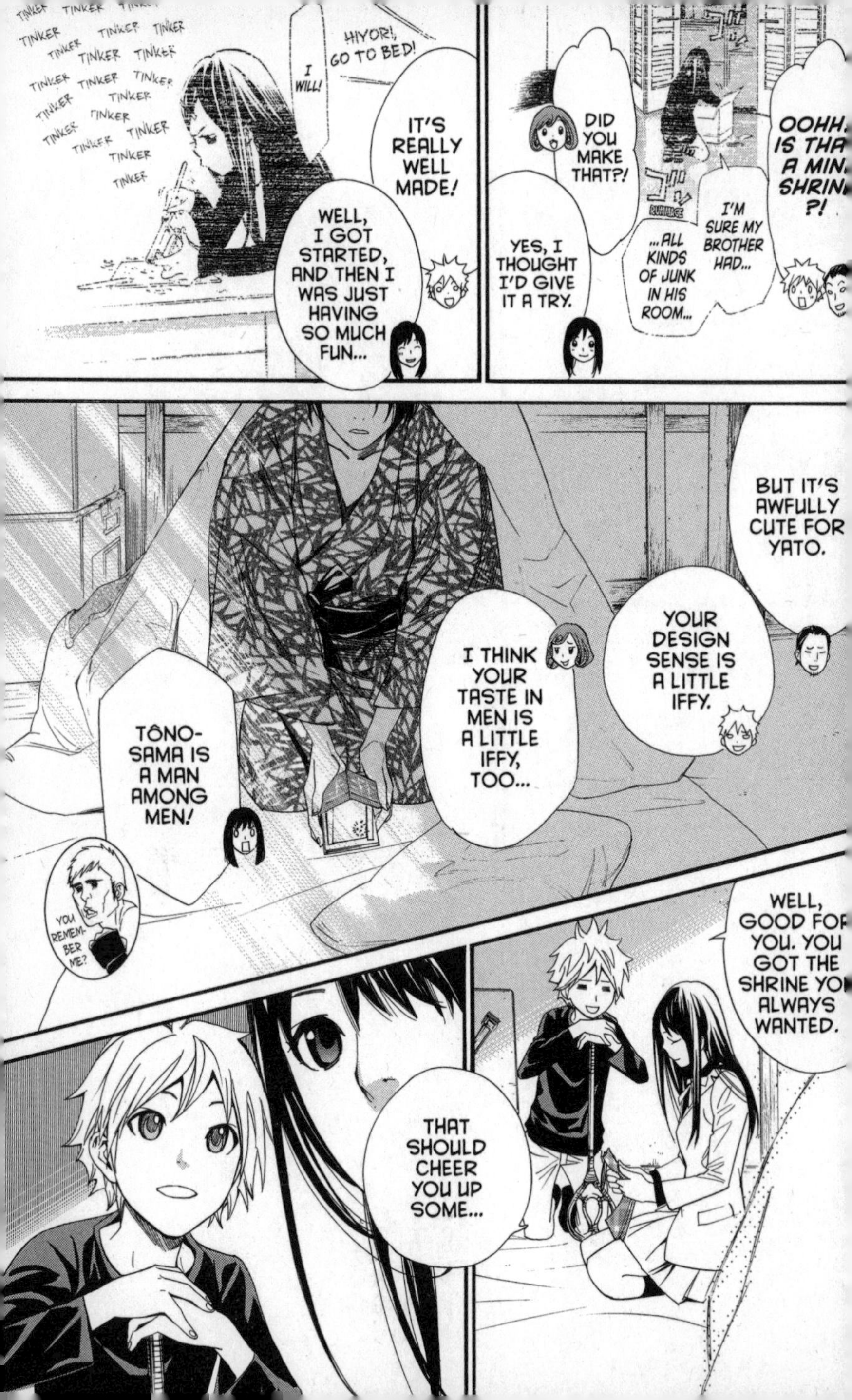
OOHH! IS THA A MIN SHRIN ?!
DID YOU MAKE THAT?!
RUMMAGE
I'M SURE MY BROTHER HAD...
...ALL KINDS OF JUNK IN HIS ROOM...
YES, I THOUGHT I'D GIVE IT A TRY.
HIYORI, GO TO BED!
I WILL!
TINKER TINKER TINKER TINKER TINKER TINKER TINKER TINKER TINKER TINKER TINKER TINKER TINKER TINKER TINKER TINKER
IT'S REALLY WELL MADE!
WELL, I GOT STARTED, AND THEN I WAS JUST HAVING SO MUCH FUN...
BUT IT'S AWFULLY CUTE FOR YATO.
YOUR DESIGN SENSE IS A LITTLE IFFY.
I THINK YOUR TASTE IN MEN IS A LITTLE IFFY, TOO...
TÔNO-SAMA IS A MAN AMONG MEN!
YOU REMEMBER ME?
WELL, GOOD FOR YOU. YOU GOT THE SHRINE YO ALWAYS WANTED.
THAT SHOULD CHEER YOU UP SOME...

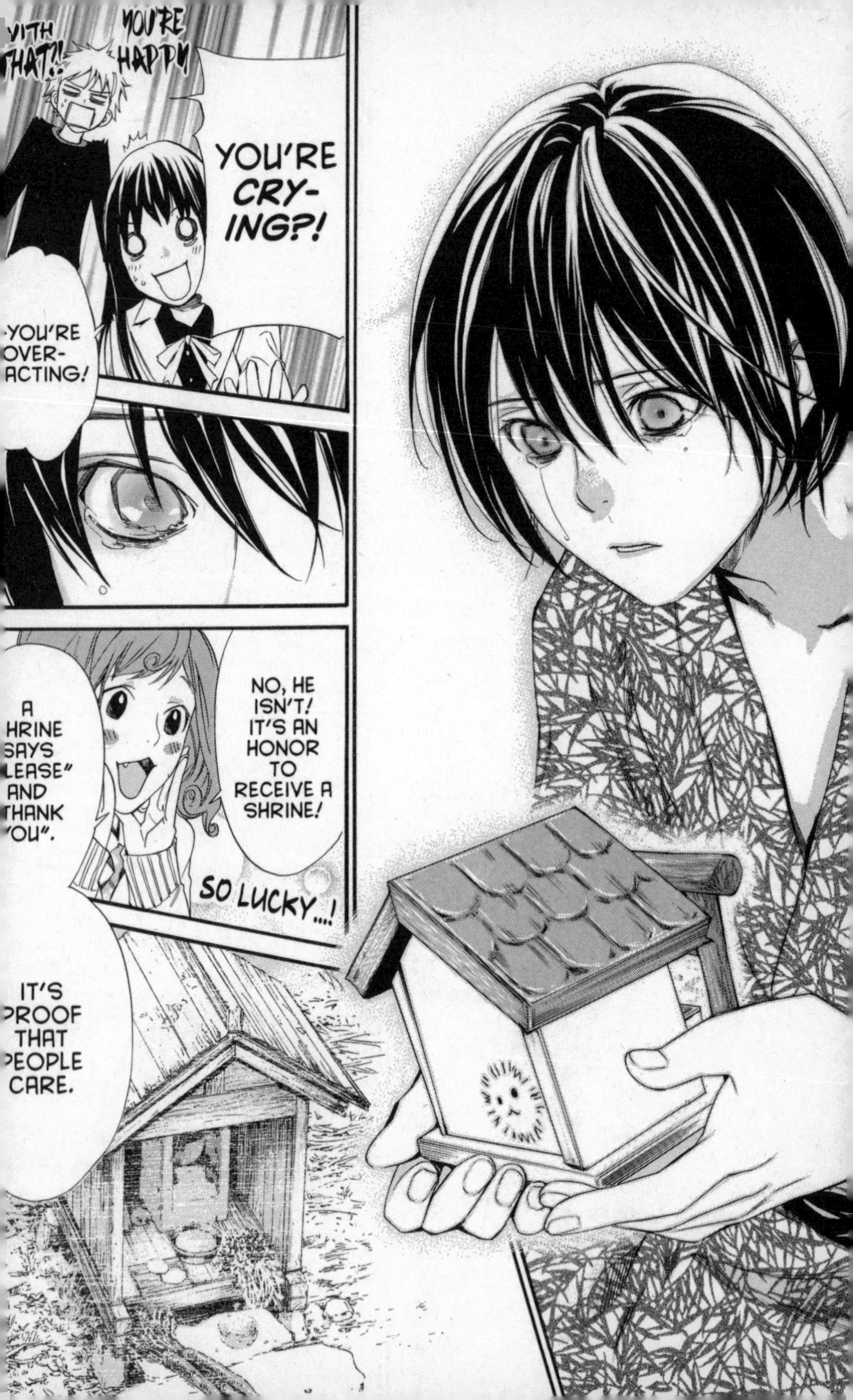

YOU'RE HAPPY
VITH THAT?!
YOU'RE CRY-ING?!
-YOU'RE OVER-ACTING!
NO, HE ISN'T! IT'S AN HONOR TO RECEIVE A SHRINE!
SO LUCKY...!
A HRINE SAYS LEASE" AND THANK 'OU".
IT'S PROOF THAT EOPLE CARE.

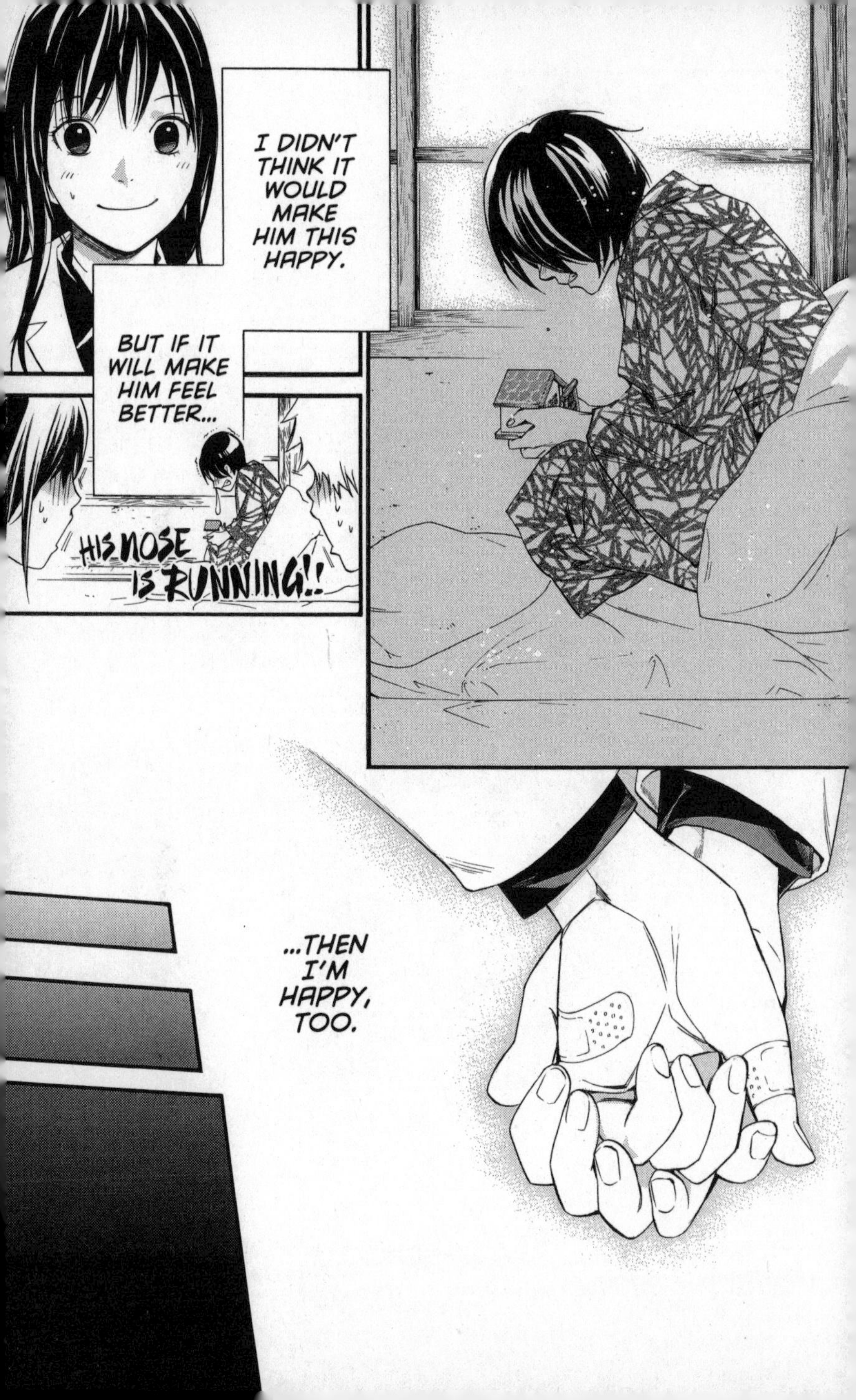
I DIDN'T THINK IT WOULD MAKE HIM THIS HAPPY.
BUT IF IT WILL MAKE HIM FEEL BETTER...
HIS NOSE IS RUNNING!!
...THEN I'M HAPPY, TOO.

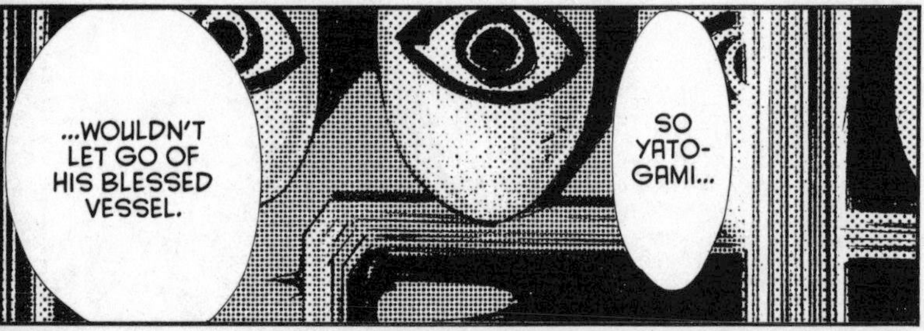
SO YATO-GAMI...
...WOULDN'T LET GO OF HIS BLESSED VESSEL.

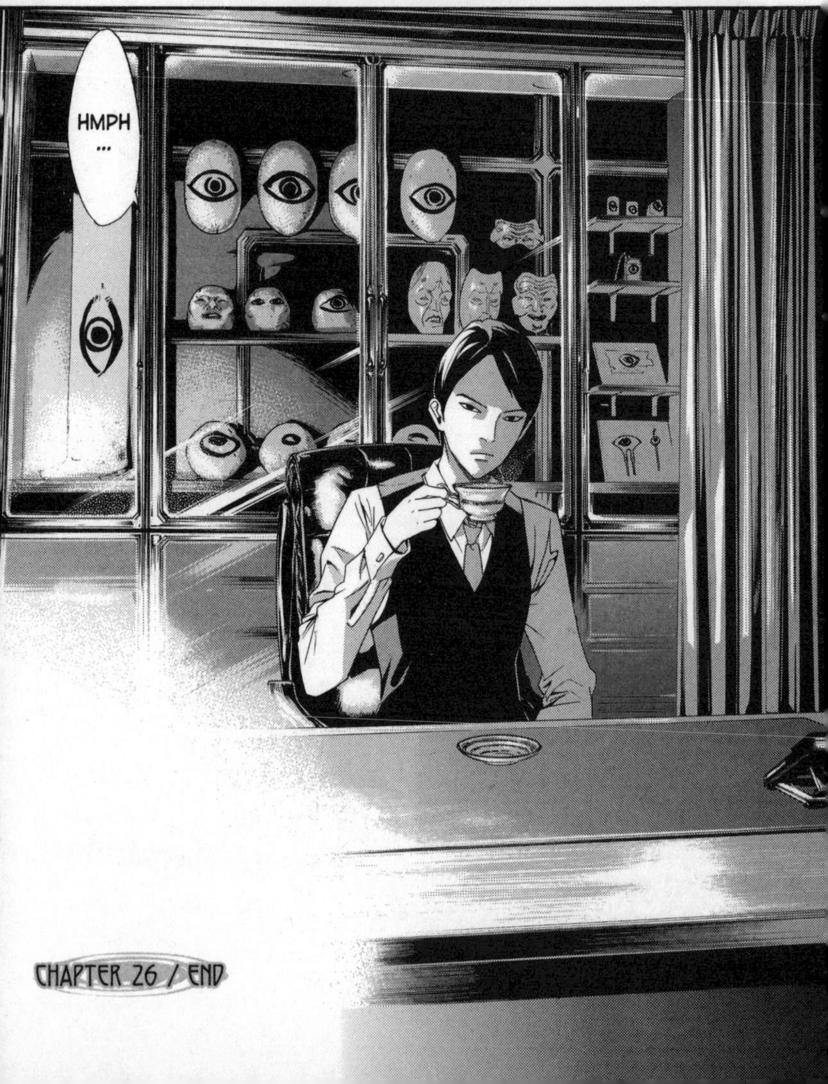
HMPH ...
CHAPTER 26 / END

封

良

神

性

[illegible]

[illegible]

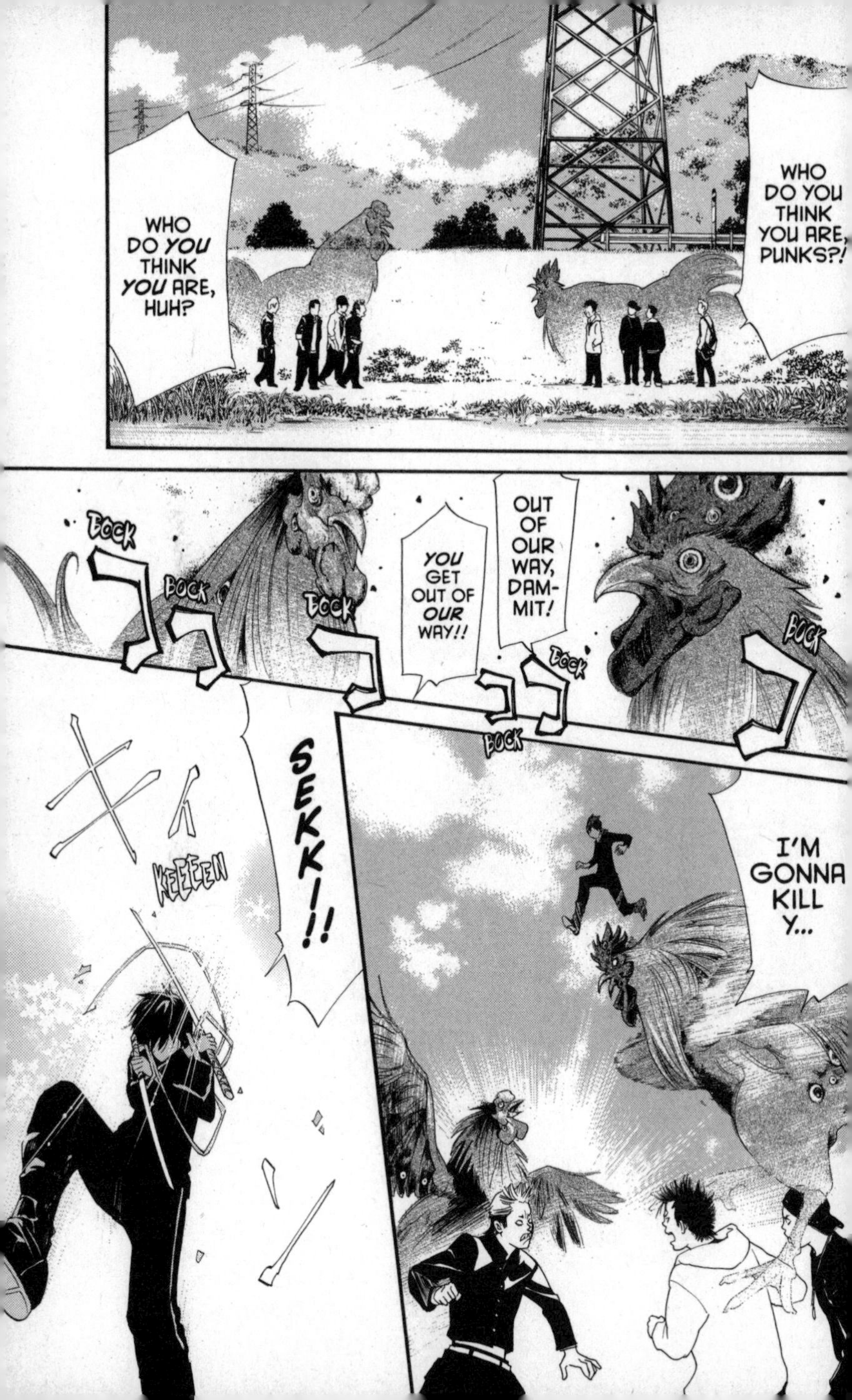
WHO DO YOU THINK YOU ARE, PUNKS?!
WHO DO *YOU* THINK *YOU* ARE, HUH?
BOCK
BOCK
OUT OF OUR WAY, DAM-MIT!
YOU GET OUT OF *OUR* WAY!!
BOCK
BOCK
BOCK
BOCK
I'M GONNA KILL Y...
SEKKI!!
KEEEEEN

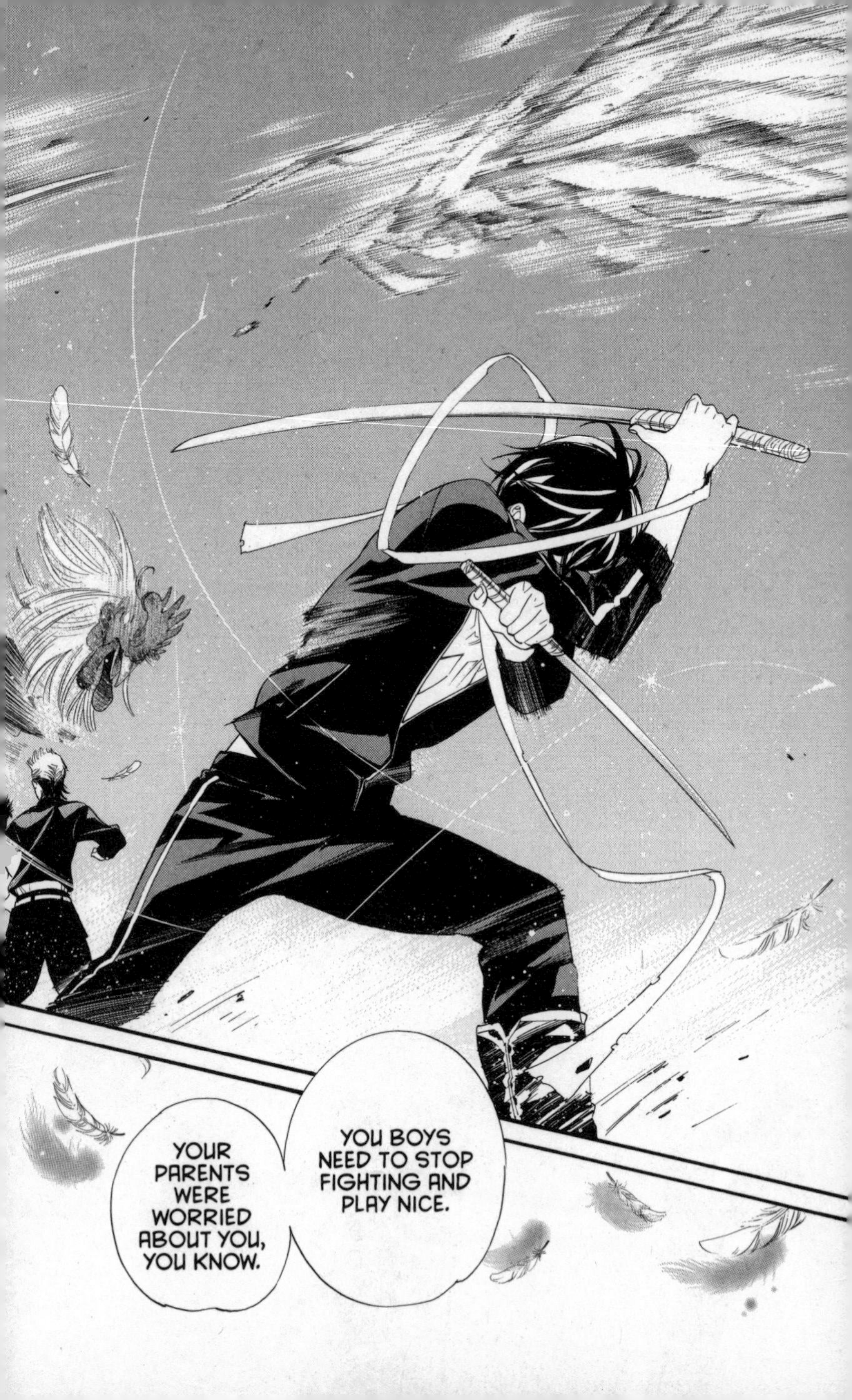
YOU BOYS NEED TO STOP FIGHTING AND PLAY NICE.
YOUR PARENTS WERE WORRIED ABOUT YOU, YOU KNOW.

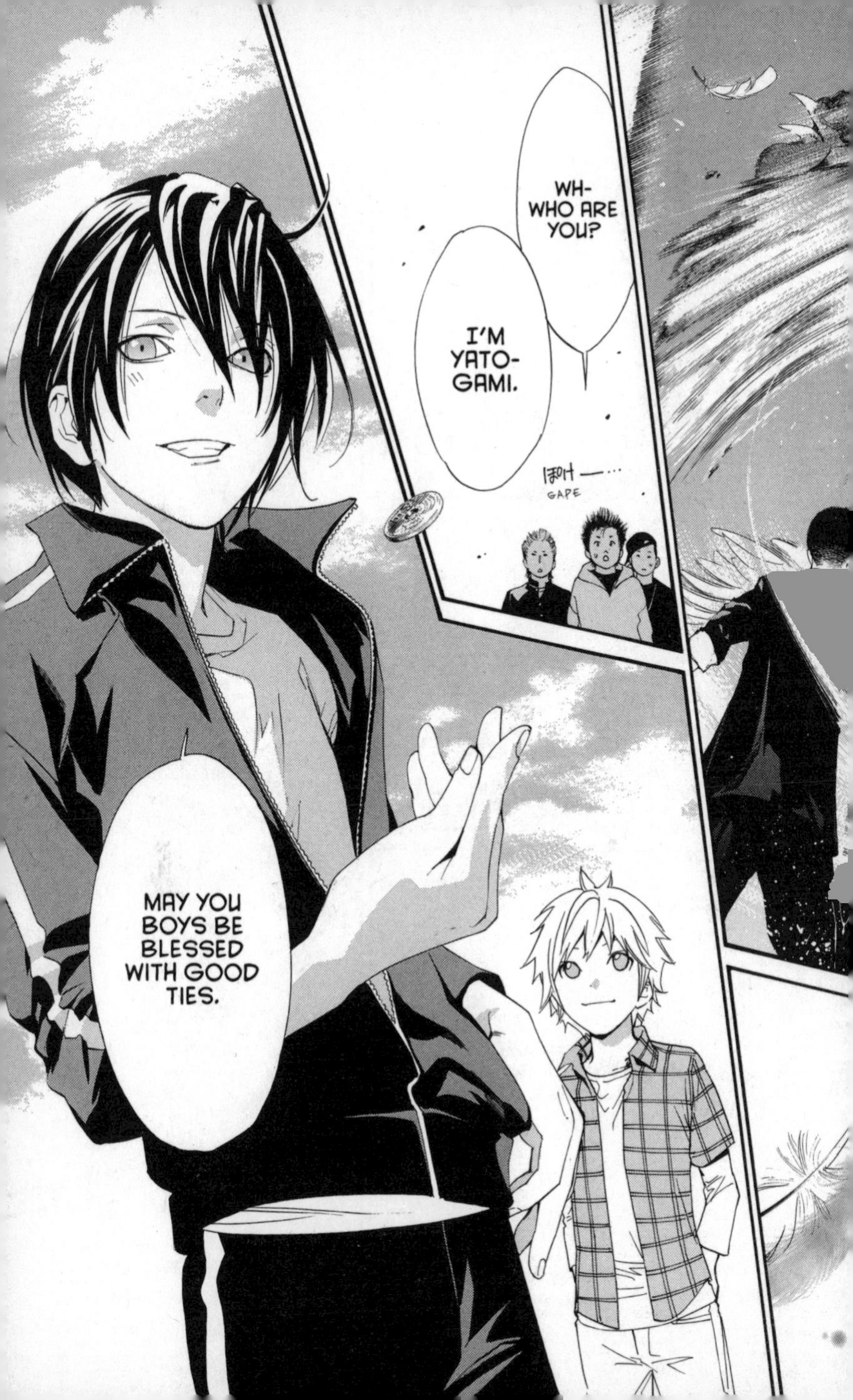
WH- WHO ARE YOU?
I'M YATO-GAMI.
ほけー…
GAPE
MAY YOU BOYS BE BLESSED WITH GOOD TIES.

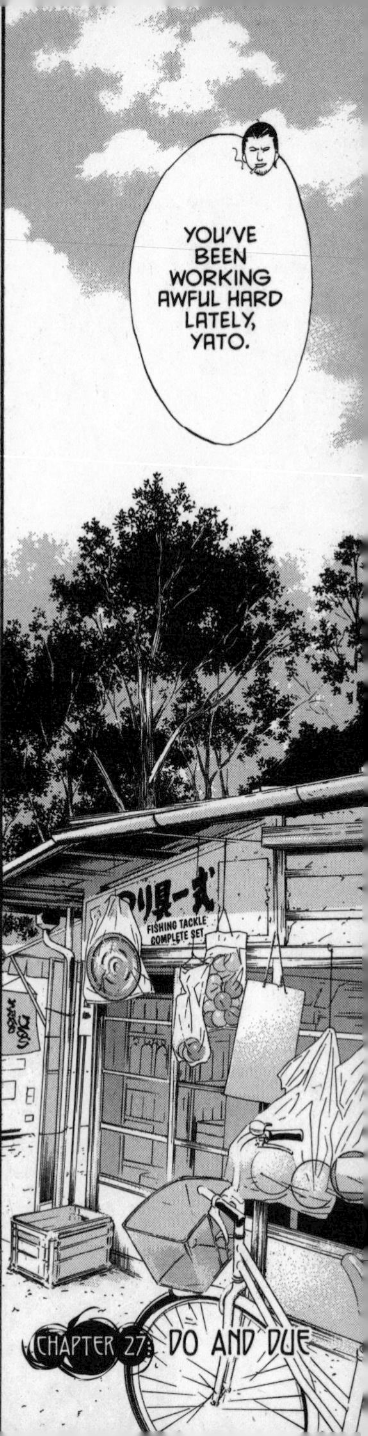
YOU'VE BEEN WORKING AWFUL HARD LATELY, YATO.
つり具一式
FISHING TACKLE COMPLETE SET
CHAPTER 27: DO AND DUE

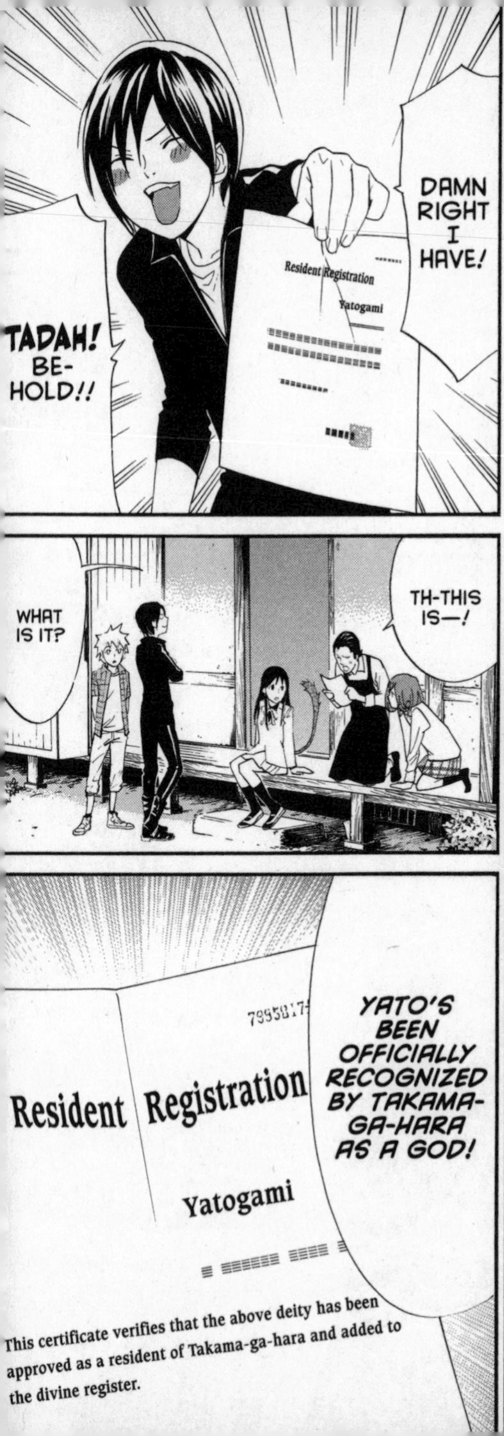
DAMN RIGHT I HAVE!
Resident Registration
Yatogami
TADAH! BE-HOLD!!
TH-THIS IS—!
WHAT IS IT?
YATO'S BEEN OFFICIALLY RECOGNIZED BY TAKAMA-GA-HARA AS A GOD!
Resident Registration
Yatogami
This certificate verifies that the above deity has been approved as a resident of Takama-ga-hara and added to the divine register.

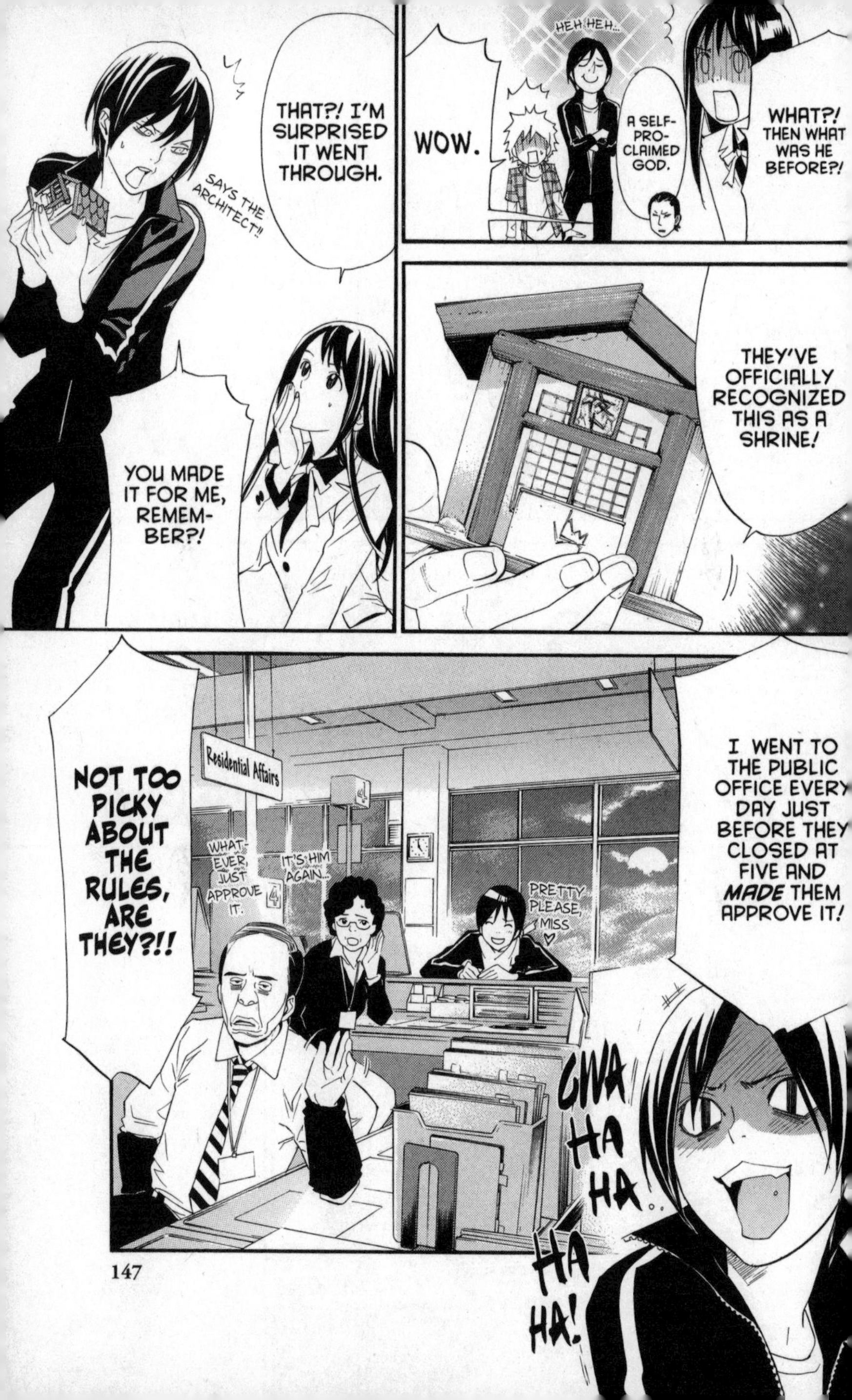
HEH HEH...
WHAT?! THEN WHAT WAS HE BEFORE?!
A SELF-PROCLAIMED GOD.
WOW.
THEY'VE OFFICIALLY RECOGNIZED THIS AS A SHRINE!
THAT?! I'M SURPRISED IT WENT THROUGH.
SAYS THE ARCHITECT!!
YOU MADE IT FOR ME, REMEMBER?!
I WENT TO THE PUBLIC OFFICE EVERY DAY JUST BEFORE THEY CLOSED AT FIVE AND *MADE* THEM APPROVE IT!
PRETTY PLEASE, MISS ♡
IT'S HIM AGAIN...
Residential Affairs
WHATEVER, JUST APPROVE IT.
NOT TOO PICKY ABOUT THE RULES, ARE THEY?!!
GWA HA HA HA.. HA HA!

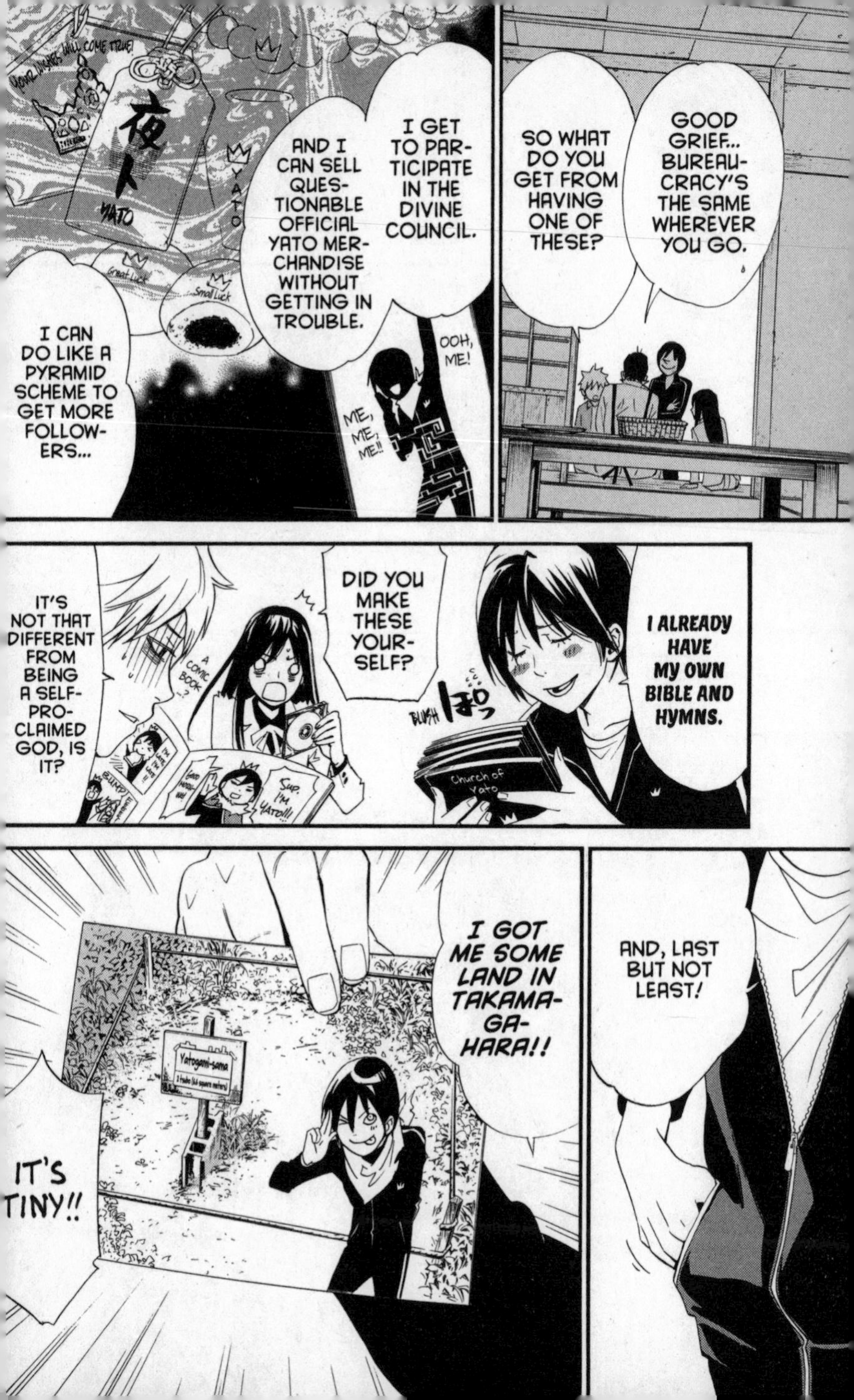

GOOD GRIEF... BUREAU-CRACY'S THE SAME WHEREVER YOU GO.
SO WHAT DO YOU GET FROM HAVING ONE OF THESE?
I GET TO PAR-TICIPATE IN THE DIVINE COUNCIL.
AND I CAN SELL QUES-TIONABLE OFFICIAL YATO MER-CHANDISE WITHOUT GETTING IN TROUBLE.
YOUR WISHES WILL COME TRUE!
YATO
YATO
Great Luck
Small Luck
OOH, ME!
ME, ME, ME!!
I CAN DO LIKE A PYRAMID SCHEME TO GET MORE FOLLOW-ERS...
I ALREADY HAVE MY OWN BIBLE AND HYMNS.
Church of Yato
BLUSH
DID YOU MAKE THESE YOUR-SELF?
A COMIC BOOK...?
Sup. I'm YATO!!!
IT'S NOT THAT DIFFERENT FROM BEING A SELF-PRO-CLAIMED GOD, IS IT?
AND, LAST BUT NOT LEAST!
I GOT ME SOME LAND IN TAKAMA-GA-HARA!!
Yatogami-sama
IT'S TINY!!

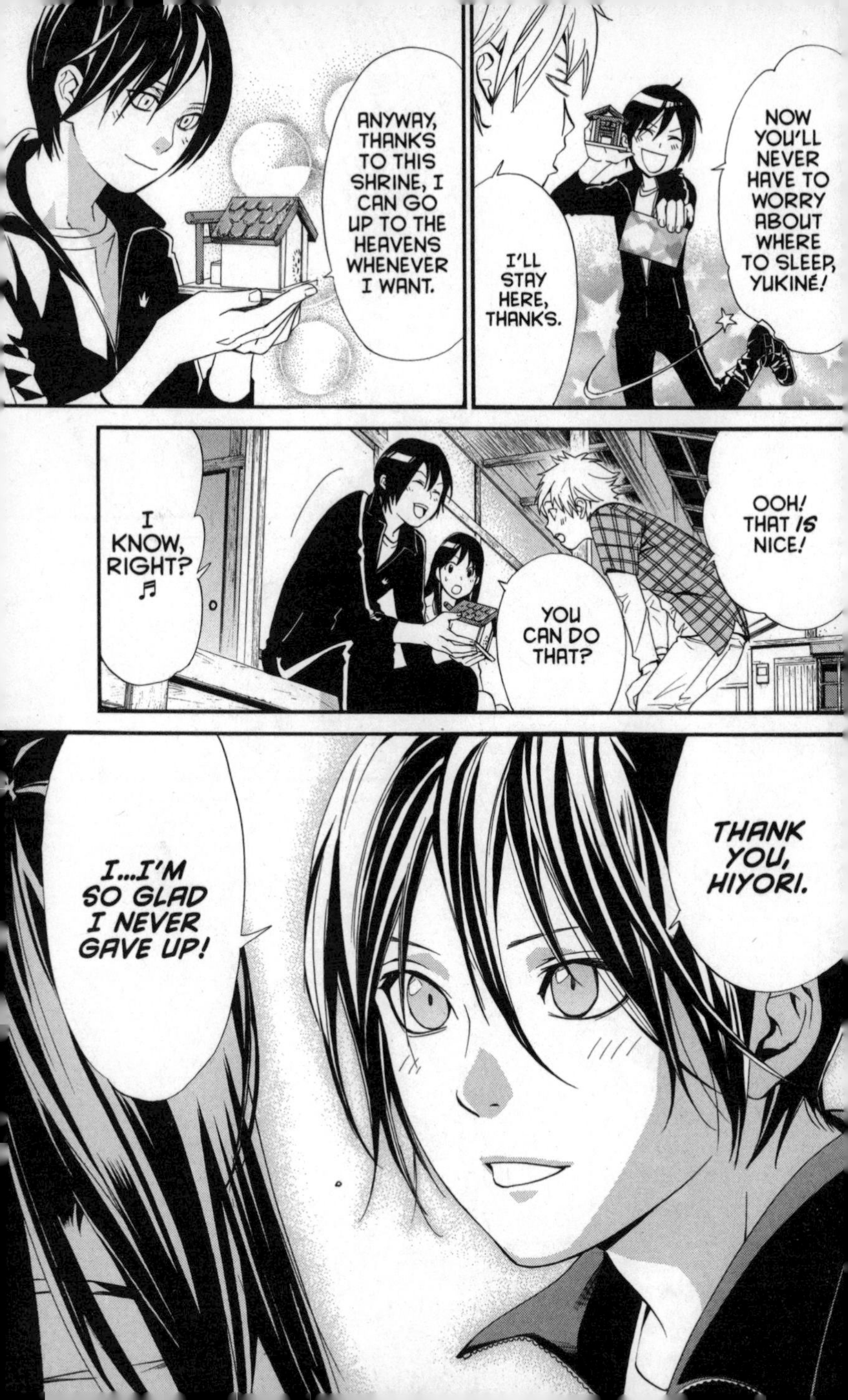
NOW YOU'LL NEVER HAVE TO WORRY ABOUT WHERE TO SLEEP, YUKINÉ!
I'LL STAY HERE, THANKS.
ANYWAY, THANKS TO THIS SHRINE, I CAN GO UP TO THE HEAVENS WHENEVER I WANT.
OOH! THAT IS NICE!
YOU CAN DO THAT?
I KNOW, RIGHT? ♬
THANK YOU, HIYORI.
I...I'M SO GLAD I NEVER GAVE UP!

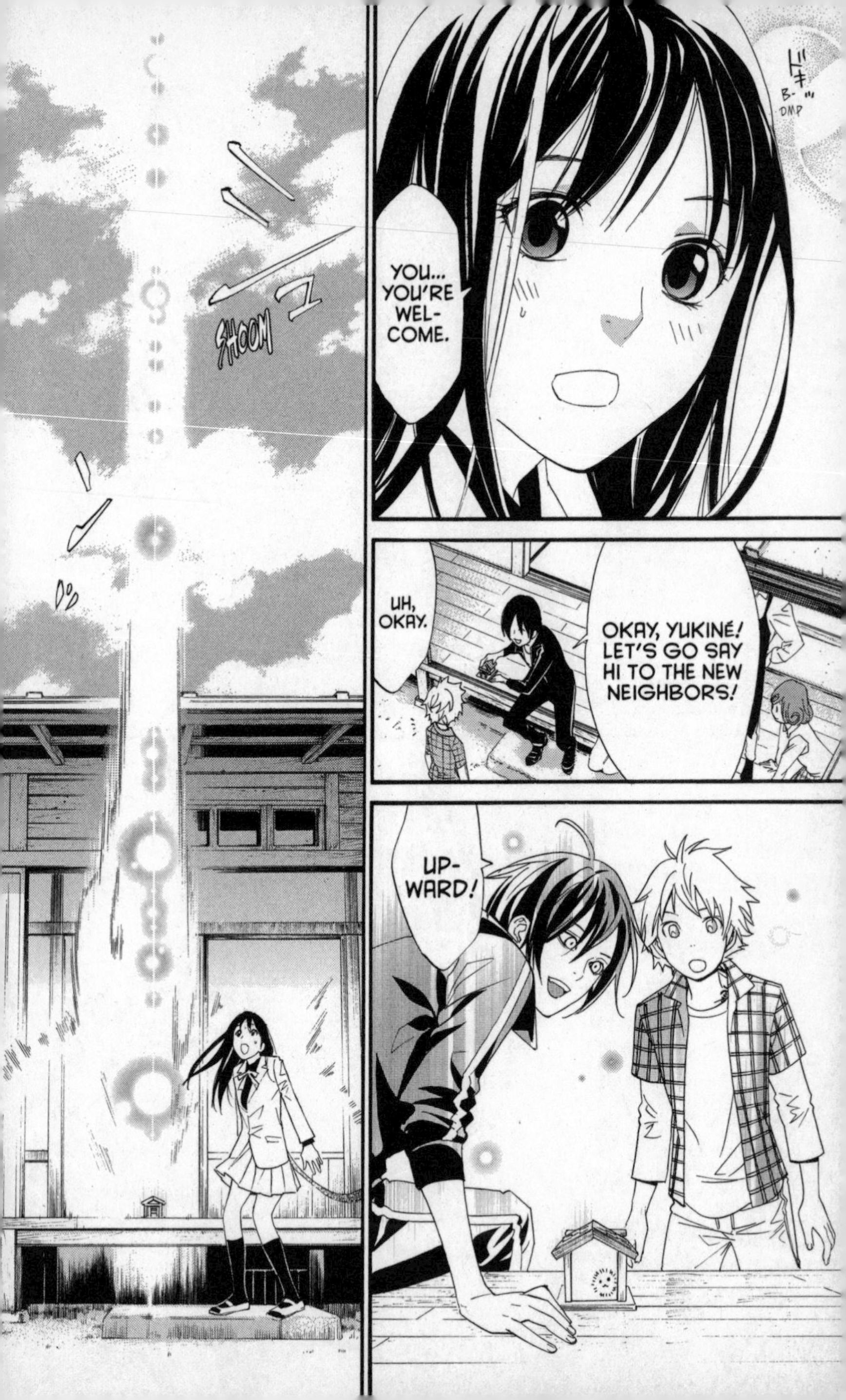
ドキ
B-DMP
YOU... YOU'RE WEL-COME.
OKAY, YUKINÉ! LET'S GO SAY HI TO THE NEW NEIGHBORS!
UH, OKAY.
UP-WARD!
SHOOM

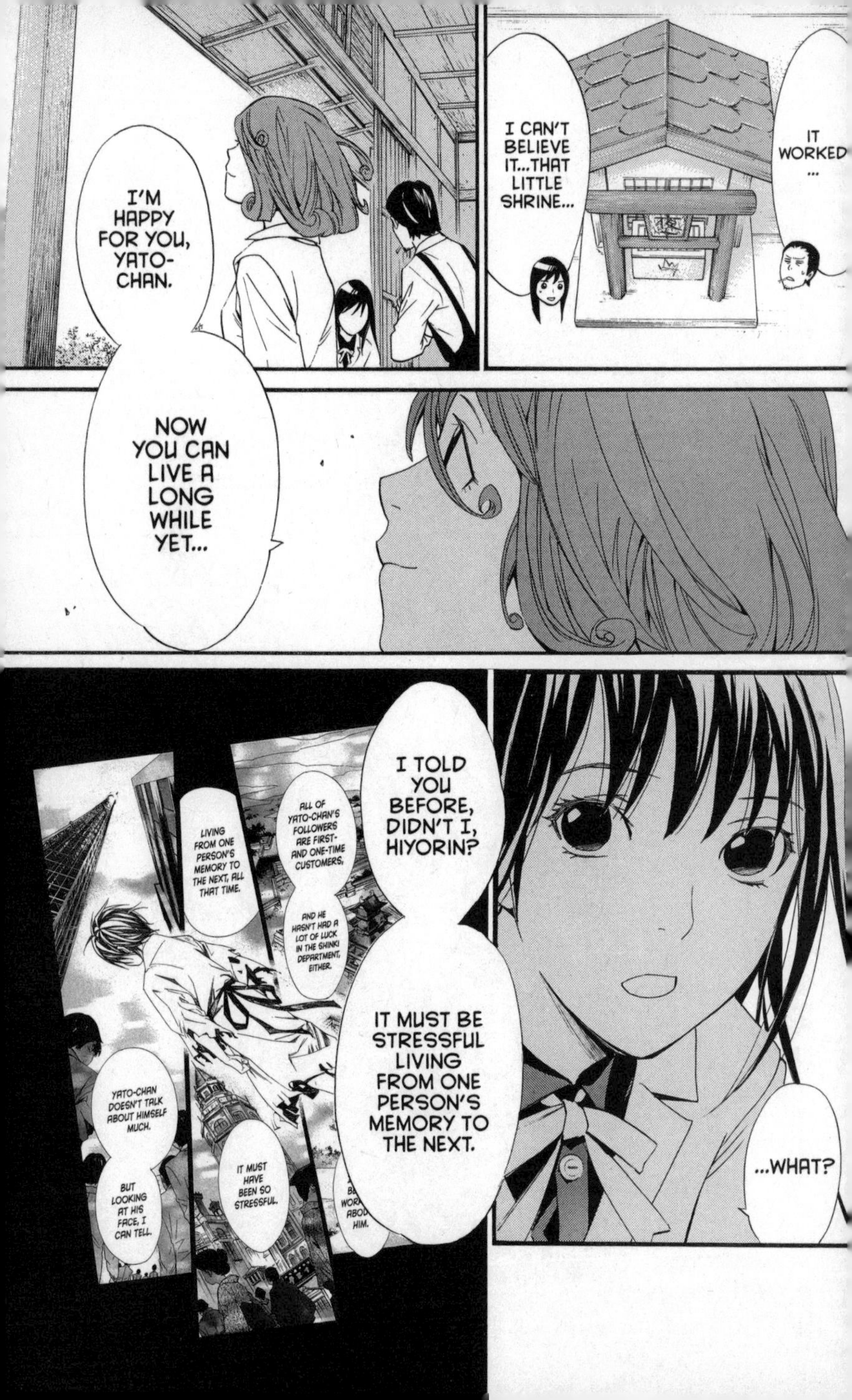
IT WORKED ...
I CAN'T BELIEVE IT...THAT LITTLE SHRINE...
I'M HAPPY FOR YOU, YATO-CHAN.
NOW YOU CAN LIVE A LONG WHILE YET...
...WHAT?
I TOLD YOU BEFORE, DIDN'T I, HIYORIN?
IT MUST BE STRESSFUL LIVING FROM ONE PERSON'S MEMORY TO THE NEXT.
ALL OF YATO-CHAN'S FOLLOWERS ARE FIRST- AND ONE-TIME CUSTOMERS,
AND HE HASN'T HAD A LOT OF LUCK IN THE SHINKI DEPARTMENT, EITHER.
IT MUST HAVE BEEN SO STRESSFUL.
LIVING FROM ONE PERSON'S MEMORY TO THE NEXT, ALL THAT TIME.
YATO-CHAN DOESN'T TALK ABOUT HIMSELF MUCH.
BUT LOOKING AT HIS FACE, I CAN TELL.

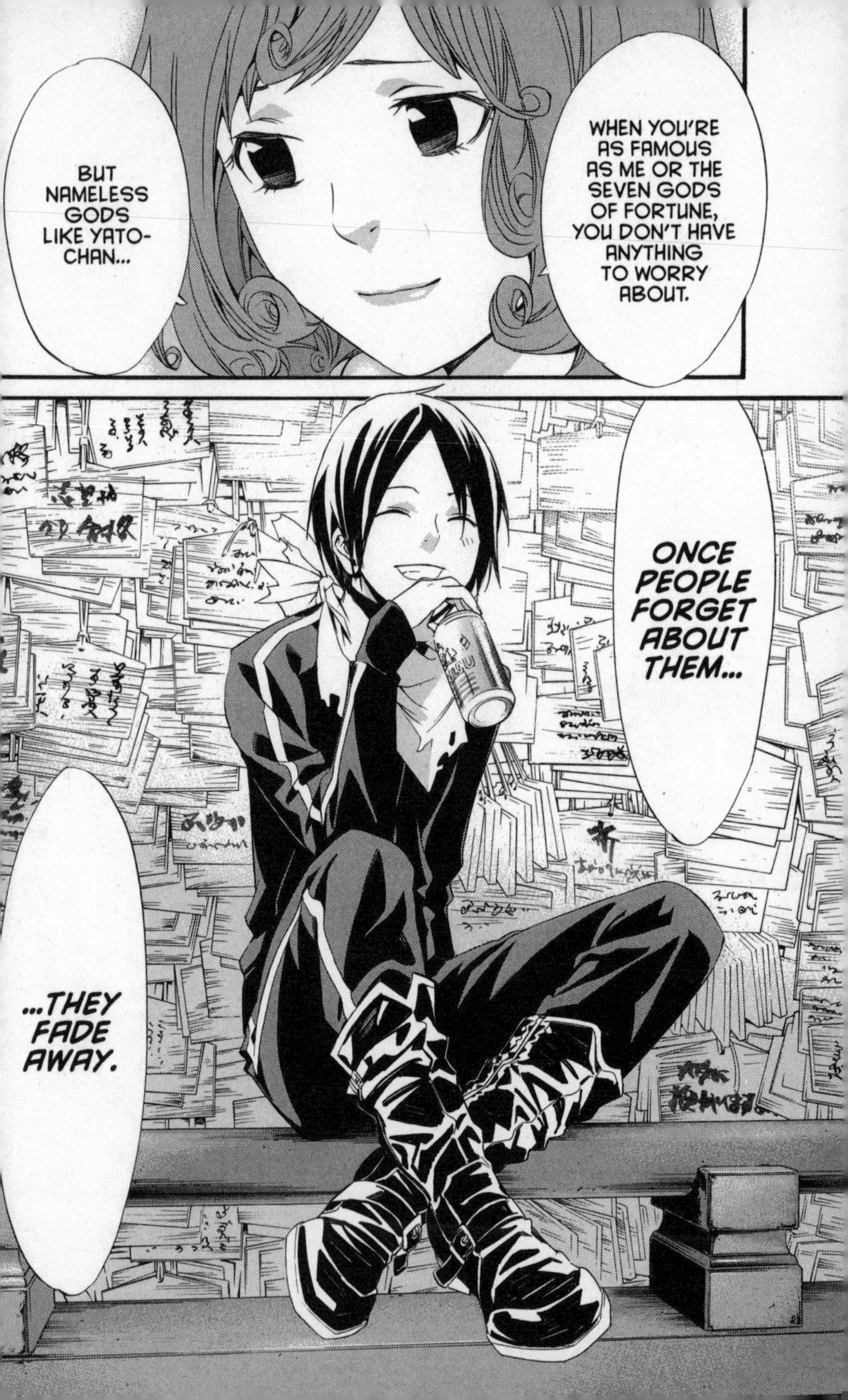
WHEN YOU'RE AS FAMOUS AS ME OR THE SEVEN GODS OF FORTUNE, YOU DON'T HAVE ANYTHING TO WORRY ABOUT.
BUT NAMELESS GODS LIKE YATO-CHAN...
ONCE PEOPLE FORGET ABOUT THEM...
...THEY FADE AWAY.

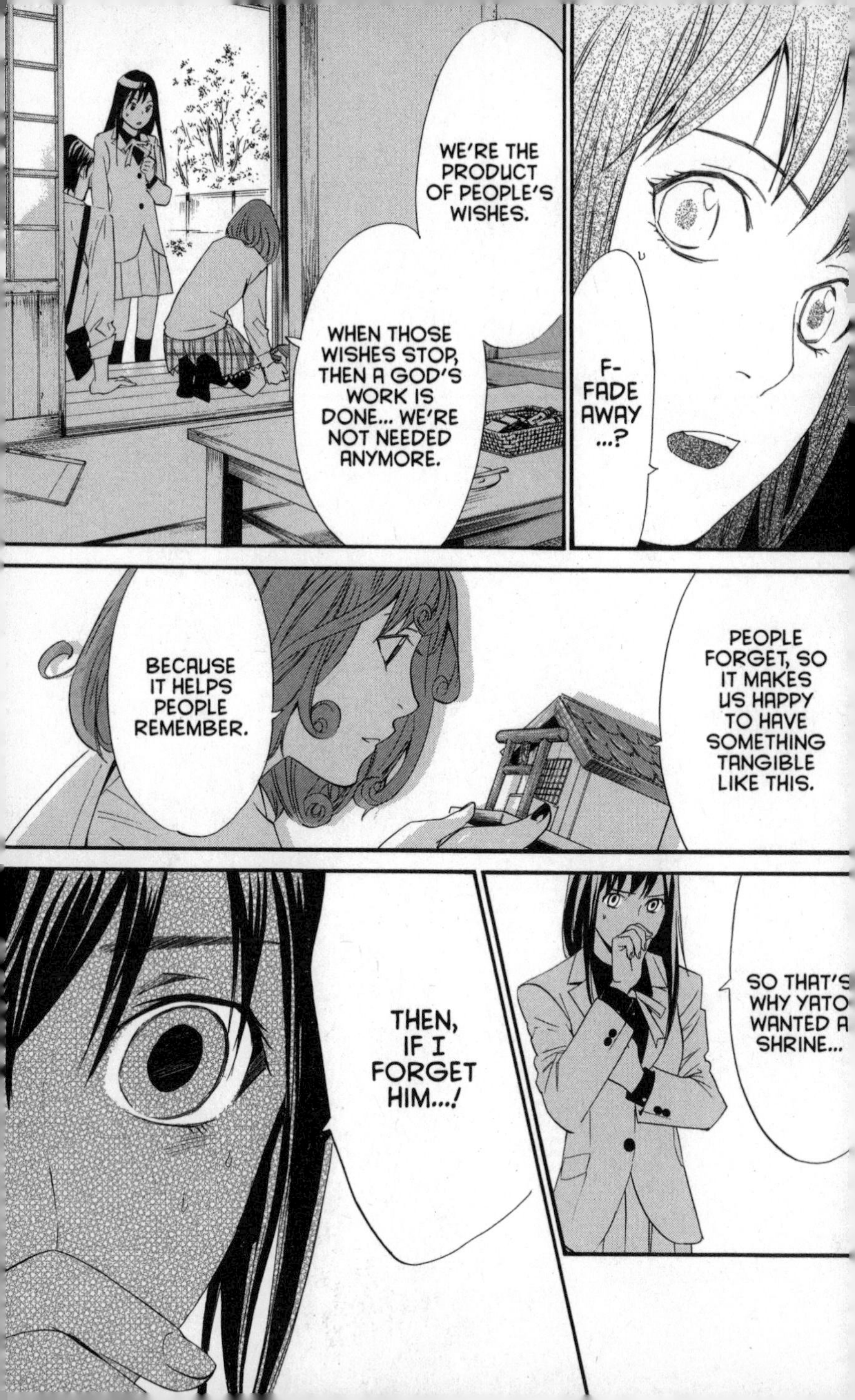
F-FADE AWAY...?
WE'RE THE PRODUCT OF PEOPLE'S WISHES.
WHEN THOSE WISHES STOP, THEN A GOD'S WORK IS DONE... WE'RE NOT NEEDED ANYMORE.
PEOPLE FORGET, SO IT MAKES US HAPPY TO HAVE SOMETHING TANGIBLE LIKE THIS.
BECAUSE IT HELPS PEOPLE REMEMBER.
SO THAT'S WHY YATO WANTED A SHRINE...
THEN, IF I FORGET HIM...!

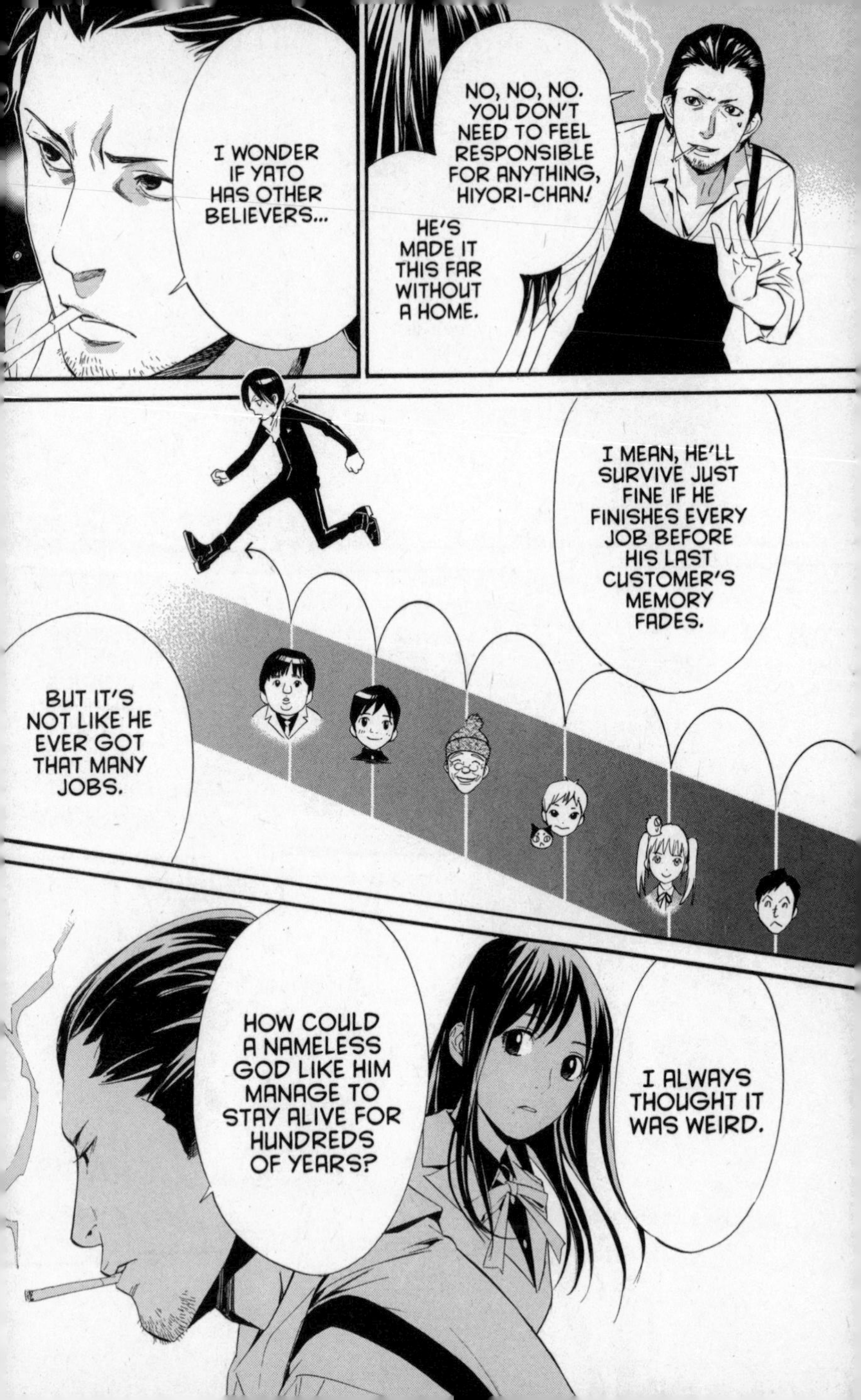
NO, NO, NO. YOU DON'T NEED TO FEEL RESPONSIBLE FOR ANYTHING, HIYORI-CHAN!
HE'S MADE IT THIS FAR WITHOUT A HOME.
I WONDER IF YATO HAS OTHER BELIEVERS...
I MEAN, HE'LL SURVIVE JUST FINE IF HE FINISHES EVERY JOB BEFORE HIS LAST CUSTOMER'S MEMORY FADES.
BUT IT'S NOT LIKE HE EVER GOT THAT MANY JOBS.
I ALWAYS THOUGHT IT WAS WEIRD.
HOW COULD A NAMELESS GOD LIKE HIM MANAGE TO STAY ALIVE FOR HUNDREDS OF YEARS?

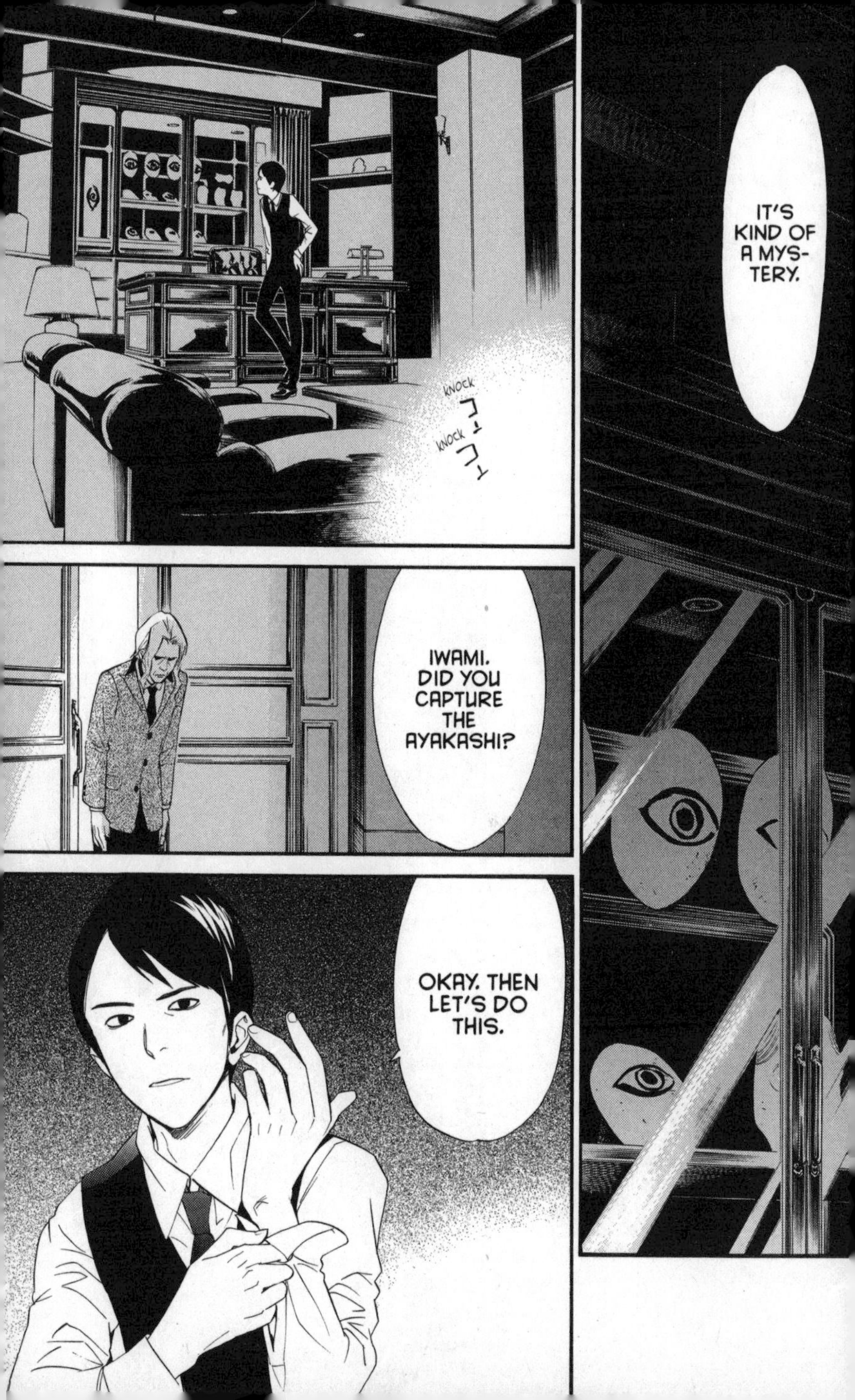
IT'S KIND OF A MYSTERY.
KNOCK
KNOCK
IWAMI. DID YOU CAPTURE THE AYAKASHI?
OKAY. THEN LET'S DO THIS.

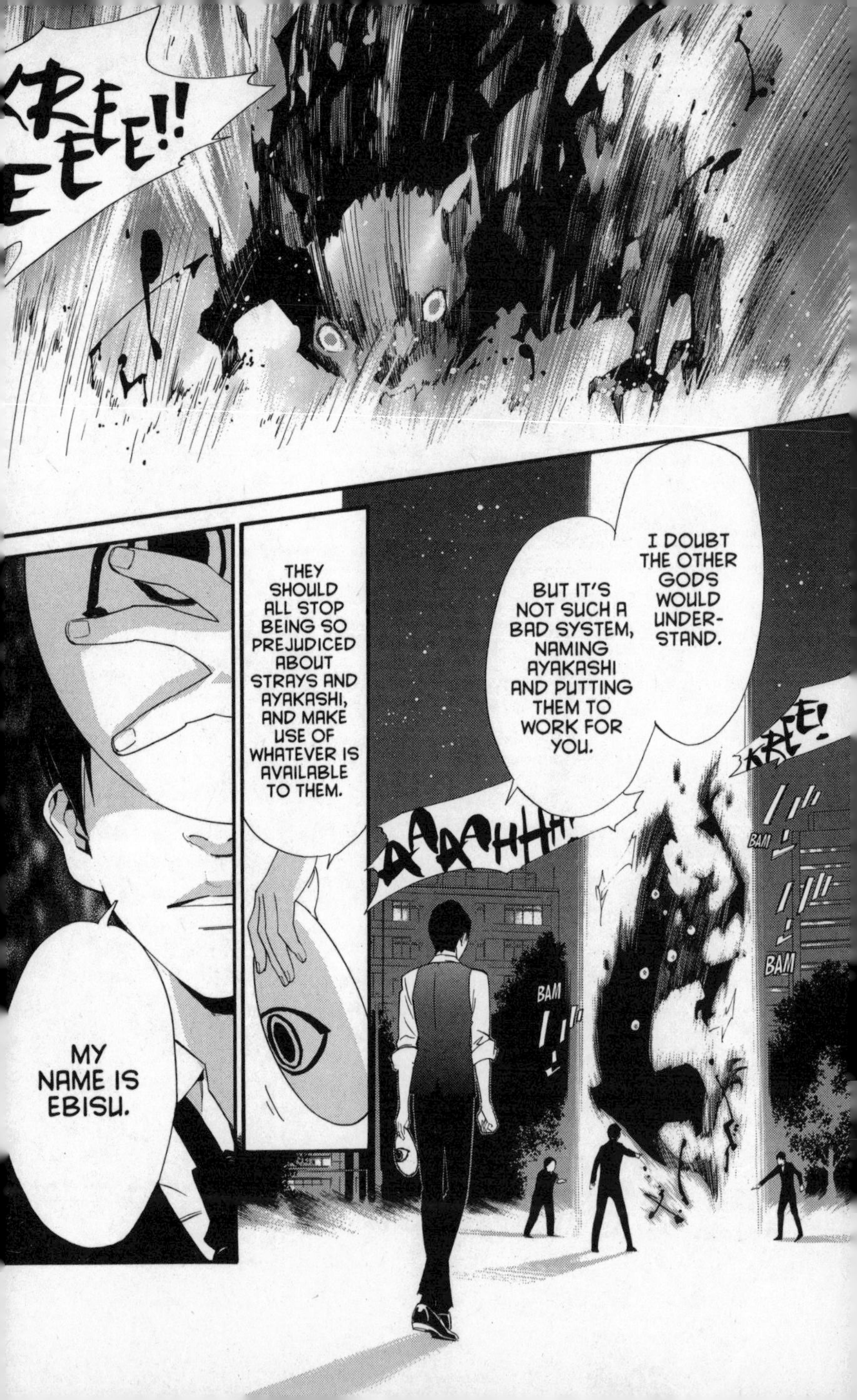
KREEEEE!!
I DOUBT THE OTHER GODS WOULD UNDER-STAND.
BUT IT'S NOT SUCH A BAD SYSTEM, NAMING AYAKASHI AND PUTTING THEM TO WORK FOR YOU.
KREE!
AAAAHHH
BAM
BAM
BAM
THEY SHOULD ALL STOP BEING SO PREJUDICED ABOUT STRAYS AND AYAKASHI, AND MAKE USE OF WHATEVER IS AVAILABLE TO THEM.
MY NAME IS EBISU.

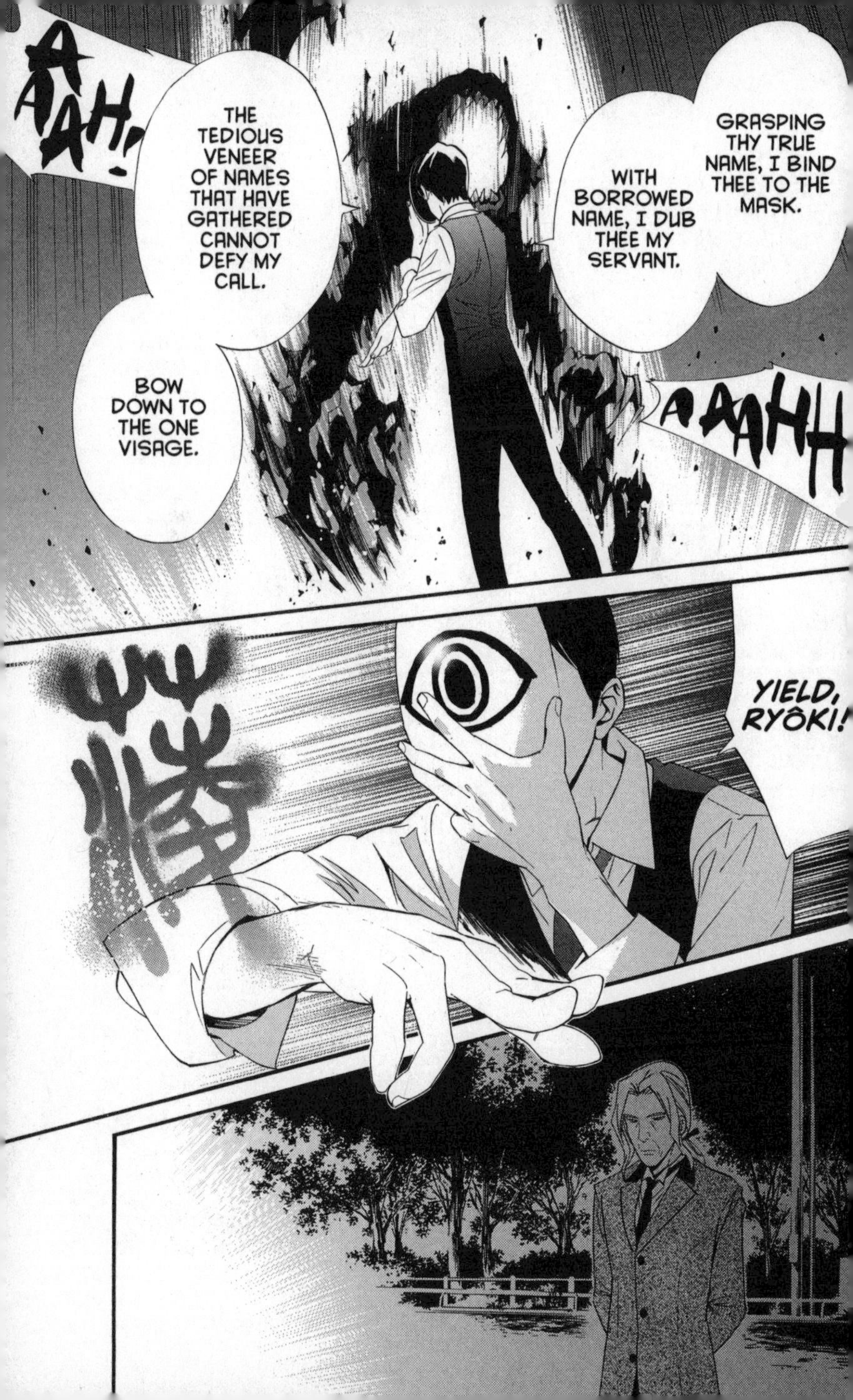
GRASPING THY TRUE NAME, I BIND THEE TO THE MASK.
WITH BORROWED NAME, I DUB THEE MY SERVANT.
THE TEDIOUS VENEER OF NAMES THAT HAVE GATHERED CANNOT DEFY MY CALL.
AAAH!
AAAHH
BOW DOWN TO THE ONE VISAGE.
YIELD, RYÔKI!

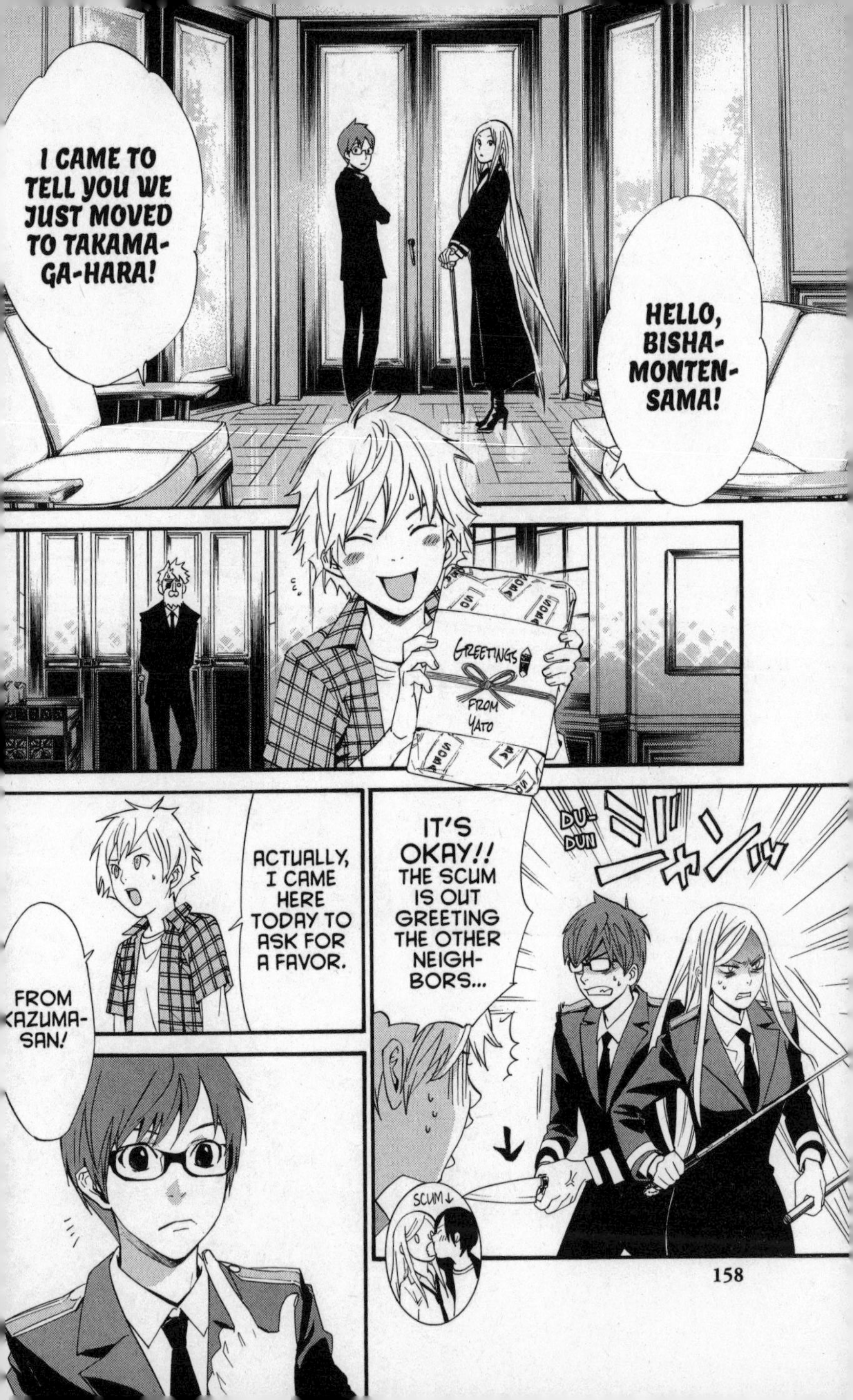
HELLO, BISHA-MONTEN-SAMA!
I CAME TO TELL YOU WE JUST MOVED TO TAKAMA-GA-HARA!
GREETINGS
FROM YATO
SOBA
DU-DUN
IT'S OKAY!! THE SCUM IS OUT GREETING THE OTHER NEIGH-BORS...
SCUM↓
ACTUALLY, I CAME HERE TODAY TO ASK FOR A FAVOR.
FROM KAZUMA-SAN!

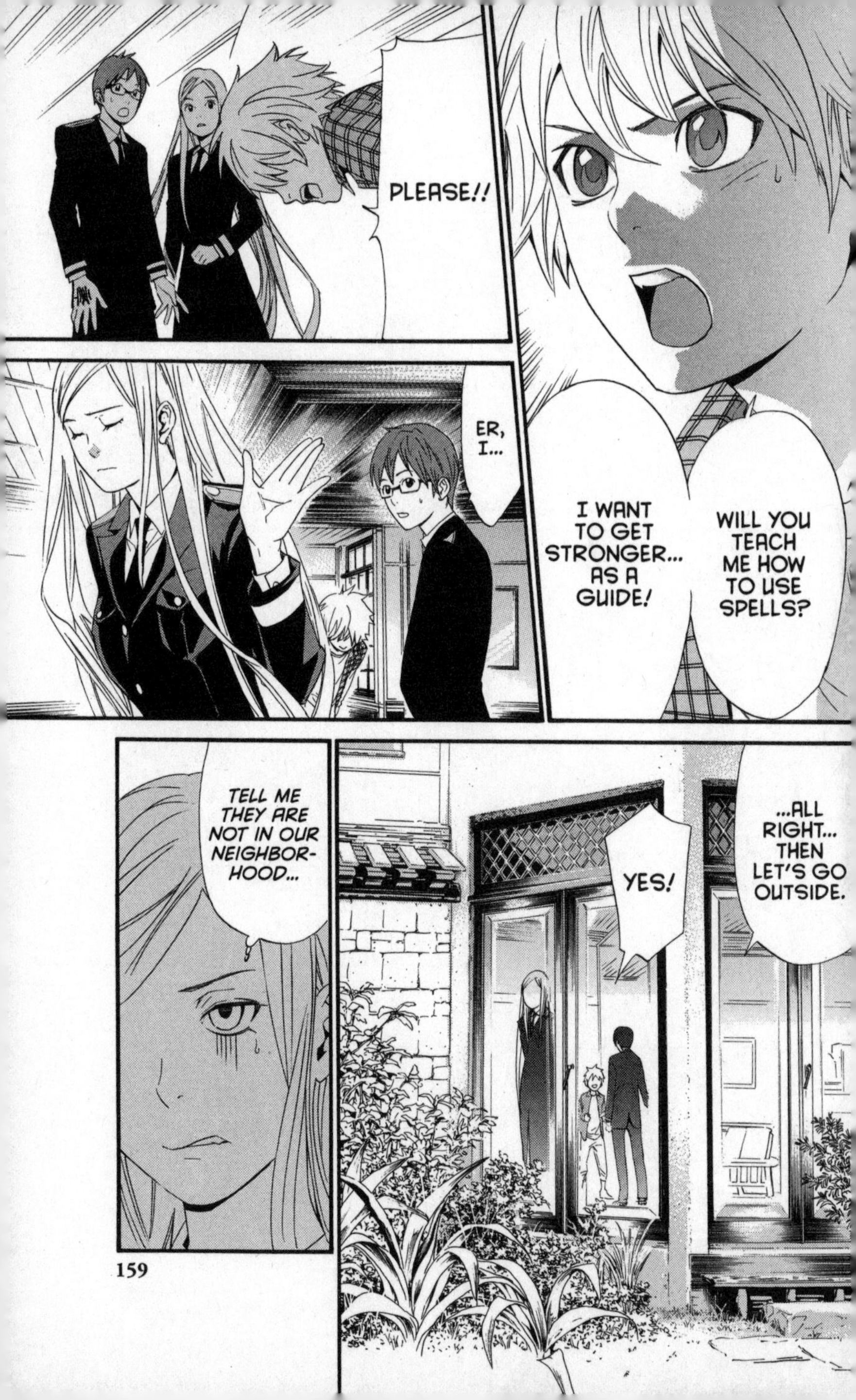
WILL YOU TEACH ME HOW TO USE SPELLS?
I WANT TO GET STRONGER... AS A GUIDE!
PLEASE!!
ER, I...
...ALL RIGHT... THEN LET'S GO OUTSIDE.
YES!
TELL ME THEY ARE NOT IN OUR NEIGHBOR-HOOD...

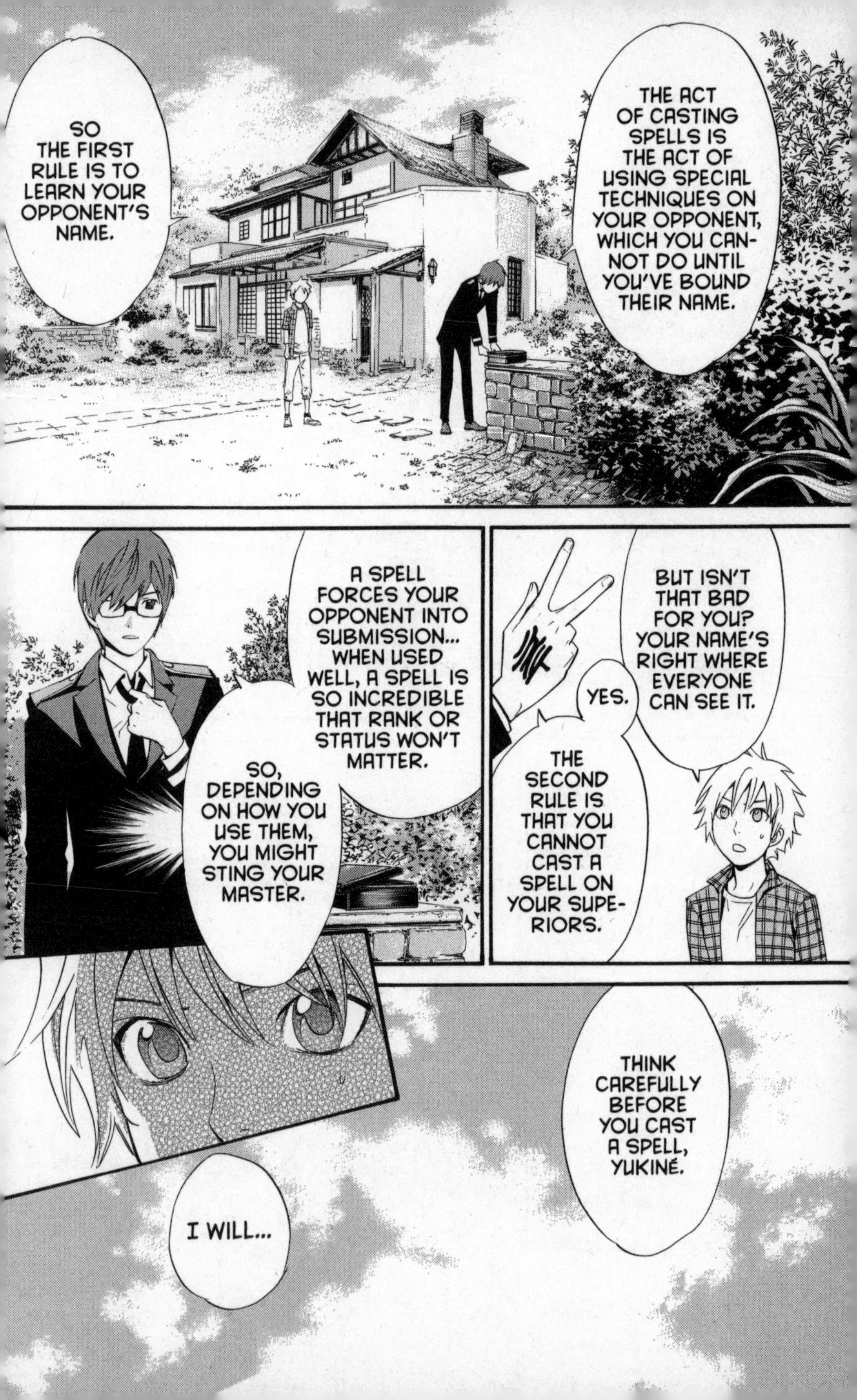
THE ACT OF CASTING SPELLS IS THE ACT OF USING SPECIAL TECHNIQUES ON YOUR OPPONENT, WHICH YOU CAN-NOT DO UNTIL YOU'VE BOUND THEIR NAME.
SO THE FIRST RULE IS TO LEARN YOUR OPPONENT'S NAME.
BUT ISN'T THAT BAD FOR YOU? YOUR NAME'S RIGHT WHERE EVERYONE CAN SEE IT.
YES.
THE SECOND RULE IS THAT YOU CANNOT CAST A SPELL ON YOUR SUPE-RIORS.
A SPELL FORCES YOUR OPPONENT INTO SUBMISSION... WHEN USED WELL, A SPELL IS SO INCREDIBLE THAT RANK OR STATUS WON'T MATTER.
SO, DEPENDING ON HOW YOU USE THEM, YOU MIGHT STING YOUR MASTER.
THINK CAREFULLY BEFORE YOU CAST A SPELL, YUKINÉ.
I WILL...

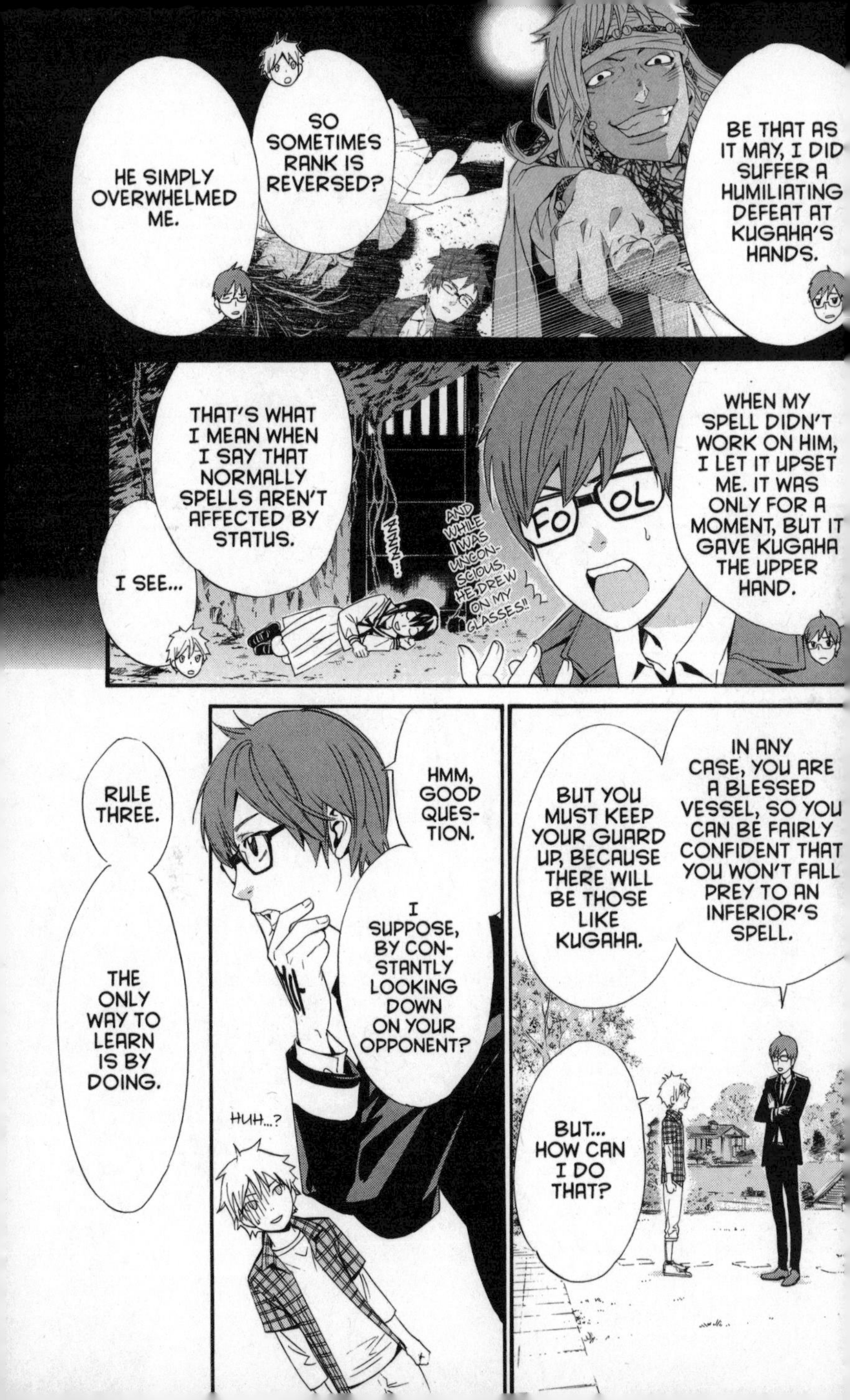
BE THAT AS IT MAY, I DID SUFFER A HUMILIATING DEFEAT AT KUGAHA'S HANDS.
SO SOMETIMES RANK IS REVERSED?
HE SIMPLY OVERWHELMED ME.
WHEN MY SPELL DIDN'T WORK ON HIM, I LET IT UPSET ME. IT WAS ONLY FOR A MOMENT, BUT IT GAVE KUGAHA THE UPPER HAND.
FOOL
AND WHILE I WAS UNCON-SCIOUS, HE DREW ON MY GLASSES!!
NNN...
THAT'S WHAT I MEAN WHEN I SAY THAT NORMALLY SPELLS AREN'T AFFECTED BY STATUS.
I SEE...
IN ANY CASE, YOU ARE A BLESSED VESSEL, SO YOU CAN BE FAIRLY CONFIDENT THAT YOU WON'T FALL PREY TO AN INFERIOR'S SPELL.
BUT YOU MUST KEEP YOUR GUARD UP, BECAUSE THERE WILL BE THOSE LIKE KUGAHA.
BUT... HOW CAN I DO THAT?
HMM, GOOD QUES-TION.
I SUPPOSE, BY CON-STANTLY LOOKING DOWN ON YOUR OPPONENT?
RULE THREE.
THE ONLY WAY TO LEARN IS BY DOING.
HUH...?

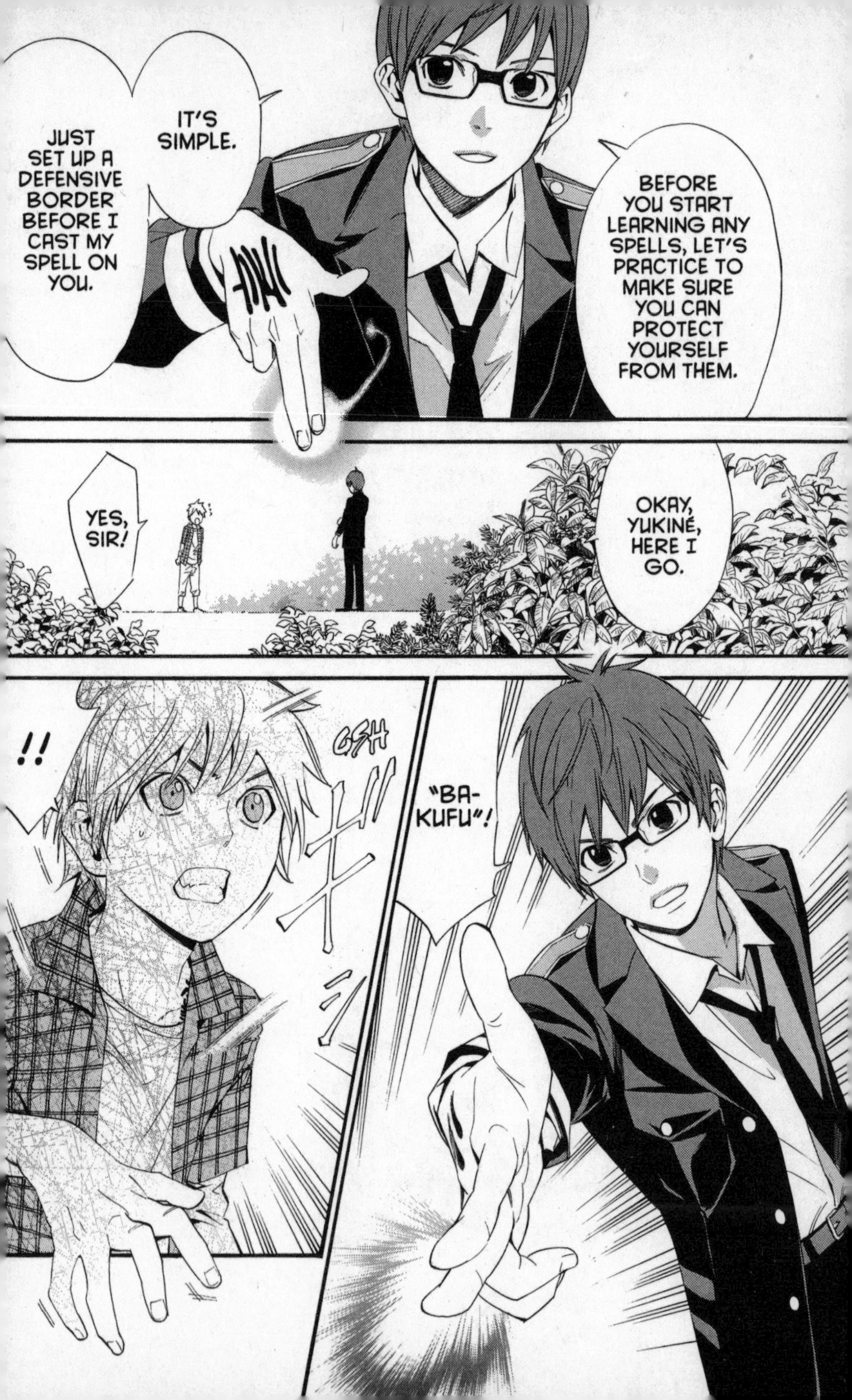
BEFORE YOU START LEARNING ANY SPELLS, LET'S PRACTICE TO MAKE SURE YOU CAN PROTECT YOURSELF FROM THEM.
IT'S SIMPLE.
JUST SET UP A DEFENSIVE BORDER BEFORE I CAST MY SPELL ON YOU.
OKAY, YUKINÉ, HERE I GO.
YES, SIR!
"BA-KUFU"!
GSH
!!

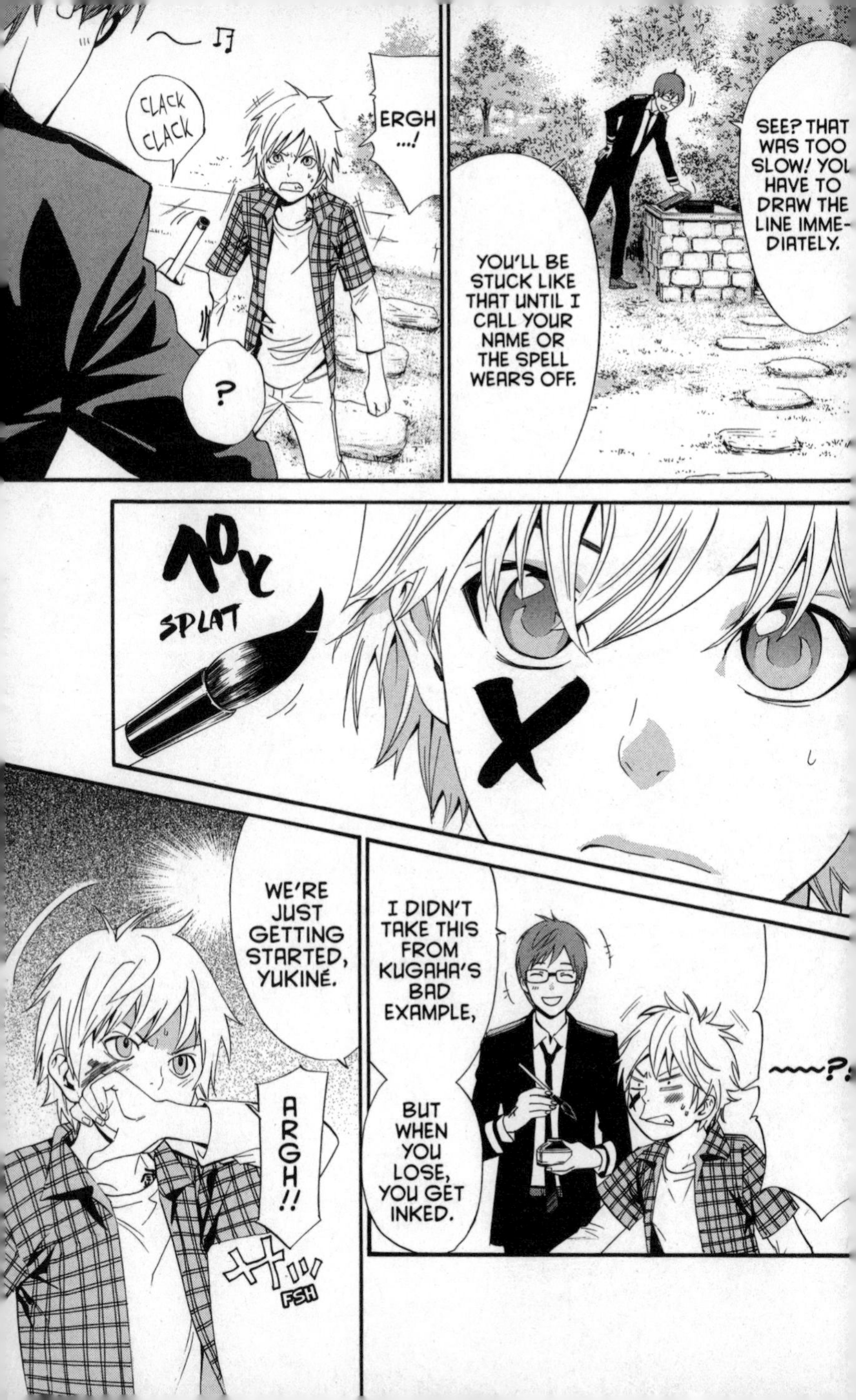
SEE? THAT WAS TOO SLOW! YOU HAVE TO DRAW THE LINE IMMEDIATELY.
YOU'LL BE STUCK LIKE THAT UNTIL I CALL YOUR NAME OR THE SPELL WEARS OFF.
ERGH ...!
CLACK CLACK
?
SPLAT
I DIDN'T TAKE THIS FROM KUGAHA'S BAD EXAMPLE,
BUT WHEN YOU LOSE, YOU GET INKED.
~~~?!
WE'RE JUST GETTING STARTED, YUKINÉ.
ARGH!!
FSH
~~~

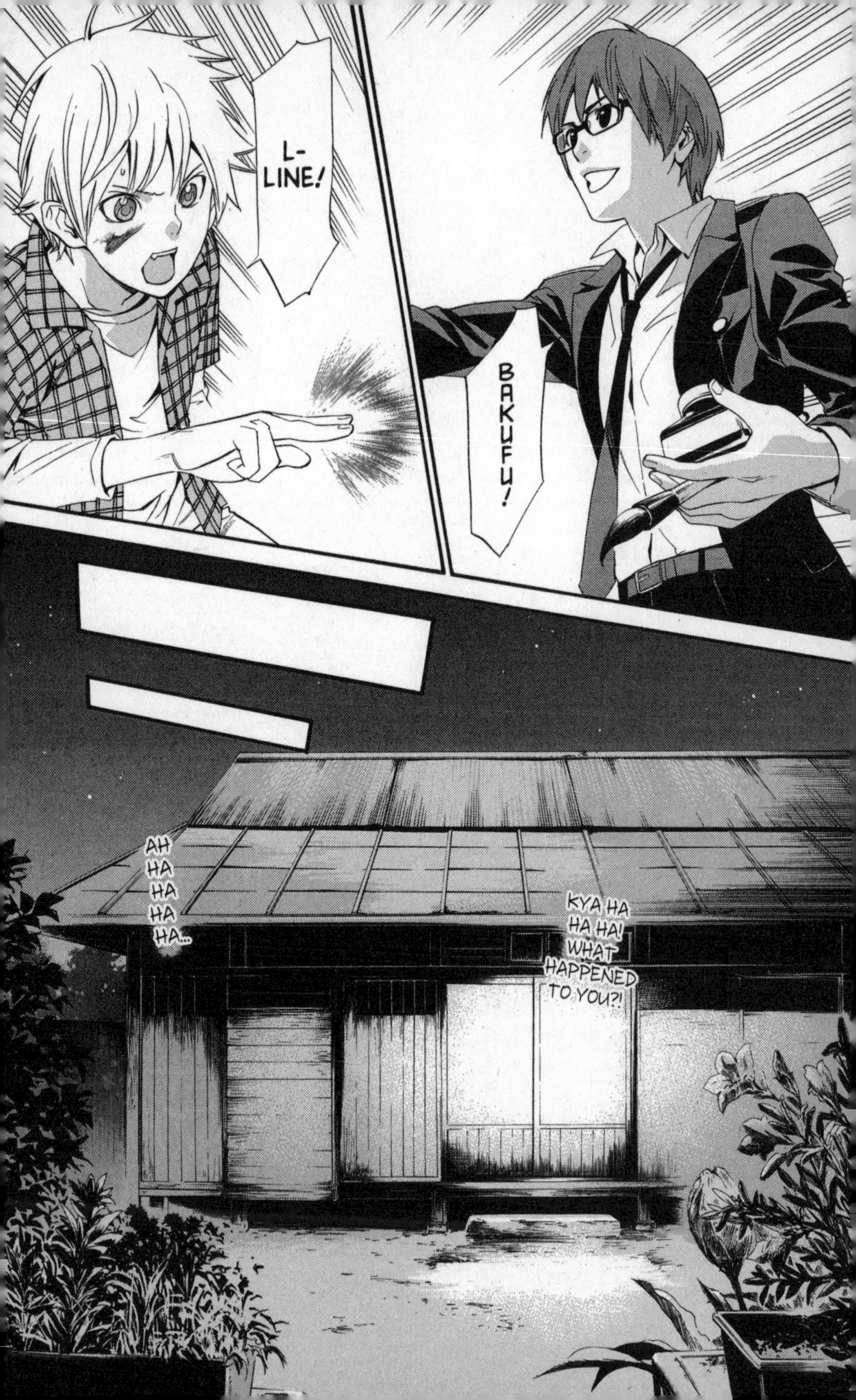
BAKUFU!
L-
LINE!
KYA HA HA HA! WHAT HAPPENED TO YOU?!
AH HA HA HA HA...

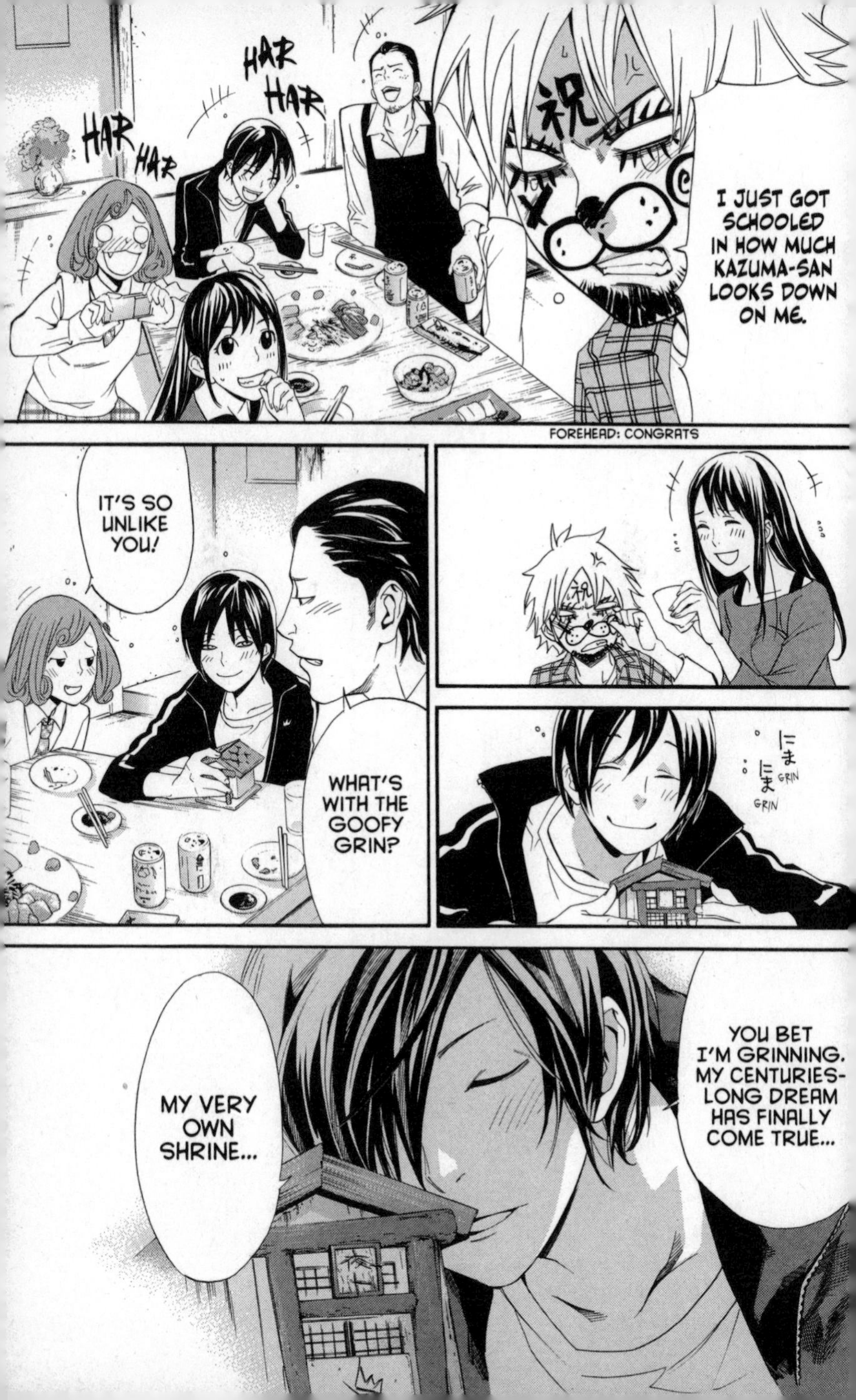
I JUST GOT SCHOOLED IN HOW MUCH KAZUMA-SAN LOOKS DOWN ON ME.
HAR HAR
HAR HAR
祝
FOREHEAD: CONGRATS
にま GRIN
にま GRIN
IT'S SO UNLIKE YOU!
WHAT'S WITH THE GOOFY GRIN?
YOU BET I'M GRINNING. MY CENTURIES-LONG DREAM HAS FINALLY COME TRUE...
MY VERY OWN SHRINE...

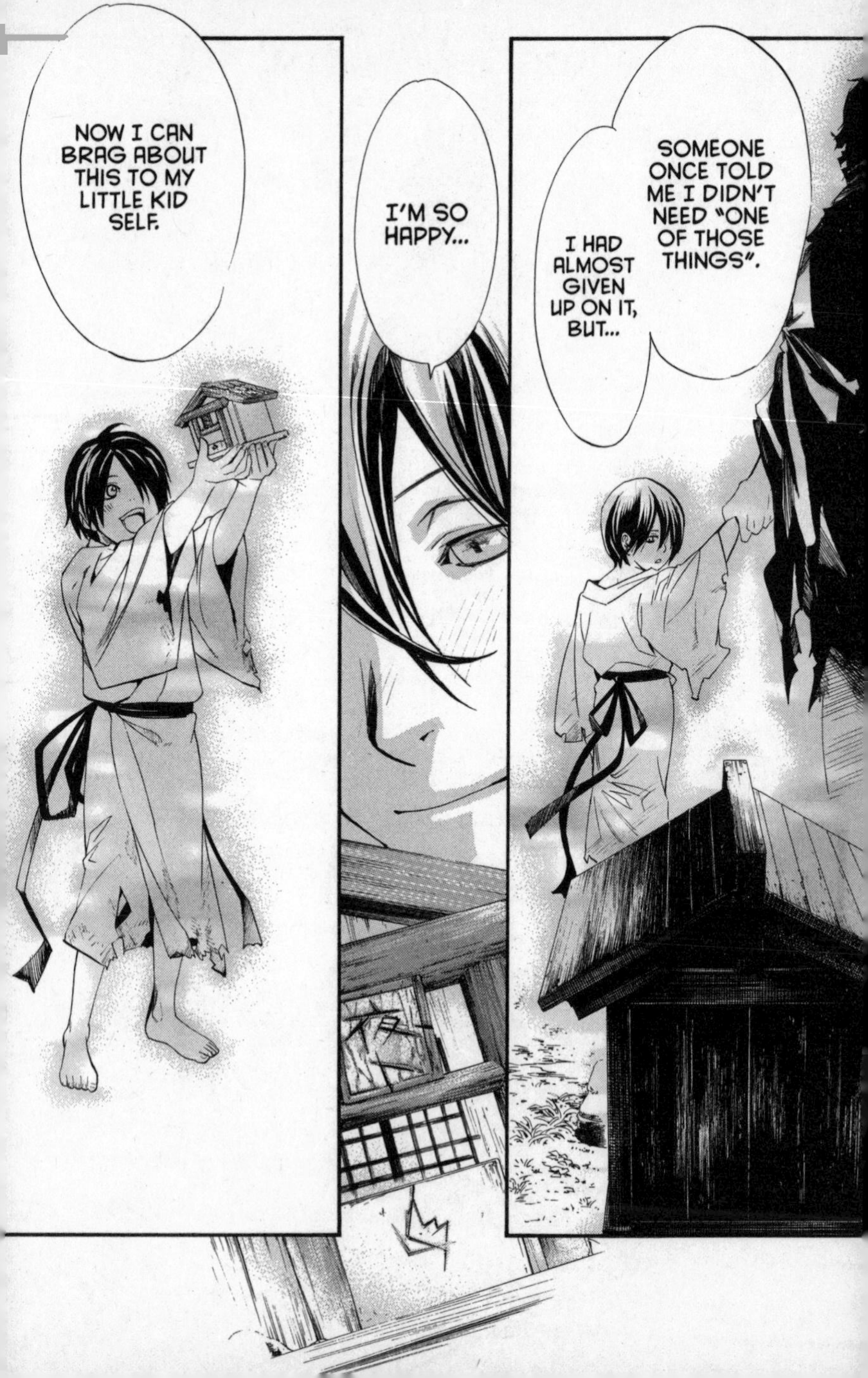
SOMEONE ONCE TOLD ME I DIDN'T NEED "ONE OF THOSE THINGS".
I HAD ALMOST GIVEN UP ON IT, BUT...
I'M SO HAPPY...
NOW I CAN BRAG ABOUT THIS TO MY LITTLE KID SELF.

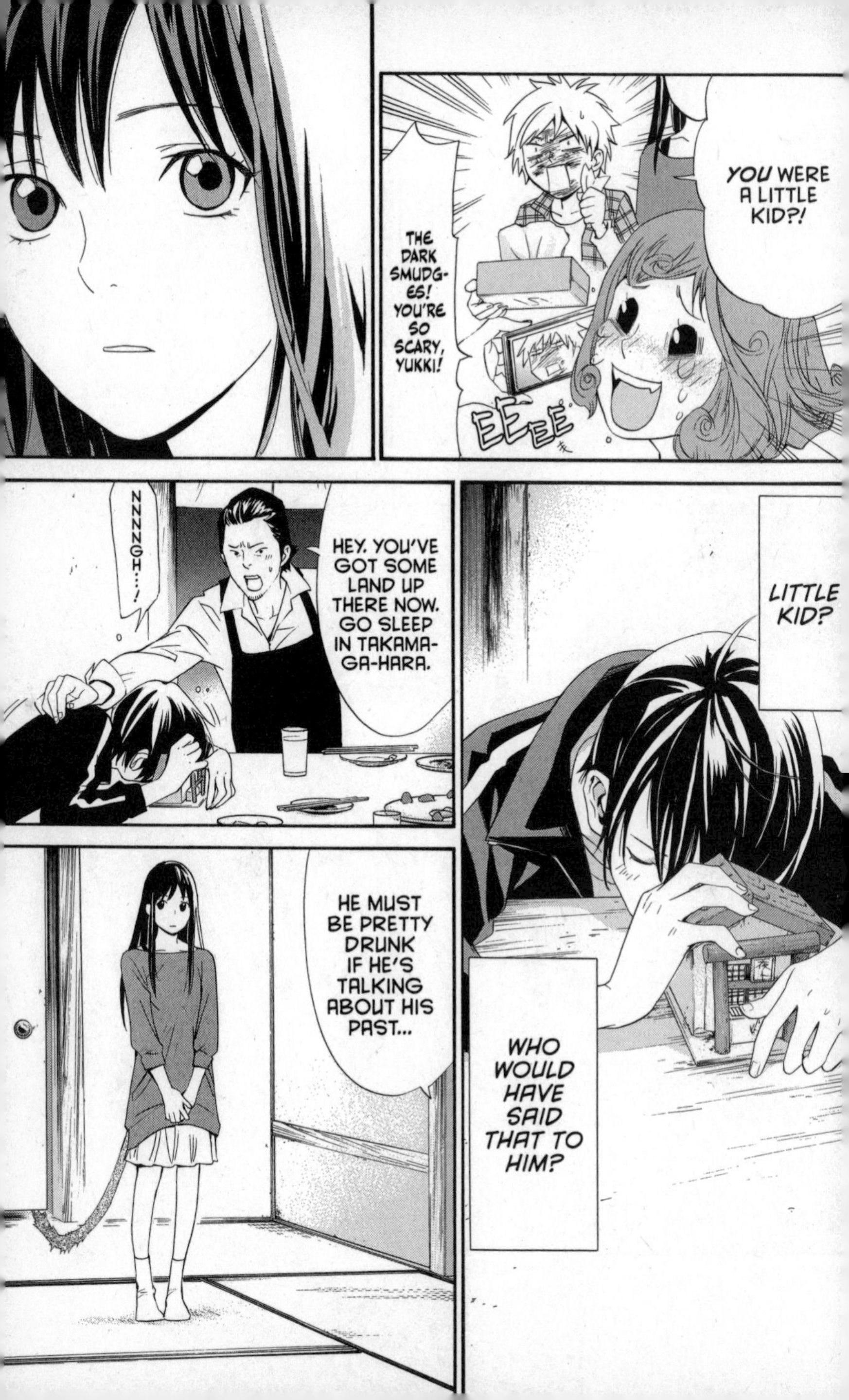
YOU WERE A LITTLE KID?!
THE DARK SMUDGES! YOU'RE SO SCARY, YUKKI!
EEEEE
LITTLE KID?
WHO WOULD HAVE SAID THAT TO HIM?
HEY. YOU'VE GOT SOME LAND UP THERE NOW. GO SLEEP IN TAKAMA-GA-HARA.
NNNNGH...!
HE MUST BE PRETTY DRUNK IF HE'S TALKING ABOUT HIS PAST...

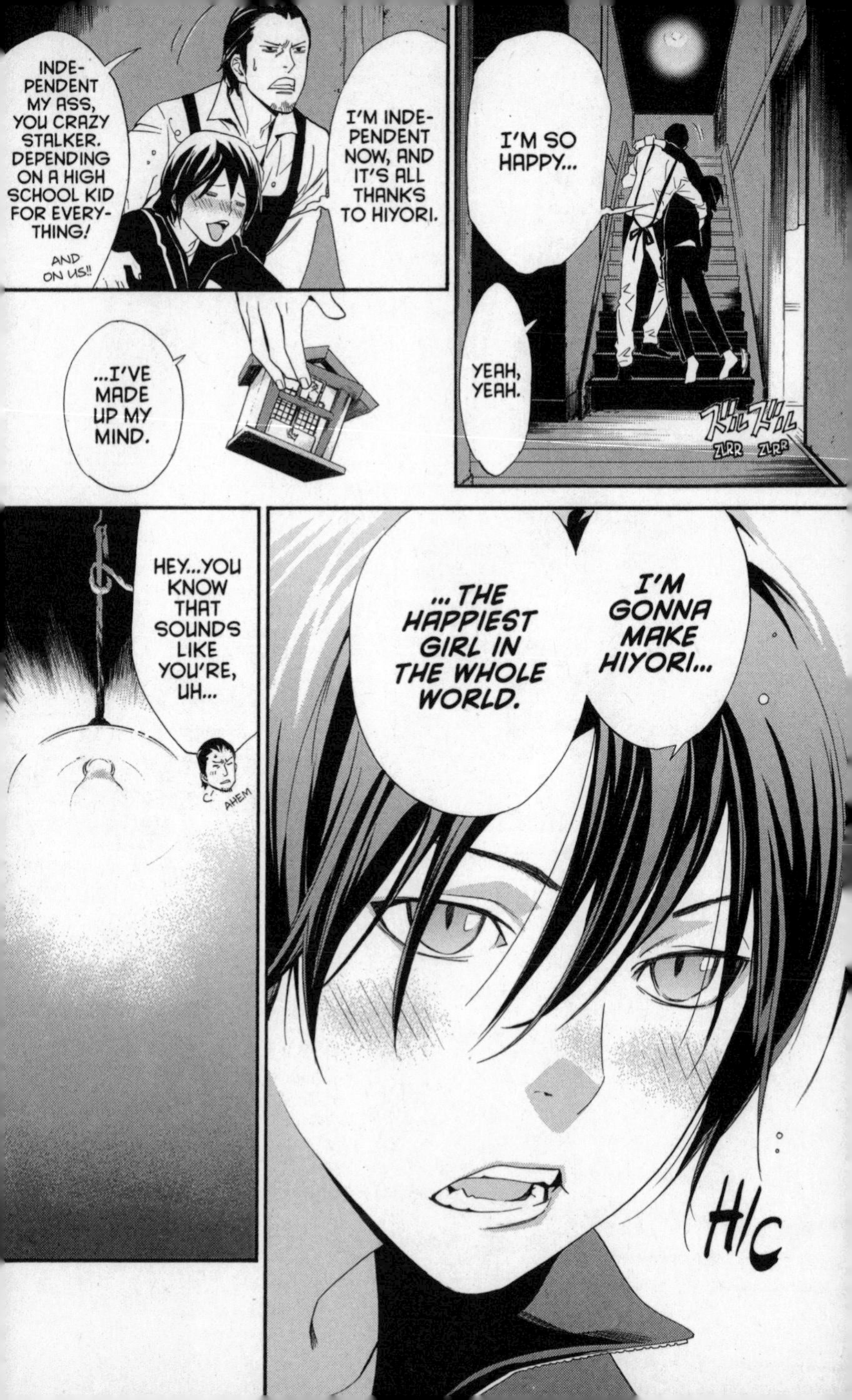
I'M SO HAPPY...
YEAH, YEAH.
ズルズル
ZLRR ZLRR
I'M INDEPENDENT NOW, AND IT'S ALL THANKS TO HIYORI.
INDEPENDENT MY ASS, YOU CRAZY STALKER. DEPENDING ON A HIGH SCHOOL KID FOR EVERYTHING!
AND ON US!!
...I'VE MADE UP MY MIND.
I'M GONNA MAKE HIYORI...
...THE HAPPIEST GIRL IN THE WHOLE WORLD.
HIC
HEY...YOU KNOW THAT SOUNDS LIKE YOU'RE, UH...
AHEM

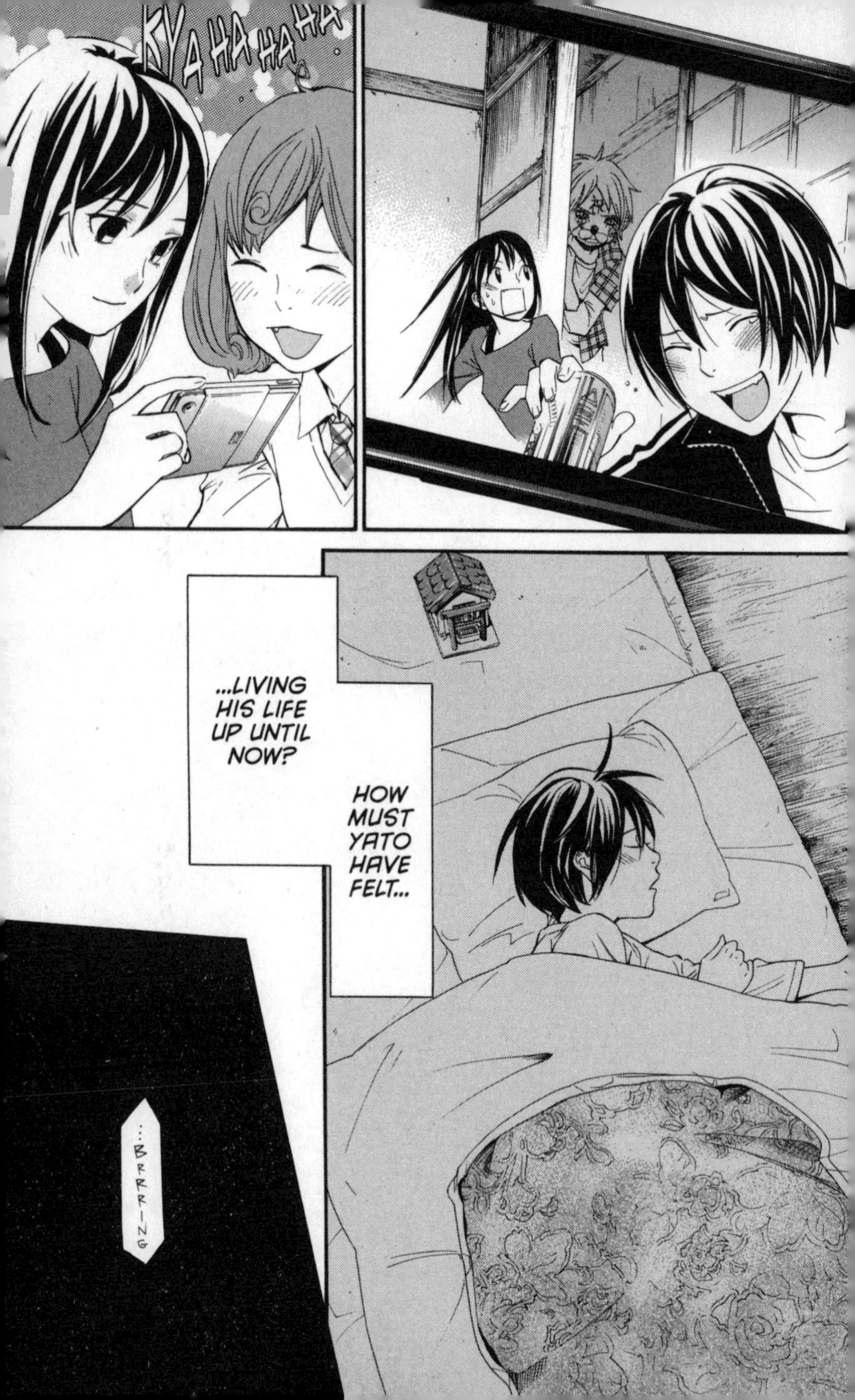
KYAHAHAHA
HOW MUST YATO HAVE FELT...
...LIVING HIS LIFE UP UNTIL NOW?
...BRRRING

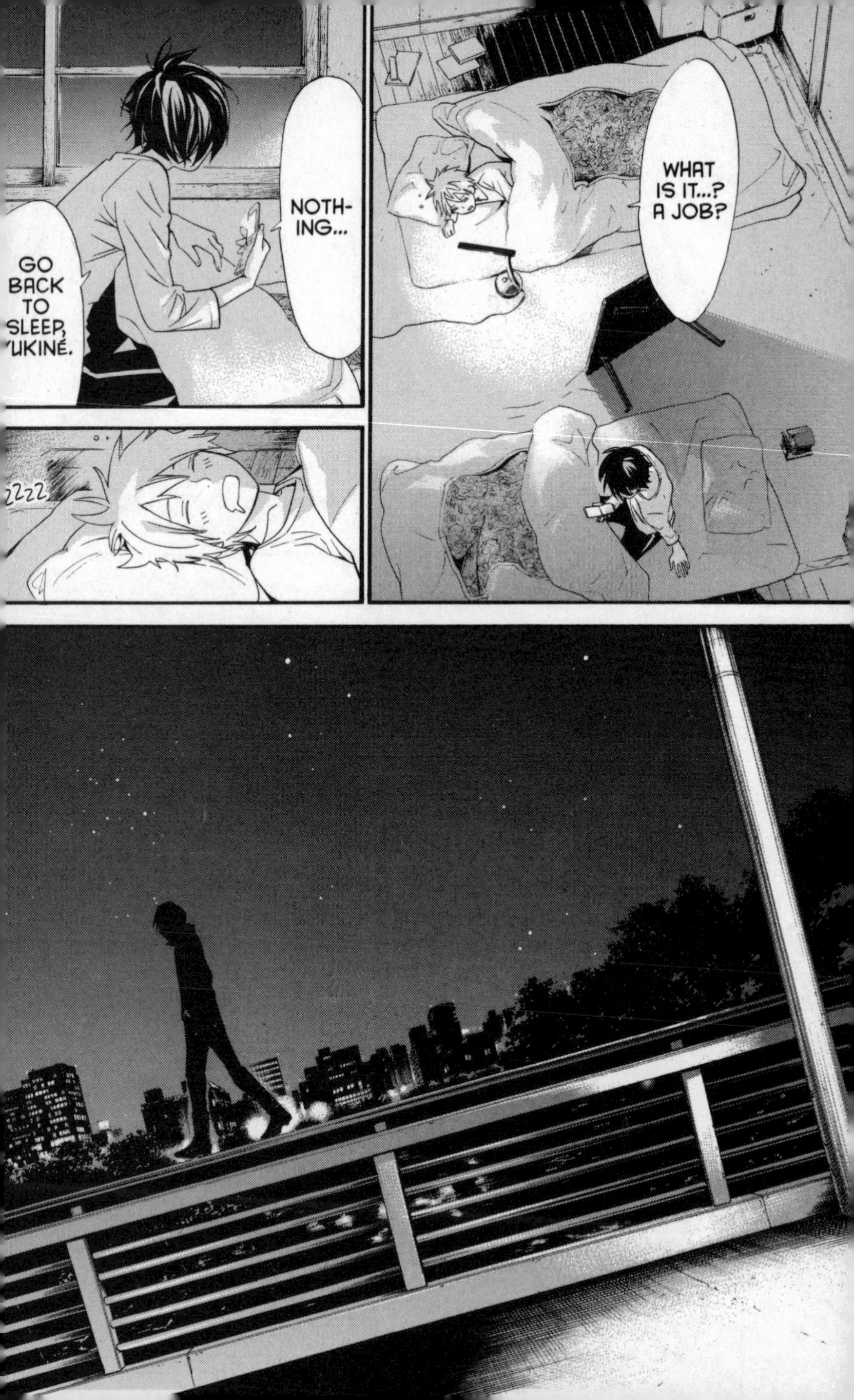
WHAT IS IT...? A JOB?
NOTH-ING...
GO BACK TO SLEEP, YUKINÉ.
ZZZZ

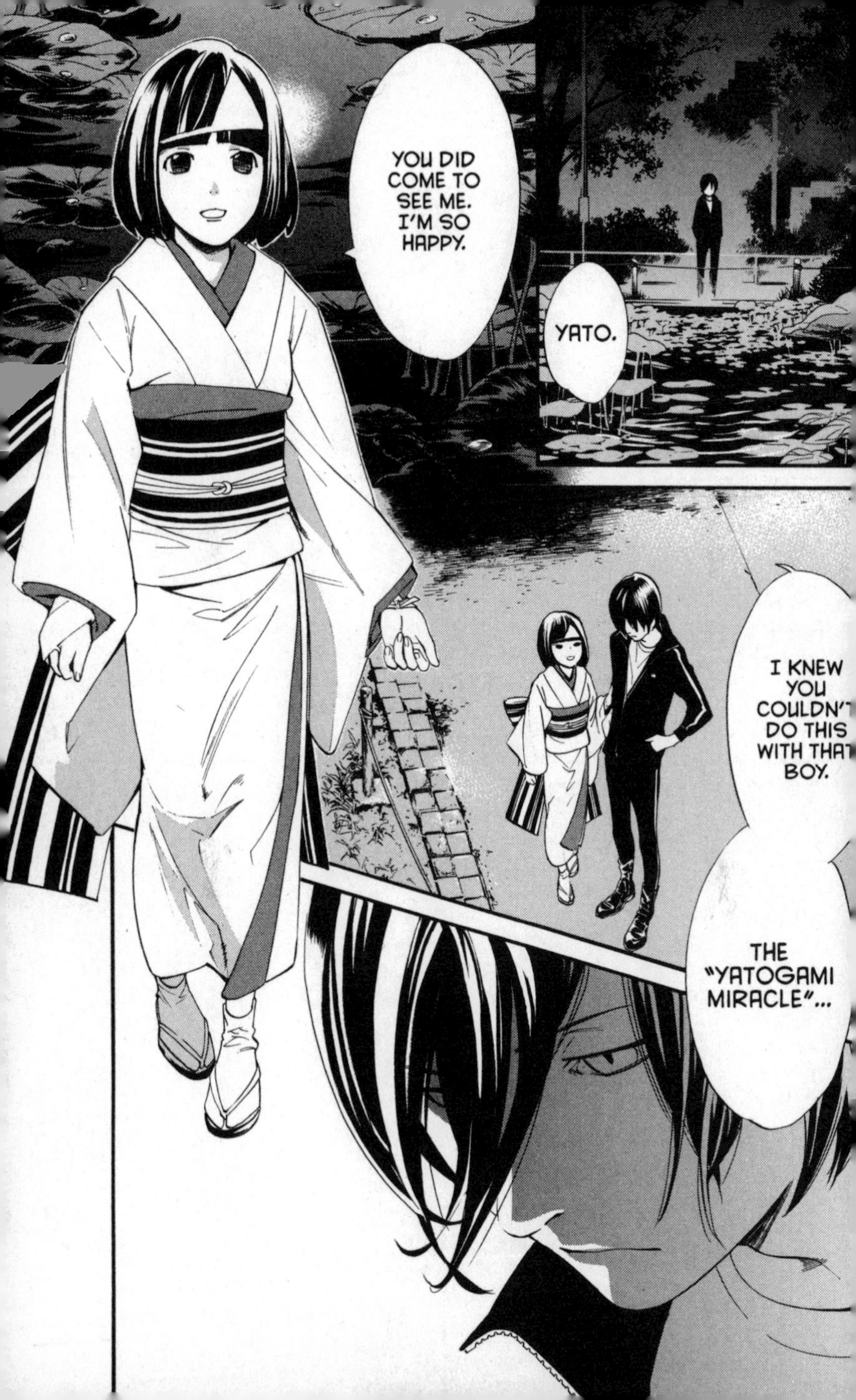
YATO.
YOU DID COME TO SEE ME. I'M SO HAPPY.
I KNEW YOU COULDN'T DO THIS WITH THAT BOY.
THE "YATOGAMI MIRACLE"...

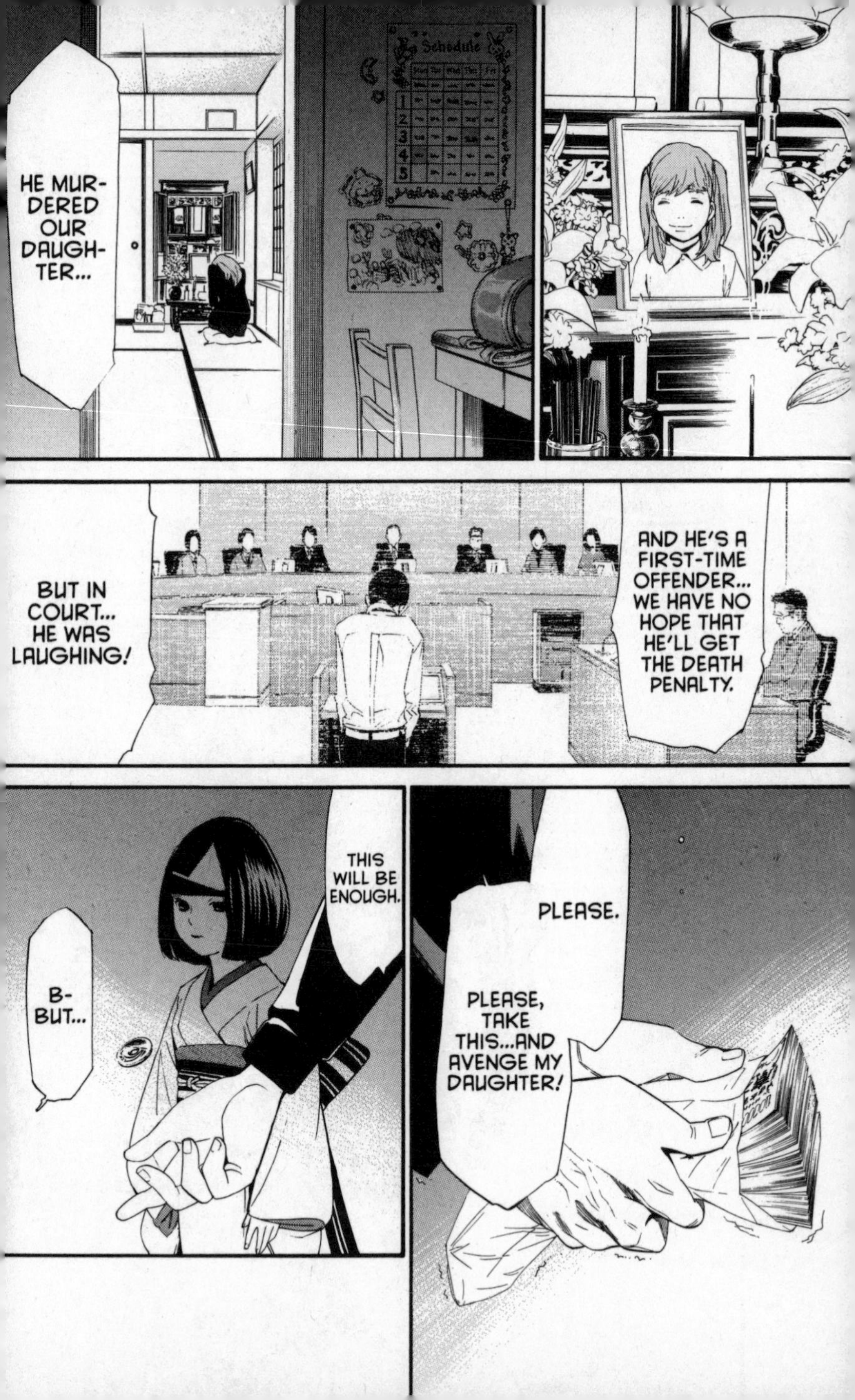
HE MURDERED OUR DAUGHTER...
AND HE'S A FIRST-TIME OFFENDER... WE HAVE NO HOPE THAT HE'LL GET THE DEATH PENALTY.
BUT IN COURT... HE WAS LAUGHING!
PLEASE.
PLEASE, TAKE THIS...AND AVENGE MY DAUGHTER!
THIS WILL BE ENOUGH.
B-BUT...

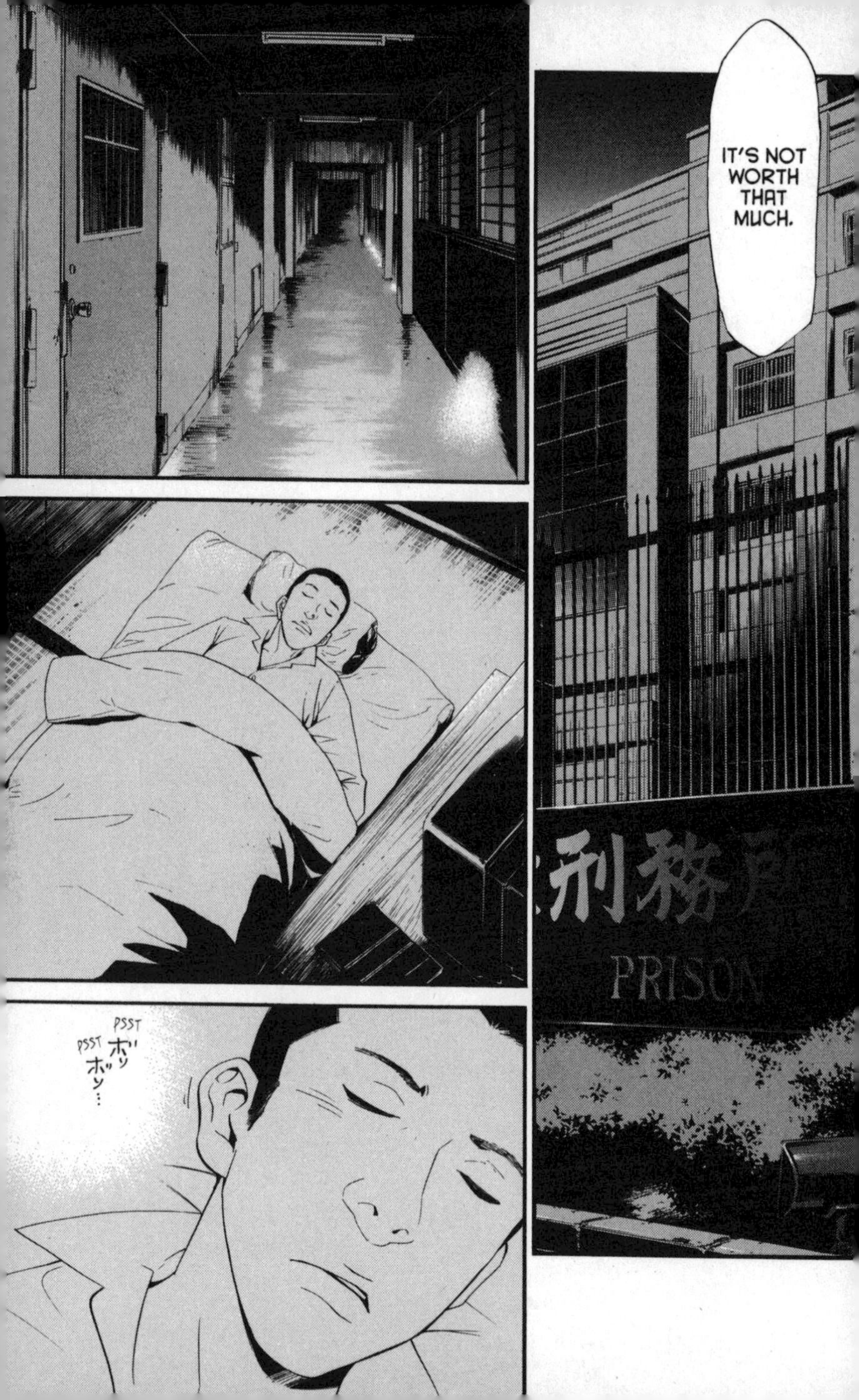
IT'S NOT WORTH THAT MUCH.
刑務
PRISON
PSST
ボソ
PSST
ボソ…

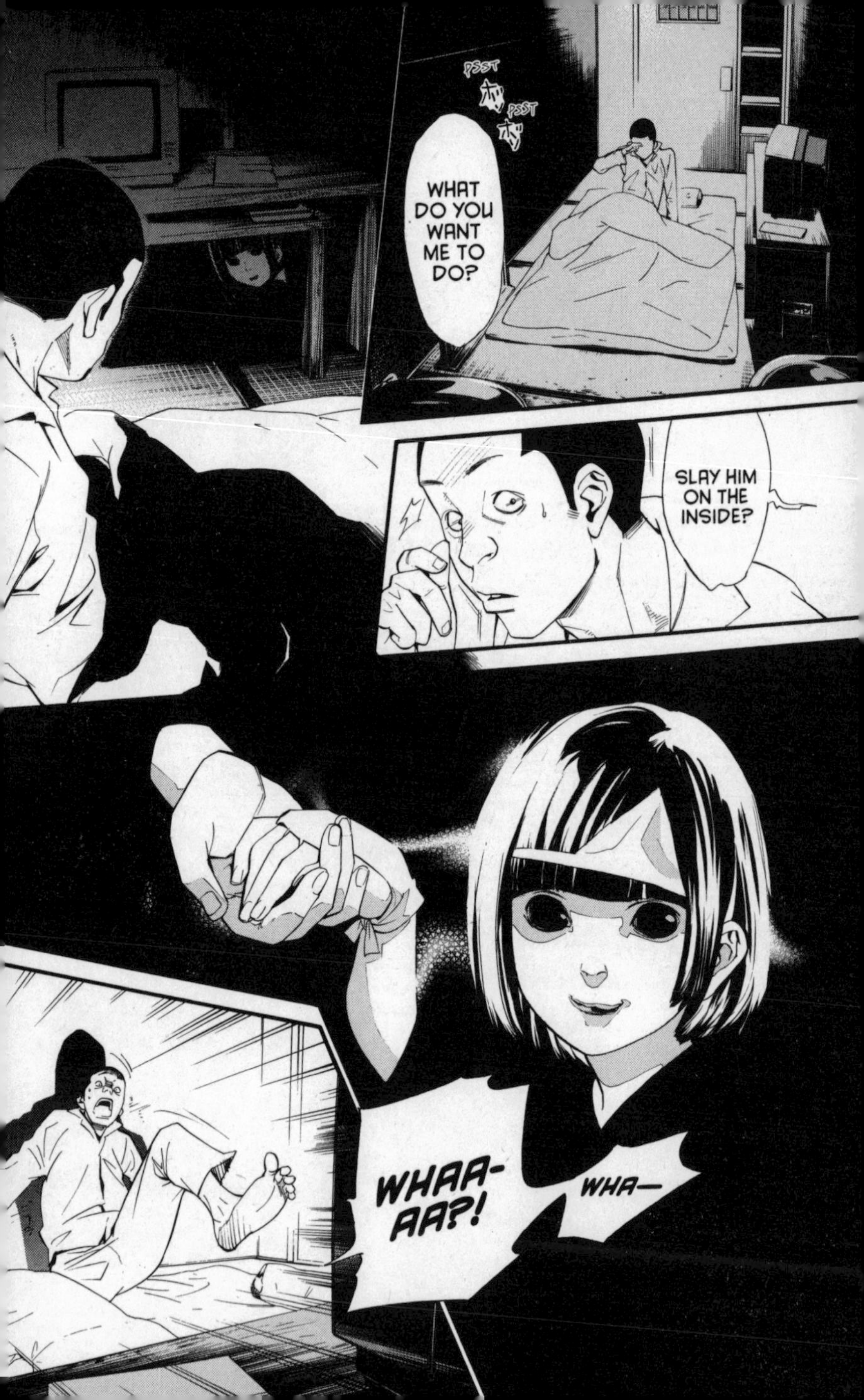
PSST
PSST
WHAT DO YOU WANT ME TO DO?
SLAY HIM ON THE INSIDE?
WHA—
WHAA-AA?!

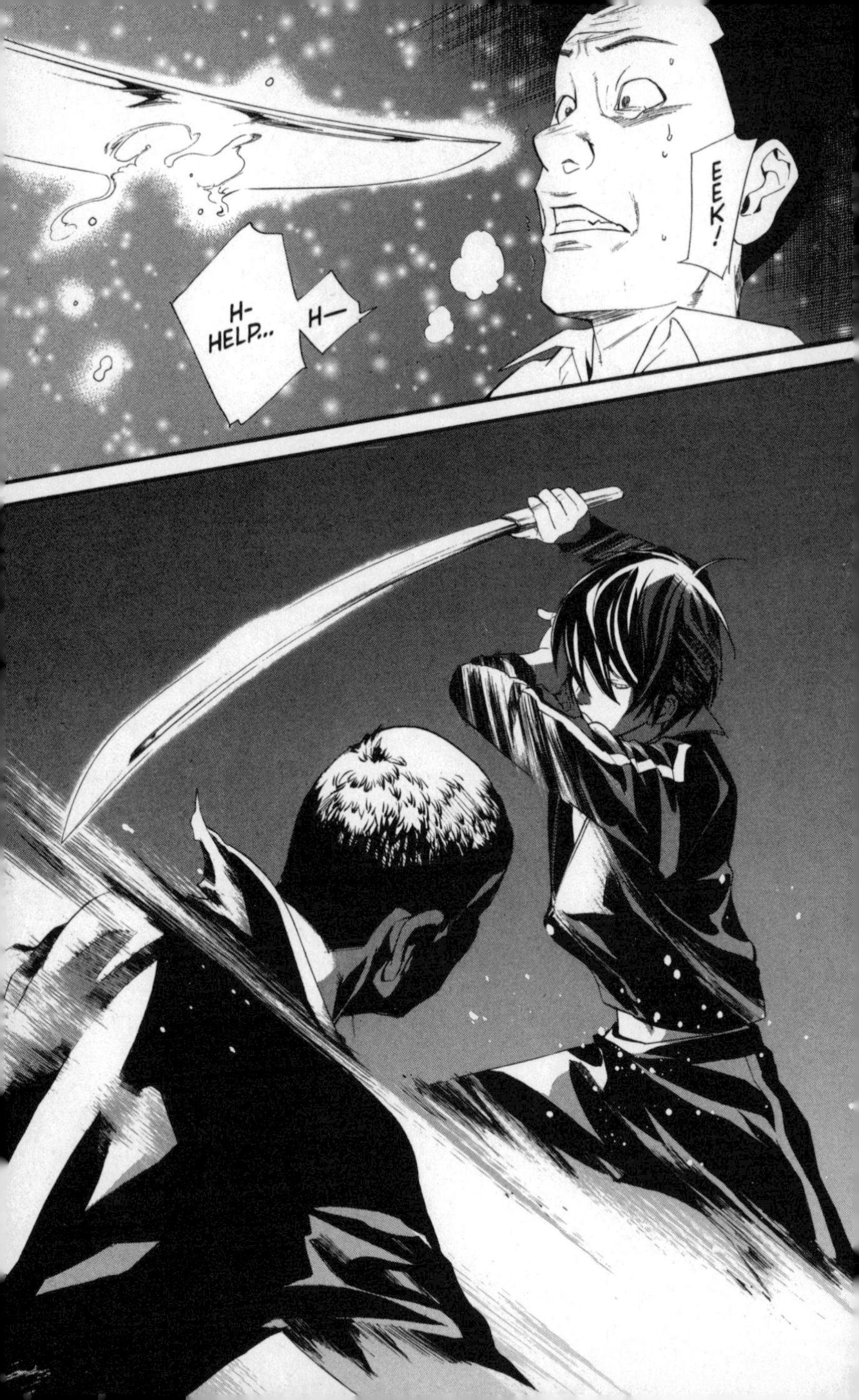
EEK!
H—
H-HELP...

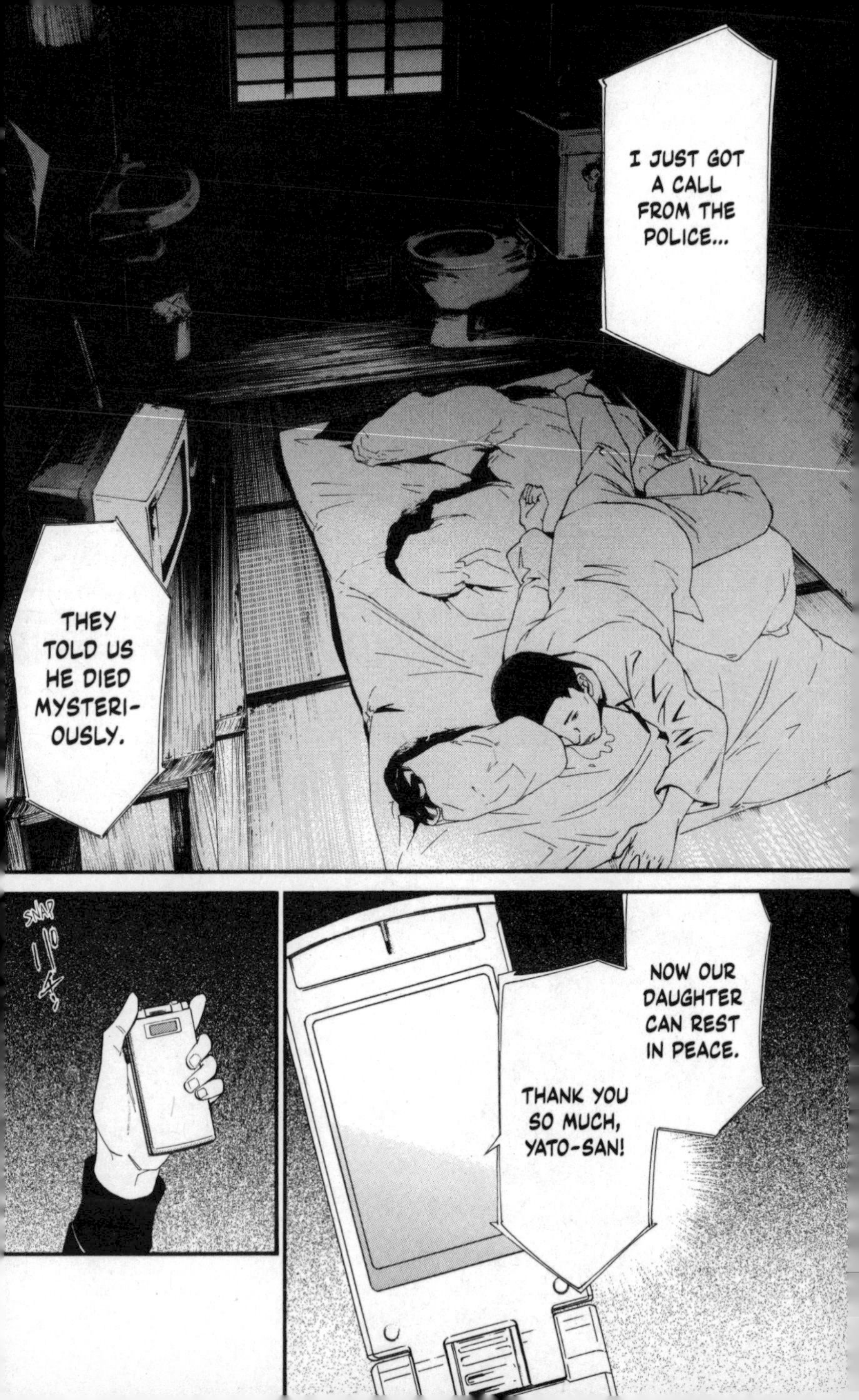
I JUST GOT A CALL FROM THE POLICE...
THEY TOLD US HE DIED MYSTERI-OUSLY.
NOW OUR DAUGHTER CAN REST IN PEACE.
THANK YOU SO MUCH, YATO-SAN!
SNAP

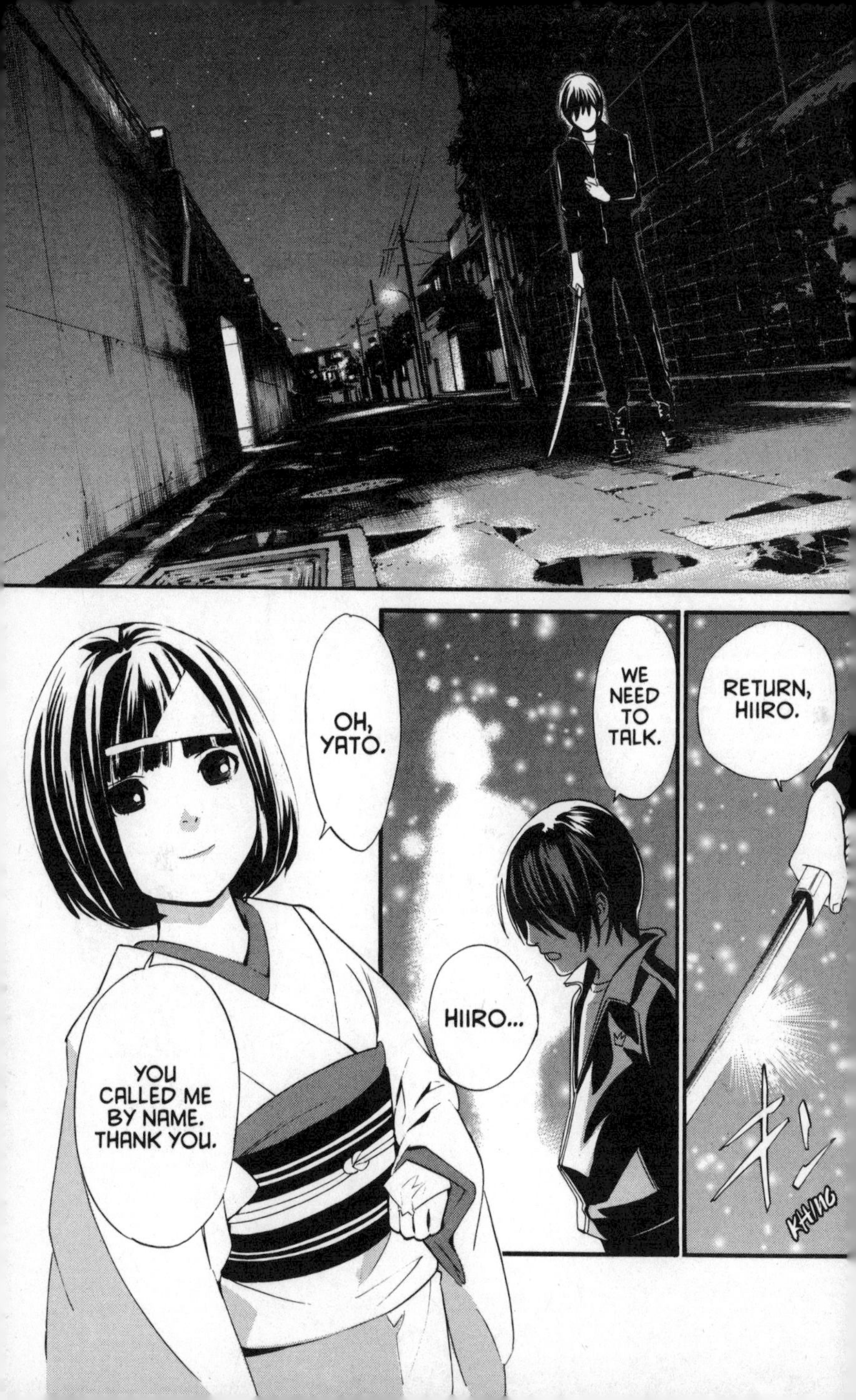
RETURN, HIIRO.
KHING
WE NEED TO TALK.
HIIRO...
OH, YATO.
YOU CALLED ME BY NAME. THANK YOU.

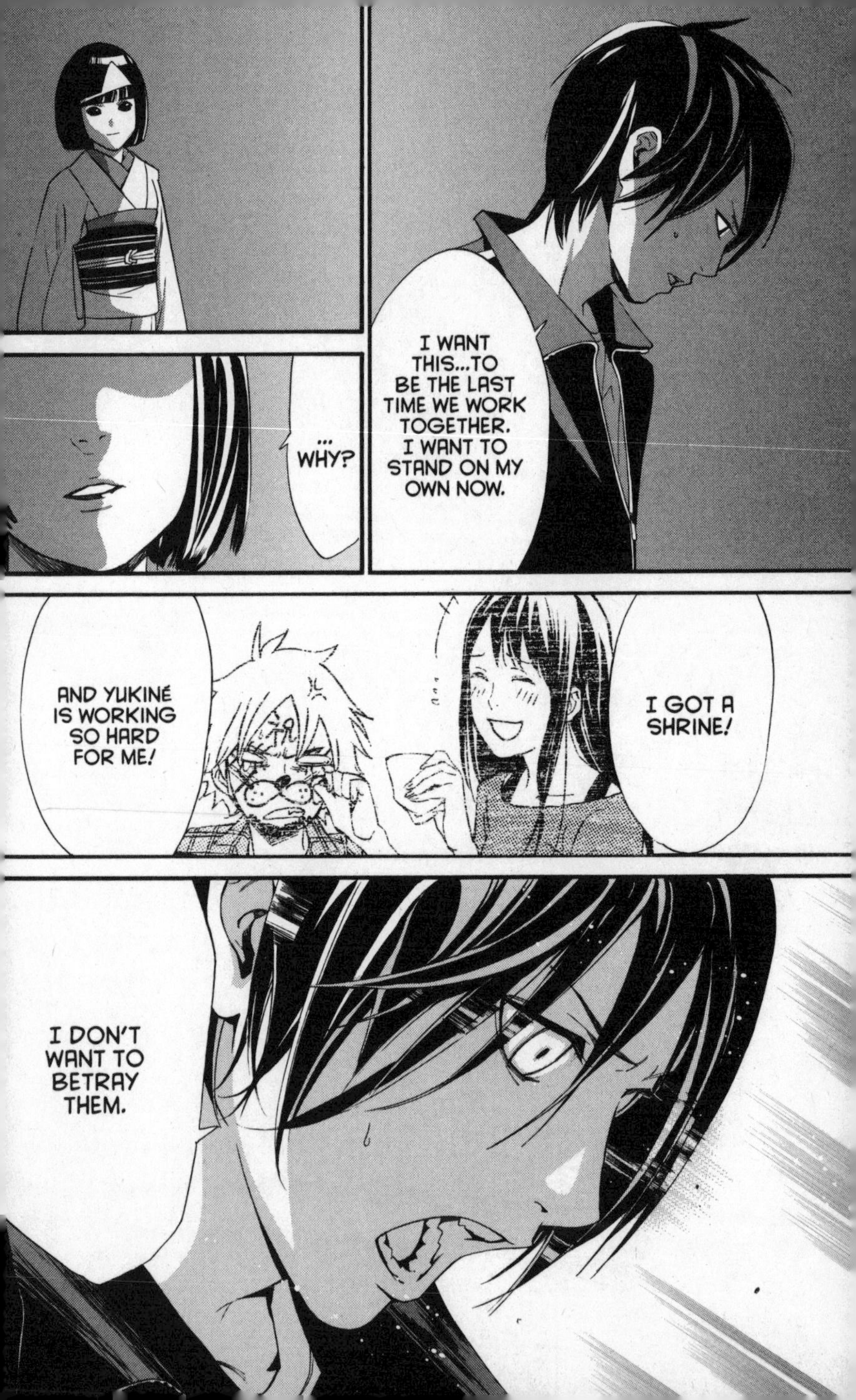
I WANT THIS...TO BE THE LAST TIME WE WORK TOGETHER. I WANT TO STAND ON MY OWN NOW.
... WHY?
I GOT A SHRINE!
AND YUKINÉ IS WORKING SO HARD FOR ME!
I DON'T WANT TO BETRAY THEM.

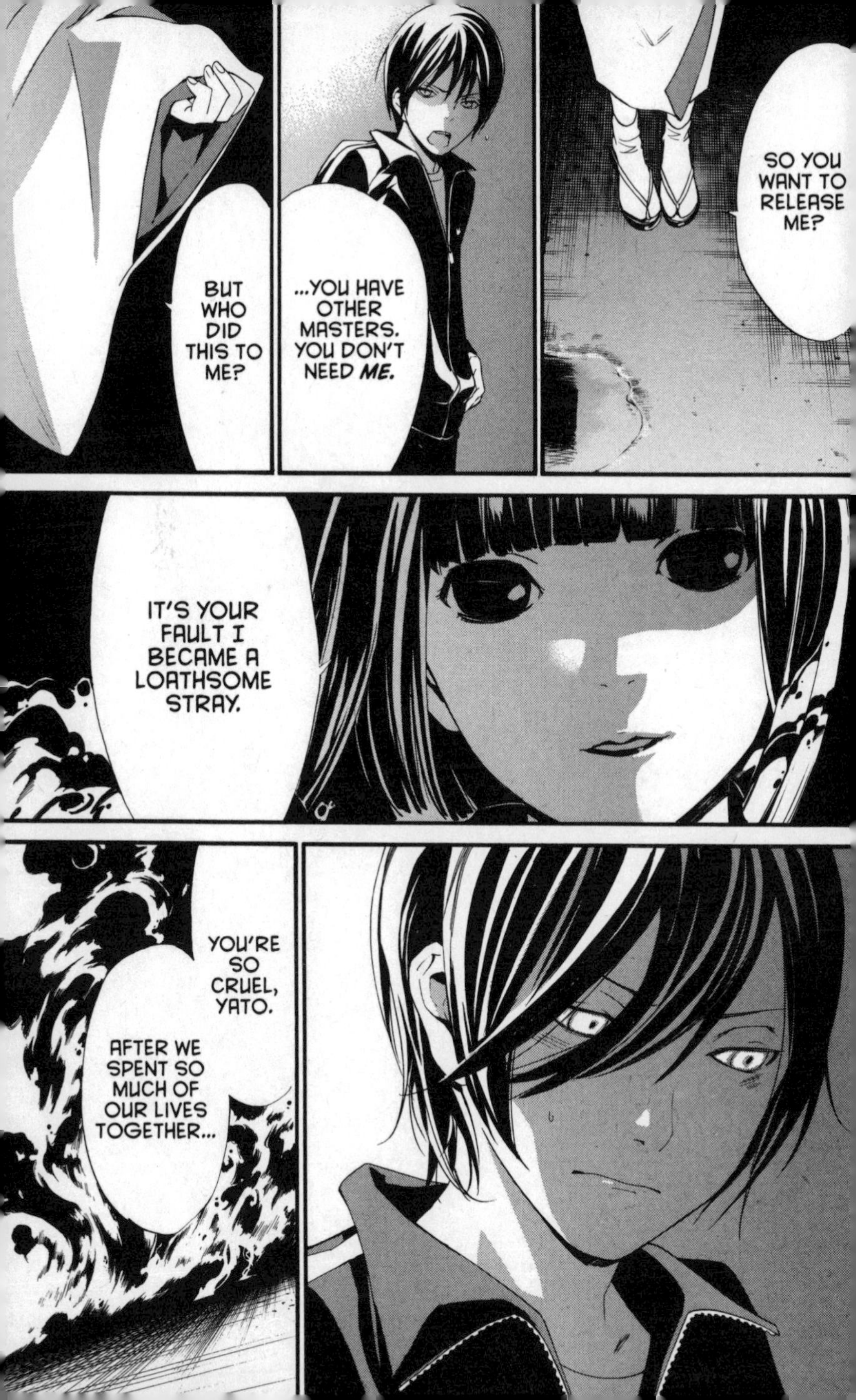
SO YOU WANT TO RELEASE ME?
...YOU HAVE OTHER MASTERS. YOU DON'T NEED ***ME.***
BUT WHO DID THIS TO ME?
IT'S YOUR FAULT I BECAME A LOATHSOME STRAY.
YOU'RE SO CRUEL, YATO.
AFTER WE SPENT SO MUCH OF OUR LIVES TOGETHER...

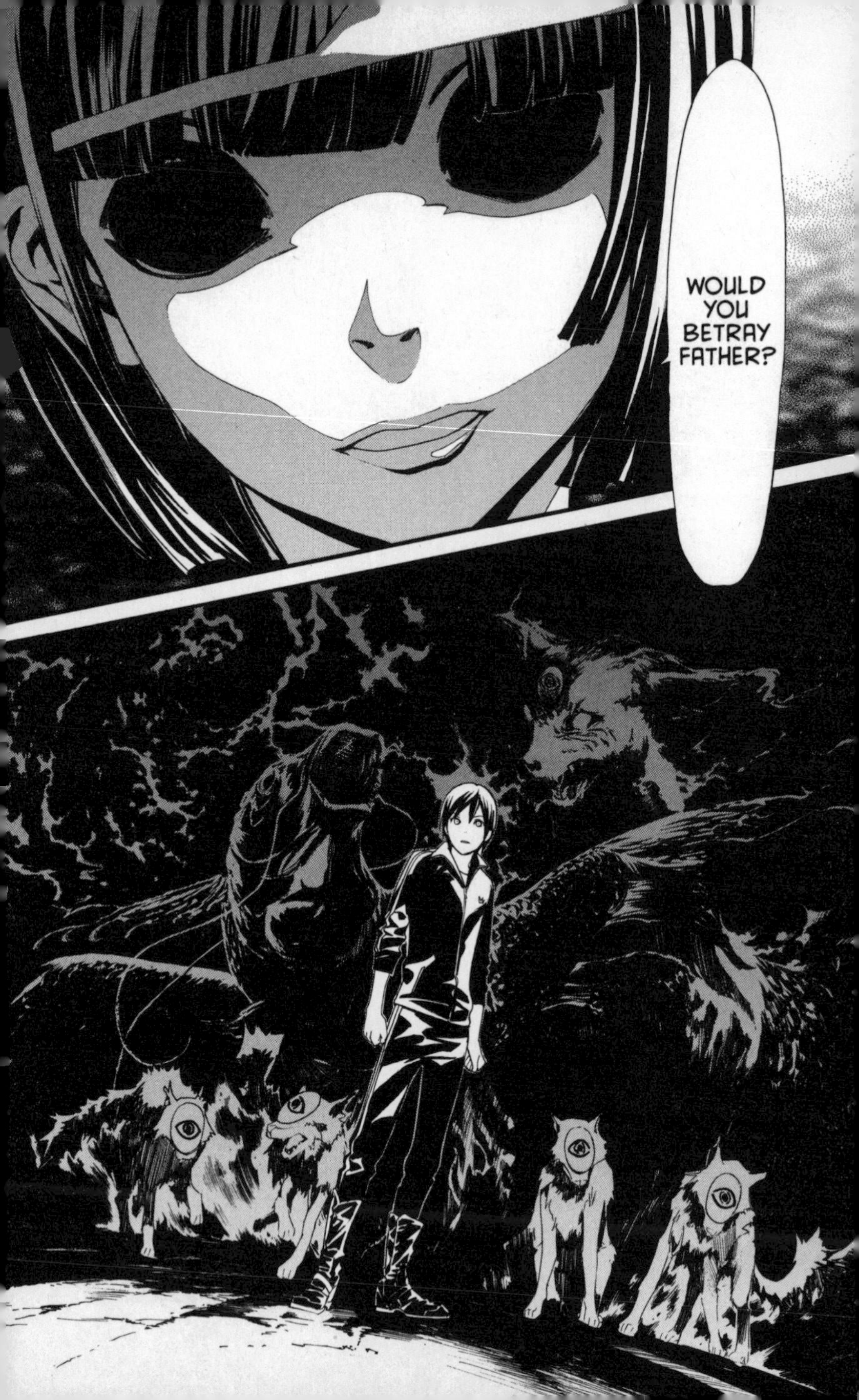
WOULD YOU BETRAY FATHER?

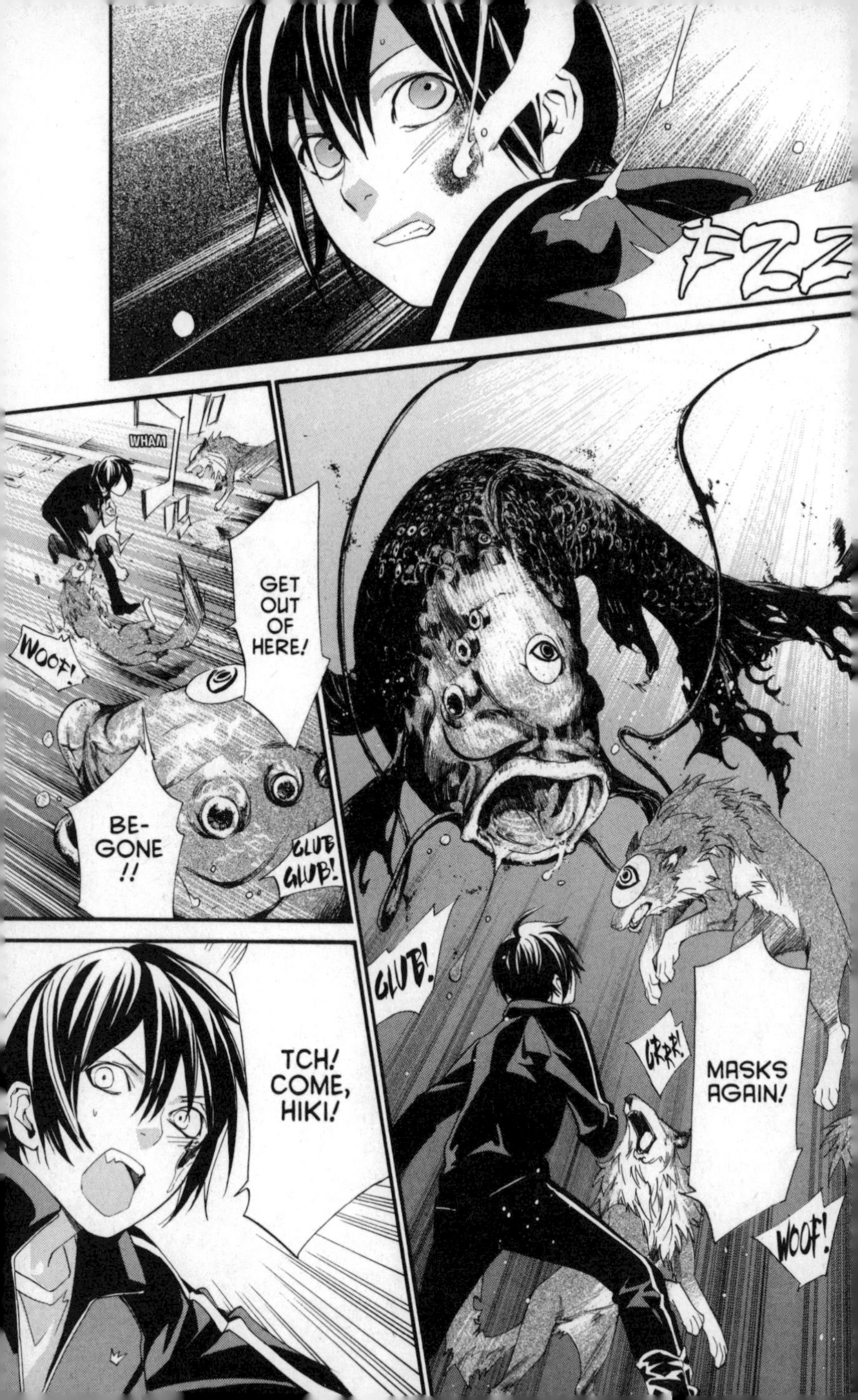
FZZ
GLUB!
MASKS AGAIN!
GRRR!
WOOF!
WHAM
GET OUT OF HERE!
WOOF!
BE-GONE!!
GLUB GLUB!
TCH! COME, HIKI!

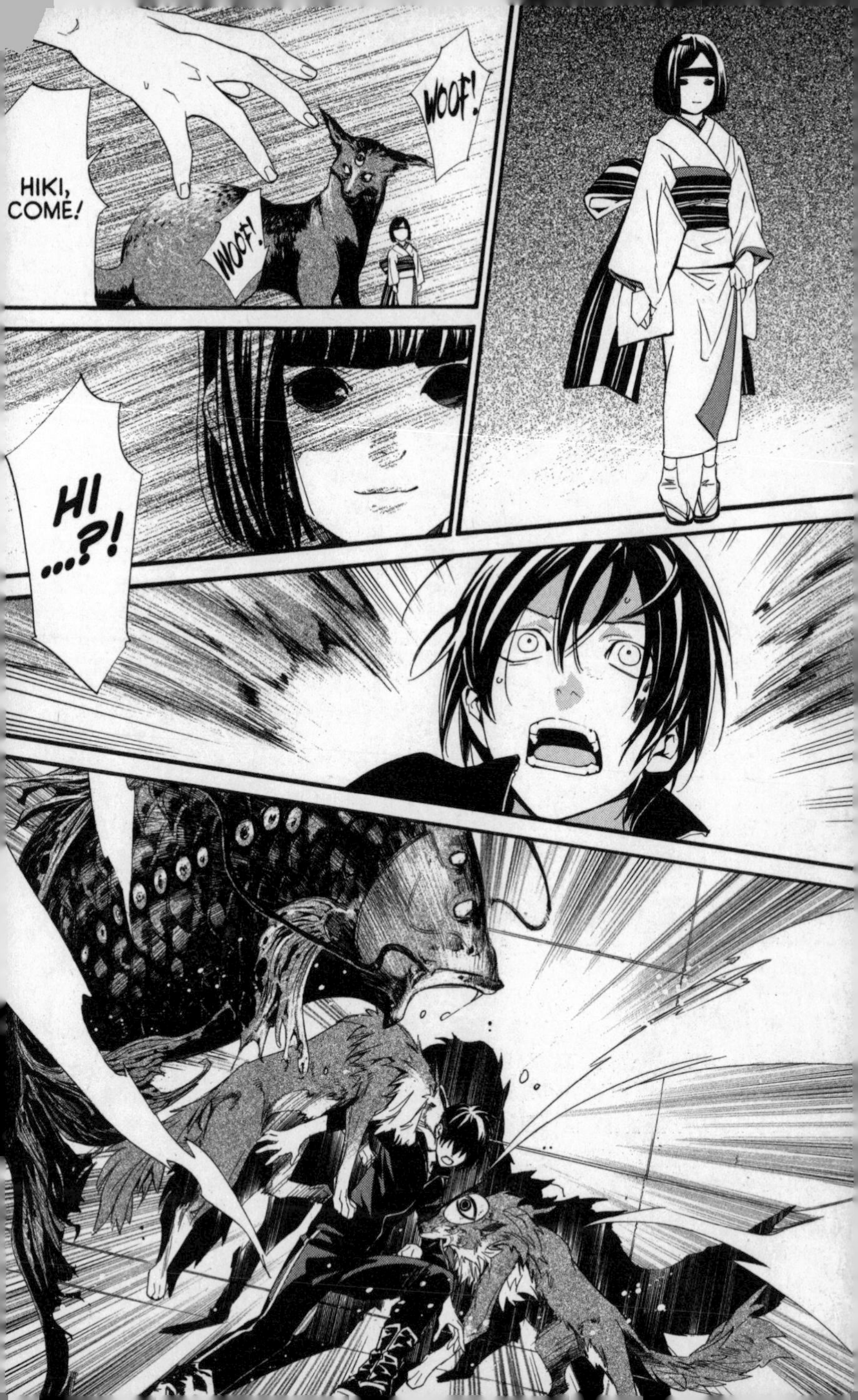
WOOF!
HIKI, COME!
WOOF!
HI ...?!

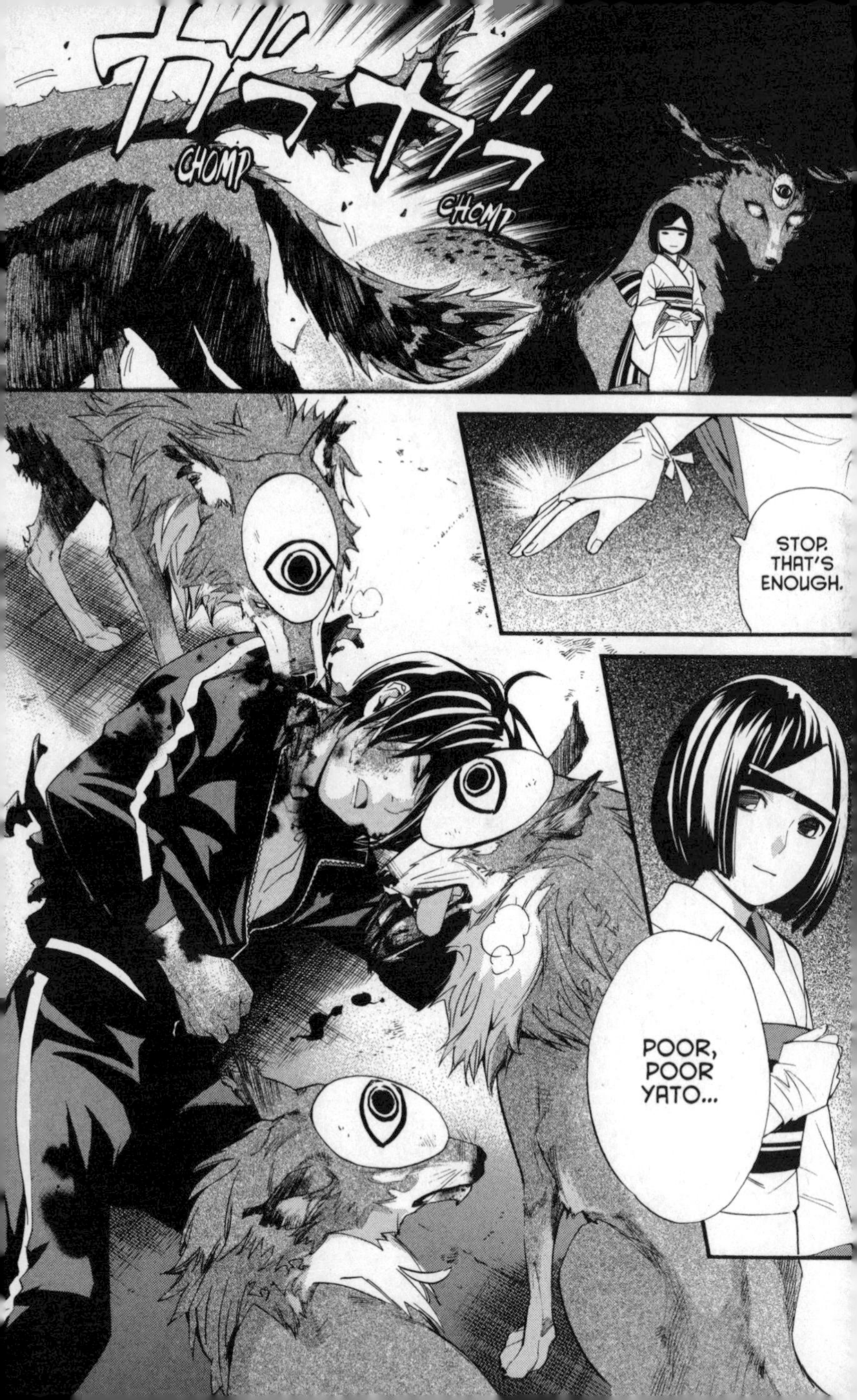
CHOMP
CHOMP
STOP. THAT'S ENOUGH.
POOR, POOR YATO...

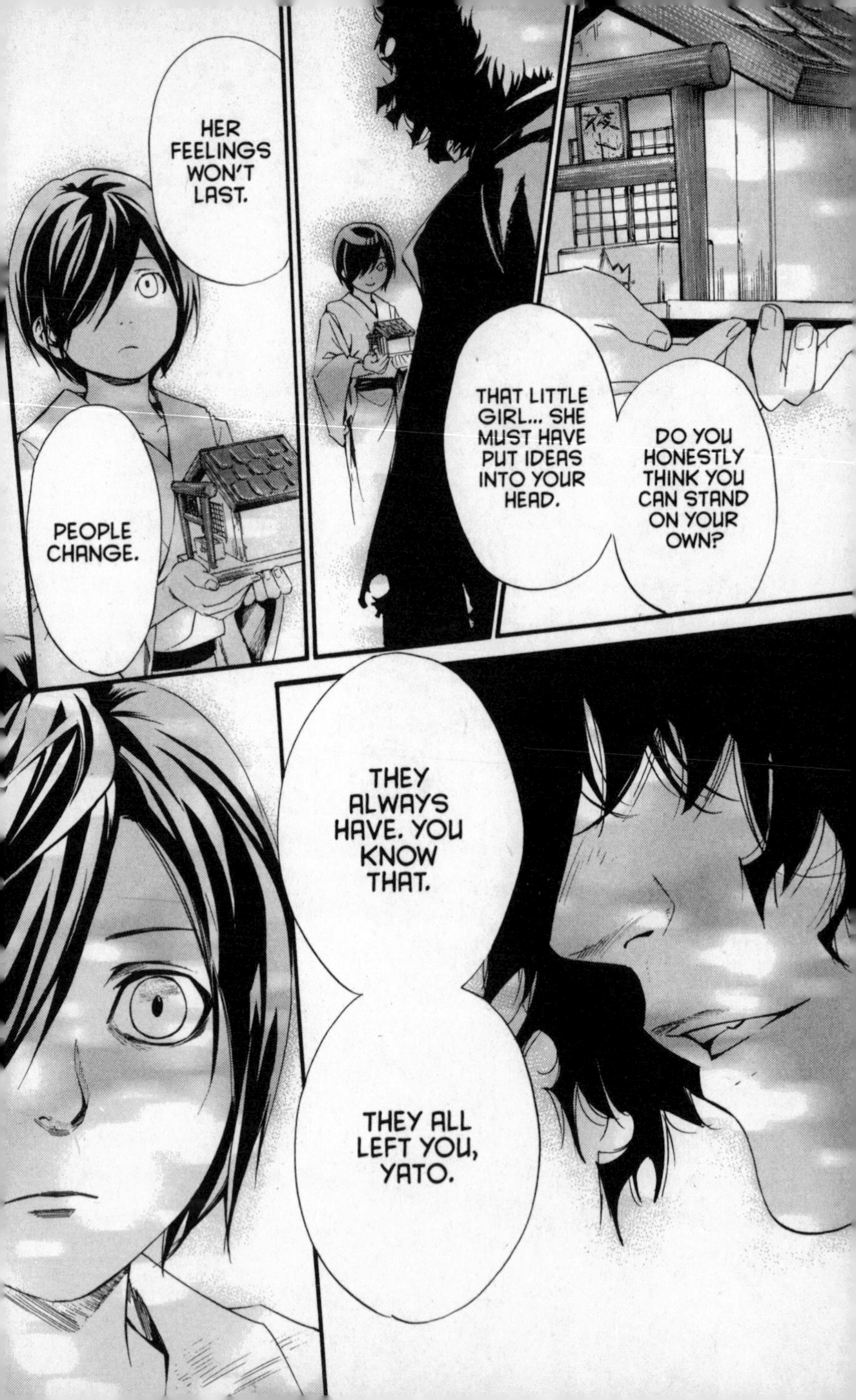
DO YOU HONESTLY THINK YOU CAN STAND ON YOUR OWN?
THAT LITTLE GIRL... SHE MUST HAVE PUT IDEAS INTO YOUR HEAD.
HER FEELINGS WON'T LAST.
PEOPLE CHANGE.
THEY ALWAYS HAVE. YOU KNOW THAT.
THEY ALL LEFT YOU, YATO.

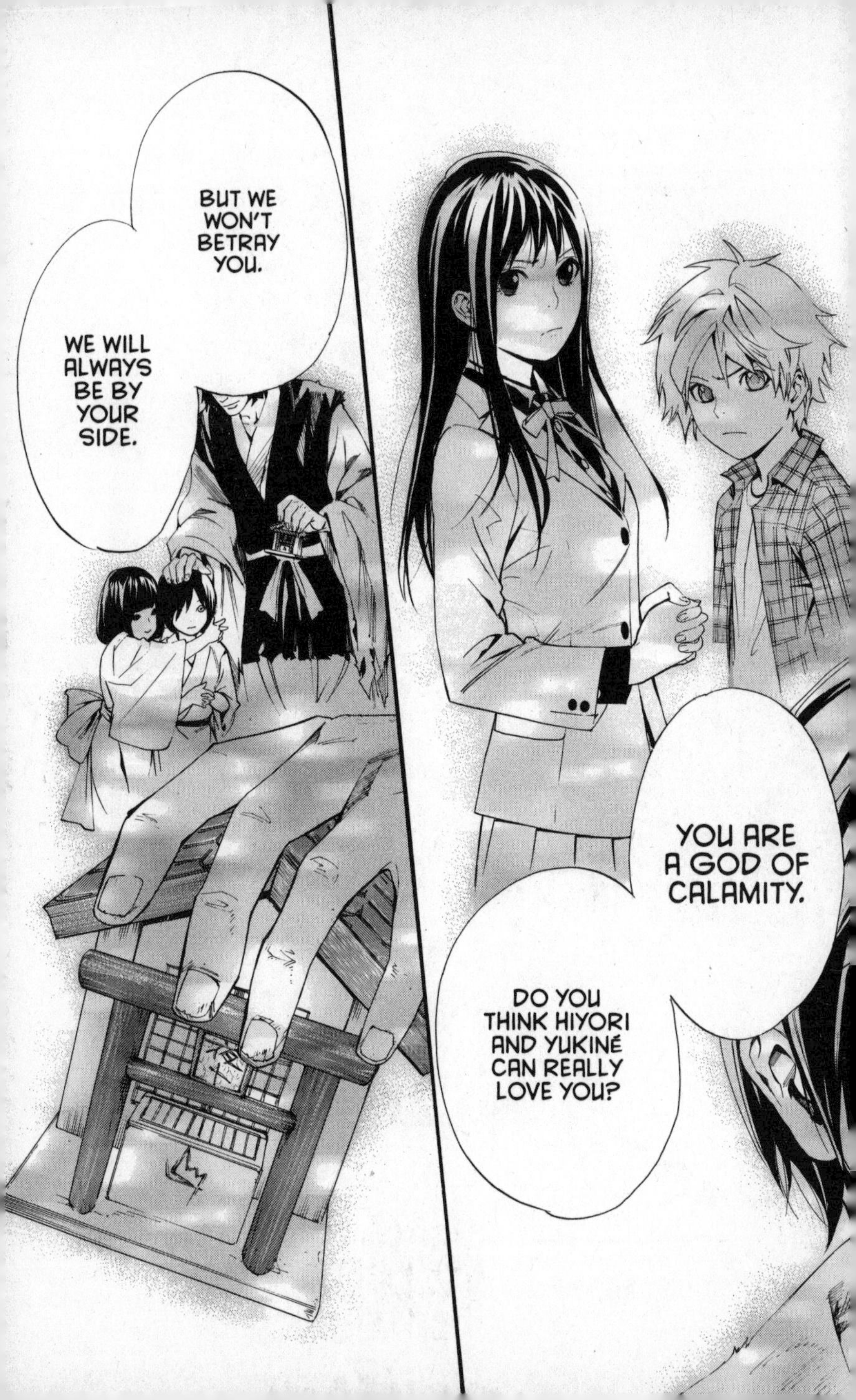
YOU ARE A GOD OF CALAMITY.
DO YOU THINK HIYORI AND YUKINÉ CAN REALLY LOVE YOU?
BUT WE WON'T BETRAY YOU.
WE WILL ALWAYS BE BY YOUR SIDE.

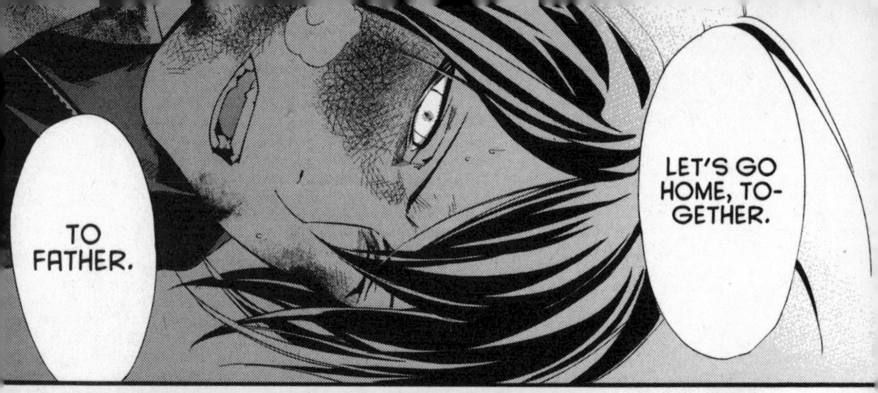
LET'S GO HOME, TO-GETHER.
TO FATHER.

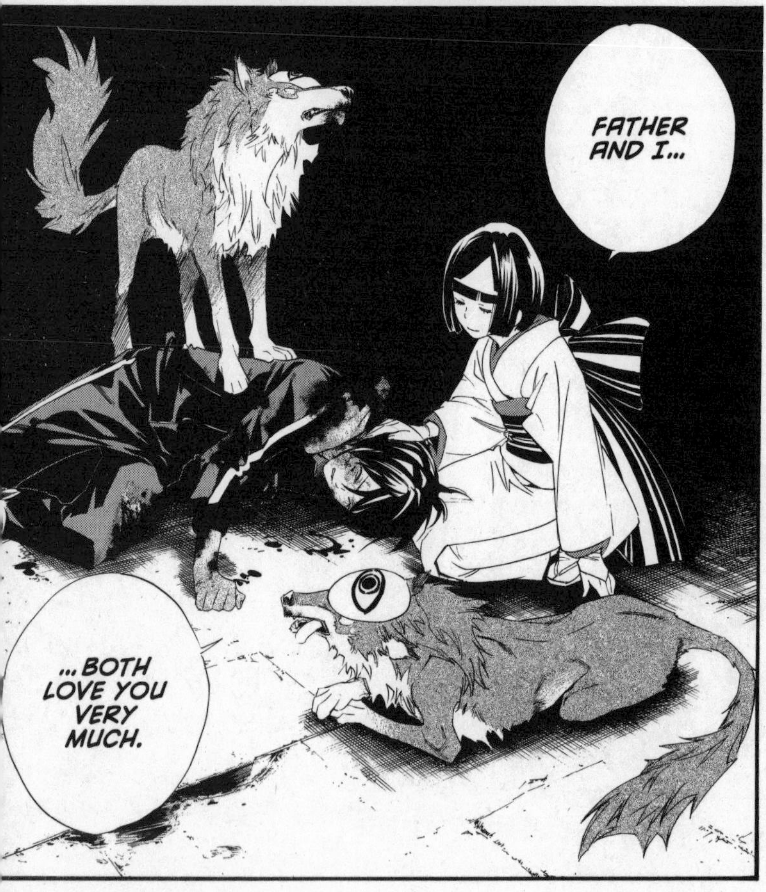
FATHER AND I...
...BOTH LOVE YOU VERY MUCH.

ORAGAMI / TO BE CONTINUED

釘

見

神

ATROCIOUS MANGA

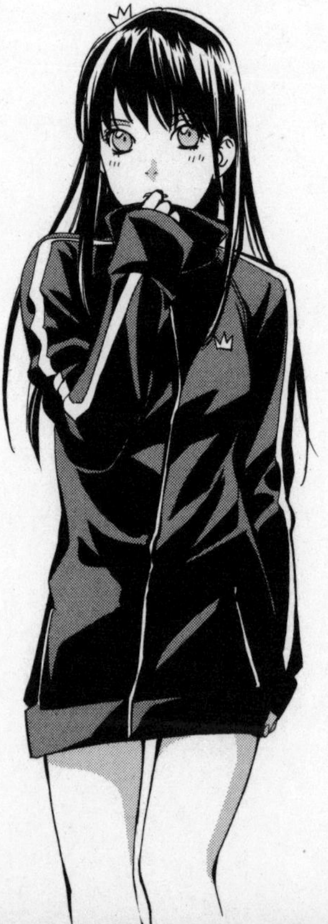

TRANSFORMATION

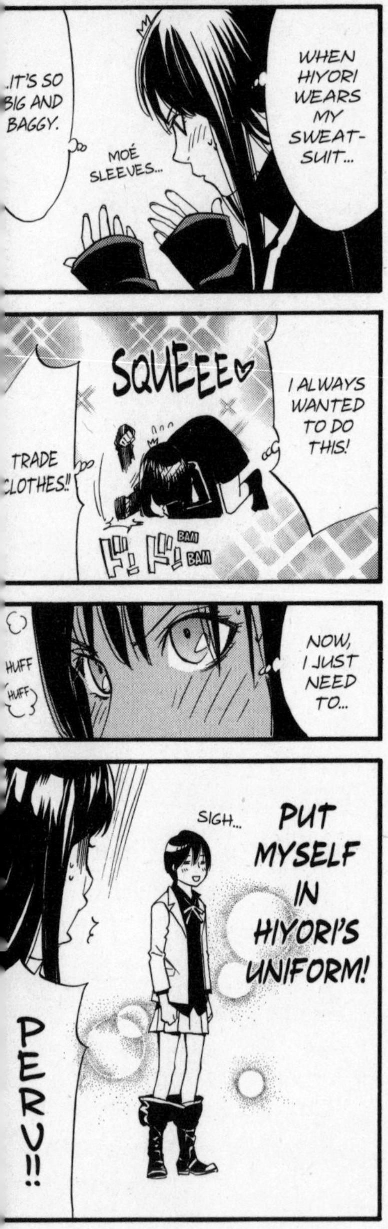
WHEN HIYORI WEARS MY SWEAT-SUIT...
MOÉ SLEEVES...
...IT'S SO BIG AND BAGGY.
I ALWAYS WANTED TO DO THIS!
SQUEEEE♥
TRADE CLOTHES!!
BAM
BAM
NOW, I JUST NEED TO...
HUFF
HUFF
PUT MYSELF IN HIYORI'S UNIFORM!
SIGH...
PERV!!

LOL

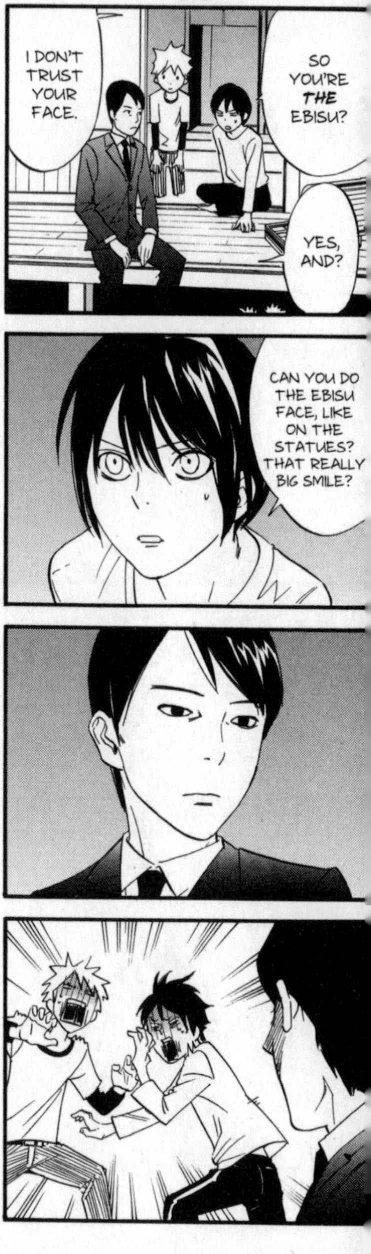
SO YOU'RE ***THE*** EBISU?
YES, AND?
I DON'T TRUST YOUR FACE.
CAN YOU DO THE EBISU FACE, LIKE ON THE STATUES? THAT REALLY BIG SMILE?

POPULAR PHASE

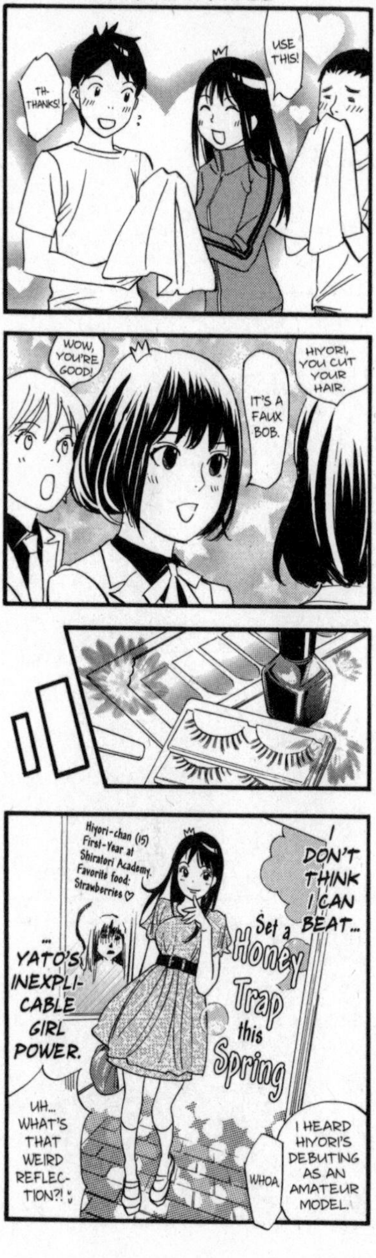
USE THIS!
TH-THANKS!
HIYORI, YOU CUT YOUR HAIR.
IT'S A FAUX BOB.
WOW, YOU'RE GOOD!
I HEARD HIYORI'S DEBUTING AS AN AMATEUR MODEL.
WHOA.
Set a Honey Trap this Spring
Hiyori-chan (15) First-Year at Shiratori Academy. Favorite food: Strawberries ♡
UH... WHAT'S THAT WEIRD REFLECTION?!
I DON'T THINK I CAN BEAT...
...YATO'S INEXPLICABLE GIRL POWER.

EXCHANGE DIARY

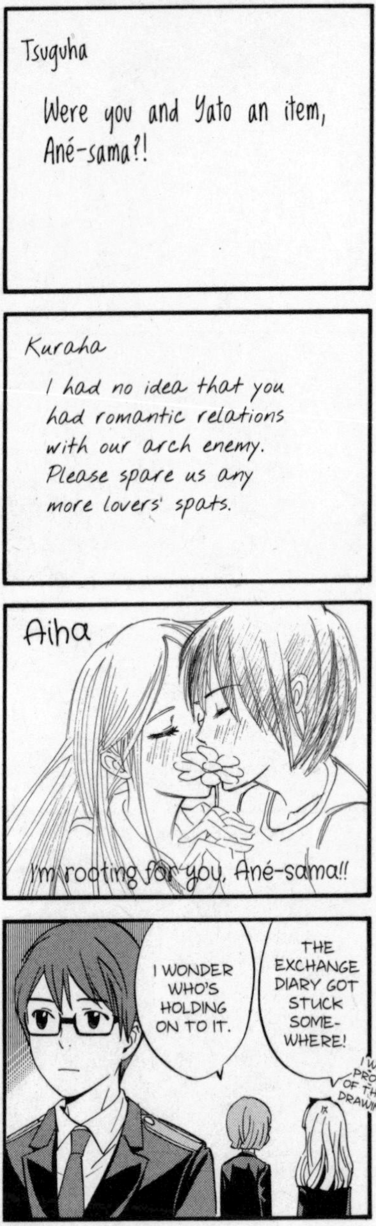
Tsuguha
Were you and Yato an item, Ané-sama?!
Kuraha
I had no idea that you had romantic relations with our arch enemy. Please spare us any more lovers' spats.
Aiha
I'm rooting for you, Ané-sama!!
THE EXCHANGE DIARY GOT STUCK SOMEWHERE!
I WONDER WHO'S HOLDING ON TO IT.
I WAS PROUD OF THAT DRAWING!

HOLY UNION

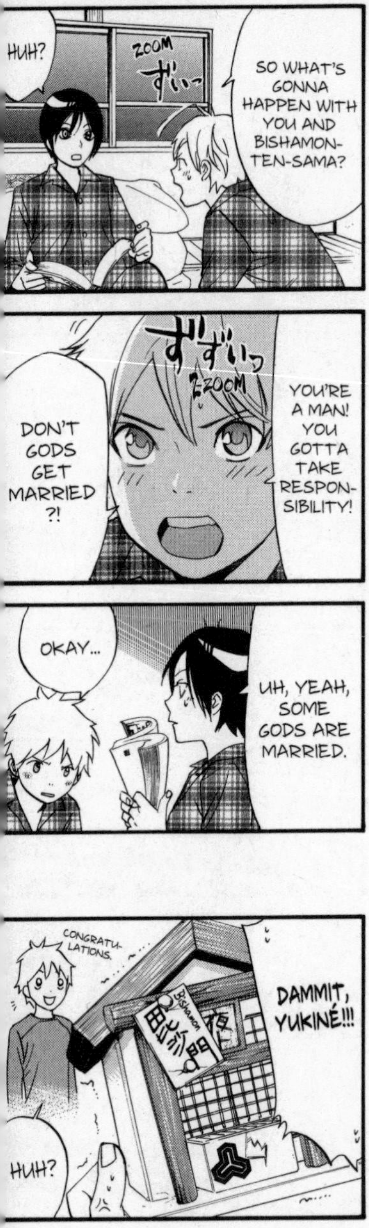
SO WHAT'S GONNA HAPPEN WITH YOU AND BISHAMON-TEN-SAMA?
ZOOM ずいっ
HUH?
YOU'RE A MAN! YOU GOTTA TAKE RESPONSIBILITY!
ずずいっ ZZOOM
DON'T GODS GET MARRIED?!
UH, YEAH, SOME GODS ARE MARRIED.
OKAY...
DAMMIT, YUKINÉ!!!
Bishamon
CONGRATULATIONS.
HUH?

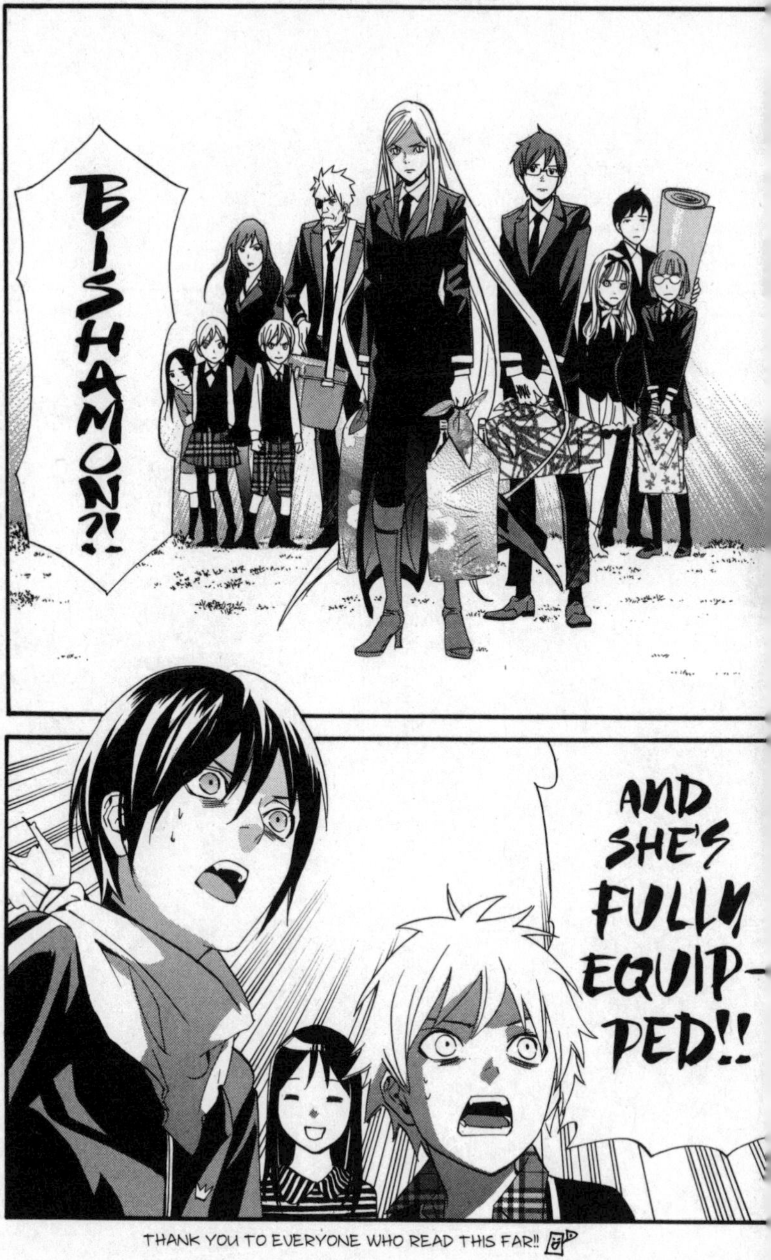
BISHAMON?!
AND SHE'S FULLY EQUIP-PED!!

THANK YOU TO EVERYONE WHO READ THIS FAR!!

TRANSLATION NOTES

Japanese is a tricky language for most Westerners, and translation is often more art than science. For your edification and reading pleasure, here are notes on some of the places where we could have gone in a different direction in our translation of the work, or where a Japanese cultural reference is used.

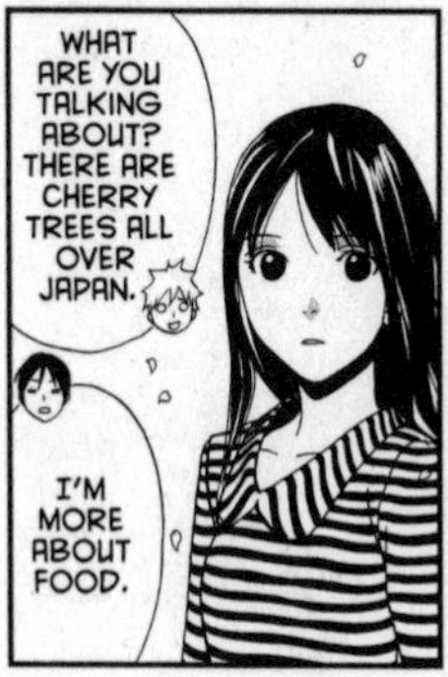
WHAT ARE YOU TALKING ABOUT? THERE ARE CHERRY TREES ALL OVER JAPAN.
I'M MORE ABOUT FOOD.

More about food, page 16
Here, Yato uses a common Japanese saying, "*hana yori dango*," which literally means "dumplings over flowers," The saying does come from flower viewing parties, like the one Yato and friends are having here, and refers to people who are more happy to come and eat than to admire the blossoms. They are more interested in practical things than aesthetically pleasing things or following trends.

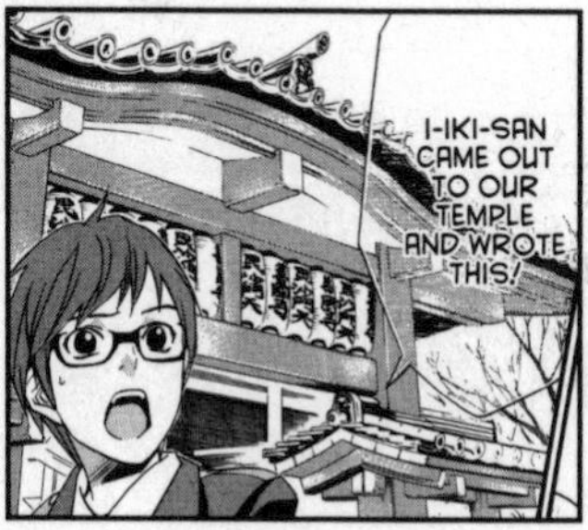
I-IKI-SAN CAME OUT TO OUR TEMPLE AND WROTE THIS!

Our temple, page 18
Bishamonten has many shrines and temples, but Hiyori lives in Tokyo, so she went to the temple that was close to home. Specifically, that temple is Zenkokuji, which houses a statue of Bishamonten that has been designated as a cultural property of the city of Shinjuku.

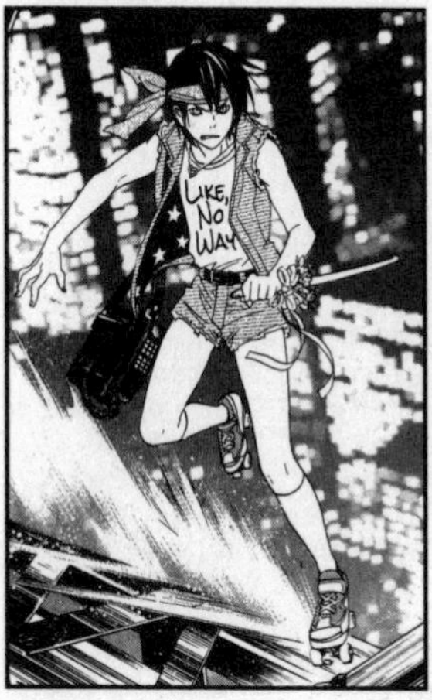
LIKE, NO WAY

Late 80's, page 25
For those interested in modern Japanese history, the time is listed here specifically as the "bubble period," referring to the Japanese economic bubble that existed from 1986 to 1991. It was a period of great prosperity until the Japanese stock market crashed, leading to years of financial stagnation. The text on Yato's shirt originally said *buttobi*, which is Japanese 80s slang for "surprise."

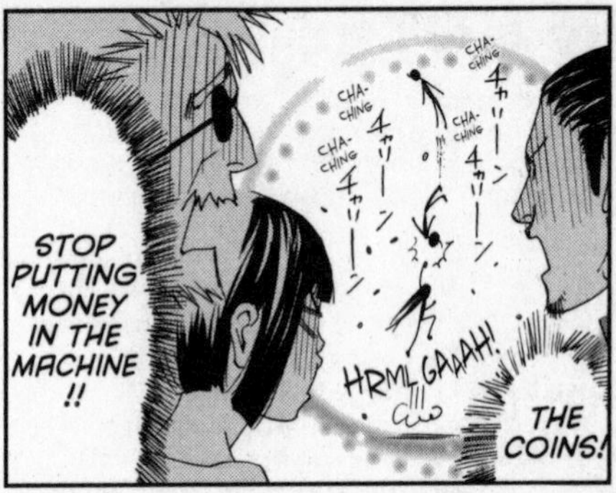
THE COINS!
CHA-CHING
CHA-CHING
CHA-CHING
CHA-CHING
HRML GAAAH!
STOP PUTTING MONEY IN THE MACHINE !!

Stop putting money in the machine, page 38
Seeing how many coins Yato is losing in this fight, the shinki use the term *renzoku koin*, or "coins in succession." This is Japanese arcade slang, referring to the act of continuously putting coins into a machine in order to keep playing indefinitely. To be polite, it is encouraged to only do this when the arcade isn't crowded and there's no one waiting to play the game one is hogging. In this case, the shinki probably aren't interested in the game in question, and are mostly shocked that anyone would throw away so much money to play it.

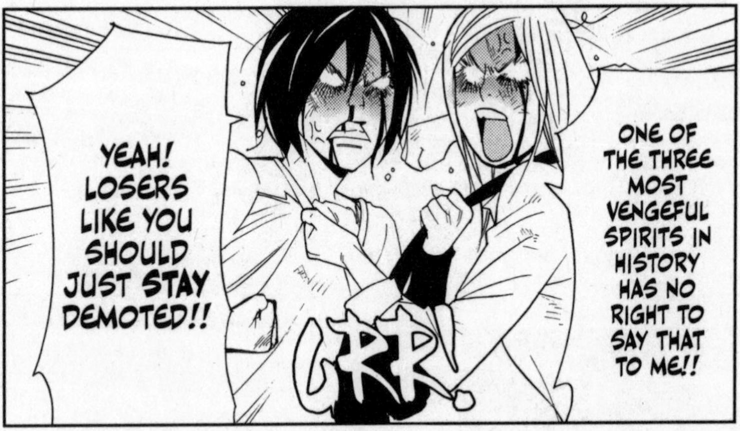
ONE OF THE THREE MOST VENGEFUL SPIRITS IN HISTORY HAS NO RIGHT TO SAY THAT TO ME!!
YEAH! LOSERS LIKE YOU SHOULD JUST STAY DEMOTED!!
GRR

One of the three most vengeful spirits, page 39
Longtime readers may remember that Sugawara no Michizane became a god when, after his death, several natural disasters occurred, leading the people to believe that they were caused by his powerful vengeful spirit. The disasters must have been terrible indeed, because to this day, Sugawara no Michizane (known in this manga as Tenjin) is recognized as one of the three greatest vengeful spirits in Japan.

Yato's insult to Tenjin is referring to Michizane's demotion due to political intrigue shortly before his death. One of the measures taken to placate his wrath and stop the natural disasters was to posthumously restore him to his former, higher rank.

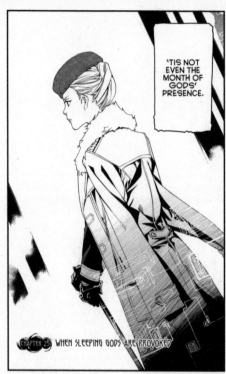

'TIS NOT EVEN THE MONTH OF GODS' PRESENCE.
CHAPTER 25: WHEN SLEEPING GODS ARE PROVOKED

When Sleeping Gods Are Provoked, page 52
The Japanese version of the English saying, "let sleeping dogs lie," can be translated to, "an untouched will not curse." The idea is that if one leaves a god alone, there's no risk of incurring their wrath. The title of this chapter is a play on that saying, and literally means "the curse of a touched god." In other words, this chapter is about what happens when sleeping gods are not allowed to lie peacefully.

The Month of Gods' Presence, page 52
In Japan, the tenth month of the year used to be called *Kannazuki*, which translates to "the Month of No Gods." Tradition has it that in that month, all the Shinto gods gather at Izumo, where the month is called *Kamiarizuki*, or "the Month of Gods' Presence." During this month, the gods meet together in a Divine Council.

So cocky now, page 67
This boy's complaint about Hiyori is nigh impossible to translate. He laments that she has become an *orekko*, which is a girl who uses the traditionally masculine first-person pronoun of *ore*. All first-person pronouns translate into English as either I or me, hence the difficulty in translating *orekko*. While it is typically men who refer to themselves as *ore*, an *orekko* doesn't necessarily act especially masculine, but she does have a tendency to be extremely confident, often to the point of arrogance, as are many men who use the same pronoun.

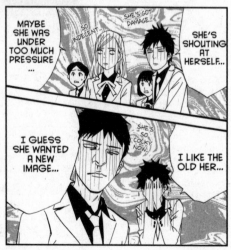

SHE'S SHOUTING AT HERSELF...
SHE'S GOT DAMAGE...
SO INDECENT...
MAYBE SHE WAS UNDER TOO MUCH PRESSURE ...
I LIKE THE OLD HER...
SHE'S SO COCKY NOW...
I GUESS SHE WANTED A NEW IMAGE...

Hiyori's sexy double personality, page 91

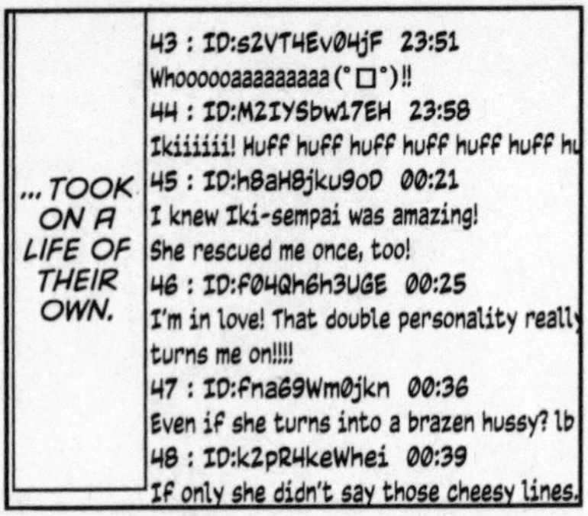
43 : ID:s2VT4Ev04jF 23:51
Whooooaaaaaaaaa (°□°)!!
44 : ID:M2IYSbw17EH 23:58
Ikiiiiii! Huff huff huff huff huff huff hu
45 : ID:h8aH8jku9oD 00:21
I knew Iki-sempai was amazing!
She rescued me once, too!
46 : ID:F04Qh6h3UGE 00:25
I'm in love! That double personality reall
turns me on!!!!
47 : ID:fna69Wm0jkn 00:36
Even if she turns into a brazen hussy? lb
48 : ID:k2pR4keWhei 00:39
If only she didn't say those cheesy lines.
...TOOK ON A LIFE OF THEIR OWN.

To be more accurate, this internet commenter uses the term gap *moé*. *Moé* refers to feelings of love and affection (and sometimes lust) that are inspired by certain characteristics. For example, someone with a glasses *moé* might feel an instant attachment to anyone wearing spectacles. A gap *moé* refers to the "gap" between what you're used to someone being like, or how you expect them to behave, and what they actually do. In this case, Hiyori is known for being much more demure, and her sudden drastic change in behavior creates a "gap," which this person finds to be very attractive.

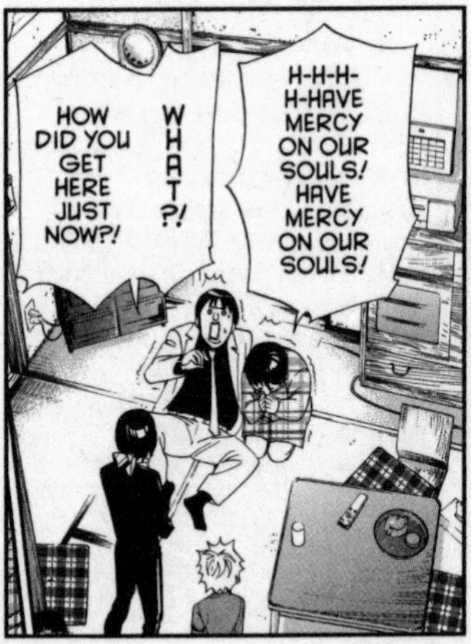
H-H-H-H-HAVE MERCY ON OUR SOULS! HAVE MERCY ON OUR SOULS!
WHAT?!
HOW DID YOU GET HERE JUST NOW?!

Have mercy on our souls, page 116

This old woman is reciting a Buddhist chant that literally means "I devote myself to Amitabha." Amitabha is the principal Buddha in the Pure Land Sect of Buddhism, and by repeating that she is devoting herself to him, she is essentially asking him to have mercy on her and save her from evil, whether that evil is a scam artist or a scary deity who appeared out of nowhere.

Who do you think you are, page 143

Specifically, these gangs are asking each other what middle school they go to (or went to). While it is not entirely clear why they would ask this specific question, it's possible that if any of them hails from a middle school with a reputation for tough, violent students, then they would have enough cred to be a worthy opponent. If not, then they need to be taught a lesson. Either way, it's probably going to end in a brawl.

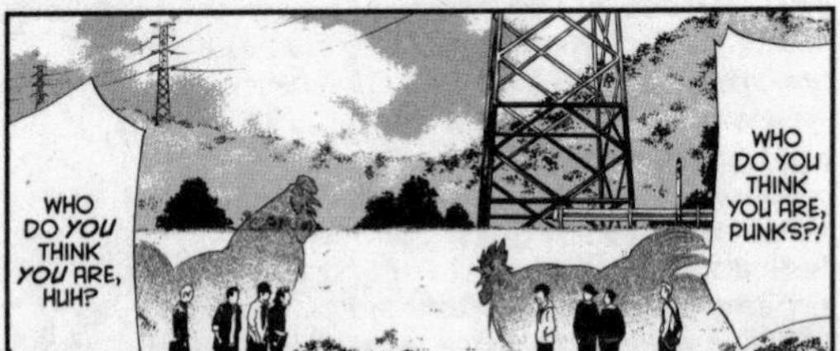
WHO DO YOU THINK YOU ARE, PUNKS?!
WHO DO *YOU* THINK *YOU* ARE, HUH?

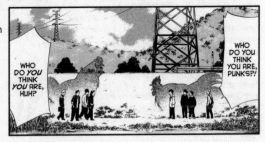

Do and Due, page 146
The Japanese title of this chapter is a play on a certain kanji (業) which can be pronounced *gyō* or *gō*. The former refers to one's occupation, business, etc.—what one does. The latter refers to karma—the good or bad consequences of one's deeds.

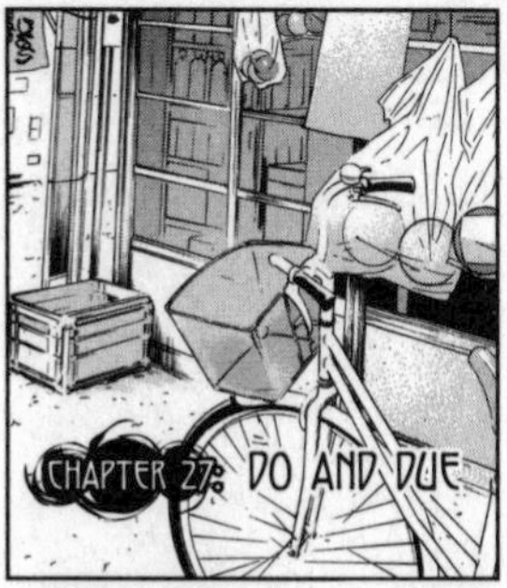
CHAPTER 27: DO AND DUE

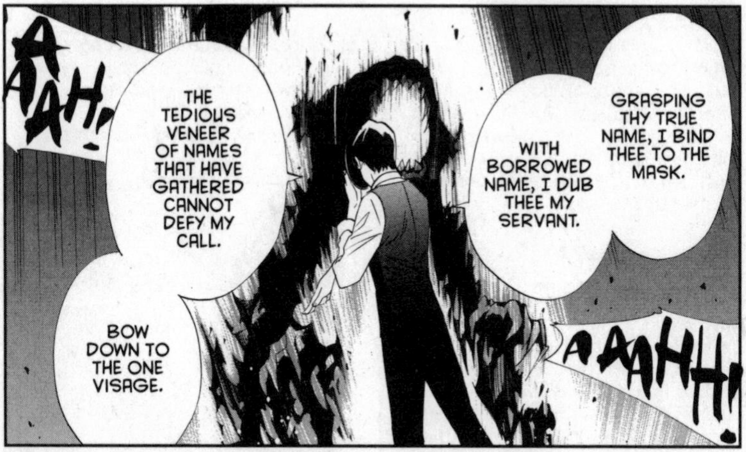
GRASPING THY TRUE NAME, I BIND THEE TO THE MASK.
WITH BORROWED NAME, I DUB THEE MY SERVANT.
AAAHH!
THE TEDIOUS VENEER OF NAMES THAT HAVE GATHERED CANNOT DEFY MY CALL.
AAAH!
BOW DOWN TO THE ONE VISAGE.

Grasping thy true name, I bind thee to the mask, page 157
Readers will probably recognize parts of this incantation from when Yato named Yukiné as his shinki back in volume one. Of course, because Ebisu is naming an ayakashi and not a human spirit, it calls for different words. As before, certain words used contain many possible meanings, and in a situation like this, usually all of them are applicable. The word in question this time is *tsuradzura-naru*, which is an adjective describing the names that have gathered. First, it is a form of *tsura-tsura*, which means "careful" or "thorough." It can also be a form of *tsure-dzure*, which can mean "careful" or "thorough" as well, but in addition, refers to a state of ennui—a melancholy that comes from boredom. The translators hope that the word "tedious" covers all of these nuances.

Finally, *tsura* is a word for "face," and repeating it makes it plural. In other words, we have a group of names that have gathered that are thorough, melancholy from boredom, and are also faces. As we saw when Yato killed Bishamon's shinki many years ago, one ayakashi can be made up of many consciousnesses, as represented by faces. Ebisu is now taking all of those names and faces and using one name to confine them to a single mask—another face. However, the "one visage" he mentions most likely refers to either the mask in question, or himself.

I JUST GOT SCHOOLED IN HOW MUCH KAZUMA-SAN LOOKS DOWN ON ME.

Yukiné's ink, page 165
Most of the writing on Yukiné's face is just scribbles, but the *kanji* character on his forehead is worth mentioning. It's seen in many places where auspicious happenings are going on, such as graduations, weddings, anniversaries, etc., and in those contexts means "celebration" or "congratulations." But Kazuma was being clever here, too, because this is also a *kanji* meaning "consecrated" or "holy," and is the same *kanji* used in "blessed vessel."

WE NEED TO TALK.

OH, YATO.

HIIRO...

YOU CALLED ME BY NAME. THANK YOU.

Hiiro, page 177
The translators would like to apologize for potentially misleading readers into believing that Yato's name for the stray in human form was Akané. In retrospect, he probably wouldn't have wanted to use his family naming system on a stray. Here, Yato refers to her only as Hiiro, which only has the one kanji character—the character that is her true name. It's possible that he gave her a different *yobina* (see volume 2), or that he didn't give her one at all, because she is a stray.

WHEN HIYORI WEARS MY SWEAT-SUIT...

...IT'S SO BIG AND BAGGY.

MOÉ SLEEVES...

SQUEEE♡

I ALWAYS WANTED TO DO THIS!

TRADE CLOTHES?!

Moé sleeves, page 188
Moé sleeves are sleeves that are too long, and therefore cover some or all of the wearer's hands. They are likely called that because people find it to be adorable.

NORAGAMI

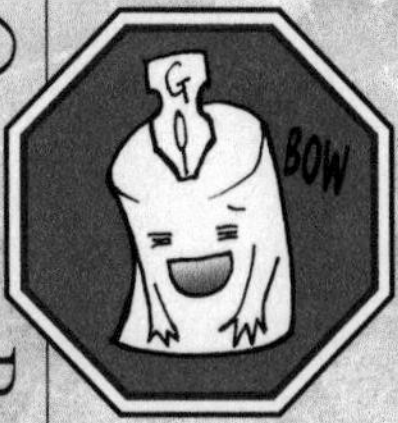
BOW

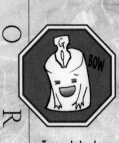

I went to Izumo for research. I also visited the head shrines for Daikoku-sama and Ebisu-sama.
The restrooms were so much bigger than Yato's piece of land, I felt like I could live in one. Marketable gods sure are different.

Adachitoka

Noragami: Stray God volume 7 is a work of fiction. Names, characters, places, and incidents are the products of the author's imagination or are used fictitiously. Any resemblance to actual events, locales, or persons, living or dead, is entirely coincidental.

A Kodansha Comics Trade Paperback Original.

Published in the United States by Kodansha Comics, an imprint of Kodansha USA Publishing, LLC, New York.

Publication rights for this English edition arranged through Kodansha Ltd., Tokyo.

First published in Japan in 2013 by Kodansha Ltd., Tokyo.

ISBN 978-1-63236-102-8

Printed in the United States of America.

www.kodanshacomics.com

9 8 7 6 5 4 3 2 1

Translator: Alethea Nibley & Athena Nibley
Lettering: Lys Blakeslee